Our Vice-Presidents
and
Second Ladies

by
LESLIE W. DUNLAP

The Scarecrow Press, Inc.
Metuchen, N.J., & London
1988

Library of Congress Cataloging-in-Publication Data
Dunlap, Leslie W. (Leslie Whitaker), 1911-
    Our vice-presidents and second ladies / by Leslie W.
      Dunlap. p.   cm.
    Includes index.
    ISBN 0-8108-2114-1
    1. Vice-Presidents--United States--Biography. 2. Vice-
Presidents--United States--Wives--Biography. I. Title.
E176.49.D86   1988
973' .09'92--dc19   88-4123
[B]

To

LESLEY and BRUCE

with love and admiration

CONTENTS

PREFACE

In a book on political figures and their spouses, a reader
might expect to encounter information dealing only with the
period in which a person held an office, but for several
vice-presidents (John Tyler and Harry Truman are examples)
the time spent in the office was too brief to reveal much of
importance about them or their spouses. Consequently, it
seemed desirable to follow each person "from the cradle to
the grave," and this I have attempted to do.

Several of the forty-three vice-presidents had more
than one wife, and I tried to represent each of them regardless of who the spouse was during the term in office. In
instances in which the wife of a vice-president had died and
another relative became his official hostess (Chester A.
Arthur's sister and Charles Curtis's half-sister are examples), I included information on these women as well.

Some of my forty-three sketches are brief because of
the obscurity of the subject (James S. Sherman and William
A. Wheeler) or the scarcity of illuminating source material
(John N. Garner destroyed his papers), and others are com-
paratively long because of the serious work already done
(Abigail Adams and Edith Roosevelt), or because of the ex-
istence of numerous published letters and memoirs (Harry
Truman and Richard Nixon). In a few cases, the availability
of a recent definitive study of a minor figure (George M.
Dallas) simplified my task; but for several others (Richard
Nixon and Lyndon Johnson) the multiplicity of studies ob-
liged me to cut fresh paths through tangled testimony.

Most of the published material utilized in the writing
of this book came from the University of Iowa Libraries,
which contain rich and readily accessible collections on American history and biography. My manuscript was typed by

Miss Doris J. Stuck, my former secretary in the University of Iowa Libraries, and I am grateful for her valued assistance. My wife, Marie G. Dunlap, waited patiently during the many hours I spent in pursuit of our forty-three vice-presidents and their ladies.

Leslie W. Dunlap
Iowa City, Iowa
May 30, 1987

JOHN ADAMS, 1789-1797

John Adams (1735-1826) was born in Braintree
(now Quincy), Massachusetts, and was graduated
in 1755 from Harvard College. His father, a
farmer, expected his son to become a minister,
but John studied law and was admitted to the
bar in 1758. He early opposed British measures
for taxation of the colonies and was chosen as
a delegate from Massachusetts to the First and
Second Continental Congress. In the latter,
through studious preparation and diligence,
Adams demonstrated his large capacities which
led to diplomatic missions from 1778 to 1788 in
France, Holland, and England. After George
Washington had been elected unanimously to the
office of president under the new government,
the sixty-nine electors cast their second votes:
John Adams led among the eleven candidates
and was named vice-president.

John Adams served during President Washington's two terms as vice-president, an office
which he did not find to be congenial or challenging, yet he held on because he aspired to
the presidency. This he achieved in 1800, but
the leader of the opposition party, Thomas
Jefferson, became vice-president. President
Adams had thorny problems with the revolutionary government of France, and his first mission
to mediate was rebuffed by French leaders.
Adams avoided a war with France by sending
a second mission which reached an amicable
agreement, but the president's bold action an-
gered leaders of his own party who were ignored
in his resolution of the crisis.

The Federalists lost the election in 1800 to

the Democratic-Republicans, and Adams retired
to Quincy where he became the patriarch of a
family which included his wife, the remarkable
Abigail Adams, and a son, John Quincy Adams,
who became the sixth president of the United
States. John Adams died at the age of ninety
on July 4, 1826, the fiftieth anniversary of the
signing of the Declaration of Independence.

                        *   *   *

On April 13, 1789, the day after John Adams received official
notice of his election to the vice-presidency, he left for New
York, the first capital of the new United States of America.
George Washington took the oath of office on April 30, and
after the ceremony, he delivered his inaugural address. His
face was "grave and sad, and his hands shook so that at
times he had trouble reading his speech...." Many (Adams
among them), remembering all that had gone before and seeing the stern, proud man so moved, wept unashamedly."

John Adams had served his country at the courts in
France, Holland, and England for ten years before he became
the first vice-president. His experiences abroad made him
aware of the importance of protocol and titles in facilitating
the business of government, but his perception of the subject
was not supported by the senators over whom he presided
as a duty under the Constitution. Adams lectured the Senate, which he was not entitled to do, and he was disturbed
by the localism of members of Congress from New England,
by a memorial from Quakers on the abolition of slavery, and
by numerous appeals from old friends and deserving patriots
for jobs in the new government. The frustrations mounted
and barely two weeks after President Washington's inauguration, the new vice-president summoned his wife from the farm
in "still, calm, happy Braintree" (her phrase). John wanted
Abigail to leave immediately; she could let his brother manage
the farm, she could borrow money for the trip, and if she
was unable to do so, she should sell their valued farm animals. "If no one will take the place," John Adams persisted,
"leave it to the birds of the air and beasts of the field, but
at all events break up that establishment and that household."

For fifty-four years John and Abigail Adams were joined
in a solid marriage which was marked by separations of month

after month while he served in the two Continental Congresses and of consecutive years while he represented the Continental government in France and at The Hague. Although he dearly loved his wife, his family, and his farm at Braintree, John Adams had politics in his blood. Toward the end of his second term as vice-president, Adams could not ignore the possibility of succeeding Washington in the presidency. "I am weary of the Game," he told Abigail, yet "I don't know how I could live out of it." Although Abigail wanted her husband at home, she was more than willing for John to participate in the two Continental Congresses. After he had demonstrated his capabilities in the debates in Philadelphia, the colonial government named him to a mission in France. Yet Abigail, who hated to see her husband go abroad, did not try to keep him at home. Indeed, the pattern of her running the farm in Braintree and of his serving as a statesman far from Massachusetts had become so familiar to Abigail and John Adams that she chose to remain at home on the farm during her husband's second term as vice-president.

These frequent and lengthy separations and their desire to keep each other informed about incidents in their daily lives including illnesses, crop and weather reports, and dealings with notables (Washington, Jefferson, Franklin, and Hamilton, to name but a few), led to exchanges of hundreds of letters despite the hazards of poor roads, stormy seas, and possible interception by an enemy. Abigail and John also wrote letters to their children and grandchildren, and when Abigail did go to Europe to join her husband, she wrote in detail about her travels and experiences in foreign lands to her sisters in Massachusetts. The thousands of letters written by John and Abigail and other members of the Adams family, preserved by the Adams Trust, were opened for study in the third quarter of this century. The extensive Adams family papers were photographed in 608 reels of microfilm, copies of which were offered for sale; selected family correspondence, John's diary, and Abigail's journal of her voyage to England were published in the 1960s and 1970s in book form. Because of the recent accessibility of this mine of personal documents, new, thorough studies of John Adams--Page Smith's two volumes entitled simply John Adams (1962) and Peter Shaw's The Character of John Adams (1976) --have appeared, as well as a separate, full-length treatment of Abigail Adams by Lynne Withey, entitled Dearest Friend (1981).

John Adams was born on October 30, 1735, at Braintree, near Boston, Massachusetts. His father, a farmer,
wanted his eldest son to attend Harvard as a preparation for
the ministry. However, after John graduated in 1755 and
taught school for several years in Worcester, he decided to
study law. While at Harvard, John Adams developed "a
growing curiosity, a Love of Books, and a fondness for
Study" which became one of his strongest traits. In 1772
while riding the legal circuit he became annoyed with his
"wandering, itinerating life" and longed for the sights and
sounds of home. After naming some of the attractions he
missed, including "my Grass and Blossoms and Corn," the
young lawyer and husband concluded, "But above all except
the Wife and Children I want to see my books." Thirty
years later he wrote to Abigail, "I read my eyes out and
can't read half enough neither. The more one reads the
more one sees we have to read."

John Adams' fondness for study led him to work for
the enlightenment of the Second Continental Congress with a
zeal unmatched by his colleagues; he was chairman of twenty-
five committees and a member of sixty-five more. According
to Dr. Benjamin Rush, "Every member of Congress in 1776
acknowledged him [Adams] to be the first man in the House."
The books he wrote, including his A Defense of the Consti-
tutions of Government in three volumes, were not popular
when new and are seldom read today. Adams succeeded as
a public speaker through "force of argument" and "strength
of language," but he often was sarcastic and uncomplimentary
toward his opponents.

Adams' personality has been described by Page Smith,
his most careful biographer, as "craggy." Ambition and the
"passion for distinction" caused him at time to be jealous of
the fame of successful contemporaries. Throughout his life,
Adams strove above all else to be independent. Adams' relations in France with Benjamin Franklin deteriorated until
Franklin wrote to the Congress, "I am persuaded ... that
he [Adams] means well for his Country, is always an Honest
Man, often a wise one, but sometimes, and in some things,
absolutely out of his senses." Adams once declared, "I have
long since learned that a man may give offense and yet succeed." This statement fairly reflects Adams' political career
for he feuded with Hutchinson, Franklin, Hamilton, and others, yet he made important contributions in many different

posts and rose to the highest office in the land. A thoughtful student has observed that Adams' behavior as president
was "as enigmatic as his complex personality."

The office of vice-president was not a congenial one
for John Adams who was obliged to preside over the Senate
but could not participate in debates; and, as is well known,
he complained to Abigail, "My country has in its wisdom con-
trived for me the most insignificant office that was the in-
vention of man." Abigail, always helpful in dispelling her
husband's dark moods, observed that if the office of vice-
president were held by a scheming politician, the country
might resort to civil war. She added that "the only fault"
in her husband's "political character" was "a certain irritabil-
ity" which sometimes placed him at a disadvantage in personal
relations. At the time, John was almost sixty and was probably unable to see real benefit in any of the things that disturbed him.

Abigail was born in 1744 in Weymouth, a town directly
south of Braintree. Her father, William Smith, was a minister, and her home gave her opportunities to learn which
were not enjoyed by many girls in New England in the middle
of the eighteenth century. Girls ordinarily learned to read
(a prerequisite for knowledge of the Bible) and to do simple
arithmetic required for household accounts, but the three
Smith girls (Abigail in particular) spent many hours in their
father's library where they enjoyed reading literature and
history. According to her biographer, "Abigail was largely
self-taught, a fact that shows in her writings.... Her spelling is unorthodox, her capitalization random, and her punc-
tuation almost nonexistent."

Regardless of stylistic faults, Abigail wrote many, many
letters of interest for their content and expressiveness of
feeling. Through her letters she could visit with her absent
husband. "I want to sit down and converse with you every
evening," she wrote. Through her simple prose Abigail
could capture the heart of a topic in beautiful English. In
a letter to John written three weeks before their marriage,
Abigail told him that her belongings would be ready for the
move to their new home after he returned from Taunton, and
added in becoming frankness, "And--then Sir, if you please
you may take me." During the Revolutionary War, Abigail
spent time in an aunt's room in Boston where she admired

the convenient arrangements for letter writing and mused,
"I always had a fancy for a closet with a window which I
could more peculiarly call my own." A year later, while
John was in Philadelphia, Abigail wrote him about the birth
of their stillborn child, "I had pleased myself with the Idea
of presenting him [her husband] a fine son or daughter on
his return ... but [those] dreams are buried in the Grave,
transitory as the morning Cloud, short lived as the Dew
Drops."

       Abigail's best-known line was written to her husband
at the Second Continental Congress, "I desire you would
Remember the Ladies, and be more generous and favourable
to them than your ancestors.... If perticular care and attention is not paid to the Ladies we are determined to foment
a Rebellion and will not hold ourselves bound by any Laws
in which we have no voice, or Representation." On the surface, Abigail's sentiment would place her at the head of the
movement to liberate women in the United States, but her
statement was written on March 31, 1776, long before any
thought of drafting a new constitution. The most careful
evaluation of Abigail's intent indicates that she was teasing
her husband. John's reply joked about the threatened rebellion of the ladies, for "as Abigail well knew, masculine
domination was more in theory than in fact."

       Abigail believed that women should receive better edu-
cation to enable them to become better mothers and teachers
for their children. She also argued that women could learn
as rapidly as men and arranged for her daughter to study
Latin, an opportunity which had not been hers. When John
learned of this innovation, he was pleased but cautioned his
daughter, "You must not tell many people of it, for it is
scarcely reputable for young ladies to understand Latin and
Greek."

       Abigail's most impressive achievement was her capacity
to do innumerable things exceedingly well. She could pamper
a husband, mother her own and other children, manage her
farm and her household, sit with the sick, and face with
fortitude every situation that she had to confront. Typical
of Abigail's remarkable ability to improve the circumstances
in which she found herself was her effort to remove the
filth that abounded on the ship in which she sailed in 1784
to Europe with her daughter, two servants, and a cow to

provide milk for the voyage. After Abigail had recovered
from a violent attack of seasickness, she organized a work
crew to make the ship livable. Under Abigail's direction,
her servant Briesler worked with a group of crewmen who
used "Scrapers, mops, Brushes, infusions of vinegar &c.
and in a few hours we found there was Boards for a floor."
Not content with one successful Herculean labor, Abigail
"taught the cook to dress his victuals, and we have made
several puddings with my own hands."

All of Abigail's relatives, friends, and neighbors admired her vigor and seemingly unlimited capacity for usefulness. After her illness in 1816, John wrote to their son,
a future president, "Your Mother is ... restored to her characteristic vivacity, activity, witt, sense and benevolence.
Of consequence she must take upon herself the Duties of
Granddaughter, Neice, Maids, Husband and all. She must
be allways writing to you and all her Grandchildren." When
Abigail suffered a stroke in October, 1818, the townspeople
of Quincy (formerly Braintree) could not believe that this
truly remarkable life was near an end. After her death on
November 10, 1818, John wrote to his son, "The bitterness
of death is past, the grim spoiler ... has no sting left for .
me." Smith phrased it succinctly, "The great music was
over."

John Adams continued to be active until shortly before
his death at the age of ninety on July 4, 1826, the fiftieth anniversary of the signing of the Declaration of Independence. In an extraordinary coincidence, his friend and fellow patriot, Thomas Jefferson, died on the very same day.

PRINCIPAL SOURCES

The Book of Abigail and John. Selected Letters.... Edited
    by L. H. Butterfield, et al. Cambridge, Mass.: Harvard
    Univ. Press, 1975. 411 p.

Peter Shaw. The Character of John Adams. Williamsburg,
    Va.: Institute of Early American History and Culture,
    [1976]. 324 p.

Page Smith. John Adams. Garden City, N.Y.: Doubleday,
    1962. 2 vols.

Lynne Withey. Dearest Friend, a Life of Abigail Adams.
    New York: Free Press, [1981].   369 p.

THOMAS JEFFERSON, 1797-1801

Thomas Jefferson (1743-1826) was the son of
Peter Jefferson, a large landowner in Albemarle
county, Virginia, and of Jane Randolph, a member of one of the most distinguished families of
the colony. The boy was tutored privately until
1760 when he entered the College of William and
Mary from which he was graduated in 1762.
Thomas then studied law under a noted teacher,
George Wythe; and, after admission to the bar
in 1767, he practiced successfully until the eve
of the Revolution.

Jefferson was a member of the Virginia House
of Burgesses from 1769 until 1794, and revealed
his exceptional skill as a writer in a document
drafted for the Virginia convention which sent
him as a delegate to the first and second Continental Congress. There his reputation as a
writer brought him a place on the committee to
draft a declaration of independence for which
he became the principal author. Jefferson left
Congress in September of 1776 to serve in the
Virginia House of Delegates until he became
governor, 1779-1781. Jefferson returned in
1783 to Congress, which appointed him in 1784
to assist Franklin and Adams in negotiating
commercial treaties in Paris, and in 1785 Jefferson succeeded Franklin as minister to France
where he remained for four years. On his return Jefferson accepted Washington's invitation
to become the first secretary of state, an office
in which he was frequently at odds with Alexander Hamilton, secretary of the treasury and
a Federalist.

Jefferson believed his resignation from the

Cabinet at the end of 1790 marked the close of
his political career, yet he continued to lead the
Republicans and agreed to be a candidate for
the presidency in 1796. Jefferson ran second
to John Adams and became vice-president, an
office which made few demands on him and paid
well. After his single term as vice-president,
Jefferson served as president for two terms,
1801-1809, during which the United States purchased the vast Louisiana Territory and struggled to keep out of a war between England and
France.

In retirement, Jefferson helped to establish
the University of Virginia, and he enjoyed international recognition as a scholar and statesman. His last years were beset with serious
financial problems and after his death on July
4, 1826, some of his valued possessions had to
be sold to satisfy creditors.

*   *   *

In the "Preface" to a compilation of The Family Letters of
Thomas Jefferson (1966), James Adam Bear, Jr. observed
the following: "Thomas Jefferson was a prolific letter writer
in a great letter-writing age: it has been estimated that he
wrote and received as many as fifty thousand letters." In
his late seventies, Jefferson received in one year 1,267 letters, "many of them requiring answers of elaborate research,
and all to be answered with due attention and consideration."
While minister to France, Jefferson broke his right wrist and
learned to write with his left hand; a few years before his
death another fall deprived him of the free use of his left
hand and writing of any kind "became very slow and painful."
Jefferson may have considered hiring a secretary to take dictation, but in his last years he was short of money and the
idea might not have appealed since he had written freely and
definitively on numerous topics for more than four decades.
Although he enjoyed correspondence with old friends, John
Adams, James Madison, and the Marquis de Lafayette among
them, his greatest pleasure came from writing loving letters
replete with fatherly advice to near relatives, especially to
his two daughters and twelve grandchildren. Regrettably,
not a single letter remains of any correspondence between
Jefferson and his wife. The editor of The Family Letters of

Thomas Jefferson concluded, "It is believed that he destroyed them after her death."

Thomas Jefferson was born on April 13, 1743, in a plain farm house at "Shadwell" in Albemarle County, Virginia. His father was a leader in the county, and his mother was a Randolph, one of Virginia's most distinguished families. On the death of his father, Thomas Jefferson at age fourteen became the owner of 5,000 acres of land and some slaves. His formal education began at home under tutors, and before he enrolled in William and Mary College, he was proficient on the violin, had learned to play chess, and was adept in riding and in judging horses. He left William and Mary after two years and began, in 1762, the study of law under George Wythe, a learned teacher who was to become a lifelong friend and mentor.

In his late twenties Jefferson commenced his courtship of Martha Wayles Skelton, an attractive widow of twenty-three who lived on her father's estate, "The Forest," near Williamsburg. Jefferson had known Martha's late husband, Bathurt Skelton, in college, and her father, John Wayles, as a lawyer and landowner who had accumulated a sizeable fortune. According to a restrained evaluation by one of her great-granddaughters, Sarah N. Randolph, Martha Skelton was "very beautiful. A little above middle height, with a lithe and exquisitely formed figure, she was a model of graceful and queenlike carriage." The young woman "was well educated for her day and a constant reader." The household accounts she kept reflect method and industry, and she loved music. Legend has it that Martha favored Jefferson over her other suitors partly because he, too, knew and enjoyed music. In the words of Dumas Malone, Jefferson's most thorough biographer, "She played on the harpsichord and pianoforte, as he did on the violin and cello."

The license bond for the marriage of Thomas Jefferson and Martha Skelton is dated December 23, 1771, and the ceremony took place on New Year's Day in 1772 at the bride's home, "The Forest." The newlyweds left promptly for Monticello and arrived after a difficult journey over mountain roads in deep snow. Their life together promised only good fortune; his income as a lawyer and landowner amounted to $5,000 per annum, and in the year after their marriage her inheritance of her father's estate almost matched Thomas Jefferson's substantial patrimony.

The Jeffersons' first child, a daughter named Martha, was born in September of 1772, and their second child, another girl, was born a year later and died at the age of eighteen months. In their ten years of married life the Jeffersons had six children; only two of them, Martha and Mary (born in 1778), survived infancy.

Despite their loss of four young children, Thomas and Martha Jefferson enjoyed a happy marriage. He prized "domestic felicity" above all else and believed that it was the wife who was mainly responsible for creating a congenial home environment. Twice a year he traveled to Williamsburg for meetings of the Virginia assembly, and his attendance was regular unless "his wife was ill or expecting." At home he was the very model of "a dutiful husband and father, the master of Monticello, and the student of everything that rubbed the surface of his mind."

In 1779 Jefferson was elected to succeed Patrick Henry as governor of Virginia, but he resigned at the end of his second year in office because of his concern for his wife's health. In 1781 British troops approached his estate, and Jefferson put his wife and children in a carriage to flee for safety while he remained behind to collect his most valuable papers. Jefferson settled his family on his estate at "Poplar Forest"; meanwhile, his plantation on the James River "was ravaged, the slaves carried away ... [and] the tobacco crop destroyed." In 1782 the Jeffersons were back at Monticello where they entertained a distinguished French visitor who described Jefferson's wife in his published Travels as "mild and amiable." During his visit, Martha was carrying their sixth child, a daughter, who was born in May of 1782. After childbirth Martha did not regain her health, and it became apparent that she would not recover.

During his wife's last illness, Jefferson, for four months, was never far from her bedside. When Martha died in September, Jefferson (as his daughter, then ten years old, recalled years later), was led from the bedroom in a state of insensibility into his library where he fainted and did not soon revive. Afterwards he remained in his room for three weeks, and when he finally came out he mounted his horse and rode aimlessly through the woods nearby and around the mountain.

Martha Jefferson left three children, Martha, Mary,
and Lucy Elizabeth, who died at age two while her father
was abroad. After Jefferson's death, locks of hair from his
deceased wife, daughter and children who had died in infancy
were found in a drawer in his room, according to a great-
granddaughter who wrote with the relics in front of her.
The packages containing the locks of hair were labelled in
Jefferson's own hand; one, which contained a few strands
of hair from the head of an infant, bore Jefferson's statement, "A lock of our first Lucy's hair, with some of my
dear, dear wife's writing."

When Jefferson resigned his commission as governor of
Virginia, he promised his wife that he would not again accept
public office. While she was alive, Jefferson twice declined
an appointment by Congress to serve as a peace negotiator
with John Adams and Benjamin Franklin, and after her death,
the offer came anew. His wife with whom he had lived for
ten years "in unchequered happiness" had been dead for two
months when Jefferson accepted the appointment, and in the
spring of 1784 Jefferson received from Congress his orders
to go to Europe. He left his two younger children with their
maternal aunt, Mrs. Eppes of Eppington. The eldest, Martha,
went with her father on the Ceres which sailed from Boston
and had a short (nineteen-day), smooth voyage across the
Atlantic.

Jefferson had served five years (1784-1789) as the
American minister to France before he obtained leave to return to America to "look after his own private affairs" and
to take his daughters to Virginia, for "they were now of an
age when they should be associating with those among whom
they were to live." His elder daughter recalled their return:

> ... we reached Monticello on the 23d of December.
> The negroes discovered the approach of the carriage
> as it reached Shadwell.... They collected in crowds
> around it, and almost drew it up the mountain by
> hand.... When the door of the carriage was opened,
> they received him [Jefferson] in their arms and bore
> him to the house, crowding around and kissing his
> hands and feet--some blubbering and crying--others
> laughing.

Before he returned to Monticello Jefferson had been

offered the post of secretary of state in the new government
by President Washington, and on December 15 he agreed to
serve.   On February 23, 1790, Jefferson gave his daughter
Martha in marriage to Thomas Mann Randolph, and a few days
later he left for New York where he arrived on March 21.
At the end of 1793 Jefferson resigned from the Cabinet with
a resolve never to return to public office.   He intended to
rebuild Monticello and to enjoy life as a private citizen.

Madison and other leaders persuaded Jefferson to stand
again for office as the leader of the Democratic-Republican
party opposed to the Federalists, and in 1796 he was elected
vice-president to serve under John Adams.   Although Jefferson described his new post as a "tranquil and unoffending
station," he recognized its attractions, "high position, good
salary, and ample leisure."   His predecessor in the office,
John Adams, in his constitutional role as presiding officer
of the Senate, had ruled on points of order without any system, and Jefferson undertook to provide a manual of procedure to be followed in debates in the Senate.   Through careful study of the rules of Parliament in his library at Monticello, Jefferson compiled a Manual of Parliamentary Practice
which was first published in 1801 and has been reprinted
hundreds of times.   Jefferson's "Manual" is included in the
current Senate Manual, and it has been adopted in part for
rules in the House of Representatives and in state legisla-
tures.

Jefferson served from 1801 to 1809 as the third president of the United States, and he was the first to be inaugurated in Washington, D.C.   He had been deeply involved
in the design and developments of the new capital, the location of which was closer to Jefferson's home than New York
and Philadelphia, the two earlier seats of government.   Jefferson, as president, advanced "the holy cause of Freedom"
and established the right of citizens to oppose the party in
power.   During his two terms in office, Louisiana was purchased in 1803 from France, the conspiracy of Aaron Burr
culminated in a drawn-out trial for treason in 1807, and an
Embargo Act was enacted in 1807 to keep the country from
involvement in the war between England and France.   The
embargo hurt New England shipping interests and damaged
Jefferson's reputation throughout the country.

As vice-president, Jefferson lived in style in Philadelphia.

He kept five horses and had four or five male servants in addition to his steward, Petit, who had followed him from France. While his younger daughter was with him in Philadelphia, she had her own maid. As president, Jefferson purchased four full-blooded bays to draw his carriage in Washington. The horses delighted both Jefferson and his coachman and cost him $1,600, surely a considerable sum for a purchase mainly for display in 1801.

Although Jefferson served in a succession of colonial, state, and national offices--he wrote in 1826 that he had devoted sixty-one years to public service--he yearned almost continuously for the freedom in which to enjoy his farms, his books, and his family at his beloved Monticello near Charlottesville, Virginia. When apart from his family he wrote numerous letters and fretted over delays in receiving replies. When his eldest daughter was but eleven, Jefferson admonished, "Take care that you never spell a word wrong," and in a postscript he instructed the young girl, "Keep my letters and read them at times, that you may always have present in your mind those things which will endear you to me." Jefferson was so concerned with the development of his two daughters that he usually wrote with great seriousness, and he counseled them as children regardless of their ages. When his younger daughter, Mary, was twenty-three years of age and married, Jefferson did not hesitate to protest her "willingness to withdraw from society more than is prudent," and encouraged her "to mix with the world, and to keep pace with it as it goes."

Whenever Jefferson was able to escape from official duties he hurried to Monticello, and he did his utmost to arrange for his daughters and their families to be there at the same time. His daughters and grandchildren delighted in his company, but his two sons-in-law must have chafed under his pervasive affection and directions. In retirement at Monticello, Jefferson devoted his mornings to correspondence, between breakfast and dinner he inspected his shops and gardens or rode on horseback to his farms, from dinner to dark he talked with his family and visitors, and from candlelight to early bedtime he read. When the demands of letter writing had become a heavy burden, "the life of a millhorse," he especially regretted the time away from his books, for as he wrote in 1822 to John Adams, "reading is my delight."

In his last years at Monticello, Jefferson found great
pleasure in planning for and serving as the first rector of
a new University of Virginia in nearby Charlottesville and
in teaching young men who came to learn from the distinguished philosopher and honored statesman. Jefferson enjoyed the society of the young men who read in his library
and listened to his counsel: "In advising the course of their
reading, I endeavor to keep their attention fixed on the main
objects of all science, the freedom and happiness of man."
Jefferson's fame brought hosts of visitors to Monticello, many
of whom intruded on his time and thoughtlessly expected to
be dined and entertained. But some of his visitors brought
great pleasure. Lafayette and Jefferson had not met since
the latter returned from France in 1789, and their reunion
at Monticello in 1824 was an emotional event:

> As Lafayette descended from the carriage, Jeffer-
> son descended the steps of the portico.... Jefferson
> was feeble and tottering with age--Lafayette perman-
> ently lamed and broken in health by his long confine-
> ment in the dungeon of Olmutz. As they approached
> each other, their uncertain gait quickened itself into
> a shuffling run ... they burst into tears as they fell
> into each other's arms.

Death came to Thomas Jefferson on July 4, 1826, the
fiftieth anniversary of the Declaration of Independence. He
was buried beside his wife and daughter Mary, and his grave
is marked by a monument which notes his authorship of the
Declaration of Independence and of the Statute of Virginia
for Religious Freedom and his part in the founding of the
University of Virginia. He also left a rich legacy of letters
and other writings which are unmatched for clarity in thought
and precision in expression.

PRINCIPAL SOURCES

The Family Letters of Thomas Jefferson. Ed. by E. M. Betts
    and J. A. Bear, Jr. Columbia: Univ. of Missouri Press,
    [1966]. 506 p.

Dumas Malone. Jefferson, the Virginian. Boston: Little,
    Brown, [1948]. 484 p. (Jefferson and His Time, I)

_____. Jefferson and the Ordeal of Liberty. Boston:
   Little, Brown, 1962.   545 p.   (Jefferson and His Time,
   III)

Merrill D. Peterson.   Thomas Jefferson and the New Nation,
   A Biography.   New York: Oxford, 1970.   1,072 p.

Sarah N. Randolph.   The Domestic Life of Thomas Jefferson.
   Third edition.   Cambridge: Univ. Press, 1939.   383 p.
   (First published in 1871)

Aaron Burr (1756-1836) was the grandson of
Jonathan Edwards, philosopher and theologian,
who became president of the College of New Jersey in 1758. Aaron graduated with distinction
from the same college in 1772 and began to study
theology, but turned in 1774 to law. His studies
were interrupted by service in the American army
from which he resigned in March 1779 with the
rank of colonel, because of ill health. After
further study Burr was licensed to practice law
in New York where his brilliance and attractive
personality brought him important cases. Yet,
his extravagant habits and speculations exceeded
his income.

In his political career in New York, Burr
found his ambitions thwarted by one faction, led
by Alexander Hamilton, and he was not sought
after by George Clinton, leader of the second.
Burr proved himself valuable enough to Governor
Clinton to be named attorney general in 1789,
and he went on in 1791-1797 to the United States
Senate. In 1798 Burr returned for two years
to the New York Assembly; through his organizational work, the Democratic-Republicans won
control in 1800 of the New York legislature and
Burr received endorsement for the vice-presidency.
While in the office, Burr lost favor with leaders
of his party, ran unsuccessfully for governor of
New York, and in 1804 killed his implacable enemy,
Alexander Hamilton, in a duel.

Unsuccessful in his efforts to advance in state
and national governments, Burr turned to a
scheme to free Spanish possessions in North
America and to possibly create a country in the

18

Mississippi Valley separate from the United States.
Burr's dream was smashed by his co-conspirator,
General James Wilkinson, and the adventurer was
tried for treason in the summer of 1807. After
acquittal Burr went to Europe where he spent
four years trying to enlist support for his fool-
hardy plan. When he did return in 1812 to New
York, Burr enjoyed a prosperous law practice
and resumed his carefree ways until his death
in 1836 at the age of eighty.

*   *   *

Madame Theodosia Bartow Prevost was the wife of a British
colonel, James Mark Prevost, who went with his regiment to
the West Indies in the early 1770s. Their home, "The
Hermitage," near Paramus, New Jersey, was a large, Gothic-
style house, where Mrs. Prevost lived during the Revolution
with some of her five children, her mother, and a half-sister.
Regardless of her husband's service in the British army,
Theodosia Prevost opened her home to American army officers
stationed in the vicinity, and her guests included General
Washington and his staff, General Charles Lee, Colonel James
Monroe, and Colonel Aaron Burr. Aaron Burr's visits to
"The Hermitage" probably began in the fall of 1777, while he
and his regiment were camped about fifteen miles away. During his many visits with Theodosia Prevost amidst her delight-
ful family and friends, Aaron Burr fell in love with his hostess who was ten years his senior and the wife of Colonel
Prevost since 1763.

Theodosia Prevost was truly a remarkable woman. Although not reputed to be a beauty, she possessed a mind and
heart which proved irresistible to Aaron Burr, who was in
his early twenties when he became enchanted with Theodosia
Prevost. She spoke French fluently (an accomplishment which
probably derived in part from living with her husband, a
native of Switzerland), and she often quoted from the better-
known French and Latin poets. She, like Aaron, was an avid
reader, and they enjoyed reading and discussing the same
authors, in particular, Rousseau and Lord Chesterfield. The
latter's Letters, in which the ideal eighteenth-century gentleman was delineated, became Burr's bible, and according to
several of his biographers, furnish the best key to his char-
acter--the style of a performance was of greater importance

than a pertinent principle which otherwise might have directed his conduct.

Theodosia's husband died in mid-October of 1781 in
Jamaica, probably of a fever which had stricken his regiment,
and she was free to marry again. Aaron pressed his suit,
but she refused to accept him largely because of concern
over her poor health, which led to spells of melancholy.
Burr pursued Theodosia to Connecticut and back to the
"Hermitage" where they were married on July 2, 1782. By
this time Aaron Burr had been admitted to the bar in New
York, and within a year the couple moved to New York City
where Burr believed a host of legal problems would follow
close on the evacuation of the British troops.

In spite of Theodosia's steadily declining health, the
couple had twelve good years together. Although the practice of law obliged Aaron to travel a great deal, they both
managed to write about the details of their daily lives.
Their first child, a daughter to be named Theodosia, was
born in Albany on June 21, 1873, and a second daughter,
named Sally Reeve after Burr's married sister, was born in
the summer of 1785. The two girls were followed by two
stillbirths, but only Theodosia would reach adulthood. His
wife was many things to him: companion, mistress, business
associate, and even his seamstress, for she designed clothes
for him which he wore with pride. He encouraged her to
read Gibbon's History of the Decline and Fall of the Roman
Empire and shared with her his discovery of Mary Wollstone-
craft's Vindication of the Rights of Women. Theodosia was
herself an admirer of Catherine the Great, the empress of
Russia who had triumphed over "the mighty Emperor of the
Turks." Aaron had reason to admire his wife's intelligence,
and this led him to question the custom of providing boys
with one kind of education and girls with another. As a
consequence, he decided to give his daughter Theodosia the
kind of an education the son of a gentleman would have had
at the end of the eighteenth century. At the age of ten his
daughter was reading Terence and Horace in Latin, studying
Greek grammar, playing the harp and the piano, taking lessons in ballet, and learning to skate.

Aaron's income as a lawyer in New York rose rapidly,
and he acquired fine houses and furnishings and enjoyed the
best books and the best wines. The removal of the federal

government from New York to Philadelphia gave Burr the opportunity to acquire the handsome residence known as Richmond Hill. The Burrs improved the grounds and filled the
mansion with expensive furniture and hundreds of books on
many, many subjects. In these spacious and handsome surroundings, Burr entertained in princely fashion. A succession of French and American dignitaries were guests at Burr's
estate in the country and at the townhouse in the city where
he had his law office.

After his election to the Senate, Burr went to Philadelphia in October of 1791 to find suitable quarters before the
next session of Congress and the onset of winter. Soon
thereafter, Aaron begged Theodosia to join him, but she
found innumerable excuses for not doing so. She finally did
visit Philadelphia but did not like it and never returned.
Whenever the couple found their separation too hard to bear,
they would meet between New York and Philadelphia in inter-
mediate New Jersey. Burr's quarters in Philadelphia improved after he became vice-president; he moved into a handsome suite of rooms near the Capitol where he entertained in
the lavish fashion he had enjoyed in New York. His daughter Theodosia frequently visited him in Philadelphia and found
much to enjoy in the Quaker City. She was her father's
daughter and shared his lifelong "hunger for excitement"
and "dread of ennui."

Burr's wife's illness, presumably cancer, did not respond to treatment; she experienced brief remissions followed
by periods of intense pain. Her last years were spent in
agony, and Aaron offered to resign from the Senate in order
to be with her but she would not let him do so. He was in
Philadelphia when she died on May 28, 1794.

There were many other women in Burr's life, and he
came to be known as a womanizer. But he seemed to have
love only for his surviving daughter, Theodosia, on whom
he doted. The second Theodosia married Joseph Alston, a
wealthy South Carolinian, and she bore him a son, Aaron
Burr Alston. Childbirth left her unwell, and her symptoms
proved to be similar to those suffered by her mother. Aaron
Burr's grandson died in his eleventh year, and both Theodosia's
father and her husband believed that a trip to New York would
improve her spirits. Her health precluded a journey by land,
and her husband booked passage for her and her luggage,

which included numerous papers Burr had placed with her
for safekeeping. The Patriot was lost at sea, and Burr's
beloved daughter was gone at the age of thirty. Her de-
spondent husband, then governor of South Carolina, died
within four years at the age of thirty-seven, and her father
lived on for twenty-four years until his death on September
14, 1836, at the age of eighty.

During his last twenty-four years Burr tried to return
to his former style of living in New York. His return to the
practice of law proved to be prosperous, and he engaged
students, assistants, and office personnel. His romantic in-
volvements with women continued unabated during this period,
and he surrounded himself with young people, some his own
children by various women for whom he arranged classical
courses of study as a requisite preparation for entrance to
Princeton. At age seventy-seven Burr married again; his
second wife was then fifty-eight, a woman of great wealth
and unenviable reputation. Within a year, Eliza Jumal Burr
filed suit for a divorce from Aaron Burr whom she charged
with adultery with Jane McManus, a young client, and other
women. During the divorce proceedings, Burr protested
that the acts charged against him were impossible to perform
at his age, but the divorce was granted and the decree became final on the day of his death.

Burr's domestic life brought him great joy and deep
sadness, and his career as a politician was an extraordinary
mixture of notable small successes overwhelmed by mistakes
and failures on a grand scale. Aaron Burr seems to have
possessed charisma which helped him to manipulate people for
the advancement of his personal goals. Although his practice
of law brought him a substantial income, Burr usually lived
beyond his means because he was able to borrow large sums
of money from friends and from persons he barely knew.
When he devoted his energies and mind to a political campaign, such as the New York election in 1800 which Burr
won for the Republicans, he was an effective vote getter,
but at other times his Chesterfieldian pose kept him from
making the bargains essential for success. His conduct during the tie election with Jefferson for the presidency revealed
a man who wanted to gain with little effort an office he did
not deserve. As vice-president Burr fought a duel with his
longtime political enemy, Alexander Hamilton, and the subsequent death of his opponent made Burr a persona non grata

in many quarters. Burr was replaced as vice-president by former Governor Clinton, and President Jefferson would not give Burr an appointment which would save his political career. Instead of turning his back on politics in Philadelphia and returning to the practice of law in New York, Burr tried to realize his Napoleonic dream of the conquest of Mexico and possibly of the creation of a country in the Mississippi Valley separate from the eastern United States.

In the furtherance of his ambitious plans Burr was able to enlist followers with reputation and wealth, including his daughter and son-in-law who journeyed to Blennerhasset Island on the Ohio River, the place designated for the launching on the projected expedition. If the United States government had declared war on Spain, as appeared possible in 1806 and 1807, Burr's grandiose plans might have made him a heroic figure; but the financial support needed from foreign countries did not materialize and Burr was betrayed by his principal co-conspirator, General James Wilkinson. Burr was tried for treason in Richmond, Virginia, and was acquitted after a lengthy, sensational trial in the summer of 1807. Again, instead of returning to the work he knew in New York, Burr went to Europe where he spent four years nursing his grand design, borrowing money wherever possible, and pleading with the French government for a passport which would permit him to return to the United States.

Almost twenty years after John Adams left the presidency he recalled that during the summer of 1798 when Hamilton, Pinckney, and Knox were to be commissioned major generals in the army to be activated in the event of hostilities with France, Burr had applied for a brigadier generalship. When Adams proposed Burr's appointment to Washington, the old general responded, "By all that I have known and heard, Colonel Burr is a brave and able officer, but the question is, whether he has not equal talents at intrigue." Burr then was but forty-two and had not appeared on the national scene except for the one term he had served in the newly formed United States Senate.

PRINCIPAL SOURCE

Milton Lomask. <u>Aaron Burr</u>. New York: Farrar, Straus, Giroux, [1979 and 1982]. 2v.

GEORGE CLINTON, 1805-1812

George Clinton (1739-1812) was born in New
York and was admitted to the bar at the young
age of sixteen. He participated in 1758 in a
military expedition against Fort Frontenac, and
ten years later he was a member of the New York
State Assembly. In 1775-1776 Clinton was a delegate from New York to the Second Continental
Congress. Clinton was appointed in 1775 briga-
dier-general of militia, a rank which Congress
confirmed in March of 1777. In the same year
Clinton became governor of New York, a position he held continuously until 1795. Although
opposed to the proposed Federal Constitution
because he believed in state rights, Clinton,
as governor, presided at the state convention
that ratified the document. Increasing opposition from the Federalists caused Clinton to decline to stand in 1795 for reelection, but a Republican victory in 1800 returned Clinton to the
State Assembly and in 1801 to the office of
governor.

Although Clinton had publicly opposed adoption of the Constitution, he was soon reconciled
to the new government. During President Washington's residence in New York City in 1789
and 1790, the first president, Lady Washington,
Governor Clinton and his wife enjoyed friendly
social occasions. Clinton received a handful of
votes for the vice-presidency in the elections
held in 1789, 1793, and 1797, but not until 1804
did Clinton win the office to succeed Aaron
Burr, vice-president during Jefferson's first
term as president. George Clinton was sixty-
nine when he was reelected to serve as vice-

president during President Madison's first term.
The weary vice-president found presiding for
three hours over the Senate to be fatiguing;
his mental faculties became impaired, and he
died in office in Washington, D.C. on April 12,
1812.

*   *   *

When George Clinton succeeded Aaron Burr as vice-president
in 1805 he was sixty-five years old and had been a widower
for almost five years. He always went to Washington in his
own carriage, accompanied by a daughter and a servant, and
he took room and board "like a common member" of Congress,
maintained no home of his own, and made no attempt to entertain. Clinton was inept as the presiding officer of the Senate, and he found sitting in the Chair for three hours to be
extremely fatiguing. One of the senators from New Hampshire found Clinton to be venerable in appearance, with a
"pleasing cheerfulness," but "too old for the office he now
holds" for "time has impaired his mental faculties much as it
has the powers of his body."

Clinton had been commissioned a brigadier general by
the Continental Congress, and in 1777 he was elected first
governor of the state of New York, a post in which he served
seven terms with exceptional vigor and considerable success.
Early on he gained the friendship of George Washington, and
the governor and the first president entertained each other
frequently during the fall of 1789 and the first half of 1790
when the new government began in New York City.

Clinton had studied law as a young man, and his practice often took him to Kingston, county seat of Ulster, where
he wooed and won Cornelia Tappen, who was related to the
Livingstons and Wynkoops, families prominent in politics in
Ulster County. Cornelia had been born in 1744, and was
about twenty-six when she married. She had a friendly manner, but there is no reason to believe that there was any
close intellectual companionship between her and her husband
during their thirty years of marriage. The nearness of Revolutionary War campaigns and the location of legislative sessions in one New York town after another caused the Clintons to move their home from New Windsor to Poughkeepsie,
to New York City, and to Albany, and Clinton was away from

his wife for weeks at a time during legislative sessions held
in Fishkill, New Windsor, Newburgh, and Saratoga. The
perennial governor complained in 1781, "One month at most,
out of the last twelve, have I enjoyed the Society of my
Family & that not without Interruption by claims from one
quarter or another."

Cornelia Clinton was not a strong and healthy woman
during many of the years of her married life, yet she bore
her husband six children, including a daughter who married
Edmund Charles Genêt, the French minister whose political
activities offended the Washington administration. The Genêts
settled on a farm on Long Island, and while the governor
and his wife lived in New York City, they enjoyed seeing the
young married couple frequently. The Clintons did less official entertaining than was expected of a governor and his
lady, and this lack was attributed to his wife's poor health.
Nevertheless, the Clintons did host dinner parties for the
leaders of the new federal government, then located in New
York City, and both George and Cornelia Clinton enjoyed
the friendship of George and Martha Washington. The Clintons named their only son and one of their daughters, George
Washington Clinton and Martha Washington Clinton.

In the late fall of 1799 Cornelia Clinton became critically
ill, and her daughter Cornelia Genêt left the farm on Long
Island to care for her mother. On Saturday, March 15, 1800,
at the age of fifty-six, Cornelia Tappen Clinton died. According to George Clinton's biographer, E. W. Spaulding, he
probably felt the loss of his wife keenly. "In his years of
widowerhood George Clinton aged rapidly.... During the
last twelve years of his life he was a solitary, almost pathe-
tic figure." Cornelia had been dead for five years when "the
aged governor" began his first term as vice-president of the
United States. He died during his second term, on April 20,
1812, and official Washington and his home state of New York
recognized the passing of a heroic figure.

PRINCIPAL SOURCE

E. Wilder Spaulding. His Excellency George Clinton, Critic
    of the Constitution. New York: Macmillan, 1938. 325p.

ELBRIDGE GERRY, 1813-1814

After graduation from Harvard, Elbridge Gerry
(1744-1814) entered his family's prosperous shipping business in Marblehead, Massachusetts. After his election in 1772 to the Massachusetts General Court, Gerry became a follower of Samuel
Adams and an active participant in raising troops
and in providing supplies for the provincial army.
As a delegate to the Second Continental Congress,
Gerry advocated separation of the colonies from
Great Britain and was a signer of both the Declaration of Independence and the Articles of Con-
federation.

During the Revolution, Gerry's business flourished and he was wealthy at the time of his marriage, in 1786, to Ann Thompson, the young and
beautiful daughter of a New York merchant. His
bride did not want to live in Marblehead, and the
couple purchased a home in Cambridge where
they entertained in grand style. Ann went with
her husband to Philadelphia when he served in
1787 as a member of the Constitutional Convention. He refused to sign the completed document
because he did not wish to see the role of the
states reduced. Nevertheless, after the formation of the new government, Gerry served successively as a member of the House of Representatives, as a member of the "XYZ" mission to
France in 1797, and as vice-president of the
United States during James Madison's second
term as president. He also served two terms
as governor of Massachusetts; at this time his
name was linked to a plan ("Gerrymandering")
to redistrict the state to increase the strength
of his political party. Gerry's public career

obliged him to turn over his interest in his family
mercantile business to his brothers who failed to
make a profit, and after his sudden death on November 23, 1814, in Washington, his family was
left in desperate financial straits.

* * *

Ann Thompson, said to be "the most beautiful woman in the
United States," became the wife of Elbridge Gerry on January 12, 1786. She was the daughter of a New York merchant,
James Thompson, and had been brought up in the gay society of New York City and had traveled to Europe to finish
her education. Shortly after her return, Ann (at age twenty) became the wife of Elbridge Gerry, who then was forty-
one years old. Gerry had been brought up in Marblehead,
Massachusetts, as a member of a prosperous mercantile family, he had graduated from Harvard in 1765, and he had
been "a Signer," a member of the celebrated convention
which advocated in 1776 separation of the colonies from the
Mother Country. Gerry's business flourished during the
American Revolution, and he possessed a fortune at the time
of his marriage.

His bride did not care to live in Marblehead, and
Gerry purchased a handsome house, "Elmwood," and acreage
in Cambridge where the couple entertained in grand style.
In May of the year after his marriage Gerry traveled to the
Constitutional Convention in Philadelphia and was accompanied
by his wife and baby daughter. Living arrangements proved
to be unsatisfactory, and Ann and their child left to live with
her parents in New York. Gerry remained in Philadelphia
where he was active in deliberations of the Convention but
was inclined to leave because of concern for the health of
his wife and daughter. According to Gerry's biographer,
George Billias, "Ann proved to be a loving and affectionate
wife," and Elbridge "always found time to sit and unburden
himself at the end of each day to the woman he addressed
as 'My dearest life.'"

Gerry did not sign the proposed new constitution because he did not wish to see the role of the states drastically
reduced, yet after ratification he agreed to support the new
government and served successively in the House of Representatives, as a member of the famous "XYZ" mission to

France in 1797, and as vice-president of the United States
during the presidency of James Madison. He also served two
terms as governor of Massachusetts, and in this office his
name became linked in 1812 to the "Gerrymander Bill" which
redistricted the state in favor of the Republicans. Gerry
believed that men with ability such as his had an obligation
to serve in public life, yet he was unhappy away from his
family and concluded that true happiness was to be found at
home with his wife and children.

Ann Gerry experienced fainting spells during the year
after her marriage, and her health was weakened by a rapid
succession of pregnancies. During the first fifteen years of
marriage, the Gerrys had ten children. She did not move
from Cambridge to Boston during Gerry's two terms as governor, and she did not accompany him to Washington, "presumably because of her frail health." In spite of a stammer
in his speech and nervous mannerisms, Elbridge developed a
courtly presence which added to his enjoyment of female companionship. At the end of a day spent presiding over the
Senate he energetically pursued the social life associated with
the office of vice-president. His regular companion on these
rounds was Madame Bonaparte, the twenty-nine year old wife
of Napoleon's youngest brother, Jerome. Gerry did not conceal his enjoyment of the relationship with this extraordinary
young woman from the son who lived with the vice-president
in Washington or from others in his family at home in Cambridge.

Gerry's unwillingness to sign the proposed Constitution
of the United States and his independent activities while a
member of a three-man team to France reflected his solid belief in the rightness of his opinions and judgments. As one
of the Founding Fathers, but not one of the first rank, he
was devoted to the principles of Republican government and
reached conclusions that seemed idiosyncratic to contemporaries
who did not understand his basic orientation. Regardless of
his inability to work with persons with whom he disagreed,
Gerry earned and kept the regard of John Adams and of
Thomas Jefferson. After the dismal failure of his part in
the "XYZ" mission, Abigail Adams, who knew him well, wrote,
"Poor Gerry always had a wrong kink in his head." He returned on October 1, 1798 to Boston where he was met with
chill from persons he greeted on the street, and he learned
that his family had been harassed by neighborhood ruffians
who shouted obscenities under his wife's window at Elmwood.

Gerry was often unhappy in the public career that he followed as a duty, and he found it increasingly difficult to support his family in the fashion enjoyed in the early years of his marriage. Gerry had left his interest in the family mercantile business in Marblehead to the management of his brothers, who could not produce a profit, and he proceeded to invest heavily in securities and in land. As vice-president he failed to obtain appointments he sought from President Madison for members of his family, and at his sudden death in Washington on November 23, 1814, he was "land poor." His family was left in a desperate plight, and an effort to furnish Gerry's widow with what would have been his salary as vice-president until the completion of his term did not succeed. John Adams, true friend and fellow patriot, summarized the unhappy circumstances which surrounded Gerry at the end: "to die at seventy, leaving an amiable wife and nine amiable children [,] nothing for an inheritance but the contempt, hatred, and malice of the world."

PRINCIPAL SOURCE

George Athan Billias. Elbridge Gerry, Founding Father and
    Republican Statesman. New York: McGraw-Hill, [1976].
    442p.

DANIEL D. TOMPKINS, 1817–1825

Daniel D. Tompkins (1774-1825) was born in
Scarsdale, New York, and attended Columbia College from which he was graduated in 1795. Two
years later he was admitted to the bar and began
a practice in New York City. In 1804 he was
elected to Congress as a Democratic-Republican,
but he resigned almost immediately to become an
associate justice of the New York Supreme Court.
In 1807 Tompkins became governor of New York,
a post he held for ten years during which important reform measures were adopted. During the
War of 1812 Governor Tompkins accepted the
command of the military district that included
southern New York and eastern New Jersey and
directed construction of defenses for the port
of New York. Expenses for these operations
were financed in part through loans for which
Tompkins pledged his personal credit, and the
records thereof were intermingled with charges
against state and federal funds.

In 1817 Tompkins was elected vice-president,
and he was reelected in 1821 to serve a second
term under President James Monroe. At times
his salary as vice-president was withheld because Tompkins was technically in debt to the
government, which had not paid him for military
expenditures made during the War of 1812.
His attendance at sessions of the Senate was
infrequent during his first term as vice-president
and worsened during his second. Tompkins'
health declined rapidly near the end of his second term, and he died on Staten Island on June
11, 1825, barely three months after he had
ceased to be the vice-president.

*   *   *

Daniel Tompkins, who served as vice-president with President
Monroe for eight years during the "Era of Good Feelings,"
was absent from the Senate nearly three-fourths of the time
during his first term. He took the oath of office for his
second term in New York, and his constitutional duty to preside over the Senate was neglected even more during his
second term. His wife, Hannah, had been seriously ill the
year before Tompkins was inaugurated in 1817 and did not
attend the event. Indeed, she seems never to have made
what was then a strenuous journey from Staten Island to
Washington and back. The vice-president found one trip by
post chaise over rough roads between New York and Philadelphia to be so unpleasant that he made the rest of the
journey by water, and he asked Hannah to ship his carriage
to Washington to permit a more comfortable return.

As vice-president, Tompkins was a tragic figure. Before the end of his first term he was broken in health and
finances, and he appeared to be prematurely old. Moreover,
his drinking to excess, which must have embarrassed his
family and friends, was noted publicly by an elector from
New Hampshire who refused to cast his vote for Monroe,
whom he criticized for unwarranted expenditures, or for
Tompkins, whom he characterized as "grossly intemperate."

Tompkins' earlier career was distinguished by good
fortune and major accomplishments. After graduation in 1795
from Columbia College he studied law, and after beginning
legal practice, he won the hand of Hannah Minthorne, whom
he had courted while an undergraduate. According to Tompkins' careful biographer Ray W. Irwin, Hannah had "charm,
intelligence, tact, wealth, family background--and a father
who was a power in the public life of New York." Her upbringing in a wealthy family in New York prepared her to
preside with particular grace at festivities in the governor's
mansion in Albany during Tompkins' four terms in office.
He was elected first in 1807 and was reelected in 1810, 1813,
and 1816, but was defeated in 1820 when he ran again near
the end of his first term as vice-president. As governor,
Tompkins led the New York Assembly to adopt measures for
reform in penal codes, better treatment of Negroes and Indians, more equitable support for the state militia, and for
improvements in the school system. During the War of 1812

Tompkins proved to be an exceptionally able leader. In spite
of bungling federal military officers, woefully insufficient
supplies needed by the militia to defend the exposed borders
of New York, and inadequate funds for the payment of troops
and supplies, Tompkins accepted the command of the military
district that included southern New York and eastern New
Jersey and directed the construction of defenses for the port
of New York. In raising money for these varied activities,
Tompkins borrowed from banks and pledged his personal
credit. The records of his transactions with state and federal funds became confused, and Tompkins was, for years,
unable to secure repayment from the state of New York and
the government of the United States. Tompkins' honesty in
handling of the monies that had passed through his office
was unquestioned, but political charges were levied against
him because he was technically in default to his state and
country. Payment of his salary as vice-president was withheld because he was legally in arrears as a creditor, and
the judgments against him included one in the amount of
$25,000 due his father-in-law, who had endorsed some of
Tompkins' many notes and found himself in financial straits
during the depression which occurred about 1820.

Tompkins lived only a few months after the end of his
second term as vice-president. During the winter and spring
months of 1825 his health declined rapidly, he drank heavily,
became morose and irritable, and at the time of his death on
June 11 at home in Tompkinsville on Staten Island he was
involved in a law suit against his son-in-law, Gilbert Thompson, over a parcel of land. Tompkins was buried at St.
Mark's where lie the bodies of two other governors of New
York. Each had served during a stormy period in New York
history, and according to the evaluation of Tompkins' biographer Ray W. Irwin, "Each man ... had performed the ex-
acting duties of his high office with vigor, courage, and re-
sourcefulness."

During most of David Tompkins' public career Hannah
remained in the background, and there are few notices of her
activities. She bore her husband four children before he
became governor and four more during his first two terms in
Albany. Hannah Tompkins and her children ordinarily spent
portions of each year with her family in New York City, and
her parents occasionally visited her home in Albany. In letters to political associates Tompkins mentioned that Hannah

had been ill, but she joined with him in entertaining President Monroe and General Lafayette on their visits to New York.

Tompkins was mindful of his responsibilities toward his wife and children and for a time enabled them to enjoy the good life then to be found in New York. While governor, Tompkins declined President Madison's offer of the post of secretary of state; one reason for doing so, he explained later, was his inability to move his large family to Washington and to support them there in the manner to which they had become accustomed. While vice-president, Tompkins once considered buying a house in Washington, but the pressure of heavy financial obligations kept him from doing so. Cognizant of his need to provide for his "numerous and beloved family," Tompkins wrote to a friend in September 1817, "I shall probably resign the office of Vice President at the next session."

Tompkins died intestate, and his widow had to struggle with the difficult problems left by her late husband. The property and buildings that Tompkins had developed on Staten Island became matters for dispute among his creditors, and the mansion that he had built was badly damaged by vandals a year before Hannah Tompkins' death on February 18, 1829. Her body was interred in the vault of the Minthorne family at St. Mark's.

PRINCIPAL SOURCE

Ray W. Irwin. Daniel D. Tompkins, Governor of New York and Vice President of the United States. New York: The New-York Historical Society, [1968]. 334 p.

JOHN C. CALHOUN, 1825-1832

John Caldwell Calhoun (1782-1850) was born
and raised in the uplands of South Carolina. He
received, from a brother-in-law, sufficient education to qualify him for admission in 1800 to Yale.
After graduation in 1804, young Calhoun studied
law in Litchfield, Connecticut. After his return
to South Carolina, Calhoun studied more law in
Charleston and began his practice in Abbeville,
near his home. His own means and additional
wealth brought through marriage to a cousin permitted Calhoun to devote his uncommon talents
to a public career.

Calhoun's father had served for a period in
the South Carolina legislature, and his seat was
occupied by his son from 1808-1809. From 1811-
1817 Calhoun was a member of the United States
House of Representatives where he supported
the war policies of the administration, internal
improvements, a national bank, and a protective
tariff. As secretary of war in President Monroe's cabinet (1817-1825), Calhoun strengthened
army organization and established several new
departments.

As vice-president under President John Quincy Adams (1825-1829), Calhoun joined with the
supporters of Andrew Jackson and continued in
office during most of President Jackson's first
term (1829-1832). After President Jackson denounced nullification, which had been espoused
by the vice-president, Calhoun resigned on December 28, 1832, and on the very next day was
appointed to the Senate by South Carolina. As
a senator for fifteen years (1832-1843 and 1845-
1850) Calhoun struggled to protect the right of

the South to expand slavery into new territory
acquired by his country. In 1844 President Tyler called on Calhoun to be secretary of state,
and in this office the South Carolinian devised
a scheme for the annexation of Texas by means
of a congressional joint resolution. After his
return to the Senate, Calhoun fought heroically
against the Compromise of 1850 because the
traditional balance in the Union between the
slave and the free states would be destroyed
thereby. Calhoun, a statesman and political
philosopher with foresight, died in Washington
on March 31, 1850.

*   *   *

As a United States senator from South Carolina, John C.
Calhoun labored mightily in the 1830s and 1840s to preserve
within the Union the way of life he knew and loved, that of
the owner of a cotton plantation worked by slaves. Calhoun
believed that a tariff for protection, as distinguished from a
tariff for revenue, bore unduly on the agricultural economy
of the South, and he developed a defense based upon his
contention that the sovereign states never transferred their
sovereignty when they formed the government under the
Constitution, only the exercise thereof. This legalistic approach to states' rights was dashed by the triumph of Union
armies in the Civil War, and the subsequent development of
a centralized national government leaves Calhoun's argument
of little interest except to political theorists. Nevertheless,
Calhoun's career of almost forty years in the federal government places him among the first rank of the country's states-
men, and his fame should not be obscured because he cham-
pioned a cause that became "The Lost Cause."

During the four decades in which Calhoun served as a
member of the House of Representatives (1811-1817), as secretary of war under President Monroe (1817-1825), as vice-
president under Presidents J. Q. Adams (1825-1829) and
Andrew Jackson (1829-1832), as secretary of state under
President Tyler (1844-1845), and as a prominent senator for
many of the years between 1832 and his death in 1850, he
was married to Floride Calhoun, the daughter of a first cousin, also called Floride Calhoun and denominated for clarity
as "old Mrs. Calhoun." Floride bore her husband nine

children, but is remembered today, if at all, for her part in the snubbing of the notorious Peggy Eaton, the tavern keeper's daughter who married Andrew Jackson's friend, Senator John H. Eaton, a few months before the old general became president. After Eaton became secretary of war in President Jackson's Cabinet, the ladies in Washington society had to determine whether to accept Peggy with her less than respectable past.

Before the composition of President Jackson's Cabinet became known, Senator and Mrs. Eaton called on the Calhouns when the vice-president was away from home. Floride Calhoun received the Eatons graciously and recognized that their visit was something of a challenge. If the Calhouns accepted the Eatons as equals and returned their call, the other leaders of Washington society probably would follow suit; if the Calhouns did not call upon the Eatons, Peggy would not be admitted to the inner circle of official Washington society. This may have meant little or nothing to the glamorous Peggy, but Floride decided to not return the Eatons' call because she would not accept the responsibility for determining "whether Peggy Eaton was or was not a virtuous woman." After all, Floride had been back in Washington for but a month after an absence of nearly three years, and she had her own family and household to think about.

A few months before his graduation from Yale, John Calhoun accepted an invitation from "old Mrs. Calhoun" to visit her and her family in Newport, Rhode Island, where they were vacationing. Calhoun immediately won the favor of his widowed cousin, her two sons, John Ewing and James Edward, and he became acquainted with her twelve-year-old daughter, Floride, who was to become his wife seven years later. John Calhoun traveled with his cousins by ship to South Carolina and returned with them by coach in 1805 when he went to Litchfield, Connecticut to study law. This was followed by work in law offices in Charleston and in Calhoun's upcountry county of Abbeville, close to the Georgia border in the northwest corner of his estate. After his admission to the bar, Calhoun celebrated the event by traveling to Bonneau's Ferry, near Charleston, the site of "old Mrs. Calhoun's" plantation. Floride then was seventeen, and her charms proved irresistible to her serious-minded cousin, ten years her senior. The couple were married on January 8, 1811, at Bonneau's Ferry: the bride was small and her black

hair and dark eyes revealed her Huguenot ancestry; the
groom was tall and loose-jointed and at age twenty-eight he
was a successful lawyer and planter, who had been elected
to represent his district in the House of Representatives in
the Twelfth Congress.

Calhoun's political career required periods of long residence in Washington, but his plantation and most of his relatives were in South Carolina. John and Floride would make
the trip to Washington together, perhaps with "old Mrs.
Calhoun" and a child or two, while their other children and
their home were left in the care of relatives, especially James
Edward Calhoun, a brother of Floride's, who had a special
talent for caring for members of Floride's family and for looking after his plantation and financial affairs when the politician was away from home.

Calhoun was late for the opening of the first session
of the Twelfth Congress because he delayed his departure
until Floride had recovered from the birth of their first
child, a boy named Andrew. Calhoun was in Washington
when their second child, a daughter, was born in South
Carolina. Floride asked her husband to suggest a name for
the child, and he tactfully deferred to the choice of his wife
and her mother but added, "my inclination would be to call
her by the name you and your mother bear." The baby
named Floride died a year later. Floride was inconsolable;
as John Calhoun wrote to her mother, "She [Floride] thinks
only of her dear child; and recalls to her mind every thing
that made her interesting, thus furnishing additional food
for her grief."

Calhoun's private life was punctuated by the births of
more babies, and his enlarging family responsibilities created
persistent demands for money which he never could resolve
as an absentee landlord with a modest government salary.
After Calhoun accepted the post of secretary of war in President Monroe's Cabinet, he moved Floride and their two children, Andrew (six years old) and Anna Maria (not yet nine
months old), to Washington where they found living expenses
to be higher than his salary of $4,500 would cover. "Cabinet
officers were expected to entertain liberally, and he shared
all the instincts and traditions of the hospitable South in this
respect. Floride was a gracious hostess and he himself was
a fascinating and willing talker." The Calhouns bought a fine

home near the Capitol for which they paid nine thousand dollars, money he sought from the sale of land in South Carolina. The high place that the secretary of war and Floride Calhoun enjoyed in Washington society is illustrated by the concern for the health of their third daughter, Elizabeth, shown by leaders in the government and the community. The little girl, not yet five months old, became seriously ill and died after sixteen painful and exhausting days. During her illness, "Fashionable ladies vied with each other for the privilege of nursing the ailing child." The wife of the secretary of state took her turn sitting with the stricken infant, and President Monroe called daily at the home of the Calhouns. This truly extraordinary demonstration was not a "mere tribute to rank" but a spontaneous expression of affection and sympathy for a couple genuinely admired and beloved.

Floride had her fourth child in the summer home acquired by her mother high in the foothills of the Blue Ridge Mountains, and "a fine boy" was born in Washington. The Calhouns sold their home in downtown Washington for the amount they paid for it, $9,000, and they soon purchased a spacious home in the present Dumbarton Oaks where another child, Martha Cornelia, was born in April of 1824. Their eighth child was born in Georgetown and named James Edward after Floride's favorite brother. The children had the usual number of colds and illnesses, and their son John had a persistent cough (whooping cough?) shortly after the birth of his youngest sister. The Calhouns left for their home in South Carolina, and the boy became so feeble that he could barely stand the motion of the carriage. However, according to his father, then vice-president of the United States, "on the very day of our arrival [at home] his cough ceased, and has not since returned."

The children had to be educated, and tutors were engaged to teach the younger ones at home in South Carolina. As they grew older they attended nearby academies and colleges, and when they grew up they needed financial aid to make a start on their own. After his marriage, Andrew purchased a plantation in Alabama with help from his father. Patrick, a graduate of the West Point Military Academy, incurred debts for gambling and extravagant living which were paid without objection by Calhoun despite repeated crop failures and the continued depressed price of cotton. Instead

of repaying his father, Andrew bought more land and more
slaves, and Calhoun had to borrow money form his son-in-
law, Thomas Clemson, to save Andrew's plantation. Calhoun's
practice of borrowing from Peter to pay Paul never extricated
him from financial difficulties, and a small group of Charleston business members undertook, without Calhoun's permission, to raise the money required to pay his sizeable bills
and to free his Fort Hill estate from the encumbrance of
heavy mortgages.

Floride became stout in her later years, and she continued to be a hostess of grace and charm. Her servants
were well trained, and, when things were running smoothly,
she delighted in her house filled with guests and noisy children. Although devoted to her children, she quarreled with
them in her intense fashion; she did not quarrel with her
husband because he wisely indulged her failings in temperament. Floride acquired enough of her mother's unpredictable
behavior to be recognized by members of her family as something of a "character." She was unduly suspicious, and she
blamed others for things that went wrong, in actuality or in
her imagination. In one quarrel between Floride and Andrew,
Calhoun believed his son to be in the right yet he counseled,
"As to the suspicion & unfounded blame of your Mother, you
must not only bear them, but forget them.... I have borne
with her with patience, because it was my duty to do so, &
you must do the same, for the same reason. It has been the
only cross of my life."

After enlarging on Floride's social and domestic accomplishments, Calhoun's most thorough biographer, Charles M.
Wiltse, observed, "Beyond the kitchen garden, however, her
interests did not extend.... For politics and intellectual
pursuits, which together with agriculture absorbed Calhoun's
major energies, she cared nothing at all." Floride was unable to properly manage her slaves when Calhoun was away,
and he had to enlist the help of one of Floride's brothers to
curb one of her periodic remodeling and building ventures.
After Calhoun returned to the Senate, his eldest daughter,
Anna Maria, took from her mother many of her household
tasks, especially caring for the younger children. Anna
Maria was truly her father's daughter; she shared his interest in politics and at age sixteen began to share in his
thoughts and aspirations in a way Floride had never done.
Calhoun was pleased to have Anna Maria with him in

Washington, and, even after her marriage to Thomas Clemson,
a mining engineer, and their subsequent removal to Belgium
when he became chargé d'affaires in 1844, Anna and her
father continued an informative and mutually supportive correspondence for years.

　　　　John C. Calhoun was never robust, and he experienced
more than his share of maladies, especially those affecting the
respiratory system.　When he received at Yale an invitation
from "old Mrs. Calhoun" to visit her and her family in Newport, the young man was "wracked with fever."　Fever overcame him again in Rockingham County, North Carolina, on
one of his annual trips to Washington, and another journey
from his home in South Carolina through mild weather around
Norfolk into damp and persistent fog along the Potomac brought
him low with influenza.　Overwork, financial problems, and
his unending concern for the future of the South undoubtedly
took its toll on his body; and at the height of the debate in
the House over the annexation of Texas, Secretary Calhoun
neglected a cold which developed into pneumonia.　Floride
and two of their children were with him during this illness,
and they nursed him back to health.　Calhoun, then secretary of state under President Tyler, conducted urgent business of his department in his bedroom in early February of
1845, and not until late in the month did he return to his
office on a restricted schedule.　Calhoun's aging, in addition
to his intense application, caused him to collapse onto the
floor of the Senate on January 19, 1849.　His physician diag-
nosed an upset stomach complicated by bronchitis, and the
beginning of heart disease were observed.　At the end of the
session Calhoun went to South Carolina to recuperate, but
he returned in November to make the case for the South in
the crisis that led to Senator Clay's proposals for a compromise in 1850.　Calhoun was ill when Clay introduced his resolutions, and he decided to write down his reply.　His carefully prepared remarks were read by Senator Mason of Virginia with the feeble Calhoun in his seat, wrapped in his
cloak.　This heroic effort and the strain caused by the devi-
sive action of Senator Foote of Mississippi and Senator Webster's dramatic Seventh of March speech exhausted Calhoun,
and friends feared that the South Carolinian might die in the
Capitol.　Calhoun did not recover, and he was attended in
his last illness by his regular physician, a Dr. Hall, his son
John (also a doctor of medicine), and by numerous friends.
One of these sent for Floride, but she had heard elsewhere

that her husband would recover and she was not with him
when he died from a diseased heart and lungs on March 31,
1850.

Calhoun's public career is another, and much longer,
story. As a young congressman he supported the development of a strong national government, but the ruinous effect
of the tariff of 1832 on the economy of the South caused him
to espouse nullification as a remedy for his state. The efforts
of abolitionists and others to keep slavery out of the territories and to brand it as immoral caused the South to become
defensive, and Calhoun developed a rationale to preserve
slavery and to protect the place of the South within the Union. His political theories are embodied in treatises and
speeches which are seldom read today: his South Carolina
Exposition and Protest (1828), "Fort Hill Address" (1831),
Disquisition on Government (1849), and Discourse on the
Constitution and Government of the United States (1850).

Although Calhoun is commonly referred to today as
"The Great Carolinian," his leadership was often challenged
by radicals within his state who wanted to leave the Union
immediately, and he did not succeed in marshalling the other
Southern States to march under his banner. He prevailed
as a leader because of "intellectual pre-eminence and force
of character alone." He shifted his ground and his allegiance
to parties as circumstances changed, and he explained his
actions in clear and logical statements. As a public speaker, he had few equals. Without the florid prose of Daniel
Webster or the mellifluous speech of Henry Clay, Calhoun
usually spoke without notes in straightforward prose which
won support because of the logic and conviction of the
speaker. Many of his speeches are models for unadorned
consistency and defy abridgement or attempts at snyopses.
When he was scheduled to speak in the Senate, the seats on
the floor would be filled with senators, members of the
House, and others who could claim a place, and the galleries
would be filled with ladies and other admirers of the magnetic
speaker. On February 15, 1847, the House of Representatives
adopted the Wilmot Proviso, which would exclude slavery from
any of the territory to be acquired from Mexico. Calhoun
made his response on February 19: "He stood there, straight
and slender, his seamed face tense, his shaggy hair shaking
with the vehemence of this speech, ... and the hand of
prophecy was on him." After predicting the "political

revolution, anarchy, civil war, and widespread disaster"
that would result from the end of a balance of power between the slaveholding and non-slaveholding states, the
senator warned his countrymen, "Wo! wo! I say, to this
Union." he closed on a personal note:

> I give no advice. It would be hazardous and
> dangerous for me to do so. But I may speak as an
> individual member of that section of the Union.
> There is my family and connections; there I drew
> my first breath; there are all my hopes. I am a
> planter--a cotton planter. I am a Southern man and
> a slaveholder--a kind and merciful one, I trust--and
> none the worse for being a slaveholder. I say, for
> one, I would rather meet any extremity upon earth
> than give up an inch of our equality--one inch of
> what belongs to us as members of this great repub-
> lic.

PRINCIPAL SOURCES

Charles M. Wiltse. John C. Calhoun, Nationalist, 1782-1828.
   Indianapolis: Bobbs-Merrill, [1944]. 477 p.

_____. John C. Calhoun, Nullifier, 1828-1839. Indianap-
   olis: Bobbs-Merrill, [1949]. 511 p.

_____. John C. Calhoun, Sectionalist, 1840-1850. Indi-
   anapolis: Bobbs-Merrill, [1951]. 592 p.

MARTIN VAN BUREN, 1833-1837

Martin Van Buren (1782-1862) was born of Dutch stock in Kinderhook, a community about thirty miles south of Albany, New York. The boy attended local schools until age fourteen when he became a clerk in the office of a local attorney. At age nineteen Martin studied law with William Van Ness in New York City; and, at age twenty-one, he was admitted to the bar and began to practice in Kinderhook. In 1808 Van Buren was appointed surrogate of Columbia county and moved to Hudson, fifteen miles to the south. From 1812 until 1820 Van Buren was a member of the New York State Senate and was active in forming the "Albany Regency," a group of editors and politicians who recognized the value of hard work and of party organization. From 1815 until 1819 Van Buren was attorney general and resided in Albany.

Van Buren was elected in 1821 to the United States Senate, but he continued to be involved in New York politics. He was reelected to the Senate in 1827, but resigned within a year to become governor of New York, a post which he left within two months to become secretary of state in President Jackson's initial Cabinet. Van Buren was a capable and efficient secretary but resigned the office to facilitate the President's reorganization of his administration. The president selected Van Buren as his running mate for his second term (1833-1837), and the New York politician presided over the Senate with exceptional skill. With Jackson's staunch support, Van Buren was nominated in 1836 for the presidency, and he won an easy victory.

The panic of 1837 resulted in widespread unem-
ployment and severe economic problems which
led to Van Buren's defeat in 1840 by William
Henry Harrison. Four years later (1844) Van
Buren received a majority of the votes in the
Democratic convention but could not muster the
required two-thirds, and the nomination went to
James K. Polk. After his defeat in 1848 as the
presidential candidate of the Free Soil party,
Van Buren retired to his estate near Kinderhook
where he died on July 24, 1862.

                    *   *   *

From February 23 until July 28 in 1842, former President
Martin Van Buren, and James Kirke Paulding, a novelist of
some reputation and secretary of Navy in Van Buren's Cabinet, traveled through the South and the Upper Mississippi
Valley, partly to test the political waters and partly to visit
old friends, especially Andrew Jackson who then was quite
ill but as keen as before. Van Buren spent a few days in
Albany with two of his sons, John and Smith Thompson, and
their expanding families, and he went on to Kinderhook, a
Dutch village thirty miles to the south where he and his wife
were born and began their married life thirty-five years
earlier. A few days later Van Buren received a letter from
his son John announcing the good news that his wife had
just given birth to a daughter. The exuberant father gave
the few bits of pertinent information ascertainable from a
newborn babe, "She weighed nine and half pounds at birth
... has dark blue eyes, regular features and a very fine
forehead." The delighted father, then aged thirty-two, continued, "... we all agree to name it after my mother--was
her name Anna or Hannah?"

    John Van Buren was but nine when his mother died,
yet he should have heard her name in family conversations
often enough for him to know it without question. Van
Buren's wife of twelve years lived her thirty-six years in
the valley of the Hudson River between Albany and Hudson,
forty-five miles to the south. She is not mentioned in Van
Buren's Autobiography written during his seventies, which
fills 782 pages in print, yet the omission probably stemmed
from a nineteenth-century distinction between private and
public life rather than from any deliberate intention to neglect
the mother of his five sons, four of whom reached manhood.

Martin Van Buren was born of Dutch stock in Kinder-
hook, New York, about thirty miles south of Albany, on
December 5, 1782, and Hannah Hoes was born in the same
village on March 8, 1783. The community numbered but thirty houses, and members of the leading families, the Hoeses,
Van Alens, and Van Burens had intermarried for generations.
Van Buren's mother was born a Hoes. She married a Van
Alen and was widowed before she married Abraham Van
Buren, Martin's father. For those who like to ponder unusual family relationships, it has been determined that Hannah Hoes, Martin Van Buren's wife, was a granddaughter of
his mother's brother.

Children in Kinderhook attended the village school until the age of fourteen. Girls left school at that age and expected to remain at home until marriage, while ambitious young
men, such as Martin Van Buren, could leave to pursue a career. Martin began as a clerk in the law office of Francis
Silvester, an attorney in Kinderhook, and in 1801, at the
age of nineteen, he entered the law office of William Van Ness
in New York City. In 1803 he was back in Kinderhook, a
member of the bar, and engaged in the practice of law with
an older half-brother, James Van Alen.

Four years later, on February 21, 1807, Martin Van
Buren and Hannah Hoes were married in the home of the
bride's sister in Catskill, New York, about fifteen miles southwest of Kinderhook. He was small in stature, only five feet
and six inches, and she was small and slender. According
to Van Buren's careful biographer, John Niven, Hannah had
a fair complexion, "she was a very proper, very religious
young lady." A contemporary described her as "a woman of
sweet nature but few intellectual gifts."

A year after marriage the ambitious young lawyer was
appointed surrogate (probate judge) for Columbia county,
and the duties of the office required Van Buren to move to
Hudson, fifteen miles south of Kinderhook, a busy town of
3,300 persons founded by New Englanders who recognized
the advantages of the location for shipbuilding. The Van
Burens bought a house on Warren Street, the main street in
Hudson, and here their first child, Abraham, was born.
Three more sons--John, Smith Thompson, and Martin, Jr.--
followed at regular intervals; a fifth named after young general Winfield Scott died in infancy. Van Buren's law practice

enlarged along with his family responsibilities. Like other successful attorneys outside of large urban areas, Van Buren attended sessions of the courts held in Albany and across the state and dined as others on the circuit did in dirty, disorderly taverns and slept in a chair or on a bed occupied by one, two, or three bedmates, fully clothed in garments soiled in their travels. Van Buren rightly appreciated the clean and modest home that his wife maintained in Hudson. After traveling the circuit in good weather and in foul and working under stress in courtrooms, Hannah's "lack of pretence, her unruffled disposition, and her thoughtfulness were just what her husband needed."

Van Buren was a very successful lawyer whose particular talents fitted him for a political career. In 1812 he was elected to the New York state senate where he formed the "Albany Regency," a group of editors, politicians and office holders who had learned the value of strict adherence to party principles and organization. In 1815 Van Buren became attorney general of New York. He soon moved his family to the capital, where he rented a house on State Street large enough for his family, three servants, and a law office in which he was joined by Benjamin F. Butler, who had learned the law under Van Buren and was to become his faithful associate through and following the presidential years.

Albany in 1815 had a population of more than 10,000 and offered superior educational opportunities for his family. His fifth son was born on January 16, 1817, and a difficult delivery left Hannah weak and feverish. Her physicians suspected tuberculosis, and the diagnosis was soon confirmed. Hannah's illness reached a critical stage by the end of 1818, and she was so ill early in January of 1819 that Van Buren stayed at her side instead of going to a meeting of a party caucus. She died on February 5, 1819, and the next day her body was taken by her husband to Kinderhook for burial. Martin Van Buren was deeply affected by the death of his wife, "so young, so self-effacing, so responsive to his needs and to those of their four young sons." At the time of her death their ages ranged from two to eleven.

Although Van Buren was defeated for reelection to the office of attorney general by a faction led by De Witt Clinton, he went on to become a United States senator, governor of

New York, secretary of state in President Jackson's first
term, vice-president in his second, and president from 1837-
1841. So successfully did Van Buren beat his politican opponents that he came to be known as the "Magician." This
sobriquet does not do justice to Van Buren's admirable working habits. He succeeded in politics because he analyzed
every facet of a situation before he reached a decision, and
regardless of whether or not he won a particular contest,
he knew that he had done his best. Van Buren was not a
"trimmer," when he was convinced that his position (on the
independent treasury system, for example) would benefit his
party and the nation, he did not equivocate. He was a Jeffersonian by education and conviction, yet he saw that Jefferson's ideals could be adapted to a later time. Van Buren
pursued a middle course; he was an advocate of states'
rights and a party regular but he never ceased to be a
New Yorker and a truly pragmatic politician. John Quincy
Adams was not fair to Van Buren when he wrote, "His principles are all subordinate to his ambitions." John Randolph,
whom Van Buren characterized in his Autobiography as "in-
scrutable," perceived the method of the "Magician" when
he wrote, [Van Buren] "rowed to his objective with muffled
oars."

     After his reelection in 1827 to the United States Senate,
Van Buren decided to base his future activities in Washington, yet he returned to become governor of his native state
and he spent his retirement there. In his responsible posts
and in his moves between, Van Buren had the help of one
or more of his four boys. While Secretary of State Van
Buren's two younger sons were with his sister in Kinderhook,
Abraham and John kept him company in Washington. One or
more of his sons served as his secretaries during his presidency, and a son usually supervised the renovation and the
decoration of a home he was to occupy. He traveled abroad
with Martin, Jr. when it was believed that his health would
improve in Southern Europe, and he was with his son when
he died on March 19, 1855, of the disease that had killed his
mother. Van Buren returned to Lindenwald, his estate near
Kinderhook which had been remodeled to induce his son,
Smith, and his family to remain under his roof. The architect Smith engaged proposed to convert a fine mansion in the
chaste Federal style into "a hybrid Renaissance Italian pal-
azzo--with Gothic revival touches!" Van Buren permitted the
changes only after his son agreed to pay part of the cost,

but he saw no need for the remodeling and expansion of Lindenwald to thirty-six rooms. He found solace in philosophy:

> What curious creatures we are. Old Mr. Van Ness built as fine a home here as any reasonable man could. Its stability unsurpassed and its taste of what was then deemed to be the best. William P. Van Ness had disfigured everything his father had done. I succeed him and pulled down without a single exception any erection he had made and with evident advantage. Now comes Smith and pulls down many things I had put up and made the alterations without stint ... what nonsense.

Although Martin Van Buren was not handsome, he often made a striking appearance. Before he decided to run for governor in 1828, Van Buren toured the western part of his state. In Rochester he attended church "in the latest fashion and in colors that complemented his fair complexion." His "beige swallow-tail broadcloth coat with matching velvet collar set off his reddish-blond hair. He wore an orange cravat with lace tips, white duck trousers, pearl gray vest and silk hose." When the parishioners gaped at the apparition, the forty-five year old Van Buren held his "yellow kid gloves in his left hand while he bowed and waved to the crowd." Nine years later, as president-elect, Van Buren "cast aside his customary brilliant attire" and wore a black frockcoat and white stock like the other men in attendance at an extravagant reception given by the Reuben Whitneys on Capitol Hill.

Van Buren's income from his legal practice, investments, and land "made him a comparatively wealthy man," and he liked to live well. As a senator in Washington, he and two convivial friends rented a furnished house in which they enjoyed "good food, good wines, and good company." He found great pleasure in gossiping with members of his family over a bottle of fine Madeira or sherry. As president, Van Buren engaged an experienced housekeeper to manage the White House staff, and the social season in official Washington lit up when his son's wife, a Southern belle, came to the White House and served as hostess for afternoon teas and dress balls.

In retirement, Van Buren had "his farm, his books, friends and always politics" to interest him, and he enjoyed riding at a gallop on horseback and fishing for bass in the ponds on his estate, for trout in nearby streams, and for salmon in the lordly Hudson. In addition, "the old man enjoyed the merry hubbub of grandchildren--John's daughter, Anna, Abraham's two sons, Martin and Singleton, and Smith's children, all of whom spent the summer [of 1849] at Lindenwald." During the coldest months of each year Van Buren lived in New York City, where he saw old friends and worked on his memoirs and a history of political parties in the United States. After 1858 he gave up historical writing, and he rewrote his will. "His affairs in order, Van Buren continued his round of activities as always, seemingly unaffected by the passage of time." After South Carolina seceded from the Union in December of 1860, Van Buren proposed a constitutional convention to close the breach; but, after the firing on Fort Sumter, the old man approved of Lincoln's call for troops to suppress the rebellion. In the fall of 1861, Van Buren was bedridden for several months from pneumonia, and he may have had several minor strokes. The end caused by arteriosclerosis and congestive heart failure came in his seventy-ninth year on July 24, 1862.

Why the sociable Van Buren, who became a widower at age thirty-seven, never married again is, according to his latest biographer, a "mystery." His relatives in Albany and Kinderhook helped him to bring up his four young sons, but they would have benefitted from growing up in a typical two-parent home. Van Buren enjoyed female companionship, and he flattered women in a manner they greatly enjoyed. Among his favorites in Washington were Jefferson's two daughters and the lovely young nieces and in-laws who surrounded President Andrew Jackson. One of the men with whom Van Buren entertained in sumptuous fashion suspected Van Buren of "licentious" conduct, but there is no record of any affair of the heart in which this eligible widower participated. This is not surprising because Martin Van Buren, skillful attorney and masterful politician, was a model for discretion in difficult personal relations.

PRINCIPAL SOURCES

John Niven. Martin Van Buren: the Romantic Age of American Politics. New York: Oxford, 1983. 715 p.

The Autobiography of Martin Van Buren. Ed. by John C.
Fitzpatrick. Washington: Gov't Printing Office, 1920.
808 p. (Annual Report of the American Historical Association for the year 1918, II)

Mary Ormsbee Whitton. "Hannah Van Buren--Four Sons and
a Tombstone," In First First Ladies, 1789-1865.... New
York: Hastings House, [1948]. pp. 136-151.

RICHARD M. JOHNSON, 1837–1841

Richard Mentor Johnson (1790–1850) was born on the frontier near the present site of Louisville where he acquired enough education at home to study law under local practitioners. At age twenty-four he was elected by his county to serve in the Kentucky legislature. Johnson served as a congressman from Kentucky from 1807 until 1819 and from 1829-37, and as a United States senator from 1819-1829. During the War of 1812, Colonel Johnson led his regiment in the battle at Thames River, north of Detroit, was severely wounded, and received credit for having killed Indian chief Tecumseh.

As a congressman and as a senator, Johnson sponsored legislation of benefit to ordinary workingmen. The popular support gained thereby, his reputation as a war hero, and his friendship with Andrew Jackson led to his nomination and election to the vice-presidency in 1836. He served during Martin Van Buren's term as president and won distinction chiefly for his singular appearance, which included rumpled hair and bright red vests.

Johnson never married, but he kept a Black mistress on his plantation in Kentucky who bore him two children. At age seventy he was elected to serve again in the Kentucky legislature, but illness and a paralytic stroke incapacitated him and led to his death in November of 1850.

*   *   *

Richard M. Johnson, the fifth child of Robert and Jemima Suggett Johnson, was born in Beargrass (Louisville),

Kentucky, in the fall of 1780 when the area was threatened
by surrounding Indians and British troops. In later life
Johnson enjoyed boasting, "I was born in a cane-brake and
cradled in a sap trough"; he did experience the hardships
of frontier life. Nevertheless, he was born into a talented
family: his father, Robert, was a leader in numerous political, religious, and educational activities; his mother came
from a long line of outstanding Virginians; and several of
his brothers, especially James, achieved more than local
prominence. Richard did not attend an elementary school in
Scott County, Kentucky. Yet, he acquired enough education, probably from his mother (who was fond of books), to
read law under George Nicholas and in 1800 under James
Brown in Lexington. Four years later he was chosen by the
voters of Scott County to represent them in the Kentucky
legislature, the first native son to be so honored.

Richard Johnson was elected in 1810 to serve in the
Twelfth Congress, and he became an authentic hero when he
was seriously wounded while leading a charge of his regiment
of mounted riflemen against Indian fighters and British troops
at Thames River, north of Detroit. Colonel Johnson showed
exceptional courage in battle, and the charge of his unit won
the day for the Americans under General William Henry Harrison. Richard Johnson sustained five wounds during the
battle on October 5, 1813, in which he was said to have
killed Tecumseh, a story which enhanced his reputation when
he returned in 1814 to his seat in Congress, "feeble, emaci-
ated, and covered with honored scars."

As a congressman, 1807-1819, as a senator, 1820-1828,
and as a congressman again, 1829-1833, Johnson sponsored
bills relating to veterans' benefits, internal improvements,
abolition of imprisonment for debt, and movement of the mails
on Sundays, all of which made him a favorite of workingmen
in all sections of the country. His reputation as a war hero
and friend of the common man led to his nomination and election to the vice-presidency in 1836.

He served one term in the office under President Martin Van Buren, but he was not renominated by the Democratic convention that met in Baltimore in May 1840, and
nominated Van Buren for a second term. No candidate was
named by the convention for the vice-presidency and Johnson
undertook to campaign for his own reelection, but the

Whigs won the election and Harrison and Tyler took office in March of 1841.

Johnson served almost continuously for forty years in Washington, where he lived most of the time in the home of O. B. Brown, the "preacher politician." He never married and did not establish his own residence in Washington until 1836 when he was the Democratic candidate for the vice-presidency. Johnson lived for a few years in his own home on Capitol Hill, but in 1840 he was again with the Browns where he enjoyed the companionship of the family and could pursue his interests in music and literature, especially the Bible. The colonel appeared frequently in social gatherings in Washington where, with his scarlet vest, ill fitting coat, and disheveled hair, he must have enjoyed the impression he made as a singular character. Harriet Martineau, English author and traveler, who sat opposite Johnson at a dinner in the White House, observed: "If he [Johnson] should become President, he will be as strange-looking a potentate as ever ruled."

Between sessions in Washington, Johnson returned to his home in Kentucky where he entertained lavishly with traditional Southern hospitality. He hosted many large parties and entertained famous visitors, including President Monroe and General Andrew Jackson in 1819 and General Lafayette in 1825.

Johnson's father, Robert, had amassed considerable wealth, mainly in land and slaves, and as his children came of age, they received respectable fortunes. One of the slaves Richard Johnson inherited from his father was Julia Chinn, who became the colonel's mistress and managed his household while he was away. She bore him two daughters, Imogene and Adaline, whom Johnson acknowledged to be his and arranged for their education under the tutelage of Thomas Henderson, superintendent of the Choctaw Academy on the Colonel's land. Johnson tried without success to present his daughters to society in Lexington, but the light-complected girls married white men and received parts of Johnson's estate. Julia Chinn died during the cholera epidemic of 1833, and Adaline died three years later. Johnson voiced his loss to the girl's tutor, "She was a source of inexhaustible happiness and comfort to me." After the death of Julia Chinn, Johnson was said to have taken another mistress,

"a fairer mulatto," who ran away with an Indian but was captured and returned. Johnson's intimate relations with attractive female slaves did not damage his reputation and influence among his friends, but his willingness to admit the pat-
ernity of children of Black mothers evoked sharp criticism in
newspapers published in Virginia, Kentucky, Washington,
and elsewhere. The Washington <u>Spectator</u> identified Colonel
Johnson as "the father of a colored family" and observed
that if he was to become president there would be "an African jubilee throughout the country."

Johnson was elected in August of 1850 to sit again in
the Kentucky legislature, but he was unable to serve. When
he took his seat on November 8, he was suffering from a
severe illness (dementia?) "which renders him totally unfit
for business." A few days later he suffered a paralytic
stroke and died in the early morning of November 19. He
was eulogized as "the poor man's friend," and his body was
buried in the Frankfort cemetery in the ground "appropriated
to the burial of Kentucky's illustrious dead." A monument
to mark "the sense of his eminent services in the cabinet and
in the field" was erected by an act of the Kentucky legislature.

PRINCIPAL SOURCE

Leland Winfield Meyer, <u>The Life and Times of Colonel Richard
    M. Johnson of Kentucky</u>. New York: Columbia Univ.
    Press, 1932. 508 p. (Studies in History, Economics, and
    Public Law, no. 359)

JOHN TYLER, 1841

John Tyler (1790-1862), the sixth child of
Judge John Tyler, was born in Tidewater Virginia and followed in his father's footsteps to
the College of William and Mary from which he
graduated in 1807. John read law with his
father and was admitted in 1809 to legal practice. He served in the Virginia House of Delegates from 1811 until 1816 where he showed
himself to be a strict constructionist and a man
of great personal charm. In the United States
House of Representatives from 1817-1821 Tyler
opposed bills for internal improvements, a protective tariff, and the Missouri Compromise.
He declined renomination in 1820 because of ill
health, but he returned in 1823 to the Virginia
House of Delegates and was governor from
1825-1827. Elected in 1827 to the United States
Senate, Tyler was a member of a Southern
states' rights group that joined with National
Republicans to form the Whig party. Tyler was
reelected in 1833 but resigned from the Senate
in 1836 because he would not follow a directive
from the Virginia legislature to expunge from
the records of Congress resolutions which cen-
sured President Jackson. Four years later
Tyler was nominated to run on the Whig ticket
with William Henry Harrison, who died less than
a month after his inauguration as president.

Tyler was the first vice-president to become
president by right of succession, and he tried
to smooth the transition by retaining members
of Harrison's Cabinet in office. Henry Clay
pressed the adoption of his American system
including a protective tariff, national improve-

ments, and a national bank, and bills embodying
these proposals were vetoed by President Tyler.
Despite his differences with politicians, Tyler
proved to be successful in a reorganization of
the Navy, the adoption of the Webster-Ashburton
Treaty, and the annexation of Texas. The
former president retired to his estate in Virginia; but after the Republican victory in 1860,
he returned to Washington as the head of a futile Peace Mission. As a member of a Virginia
State Convention, Tyler advocated secession;
and he was elected to a seat in the Confederate
House of Representatives but died in January,
1862, before the first meeting of that body.

*   *   *

After the inaugurations of President William Henry Harrison
("Tippecanoe") and of Vice-President John Tyler on March
4, 1841, the latter returned to his home in Williamsburg,
Virginia, in the expectation that the next four years would
be quiet and peaceful. No word of the president's illness
had been sent to Tyler, and not until after the old soldier's
death did Fletcher Webster, son of the secretary of state and
an officer of the Senate, leave for Tyler's home. At sunrise
on April 5, young Webster, who had traveled all night, told
John Tyler that he was to become the president. Two hours
later, at seven in the morning, Tyler left Williamsburg for
the capital, which he reached at four in the morning of April
6. He had covered the 230 miles by boat, train, and horseback in record time. Although he believed that the oath he
had taken on March 4 as vice-president was sufficient, he
was persuaded to be sworn in by a federal judge to forestall
any questions about his succession to the presidency that
might arise.

As the first vice-president to succeed a president in
office, there were some influential Whigs (former President
John Quincy Adams was one), and several important newspapers that regarded Tyler as "Acting President" or "Vice-
President-Acting President." However, the new president
believed that the powers and duties of the office belonged
to him and he was recognized as "President of the United
States" by the Congress in a special session convened on
May 31, 1841.

Tyler's incumbency in the office, which he was to hold
for three years and eleven months, was fraught with difficulties. Although he had become the titular head of the Whig
Party (better, "Whig Coalition") he was at heart an anti-
Jackson Democrat who had been named to run with Harrison
in the hope that his record would attract the votes of states'
rights Southerners. Because of his desire to facilitate the
transfer of power, Tyler requested members of the Cabinet
who had accepted their places under Harrison to continue to
head their departments, yet the officials were not loyal to
Tyler or his principles. Worst of all, Henry Clay, who had
been passed over by his party in favor of Harrison, recognized that the peculiar circumstances existing at the time
would enable him to win the adoption of his American system,
which included a protective tariff, internal improvements,
and a national bank. Tyler's position on these and related
measures was well known, since he had voiced his conservative opinions with vigor during his five years in the House
of Representatives (1816-21) and nine years in the United
States Senate (1827-36). President Tyler vetoed two national
bank bills that Congress had passed in special session, and
on the day of adjournment (September 13), the Whigs in
Congress publicly broke with Tyler; his Cabinet, with the
exception of Secretary of State Webster, resigned in protest
of his second veto. In less than six months Tyler had become "a President without a party."

Regardless of the near disaster at the beginning, Tyler's term as president did achieve some important benefits.
Chief among these were the reorganization of the Navy, the
adoption of the Webster-Ashburton treaty on the Northeastern boundary, and the annexation of Texas. Tyler was a
Virginia gentleman whose gracious manner and ability as a
public speaker helped in personal relations and in his effi-
ciency as an administrator. His reputation as a leader has
suffered because historians "find a record of courageous
consistency bewildering." During his last three years in
the White House, John Tyler experienced major changes in
his private life: his first wife (Letitia Christian Tyler)
died on September 10, 1842, and on June 26, 1844, he was
married to his second (Julia Gardiner Tyler).

John Tyler was born on March 29, 1790, on his father's
plantation, "Greenway," on the James River midway between
Richmond and Williamsburg. His father, "Judge" John Tyler

served from 1808-11 as governor of Virginia, and his mother
was the only daughter of a prominent planter in a nearby
county. Judge Tyler was an admirer of Patrick Henry and
a friend of Thomas Jefferson, and he was educated at William
and Mary College and read law in an office in Williamsburg.
His son, John, followed in the Judge's footsteps by graduat-
ing from William and Mary College at the young age of seventeen and he was admitted to the bar while but nineteen.
While studying law in Richmond (during his father's term as
governor), John Tyler began his courtship of Letitia Christian, daughter of Robert Christian of "Cedar Grove" in New
Kent County.

     Young Tyler's pursuit of the beautiful young lady,
several years his junior, was marked by uncommon restraint.
Although he courted Letitia for four years, he never dared
to kiss her hand until three weeks before the wedding which
took place at "Cedar Grove" on the bridegroom's twenty-
third birthday, March 29, 1813. Letitia and John were married for twenty-nine years during which she bore him nine
children, two of whom died in infancy. Unfortunately, no
letter of Letitia's has survived (her husband's papers were
destroyed in the fall of Richmond in April of 1865), so our
knowledge of her must come from the accounts of others.
According to all of these, she was a lovely woman who
"knitted and stitched and gardened (she loved flowers),
supervised her household slaves with humanity and kindness,
raised her seven children, and minded her own business."

     While John Tyler served in the House of Representatives
(he entered in December of 1816 while but twenty-six) he
lived in a boarding house, as did many of his fellow congressmen, and his family remained at home. The mistress of
a Virginia plantation had duties regarding the clothing and
feeding of her family and the servants to superintend, and
these Letitia Tyler performed admirably. Her social life while
her husband was away was confined to a small group of
friends and neighbors. While Tyler served as governor of
Virginia (1825-1827), he and his wife were qualified by background and experience to entertain the society of Richmond
in handsome fashion; the only problem they confronted was
the inadequate income of the governor. In an effort to inform
the legislators of his need for funds for entertainment, the
governor invited them all to the Mansion to feast on Virginia
ham, cooked corn bread, and cheap Monongahela whiskey,

but his tactic did not succeed. His salary was not raised,
and in January 1827, when Tyler accepted his election to
the United States Senate, he had serious financial problems.

Tyler's nine years in the Senate were happy ones; his
personal charm showed to advantage in his dignified surroundings and his official duties left him time to read and
to reflect on his position regarding slavery and other current topics. His wife visited Washington only once or twice
during this period, and while there she won the admiration
of his friends and associates. After Tyler resigned his place
in the Senate (because he was unwilling to expunge from the
record of the Congress a vote of censure against Andrew
Jackson as he was instructed to do by the legislature of Virginia), he and his family made their home in Williamsburg, a
town in which he had attended college and which still (in
1837) had some of the stimulating culture that had flourished
there in the eighteenth century.

After Letitia suffered a paralytic stroke in 1839, she
retired to her "chamber" where she continued to live and
manage her home as best she could. According to a letter
her daughter-in-law wrote in October 1839 from Williamsburg
to her sisters in Bristol, Pennsylvania:

> The room in the main dwelling furthest removed
> and most retired is the "chamber," as the bedroom
> of the mistress of the house is always called in
> Virginia ... here mother [Mrs. Tyler] with a smile
> of welcome on her sweet, calm face, is always found
> seated on her large arm-chair with a small stand
> by her side, which holds her Bible and her prayer
> book ... with her knitting in her hands....
> Notwithstanding her delicate health, mother at-
> tends to and regulates all the household affairs, and
> all so quietly that you can't tell when she does it.

After John Tyler had moved into the White House his
wife joined him in Washington, but her illness kept her from
her social duties as the First Lady. This role was performed
until his second marriage by two of Tyler's daughters and
by a daughter-in-law, Priscilla. When the wedding of daughter Elizabeth was celebrated on January 31, 1842, in the
White House before members of the families and a few intimate
friends, Letitia made her only appearance on the ground floor.

Her illness, which began with a paralytic stroke four years
before, worsened, and she died on September 10, 1842. Her
funeral was held on the twelfth in the White House, and her
body was taken to Richmond by train and on to the Christian
plantation, "Cedar Grove," in New Kent County for burial.

John Tyler's courtship of Julia Gardiner and their life
together is a story decidedly different from that of his first
marriage. Letitia Christian came from the planter aristocracy
in Virginia, and she was disinterested in the world outside.
She did not care for politics and did not want to live in
Washington. Only once did she travel to spas in the North;
she much preferred the familiar resorts in her native Virginia. Julia Gardiner belonged to a family that had long
been prominent in Connecticut and on Long Island. Her
father's marriage to Juliana McLachlen brought him wealth
and enabled him to retire at the age of thirty-two and to
travel for a year with his wife and daughters in Europe and
to follow the tour with a lengthy residence in Washington.
Julia's first meeting with President Tyler, their courtship,
their married life together, and her widowhood are an open
book, because she, her sister Margaret, her mother, and
her children (the seventh was born when John Tyler was
seventy!) wrote many frank, personal letters which have
survived and were utilized by Robert Seager in the writing
of And Tyler Too, a Biography of John and Julia Gardiner
Tyler (1963).

Before their trip to Europe Julia visited Washington
for about a week in early August of 1840 with her sister
and parents, and the four made a second visit to the capital
in January and February of 1842. Julia was twenty-two at
the time and her sister was but twenty, and the young pair
enjoyed the excitement of the social whirl in which they
moved. Their father was wealthy and had served in the
New York Senate, and his credentials opened doors for his
family in Washington's top society. After this taste of life
in the capital, the girls were bored at home in East Hampton
on Long Island and pleaded with their father to return to
Washington. When the Gardiners returned in December of
1842 they resided again at Mrs. Peyton's boardinghouse.
Here the Gardiners began their preparations for the coming
social season which proved to be truly sensational.

The Gardiners set the wheels in motion by having a

servant deliver their calling cards to the White House, to
members of the Cabinet, and to all of their New York friends
and acquaintances known to be in Washington. This brought
a host of callers, so many in fact that the Gardiners were
obliged to engage a private parlor in the Peyton boardinghouse. Among the first of the callers was John Tyler, Jr.,
a son of the president, and shortly an invitation came from
the White House to have Christmas dinner with the president
and his family. Subsequent exchanges of visits between the
Tylers and the Gardiners occurred throughout January, and
on February 7, 1843, the president asked the Gardiners to
join him upstairs in the White House after the other guests
had left. At the end of a friendly chat before the fire,
President Tyler, almost fifty-three years of age, kissed Margaret's hand and proceeded to do the same with Julia's who
pulled her hand away "and flew down the stairs with the
President after her around chairs and tables until at last he
caught her." Margaret, the narrator, observed in a classic
understatement, "It was truly amusing."

President Tyler had been a widower for but five months
and he was in everyone's eye, but he could not resist the
charms of the vivacious Julia Gardiner. On Sunday, February
12, Tyler walked home from church with the Gardiners, and
at the Washington's Birthday ball on the 22nd, the president
asked Julia to marry him. She "was dressed in a white tar-
latan and she wore a crimson Greek cap with a dangling tassel. With her, 'No, no, no,' she shook her head with each
word, and this flung the tassel in the face of her suitor."
Several days later the Gardiners went to the White House for
tea where Margaret participated in "a real frolic with the
P[resident]." Her account conveys the excitement of the
gambols in the White House: "Julia and I raced from one
end of the house to the other, upstairs and down, and he
[President Tyler] after us." The president abandoned
subterfuge and escorted Julia to exhibitions and entertainments, and delighted onlookers surmised that they were engaged, but no announcement was forthcoming before the
Gardiners returned to East Hampton at the end of March.

Julia's conquest was complete, and at the end of summer the president implored the Gardiners to return to Washington. David Gardiner and his two daughters did return
in February of 1844, this time to a house on Lafayette Place,
but Juliana, who had suffered a series of migraine headaches,

chose to remain in New York. The two girls immediately
joined in Washington social activities, and on the twenty-
seventh they danced the night away at the White House.
The next day many of the guests, including the three Gardiners, were to cruise down the Potomac on the Princeton,
a new steam frigate. The ship carried the "Peacemaker,"
the world's largest naval gun, which was to be fired for the
amusement of the president's party. The gun had been fired
twice and was to be fired again at the hour when the president and special guests, including Julia, gathered in the
salon to toast the Navy, the great gun, and the skipper of
the Princeton. On this firing the breach of the "Peacemaker" exploded spraying chunks of hot metal around the deck;
many were wounded and among the dead were A. P. Usher,
the secretary of state, and Julia's father. His body and
those of the other victims of the tragedy lay in state in the
East Room of the White House, and after the funeral David
Gardiner's remains were taken to Long Island for interment.
Julia's sudden departure from Washington on March 5 depressed the president. "Saddened as he was by David Gardiner's death, vexed by gossip about the state of his private
relations with Julia, Tyler made haste to the altar."

    Julia Gardiner, age 24, and President John Tyler, age
54, were married on June 26, 1844, in New York at the Episcopal Church of the Ascension in a private and seemingly
clandestine ceremony. Despite their difference in ages and
needlessly abrupt marriage, the couple was received with enthusiasm wherever they went, from Philadelphia to Washington, and from Washington to Tidewater, Virginia, and back
to the White House in early August. Tyler had presidential
affairs that demanded attention, including the election to
come in November, and Julia set out to improve the style of
living in the White House and to lay plans for the social season to follow. Julia shared her enthusiasm with her mother,
"This winter I intend to do something in the way of entertaining that shall be the admiration and talk of the Washington world."

    With Gardiner money Julia put the White House coach-
men and footmen into new livery, and she induced her husband to obtain for her through the American consul at Naples
an Italian greyhound, a breed then in fashion, which would
add a touch of Continental elegance to her surroundings. A
stock of fine French wine was ordered in addition to a number

of pieces of expensive French furniture. Young women in
Julia's family came to Washington to enjoy the social activities
and to assist the First Lady, and crusty Juliana Gardiner
arrived to chaperone the girls but retreated from their chat-
ter to her room to read the Bible and to pursue her new interest in spiritualism.

Julia set Saturday for her regular reception day, and
at these functions she ordinarily was attended by six to
twelve maids of honor dressed in white. Her public reception on New Year's Day was described as a glorious success
by a New York newspaper correspondent, but a private
White House ball a week later had so few invited guests that
the hostess was criticized for being "unnecessarily select."
Julia had a gala evening on January 21; the president was
pleased with the progress on the annexation of Texas and
his wife was stunning in a new white satin dress, a white
satin headdress with three ostrich feathers, and her set of
diamonds. Julia's receptions on February 4 and February 11
were splendid successes, and she laid plans for a noteworthy
final ball. Two thousand were invited, six hundred candles
illuminated the East Room, and wine and champagne flowed
freely. The First Lady was beautifully dressed, and she and
her delighted husband received their guests in the Blue
Room. When he was being congratulated on the success of
his social swan song, Tyler laughed and responded, "Yes,
they cannot say now that I am a President without a party!"

The Tylers left Washington for "Sherwood Forest," an
estate of 1,150 acres which the former president had purchased for his retirement. Although Julia missed, at the
outset, her gay life in Washington, she soon found beauty
and satisfaction in her congenial surroundings. Her husband
did not return to his legal practice; instead he became a
gentleman farmer and enjoyed his hours in the saddle. Together they visited Sweet Springs and White Sulphur Springs,
and part of the summers of 1847 and 1854 were spent at
Saratoga. Tyler wanted Julia to "look out on the world
once a year," but childbearing and her husband's illnesses
kept her close to "Sherwood Forest."

As the dark cloud of the extension of slavery became
large and more ominous, Tyler as a slave holder and strict
constructionist opposed restrictions of slavery, such as the
Missouri Compromise, adopted by Congress. After the

Republican victory in 1860, Tyler headed a Peace Mission in
Washington to consider measures that would avoid the breakup of the Union.   Julia and two of the younger children accompanied the former president to Washington, where she
enjoyed the countless courtesies she received on her first
return visit.

The Peace Commission accomplished little of consequence,
and Tyler on March 1 took his seat in the Virginia State
Convention to determine the course to be followed in the
secession crisis.   Tyler argued eloquently for secession and
advocated adoption of the Ordinance of Secession when it
was laid before the people.   In June of 1861 Tyler was chosen
by the Covnention to a seat in the Provisional Congress of
the Confederacy, and his district named him to a seat in the
Confederate House of Representatives.   Tyler never served
in the Confederate Congress, because he died in Richmond
on January 18, 1862, about a month before the first session
of that body.

Julia Tyler stayed for a time at "Sherwood Forest,"
but the nearness of military operations caused her to take
her family north to her mother's home on Staten Island.   Her
loyalties were with the South, and she was outraged when
"Sherwood Forest" was taken over by Negro troops in Yankee
uniforms.   After the death of her mother, Julia was involved
in a lengthy contest over her will, because one of her brothers believed she had exerted improper influence on her mother while she was on her deathbed.   After the Civil War,
Julia tried to gain payment for the use of her vacation cottage at Old Point Comfort and for damages done to her home
in Charles City County.   These efforts yielded little, but
Julia was successful in one of her campaigns: in 1881 she
was awarded a widow's pension of $1,200 per annum, less
than half the amount being paid to Mary Todd Lincoln.   The
assassination of President Garfield left the country another
president's widow, and on March 31, 1882, Congress provided pensions of $5,000 each for the four widows (Tyler,
Polk, Lincoln, and Garfield).   This income permitted Julia
Tyler to live comfortably in Richmond until her death on
July 10, 1889.   She died in the Exchange Hotel in a room
only a few doors down the hall from the room in which John
Tyler had died in 1862.

PRINCIPAL SOURCES

Oliver P. Chitwood. John Tyler, Champion of the Old South.
    New York: Appleton-Century, [1939].   496 p.

Robert Seager II. And Tyler Too, A Biography of John Ty-
    ler & Julia Gardiner Tyler. New York: McGraw-Hill,
    [1963].   681 p.

GEORGE M. DALLAS, 1845-1849

George Mifflin Dallas (1792-1864) was the son
of Alexander James Dallas, a prominent Philadelphia lawyer and secretary of the United States
Treasury from 1814-1816. George was graduated
in 1810 from Princeton, and in 1813 he served
as secretary to Albert Gallatin on a mission to
Russia. In 1816 George Dallas married Sophia
Chew Nicklin, the daughter of a prominent Philadelphia businessman. His wife was a woman of
spirit with expensive taste in clothes and in living, which her husband could not support from
a career in politics and public affairs. Consequently, Dallas developed his practice of law
while he dabbled in the complicated party politics that prevailed in Pennsylvania in the first
half of the nineteenth century. He was appointed in 1831 to fill out a term in the United
States Senate, but his wife did not accompany
him to Washington and discouraged him from
seeking election to a regular term.

In 1837 President Van Buren appointed Dallas
minister to Russia, and he took his wife and
seven children with him to St. Petersburg where
they remained for two years. Back in Philadelphia, Dallas renewed his earlier pursuits, law
and Pennsylvania politics. After James A. Polk
won the Democratic nomination for president in
1844, Dallas was named to the second place on
the ticket. After the conclusion of his term as
vice-president, Dallas devoted himself to his
family and the law. He agreed in 1856 to become
minister to Great Britain, a post in which he
performed effectively under two presidents. In
May of 1861 Dallas returned to his prominent

place in Philadelphia where he died on December
31, 1864.

*   *   *

George M. Dallas was born on July 10, 1792, into a distinguished upper-class family which admirably prepared him for
a high place in the social and intellectual life of Philadelphia.
He was tall, even handsome, with a compelling voice and
long, prematurely white hair, which fell gently on his neck.
Dallas was conscious of his good looks, and he enhanced
them by wearing expensive clothes and cultivating aristo-
cratic manners. His appearance and bearing appealed to
women in drawing rooms, and he did not enjoy the camaraderie of rough and ambitious political workers.

George Dallas began to court Sophia Chew Nicklin, the
eldest daughter of a prominent Philadelphia businessman,
Philip Nicklin, and he proposed the following spring. The
couple were married on May 23, 1816, as soon as Dallas was
established in his legal practice, and the wedding joined two
influential families as well as two individuals. George fell
quickly into the routine of a family man and provider for a
wife and, in time, their eight children. Sophia was a spirited
woman who kept herself informed about political developments,
and she had expensive tastes in clothes and in living which
required funds larger than her husband could earn in politics
and public affairs.

In addition to his law practice, George Dallas held numerous political offices in Philadelphia, and he became a leader
in one of the factions that dominated the Democratic Party in
Philadelphia during the first half of the nineteenth century.
Dallas accepted an appointment to fill out a term in the United
States Senate, and the separation that followed during most
of his two years in Washington was hard for Sophia to bear.
She wrote to her husband about her loneliness, envy, and
poverty and chided him for enjoying the lively society in
which he moved. Dallas enjoyed fine sherry and cigars and
obtained both from Philadelphia; he spent his free hours in
Washington playing whist or chess, riding horseback, and
dining out. Meanwhile, Mrs. Dallas sought relief for her
loneliness in the theater, opera, parties, and in shopping
for new clothes. Although proud of Dallas' contributions as
a senator, she wanted him home and persuaded him not to
seek a new term.

President Van Buren appointed Dallas minister to Russia in 1837, and the Dallases--George, Sophy, and their seven children--sailed from Boston to London where they spent a month shopping and sightseeing. They landed at the port of Kronstadt on July 29, and on August 6, Dallas and Sophia were presented to Emperor Nicholas I and the Empress Alexandra at the Peterhoff Palace.

There was little of consequence for the new minister to accomplish, and he did not like the court practice of handling diplomatic contacts at parties and other social events. Sophia and their daughters delighted in the social life that surrounded them, as many as four parties in a single evening, but Dallas permitted his girls to attend but two a week. Dallas and his wife lived extravagantly in St. Petersburg; the family had twelve servants, and his salary of $9,000 per year was inadequate to support them in the manner enjoyed by wealthy associates. Sophy wrote to her mother, "The expense of this place swallows up everything," and she had decided that without "an increase in salary we cannot brave another winter here." Dallas became frustrated with his secondary place in Russian diplomatic circles; he requested a recall, which came on July 6, 1839, and he left St. Petersburg the day after a final audience with the Czar on July 23. After a journey of two months, Dallas and his large family reached New York on October 20.

Dallas spent the next four years in the practice of law and in the rivalries of Pennsylvania politics. At the Democratic convention in 1844 James A. Polk won over Van Buren, Cass, and Buchanan, and Dallas accepted the nomination to the second place on the ticket after it had been declined by Silas Wright. Dallas' expectations for patronage did not materialize, and his relations with Polk declined until the two rarely met. At the end of his term Dallas understandably looked forward to taking up his former life on Walnut Street. Sophy never moved to Washington, but she did visit him frequently. Despite his straitened financial position, Sophy urged her husband to take the family on a European tour. In order to supplement his salary as vice-president, Dallas tried to maintain his law practice throughout his four-year term.

During the next six years Dallas devoted most of his attention to the practice of law and to his family. He continued to dabble in Pennsylvania and national politics, but

when Buchanan received in 1856 the Democratic nomination
for the presidency, Dallas realized that his own hope for the
highest office would not be realized. Consequently, he
agreed in January of 1856 to become minister to Great Britain, a post he held for five years under two presidents.
In March he departed for London with his wife, his sister,
three unmarried daughters, and a son who would serve as
secretary of the legation. As a diplomat in London, Dallas
was tactful and effective, and his family enjoyed the parties
they attended and the attention they received. Again, financial limitations caused Dallas to long for his orderly and
prosperous life in Philadelphia. The weather in London obliged Dallas and his family to remain within their home, but
his wife and daughters forced him to attend numerous parties
and concerts. "Sophy reveled in her flirtation with European
nobility who represented a welcome relief from her ... position in Philadelphia."

Dallas left London in May of 1861 with a sense of
weariness and relief. He returned to his place in society in
Philadelphia where he died suddenly on December 31, 1864.
Sophy died five years later and is buried near her husband
and son in St. Peter's Churchyard.

PRINCIPAL SOURCE

John M. Belohlavek. George Mifflin Dallas, Jacksonian Patri-
    cian. University Park: Pennsylvania State Univ. Press,
    [1977]. 233 p.

MILLARD FILLMORE, 1849-1850

Millard Fillmore (1800-1874) was born into
the family of a poor farmer in Cayuga County,
New York, and was appointed at age fourteen,
to work in a cloth-dressing mill. Millard voraciously read books obtained from a circulating
library, and during slack periods in the mill
he pursued classes in a local academy. As a
young man, Fillmore struggled with school
teaching and law clerkships in towns near his
family and in 1822 at Buffalo. He first practiced law in East Aurora, from which he was
elected to three terms in the New York Legislature. Further independent study of law
brought Fillmore important cases and a partnership with a former mentor in Buffalo, the
city that was to be his home for the rest of
his life.

After his removal to Buffalo, Fillmore
served as a Whig from 1833-1835 and from
1837-1843 in the United States House of Representatives. He chose to retire in 1842 from
Congress, but in 1848 he became controller
of New York, which required him to locate in
Albany. After the nomination of Zachary
Taylor for the presidency in 1848, Fillmore
was chosen for his running mate because the
Whig Convention wanted a Northerner who
represented the Henry Clay faction in the
party. After the death of President Taylor
on July 9, 1850, Fillmore became president
and mustered the support of moderates in
Congress needed for the adoption of the
Compromise of 1850. In 1852 the Whig
nomination for the presidency went to General Winfield Scott, and in 1856 Fillmore ran

unsuccessfully for the White House as the candidate for the short-lived American party. After his brief terms as vice-president and president of the United States, Fillmore returned
to Buffalo where he devoted his energies to
the formation and development of important cultural and educational institutions. He was chan-
cellor of the University of Buffalo from 1846
until his death in his adopted city on March
8, 1874.

*   *   *

The romance of Abigail Powers and Millard Fillmore was of
classic simplicity. When they met in 1819 in the New Hope
(N.Y.) Academy she was twenty-one, and he was but nineteen. Her father was a minister in Moravia, halfway between
Auburn and Ithaca, and his father had worked hard but unsuccessfully to farm poor land near Bennington, Vermont,
and in several locations in central New York near the Finger
Lakes, and again near East Aurora, eighteen miles from Buffalo. Millard's father saw little future in farming and ap-
prenticed his fourteen-year-old son to cloth-dressing mills.
In his free hours the youth voraciously read books borrowed
from a local circulating library, and when an academy was
established in the mill town he enrolled for classes to be
pursued during the slack months in the mill. Abigail pursued studies to acquire polish; young Millard aimed at obtaining the rudiments of an education which would enable
him to escape from impoverished surroundings. The young
couple became acquainted in their classes: her beauty and
gentle manners appealed to him, and his dignified bearing
and sturdy manhood evoked her admiration. Their attraction
for each other shortly blossomed into love, but Millard's
financial situation and prospects did not permit him to take
a wife.

Millard struggled with school teaching and law clerkships in towns near his parents, first at Montville, then at
East Aurora, and finally in 1822, at Buffalo. There he
showed the character traits, industry, integrity, and courteous bearing which earned the respect of his associates and
led within a few years, instead of the customary seven, to
his admission to the bar. He opened a law office in East
Aurora, and his practice as a small-town lawyer grew rapidly;

within two years he was able to conclude the engagement
made six years earlier. Abigail and Millard were married in
her hometown of Moravia on February 5, 1826, and they
soon left to live in East Aurora. Millard resolved to enlarge
his knowledge of the law through intensive study on his own,
and his efforts led to more important cases, and in 1830 to
a partnership in the office of Joseph Clary, under whom Millard had studied law, and a removal to Buffalo, the city that
was to be home for the rest of his life.

The married life of the Fillmores was almost idyllic.
The couple purchased a six-room frame house near the center of the rapidly growing city, and both Abigail and Millard
participated in the many social activities to be found in their
lively surroundings. In addition to the dinners, parties,
plays, and musical entertainments which the Fillmores enjoyed, the young couple continued their studies in their library, which Millard developed through frequent visits to
bookstores. A son, Millard Powers, was born in 1827, and
a daughter, Mary Abigail, was born in the spring of 1832.
The Fillmores joined the Unitarian church and attended
services regularly. Millard was active in the Buffalo Ly-
ceum, and he continued "to promote libraries, learning, and
knowledge."

Fillmore's qualities of intense application, unselfish
service, loyalty to his friends, congenial composure, and
quiet competence which had brought him prominence in the
legal profession in western New York soon led him into
politics. His three terms in the New York legislature began while he was a resident of East Aurora and a member
of the Antimasonic party, and after he moved to Buffalo,
he served for almost a decade in the United States House
of Representatives as a Whig, the new party concerned
with advancing the business interests of Americans. After
Fillmore became chairman of the important Ways and Means
Committee he developed and sponsored the tariff bill passed
in 1842. He chose to retire from Congress, but was pres-
sured by Thurlow Weed into running for the post of governor of New York, a contest in which Fillmore was defeated.

Free of political duties, Fillmore devoted his energies
to his lucrative practice of law, but he found time to enjoy
domestic life with his wife and two children. In 1844 his
son reached age sixteen and entered his father's law office

as a student, and his daughter made encouraging progress
with her music lessons. His wife, Abigail, was treated by
her husband with tender respect, and it became a habit with
Millard to show his wife innumerable courtesies. Three years
later Fillmore was elected to the important post of controller
of New York. This required his removal to Albany, so Fillmore ended his law partnership in Buffalo, sent his son to
Harvard to obtain a formal education, and his daughter went
to a finishing school in Massachusetts.

Throughout his political career, Fillmore had many encounters with Thurlow Weed, the boss of the Whigs in New
York, who controlled a large portion of the patronage in the
Empire State and seldom missed an opportunity to advance
his favorite protégé, William H. Seward. Fillmore was largely ignored by President Taylor in the filling of important
political positions in New York, and after Fillmore became
president he did not remove the officers named by Weed because he wanted harmony in his party and administration.
Fillmore had become the vice-presidential nominee of the
Whigs after Taylor received the nomination for president,
mainly because the convention believed that the ticket needed
a Northerner who represented the faction in the party led
by Henry Clay.

Fillmore's wife and daughter had left Washington in
June of 1850 to escape summer heat in the capital, and the vice-
president was alone in his rooms when a messenger from the
White House brought word of the death of Zachary Taylor.
Upon learning this momentous news, the three members of
Fillmore's immediate family hurried to Washington. His wife
was unwell and could not perform the duties of the First
Lady without assistance which was furnished with "inborn
felicity" by their daughter. The son, now himself a lawyer,
became President Fillmore's private secretary.

Fillmore's brief term as president was notable for his
effort to muster the support of men of the North and of the
South who would vote for the legislation embraced by the
Compromise of 1850, and therein he showed himself to be an
effective political leader. Fillmore did not seek another term
in office, and the nomination of his party went to General
Winfield Scott who lost the election in 1852.

Fillmore planned to make an extended tour of the South

soon after his term as president had ended (March 4, 1853). However, his wife, who had been in poor health for months, suffered from exposure to raw March weather during the inaugural ceremonies for President Pierce. Her severe cold developed into pneumonia, and before the end of the month, Abigail Fillmore was dead. Less than a year and a half later, Fillmore suffered another great loss: his daughter, Mary Abigail, who had enjoyed perfect health, died a few hours after the first signs of an illness when she was but twenty-two years old. The loss of his daughter, who had succeeded her mother in the management of the Fillmore household, may have caused the former Whig president to agree to become the candidate of the American party for the presidency in the campaign of 1856, which was won by the Democratic candidate, James Buchanan.

Now in permanent retirement from political life and from his practice of law, which he considered to be an improper occupation for a former president, Fillmore married a wealthy widow, Mrs. Caroline C. McIntosh, and settled into a comfortable and useful life in Buffalo. The former president accepted a prominent place in many cultural institutions in his adopted city, and he enjoyed remarkably good health until shortly before his death from paralysis on March 4, 1874.

PRINCIPAL SOURCE

Robert J. Rayback. Millard Fillmore, Biography of a President. Buffalo: Buffalo Historical Society, 1959. 470 p.

WILLIAM R. KING, 1853

William Rufus Devane King (1786-1853) was
born in North Carolina where his family had large
land holdings and his father was a leader in political affairs.   William attended academies in nearby counties before he enrolled in 1861 in the
University of North Carolina.   He spent three
years in the Unviersity before he left to study
law; after a year of preparation, he was licensed
to practice.   Three years later he was elected
to the United States House of Representatives.
He was reelected in 1813 and again in 1815.
At age thirty King resigned from the House to
become secretary of a mission to several Italian
states and to Russia.

Duing his travels in Europe, King decided
to sell his North Carolina estate and to move
to Alabama where he bought 750 acres of land
on the Alabama River.   King had an important
role in the Alabama constitutional convention that
met in 1819 in Huntsville; he obtained one of
Alabama's two new seats in the United States
Senate, where he won the respect of his colleagues for his work as a mediator.   In 1844
President Tyler named King minister to France,
where he dissuaded the French from joining
with the British in actions that would interfere
with American interests in Texas, Oregon, and
elsewhere.   After King returned in 1846, he
was appointed in 1848 to the United States
Senate where he served until late in 1852, the
year in which he was nominated to the second
place on the Democratic ticket with Franklin
Pierce of New Hampshire.   King was weakened
by tuberculosis and went in January of 1853

to Cuba to regain his health. He was permitted
by special legislation to take the oath of office
on foreign soil and did so on March 4, although
he was too weak to stand alone. The vice-
president returned to his estate in Alabama where
he died on April 18, 1853.

*   *   *

Franklin Pierce of New Hampshire, who had served in the
United States Senate and rose to the rank of brigadier general in the Mexican War, was elected to the presidency in
1852. His running mate, William Rufus King of Alabama,
is the only vice-president who took the oath of office on
foreign soil and is one of the two vice-presidents who never
married. Although King held public office during most of
the forty-five years between 1808 (when he was but twenty-
two) and 1853 (when he died at sixty-seven), only the out-
lines of his life are known because he left no diary or extensive correspondence files that would reveal the man behind his offices.

King's three decades in the United States Senate began before the adoption in 1820 of the Missouri Compromise
and continued through the Compromise of 1850. The great
issues of the period, the extension of slavery into the territories, internal improvements, tariffs for revenue or for
protection, and the sale of public lands, were debated eloquently by the spokesmen for the three large sections of the
country: John C. Calhoun for the South, Henry Clay for
the West, and Daniel Webster for the Northeast. King's
role in the titanic struggles was that of mediator, for he
loved both his adopted state of Alabama and his native country.

Although King usually occupied a middle ground where
he sought to calm Southern firebrands and to obtain better
treatment from the North, he enjoyed the respect of his
political associates. He was repeatedly named president pro
tempore of the Senate, and King's close friend, James Buchanan, later a president of the United States, wrote to President-elect Pierce: "He [King] is among the best, purest,
& most consistent public men I have ever know, & is, also,
a sound judging and discreet counsellor."

William Rufus Devane King was born on April 7, 1786,
in Sampson County, North Carolina, the second son of William King and Margaret Devane. William King owned considerable land in North Carolina at the beginning of the
American Revolution, and he added frequently to his holdings of land and slaves. The Kings had three sons and four
daughters, and whenever a son reached his majority he received enough land and slaves to establish him in the planter class.

William King served briefly in the Revolutionary Army,
and he was a leader in political affairs in Sampson County.
He was a justice of the peace until he resigned the office in
1791, and he was a delegate to the Fayetteville Convention
called in 1789 to ratify the new Constitution for the United
States. King opposed ratification, but the Constitution was
approved in North Carolina by a vote of 194 to 77. William
King served in four sessions of the North Carolina House of
Commons, where he was not active in debate and was invariably a strict constructionist. His son William Rufus probably heard his father expound his views with neighbors and
political associates.

William King, one of the wealthiest men in the community, could give his children exceptional advantages. His son
William Rufus was able to attend Grove Academy near Ken-
ansville in Duplin County and Fayetteville Academy in Cum-
berland County before he enrolled in the University of North
Carolina preparatory school in 1800, where the youth cor-
rected a deficiency in reading and won recognition for superior work in Latin and French. At the age of fifteen, William Rufus King was eligible for admission to the University
of North Carolina which he attended for three years. Soon
after entering the University, King joined the Philanthropic
Society, which encouraged recreation and public speaking,
and the young man held offices in the organization and participated in several debates. William Rufus left the University after his junior year, probably because he had arranged
to study law under William Duffy of Fayetteville, one of the
leading lawyers of the state. After a year of tutelage in
law, King was licensed at age nineteen, and he opened a
law office in Clinton in Sampson County.

King practiced law in Clinton from 1805 until 1808,
when at age twenty-one, he first sought public office. He

was elected to the North Carolina Legislature, and a year
later he became solicitor of the state Superior Court, a post
that required him to travel twice a year through ten counties of North Carolina. Four of the counties on King's circuit were in the Wilmington congressional district which was
represented by Thomas Kenan. When the congressman decided not to seek reelection, the door was open for King,
who, at age twenty-four, was probably the youngest representative in the House when President James Madison called
a special session in November, 1811.

Congressman King affiliated with the War Hawks led
by Henry Clay, and he voted for the war with England
called for by President Madison in June, 1812. Not all of
Madison's program received the North Carolinian's support,
but his positions must have been approved at home because
he was reelected without opposition in 1813 and again in
1815.

At age thirty King resigned from the House of Representatives to accept a commission as Secretary of the Legation
headed by William Pinkney to the Court of Naples and the
Two Sicilies and to the Court of Russia. The Pinkney mission left Baltimore on June 8, 1816, aboard the seventy-four
gunship Washington, and reached Gibraltar twenty-four days
later. King enjoyed the voyage after he overcame his initial seasickness, and he delighted in the sights of Gibraltar
and Naples. The mission sought to obtain reparations for
ships seized in the harbor by a government headed by a
brother-in-law of Napoleon, but the Marquis di Circello, the
new Neopolitan foreign minister, denied responsibility for
acts of his king's predecessors.

In late September, King left Naples alone for St.
Petersburg and he arrived in early November. Two months
later King wrote a long letter to Secretary of State Monroe
in which he described Russian military power and complained
of the climate. King was presented at court, and he probably enjoyed the social activities that preceded the marriage
of the Grand Duke Nicholas and Princess Charlotte of Prus-
sia. About a month after the wedding, Pinkney reported
to John Quincy Adams that his Secretary had "quitted" him.
Pinkney did not say whether King had left unceremoniously
because of the severe weather in the Russian capital, a
rumored affair of the heart at court, or his eagerness to make
a new start in the territory of Alabama.

Before he went to Europe, King had learned of the
possibilities for economic development in Alabama, and he
had sold his North Carolina estate. After his return, King
purchased in 1818 750 acres of land on the Alabama River
near the town of Cahawba in Dallas County. His plantation,
"King's Bend," was about fifteen miles from the site of the
projected city of Selma, a development in which King purchased ten shares of stock for $80 and five lots for $990.

The new resident of Alabama was named to the state
constitutional convention that met in July 1819 in Huntsville. Among the forty-five members of the convention there
were many men who later held high office; but King stood
out among them, for he was appointed by President John E.
Walker to the Committee of Fifteen to draft the constitution
and he was subsequently named to a committee of three to
revise the rought draft prepared by the larger group. In
the debates on provisions of the proposed constitution, King
argued for a conservative document, but he lost when popular elections for sheriffs and clerks prevailed.

After the adoption of the constitution for Alabama,
there was a contest for her two seats in the United States
Senate. One went to John S. Walker, president of the constitutional convention, and the second went to King despite
a strong contest from Charles Tait, formerly a senator from
Georgia. At the time of his first election to the Senate,
a friend commented, King is "a very gay, elegant looking
fellow, ... a fluent speaker and a man of respectable talents." An early Alabama historian wrote that King "was
tall and slender. His figure was gracefully erect, and his
manners were as courtly as Chesterfield's."

Alabama's two new senators drew lots to determine the
lengths of their terms and King's expired in 1822. He was
opposed once more by Charles Tait and by others, but King
was reelected on the second ballot. In his second term King
opposed the "Tariff of Abominations," but he counseled constitutional resistance instead of nullification. Reelection to
the Senate in 1828 came readily with Andrew Jackson's poli-
ticial sweep, and as King moved closer to President Jackson's
policies, his reelection in 1834 was assured. In 1837 President Van Buren offered King the post of minister to Austria,
but he preferred to remain in the Senate.

When King began his fifth term in 1841, the Whigs, headed by Harrison and Tyler, won the national election. King continued to oppose the Whig policies of a second national bank, high tariffs, and distribution of proceeds from the sale of public lands, and he defended the annexation of Texas and of the Oregon country. After the death of Harrison, John Tyler, more of a states' rights Democrat than a Whig, became president, and he wanted to join the independent Republic of Texas to the United States. In order to achieve this end it was necessary to obtain tacit acquiescence from France and Great Britain.

King was named minister to France by President Tyler on April 4, 1844, and his nomination was unanimously confirmed by the Senate. The new minister, his favorite niece, Catharine Ellis, and Joshua L. Martin, Secretary of the Legation, sailed from New York on May 16 and arrived in La Havre on June 7. King had an audience with King Louis Phillipe on July 1 and was his guest for dinner on July 4. After dinner the King expressed the interest of his country in commerce with Texas, and William Rufus King assured his host that this would not be impaired by American annexation. In his relations with Guizot, the French Minister of Foreign Affairs, King was remarkably forthright and especially adept at forestalling collusion between France and Great Britain which would interfere with American interests in the annexation of Texas, negotiations pertaining to the Oregon country, and the war with Mexico.

King also gained high marks for his country from the leaders of Parisian society; the ball he gave on George Washington's birthday in 1846 was attended by four hundred guests and was recognized as "one of the most pleasant affairs of the season." The American minister's only insurmountable problem was the deleterious effect of the climate on his health, and King requested on July 15, 1846, a recall from his important post. After traveling on a ship that struck a rocky ledge off the north coast of Ireland, King and his party returned to Liverpool and embarked on a packet which brought them to New York in early November.

King returned to Alabama where he hoped to be reelected to a seat in the Senate. He lost the first contest to Dixon H. Lewis who represented the state-rights wing of his party. However, he was returned to the Senate when

Governor Chapman appointed King to the place vacated by
Senator Bagley, who resigned to become minister to Russia.
After he returned to the Senate, King was named chairman
of the Foreign Relations Committee, and in this capacity he
secured approval for the Clayton-Bulwer Treaty in which
Great Britain and the United States agreed not to acquire
territory in Central America. King supported the Compromise of 1850, and he appealed for moderation from both sides.
His position was clear:

> I am disposed to yield, all I can, in honor--all I
> can do without the sacrifice of essential rights--in
> order to settle this [slavery] question.

King hoped that the Democratic National Conventions
in 1840 and 1844 would nominate him for a national office,
but he did not gain this prize until 1852. At the Convention held that year in Baltimore there were five or six leading candidates for the nomination for president, and Pierce
won on the forty-ninth ballot. Delegates from Maine proposed that a Southerner should be named to be the candidate
for vice-president, and King was nominated on the second
ballot. King was pleased, and in the same month (June
1852) he was optimistic about the result, "The skies are
bright, and I cannot doubt our success."

King was never robust, and he was weakened by tuberculosis late in 1852. He declined to attend dinners in his
honor in his old North Carolina congressional district and in
Selma, but he returned to Washington for the session of
Congress that began on December 6. Pierce and King defeated the Whig candidates, but King's health declined and
he left Washington. On January 17, 1853 the vice-president-
elect left for Cuba where he hoped to regain his health, and
special legislation was passed that would permit the United
States Consul in Cuba to swear King into his high office.
On March 4, King was too feeble to stand without support,
and he was aided by a congressman from Texas on one side
and a consular official on the other. The vice-president returned to Mobile on April 11, 1853, and to his plantation,
"King's Bend," near Selma on April 17. He died there on
the following day, April 18.

President Pierce noted in his annual message that the
vice-president's death had occurred "since the adjournment

of Congress." When the members reconvened, both the House and Senate voted resolutions for the observance of periods of official mourning and listened to obituary addresses delivered in the House of Representatives and in Senate on December 8, 1853. Although several of the speakers had served in the Congress with the late vice-president for more than two decades, they had little to say except to mention his long period of service and his gentle mien. Ten thousand copies of the speeches were printed in the next year in a booklet which included a portrait of King as its frontispiece.

PRINCIPAL SOURCE

John Milton Martin. William Rufus King: Southern Moderate. Ph.D. dissertation accepted by the University of North Carolina, 1955. 385 l.

JOHN C. BRECKINRIDGE, 1857-1861

John Cabell Breckinridge (1821-1875) was the
son and grandson of men who had practiced law
and had held important political offices in Kentucky. John prepared himself for a similar career through collegiate studies at Centre College
and legal work at Transylvania University. At
age twenty-five the young attorney was commissioned major in the Third Kentucky Volunteers
and led his troops to Mexico but did not arrive
until the war had ended. Breckinridge demonstrated exceptional leadership qualities while his
troops were in training and in transit, and he
became acquainted in Mexico City with officers
who were to achieve lasting fame during the
Civil War.

Breckinridge was elected in 1850 to represent Kentucky's Eighth Congressional District
in Congress, and he was reelected in 1852. He
went in 1856 to the Democratic National Convention in Cincinnati resolved not to accept a
nomination to a national office but was chosen
to be James Buchanan's running mate. Breckinridge and President Buchanan were poles apart
in many respects, but neither had a workable
solution to the deepening controversy over slavery. Breckinridge was nominated in 1860 for
president by Southern Democrats who would not
support Stephen A. Douglas, and both lost to
the Republicans.

After the end of his term as vice-president,
Breckinridge became a senator from Kentucky;
but, after his state abandoned its neutrality in
September 1861, he joined the Confederate Army.
Breckinridge's treason brought expulsion from

the Senate. Although he lacked experience in
combat, Breckinridge proved to be an able general in important battles in the Western theater,
and he was called in 1864 to lead a division in
Lee's army. He served for a few months as
secretary of war in President Davis' Cabinet
and fled the country after Lee's surrender.
Breckinridge returned in 1869 to practice law
in Lexington, Kentucky, where he died in 1875.

*   *   *

During the summer of 1843 Mary Cyrene Burch of Lexington,
Kentucky, a seventeen-year-old cousin of Thomas Bullock,
became engaged to John C. Breckinridge, and the couple
were married on December 12 of that year. Breckinridge
was also a cousin of Thomas Bullock and his law partner.
The young men had practiced law for two years in Burlington, Iowa, but the partnership was dissolved after Breckinridge and his fiancée determined to make their home in Kentucky. Breckinridge formed a new partnership with Samuel
Bullock, another of Thomas' cousins, who was to handle the
business in Lexington while the partner practiced in nearby
Georgetown. The young Breckinridges bought a house in
Georgetown; his business flourished for a few years, and
Mary had her first child under circumstances in which she
almost lost her life.

After the legal business in Georgetown began to decline, the partners decided to handle all of their cases out
of their office in Lexington, the city in which Mary and
John Breckinridge lived longer than in any other and in
which they spent some of their happiest years. Here their
second child was born in 1846, and here the young lawyer
became prominent as a public speaker and budding politician.
The war with Mexico had begun in May of 1846, and John C.
Breckinridge was commissioned major of the Third Kentucky
Volunteers on September 4, 1847. The fighting was over by
the time Breckinridge and his regiment reached Mexico City
in mid-December of 1847, but during the two months of training and six weeks in transit the young major exhibited exceptional qualities of leadership. In Mexico City Breckinridge joined the Aztec Club, formed by officers of the troops
who took the city, and there he met some of the young
soldiers who were to achieve fame in the Civil War:

Beauregard, Grant, McClellan, Lee, Johnston, and Franklin
Pierce. The Kentucky regiments returned in the summer of
1848, and as soon as his ship docked at Louisville, Breckinridge hastened to Lexington where a daughter had been born
while he was away.

John C. Breckinridge's father won a seat in the Kentucky House of Representatives, and his father had served
in the Kentucky legislature and in Jefferson's Cabinet. The
father, Cabell, and his father, John, attended college and
practiced law in Kentucky, and "Cabell's John" studied classics at Centre College, read law in the office of William Owe-
ley and studied law at Transylvania University. In college
he developed his speaking ability which, in addition to his
respected family name and manly physical appearance, qualified him for a political career.

Mary also had important family connections in Kentucky;
a cousin, George W. Johnson, was elected governor of the
provisional anti-Union government of the state. Mary's love
for her husband was unrestrained; in her words, "I never
saw him come without being glad, or leave without being
sorry." On the day of his first political victory, Mary gave
birth to another son, and shortly before he attended the
Democratic state convention in January of 1851, she had
another boy. Mary accomplished this rapid succession of
childbirths despite the poor health which persisted during
much of her married life.

At the state convention in 1851 Breckinridge was nominated to fill the seat for Kentucky's Eighth Congressional
District, and through hard campaigning and his popularity
in his section of Kentucky, he won the election, an exceptional feat for a Democrat in the state dominated by Henry
Clay and his Whigs. In April of 1852 Congressman Breckinridge visited Lexington, and Mary returned with him to
Washington. She was pregnant again, and her husband's
income had not grown as rapidly as their expenses. Before
the end of his first term in Congress, Breckinridge was offered the governorship of Washington Territory by President
Pierce, and the young politician sought advice from his wife.
She left the decision to him, and he declined the offer to
run for reelection. During a slow period in April of 1854
John and Mary lived in a rented house on C Street, and before the end of the session Breckinridge completed a special

report which added to his reputation. President Pierce offered the Kentuckian the post of minister to Spain, and he
at first intended to accept the appointment, partly because
he thought a change in surroundings might help to improve
his wife's persistent poor health. However, Mary wanted her
husband to leave the national political scene, and he declined the appointment in February, 1854.

    Although Breckinridge intended to devote his attention
to his legal practice, developments such as the rise of the
Know-Nothing Party and the turmoil in "Bleeding Kansas" concerned him greatly. He attracted attention through speeches
on these topics, yet he went to the Cincinnati Democratic
convention in 1856 resolved not to accept nomination for a
national office. Almost in spite of himself (his eloquent
declination of his nomination for the vice-presidency brought
him greater support), he became Buchanan's running mate,
and he helped to win the election by speaking around the
country, something that a candidate for a national office had
not done before. On a trip to the East, Breckinridge met
Buchanan for the first time, and the latter was mindful that
his running mate had supported Pierce and then Douglas for
first place on the ticket at the Democratic convention. The
Democratic ticket easily defeated the Republicans led by
Fremont and the Americans (Know-Nothings) headed by Fillmore, and Breckinridge was slated to become within a few
months the youngest vice-president in history. His record
is hard to surpass since the Kentuckian met the age require-
ment for the office less than a year before he was elected.

    Mary left Lexington on February 19 to go with her
husband to Washington for his inauguration. While in Washington Breckinridge looked for a residence for his family
during his term in office and settled on an arrangement with
two others for the purchase of two city blocks. On one of
these, two houses would be built and the other would be
sold in lots to pay for both the land and the construction.
The houses were to be quite large: four floors high, with
a library, two parlors, a dining room, seven bedrooms, and
a bathroom. Breckinridge had to sell a slave with her baby
and his home in Lexington to pay for his projected house in
Washington, because his monthly salary ($666) was needed
for current expenses. After two years in office his new
house was not ready for occupancy, and Mary did not want
to live in any of the quarters that could be rented in

Washington. Only her love for her husband, which a biographer termed "almost reverential," caused her to remain.

During most of his term as vice-president, Breckinridge was largely ignored by Buchanan, who was inadequate to the demands created by deep divisions in the country over the question of the extension of slavery. Almost at the end of his administration, the president summoned Breckinridge to the White House. By then, December of 1860, Lincoln had been elected to become president in March of 1861, and Breckinridge had lost his effort to win the election for the Democrats and the South. Buchanan, with great seriousness, unlocked a drawer in his desk and explained that he had called on the vice-president to learn whether or not he would favor issuance of a proclamation designating a day of humiliation and prayer. Breckinridge was stunned at first, made a few polite and complimentary remarks, and then smiled and left. Later Breckinridge would be amused by the absurdity of the incident in which the president demonstrated anew his incapacity to deal with his country's major problems.

Although Buchanan and Breckinridge were poles apart in their personalities and life styles, the younger man had no better solution to the impending crisis than the president's. As vice-president, Breckinridge could not participate in debates in the Senate, but he did vote several times to break ties and he made an eloquent address when the Senate moved from the chamber once occupied by Calhoun, Clay, and Webster to larger quarters. He was away from Washington during a crucial vote on the Lecompten (Kansas) constitution, and as a candidate of the Southern wing of the Democratic party for the presidency he never answered the "Norfolk Questions" which Douglas, the candidate of the Northern Democrats, had been asked during the presidential campaign. Douglas responded unequivocally that the Southern states should not secede in the event of a Republican victory, and, if they did so, force might be warranted in resisting secession. Throughout his vice-presidency, Breckinridge avoided facing issues in which declaring himself might cause him to lose the support of his party, which had failed to respond to the pressures of the newly formed Republican party.

After the conclusion of his term as vice-president,

Breckinridge was pleased to become one of Kentucky's senators, because this would enable him to participate in the
great debate in progress before the beginning of the Civil
War.   Here, blind to the significance of the Republican victory in the recent election, Breckinridge strove with leaders
of border states to develop a compromise that would protect
slavery where it existed and preserve neutrality for states
that did not wish to secede or to prevent secession.   After
Breckinridge returned to Lexington he continued to speak in
public against "Lincoln invaders."

     The Kentucky legislature voted on September 18 to
end its neutrality and to lend support to the Union, and the
arrest of Breckinridge was recommended by the heads of the
two houses in Frankfort.   When word of his possible arrest
reached Breckinridge, he decided to "go South," and at
night, late in September, he left Lexington to join the army
of the Confederacy.   This act led to an indictment for
treason by a federal court in Frankfort, and on December
2, 1861, to his expulsion from the United States Senate.
Through all of this and in later years Breckinridge was
convinced he had taken the right course because he persuaded himself that rights guaranteed by the Constitution
would be lost if the Southern states had to submit to the
federal government.   His identification with the aspirations
of the Southern states caused him to turn his back on the
government to which he had sworn allegiance as an officer
in the United States Army, as a member of Congress, as
vice-president, and as a senator.   In Breckinridge's myopic
view, the new administration in Washington represented rule
by dictators who did not deserve his loyalty rather than
that of a government that had won a national election fairly.

     There is no need to review here Breckinridge's career
as a general in the Confederate Army, his brief service as
secretary of war in Jefferson Davis' Cabinet, or his years
of self-imposed exile in Canada and Europe before he returned to live out his remaining years in Kentucky, but his
wife's role after 1861 can be suggested.   Although her health
continued to be poor, Mary never missed an opportunity to
be near her husband whether he was in or out of uniform.
He served in different theaters of the Civil War, and she
visited him in several of them.   During her stay with him
at Winchester, Virginia, late in the War, she and other wives
of officers stationed there stood in the streets and pleaded

with the troops routed by Sheridan to stand and fight, but without success. A few days before the surrender of Lee's army at Appomattox, Davis' Cabinet discussed ways the impending tensions might be reduced, and a Confederate general proposed that while Grant met with Lee, "the wives of the ranking officers in both armies should pay calls, escorted by officers, on the wives of generals in the other army." Several hours were spent on February 21 in discussion of the proposal, and Breckinridge, who had repeatedly shown great courage under fire and had seen the carnage of battle, approved, "especially pleased by the imaginative use of the wives."

The war years and three years in exile injured Breckinridge's health, and he experienced recurrent illness during the rest of his life. He died in Lexington on May 17, 1875, and was buried near Henry Clay's monument. Mary recovered her health and survived her husband by thirty-two years; she was buried beside him in 1907.

PRINCIPAL SOURCE

William C. Davis. Breckinridge: Statesman, Soldier, Symbol. Baton Rouge: Louisiana State Univ. Press, [1974]. 687 p.

HANNIBAL HAMLIN, 1861-1865

Hannibal Hamlin (1809-1891) was born in Paris
Hill, about forty miles north of Portland, Maine,
attended local schools and nearby Hebron Academy, and practiced law in Hampden, ten miles
south of Bangor. Hamlin's political career began
in the Maine House of Representatives, where
he represented his district for four years, 1836-
1840, and was the speaker for three of these
years. In the Maine Legislature, in the United
States House of Representatives from 1843-1847,
and in the Senate from 1848-1857, Hamlin was a
loyal Jacksonian Democrat until he broke in 1856
from his party because of its stance on slavery
and joined the Republicans. In the same year
the new Republican became governor of Maine,
but, after less than two months in the office,
Hamlin returned to the United States Senate.
Hamlin's New England background, his legislative experience, and his outspoken opposition
to slavery qualified him for the second place
on the Republican ticket with Abraham Lincoln
in 1860. As vice-president, Hamlin had few
duties of consequence, and the president gave
him no special assignments. Hamlin was replaced in 1864 as Lincoln's running mate, and
was appointed in the summer of 1865 to the
lucrative post of collector of the Port of Boston. He resigned the post a year later to
show his disapproval of President Johnson's
leniency toward the South. Hamlin returned
in 1869 to the Senate, where he worked harmoniously for two terms with the Radical Republicans. He declined to run again in 1880,
but he did accept in 1881 an appointment as

minister to Spain. Hamlin traveled to Madrid by
way of London and Paris, but the former vice-
president was not favorably impressed with Europe. He was glad to return in 1882 to Bangor,
where he spent nine years in comfortable retirement before his death from a heart attack on
July 16, 1891.

*   *   *

At the age of nineteen or twenty Ellen Vesta Emery became
the second wife of Senator Hannibal Hamlin, then in his
forty-seventh year. The marriage took place in the bride's
home in Paris Hill, Maine, a small town about forty miles
north of Portland, where Hannibal had been born and had
grown to manhood. His first wife had been Sarah Jane
Emery, Ellen's older step-sister, who bore him four children
and maintained their home in Hampden, Maine, while Hannibal
served in Washington as a member of Congress and as a
senator. In the summer of 1854 Sarah Jane developed a
severe cold and lung inflammation which continued into the
fall and worsened during the winter. Hannibal returned in
December from Washington to be with his wife, who was
recognized as consumptive. In early April Hannibal summoned his son, and his wife's father and half-sister, Ellen,
came from Paris City to the Hamlin home in Hampden.

After the death of his first wife, Hannibal's grief was
severe for months but was assuaged in time through physical
labor on his farm, participation in a reunion at Hebron Academy, and by his return at the end of the year to Washington
to begin a momentous session of Congress. How the senator
courted Ellen Emery, Sarah Hamlin's younger half-sister,
is unknown; but the young woman, said to be "a rather
plain but witty and warm-hearted girl" became his wife on
September 25, 1856. Shortly after their wedding Ellen made
a campaign trip with her husband in New Jersey and Pennsylvania. Ellen found politics "novel and exciting" and was
thrilled by the four-mile-long procession of Republicans she
saw in Lancaster. Although but a few years older than the
three surviving children of Hannibal's first marriage, Ellen
became their stepmother, and the new Hamlin family was enlarged by the birth of two sons, Hannibal Emery, born in
August of 1858, and Frank, born in September of 1862.

After serving as a loyal Jacksonian Democrat in the
Maine Legislature from 1836 to 1841 and in 1847, as a member of Congress from 1843 to 1847, and as a United States
senator from 1848, Hamlin became dissatisfied with the policy
of his party toward slavery, renounced his allegiance to the
Democrats, and became in 1856 a Republican. As a Republican Hamlin was elected governor of Maine in the fall of 1856,
but left the post after a few weeks to become a United States
senator once again. This office provided Hamlin with a salary five times as large as that of the governor of Maine, a
factor that loomed large in his plans for the education of his
children.

As a senator with little secretarial help, Hamlin con-
scientiously answered thousands of letters from constituents,
and he wrote almost daily to Ellen and frequently to each of
his three older children. Hamlin did not like Washington
and probably did not consider establishing a family residence
there. Instead, as a congressman, senator, and vice-
president, he lived in a succession of boarding houses and
hotels, usually without his family. Hannibal Hamlin enjoyed
a good dinner and received in a week about ten invitations
to dine, but he was not convivial. He wore coats and col-
lars long out of fashion, and his latest biographer, H. Draper Hunt, characterized Hamlin as "the stalwart but rather
dull man from Maine."

After the nomination of Abraham Lincoln for the presidency by the Republican Convention in 1860, the party leaders secured the nomination of vice-president for Hamlin on
the second ballot. Hamlin's obvious qualifications for the
nomination were his antislavery record, his New England
background and residence, and his seasoning as a legislator.
He wrote to Ellen that he "neither expected or desired" the
nomination, but, as a faithful member of the party, he had
an obligation to accept, which he did in a letter much longer
than Lincoln's.

President-elect Lincoln invited Hamlin to visit him in
Chicago to become acquainted and to discuss the formation
of the new administration. Hannibal responded to the warm
informality of the President-elect and his wife, "a small,
plump, handsome woman" whom the senator was sure Ellen
would like. "I think she is one of your kind of women ex-
actly," Hamlin wrote from Chicago. Hamlin had to miss the

wedding of his son, Charles, in order to meet the Lincolns
shortly after the receipt of his invitation, but he saw the
young couple in Washington soon after the beginning of the
new year. Ellen was told by her husband, "You will find
her [their new daughter-in-law] a modest and pleasant
woman--and they are the brightest jewels that can adorn a
woman."

Ellen traveled with her husband in February 1861 to
Washington to attend his inauguration as vice-president.
The first night of their journey was spent in the Revere
House in Boston and the second with relatives at Windsor
Locks in Connecticut. On the 20th the Hamlins reached the
Astor House in New York. According to the New York
Tribune: "Mrs. Hamlin is about twenty-five years of age,
smaller, and not as full in form as Mrs. Lincoln. She has
a mild blue eye, rather sharp features, but a gentle expres-
sion of face." The Hamlins dined that evening with the
Lincolns in the latter's suite, and afterwards the two couples
went to a performance of Verdi's The Masked Ball at the
Academy of Music where they were roundly cheered. The
presidential party left the opera after the first act and returned to the Astor House where Ellen Hamlin and Mary
Todd Lincoln hosted a reception. Later Ellen held a second
reception in her own parlor.

The Lincolns left New York for Washington on the
21st, and the Hamlins followed early on the 22nd. The Hamlins crossed the Hudson in a gaily decorated ferryboat, were
escorted to Newark in a special train by a vice-presidential
party which included Lincoln's friend, David Davis, and
traveled the last leg of the trip to Washington in a special
car which was scheduled to leave Philadelphia at noon on the
23rd.

From her seat in the balcony of the Senate Chamber,
Ellen saw her husband sworn in at noon on March 4 by his
predecessor, John C. Breckinridge. In the evening she attended the inaugural ball in the "Palace of Aladdin," a temporary plank structure built next to City Hall and decorated
with red and white muslin and seals of the federal government and of the states. Music for dancing began at 11:00
p.m., but ten minutes later the band played "Hail to the
Chief" as the president and his party arrived. Lincoln was
escorted into the hall by Hamlin, the mayor of Washington,

and Senator Anthony of Rhode Island. Mrs. Lincoln entered
on the arm of Senator Douglas, and Mrs. Hamlin was escorted
by Senator Baker of Oregon. Mrs. Lincoln wore a rich blue
gown set off with a necklace of gold and pearls, and Ellen
created a "marked sensation" in a dress of white silk trimmed
with blonde lace and rosebuds, a flowered headdress, and
jewelry of pearls and diamonds.

At the beginning of April, Ellen and Hannibal Hamlin
left for Maine. They reached Bangor on the 4th and went
at once to nearby Hampden. Hamlin left Bangor on April 22
for New York City, and on May 26 he returned to Washington.
As vice-president he had no duties of consequence, and
President Lincoln gave him no assignments. He once complained that he was "the most unimportant man in Washington,
ignored by the President, the Cabinet, and Congress." Ellen
was with her husband in Washington at the end of March,
1862, and the couple were members of a group of dignitaries
who traveled in a steamboat from Washington to Hampton Roads
to go aboard the U.S.S. Monitor, shortly after its much publicized battle with the C.S.S. Virginia (formerly the Merri-
mac). After dining with General Wool who came from Fortress
Monroe to join the distinguished visitors, the Hamlins and
others in the party returned to Washington.

Hamlin was replaced in 1864 as Lincoln's running mate
by Andrew Johnson, and the vice-president realized that in
a contest for a seat in the Senate he would lose to William P.
Fessenden. Hannibal wrote to Ellen that his chief concern
for their future was his reduction in income. "But be of
good cheer ...," he wrote, "if Heaven will continue my
health I can work, and if necessity required more frugality
we will have still a quiet, cozy and happy home." Hamlin
left Washington with the feeling that he had been betrayed
by political associates whom he had helped to advance, but
he was relieved to return to his comfortable home in Bangor
where he could be happy with Ellen and their two youngest
children.

In the spring of 1865 Hamlin had purchased a small
farm on which he was working diligently when he received
in August an appointment as Collector of the Port of Boston,
a post with an income twice that of his salary as a senator.
He resigned a year later to show his disapproval of President Johnson's restrained treatment of the treasonous South.

In 1869 Hamlin won reelection to the Senate, and he enjoyed the confidence of the new party leaders, President
Grant and Speaker James G. Blaine. Before the end of his
second term, Hannibal had decided not to run for relection,
but he attended the 1880 Republican National Convention to
help Blaine obtain the nomination for president. Garfield
won the nomination and the election, and Blaine became his
secretary of state. As one of his first acts, he offered a
post as minister or ambassador to Hamlin, who responded
that he would be pleased to have such a place in Spain,
Italy or Austria. On June 30, President Garfield appointed
Hamlin minister to Spain, and his appointment was unanimously approved by the Senate.

Ellen and the new minister to Spain sailed from Philadelphia on November 5, 1881, and ten days later they arrived in Liverpool. After sightseeing in London and in
Paris, the Hamlins reached Madrid by the middle of December. On December 20, 1881, Hannibal was presented to the
King and Queen of Spain, and the cordiality of his reception
delighted the new envoy. Fortunately for Hamlin, who knew
little French or Spanish, the King spoke English "quite
well." Hamlin had little fondness for monuments of older
culture, and his travels in western Europe increased his
devotion to his own government and "its plain republican
character."

After the Hamlins returned to Bangor, the politician,
then seventy-four, wrote that he was "out of official life"
and nothing could induce him to leave his family and friends.
His nine years in retirement were spent in farming, fishing,
reading, and merely sitting in front of the fire in his favorite rocking chair. He enjoyed playing cards with old cronies
at a club he had helped to organize, and there he experienced (on July 4, 1891, in his eighty-first year) a heart
attack from which he did not recover.

We know little of Ellen's reaction to her trip to Europe
with Hannibal, of her life with him in retirement, or of her
years of widowhood. She was not the letter writer of the
family, and we do not have her reaction to the years she
maintained the Hamlin home in Maine while her husband
lived in Washington or Boston and traveled to political gatherings around the country. Once, late in his career, the
senator wrote to Ellen, "some times I think I will resign my

seat and go home. I know that there are not many years
for me to be with my loved ones," but this sentiment reflected an uncommon mood because he repeatedly sought
public office. The two biographies of Hannibal Hamlin do
not tell us how long Ellen survived her husband nor the
circumstances of her death. This information and details
about Ellen's life in Hampden and Bangor--with and without
her husband--could probably be found through a careful
perusal of Bangor newspapers published in the late nineteenth and early twentieth centuries.

PRINCIPAL SOURCES

Charles Eugene Hamlin. The Life and Times of Hannibal
    Hamlin. Cambridge: The Riverside Press, 1899. 627 p.

Harry Draper Hunt. Hannibal Hamlin of Maine, Lincoln's
    First Vice-President. [Syracuse]: Syracuse Univ.
    Press, [1969]. 292 p.

ANDREW JOHNSON, 1865

Andrew Johnson (1808-1875) was the son of
a porter in Raleigh, North Carolina, who died
in 1811 leaving his widow and two young sons
without means of support. His mother remar-
ried and the pair bound out Andrew to a local
tailor in February 1832, but the boy ran away
and opened tailor shops in South Carolina and
in Tennessee where he finally settled in 1826
in Greenville. Somehow Andrew learned to
read simple words; and his wife, whom he married in 1827, taught him to write. He was recognized by workingmen in Greenville as a
powerful speaker, and they elected him alder-
man and then mayor of the town. In 1835,
1836, 1839 and 1841 Johnson served in the
Tennessee Legislature. In 1843 he was elected
to the United States House of Representatives,
where he served for ten years and vigorously
supported the "Homestead Bill." After two
terms as governor of Tennessee (1853-1857),
Johnson returned to Congress but this time
(1857-1862) as a senator.

Although Johnson favored most liberal legislation, he defended slavery as a Constitutional
right; yet, when other Southern senators withdrew at the outbreak of the Civil War, Johnson
proclaimed his loyalty to the Union. In 1862,
President Lincoln appointed Johnson military
governor of Tennessee, an office in which he
showed the wisdom of Lincoln's tolerant reconstruction policy. As a result of President
Lincoln's desire to seek reelection as the head
of a national party, the National Union Convention in June 1864 chose the loyal Tennessean

to be Lincoln's running mate. After the death
of President Lincoln, President Johnson tried
to continue his predecessor's plans for reconstruction. Radical Republicans disliked Johnson's leniency toward the former Confederate
states and harsh disagreements between the
president and Congress led to an attempt to
impeach him. Johnson returned in March of
1869 to Tennessee where he tried for seven
years to regain a seat in the Senate. He did
so in 1874 and attacked anew his former enemies. Senator Johnson died on July 31, 1875,
at Carter's Station in Tennessee.

*   *   *

On the day Abraham Lincoln died and Andrew Johnson became president of the United States, April 15, 1865, the
latter's family in Nashville anxiously waited for news. At
noon his eldest child, Martha Patterson, wrote:

My dear, dear Father:
    The sad, sad news has just reached us, announc-
ing the death of President Lincoln. Are you safe
and do you feel SECURE?.... Poor Mother, she is
almost deranged fearing you will be assassinated....
Our city is wild with excitement. It presented a
gala appearance this morning but our joy suddenly
turned to grief.... How I long to be with you this
sad day that we might weep together.

Six weeks before, on March 4, Johnson had brought
disgrace on himself by delivering his inaugural address while
under the influence of liquor, and now he was the president.
He had earned his nomination to the vice-presidency through
years of hard work as a member of Congress for five successive terms, as governor of Tennessee for two terms, and
as a United States senator before President Lincoln appointed
Johnson military governor of Tennessee, a very difficult role
in which he had performed admirably. Johnson, a Democrat,
was selected to run with President Lincoln on the National
Union ticket, but little thought was given to Johnson's place
within the organization of the Republican party if he did
succeed to the presidency. At the time of his nomination
and election to the vice-presidency, Andrew Johnson was little

known outside of Tennessee and Washington. He had not
delivered a major speech in a large eastern city, and he
had never visited New England. The new president was a
Southerner but not of the mold of Southern leaders familiar
in the North or the South.

Andrew Johnson's early years were replete with grind-
ing poverty. He was born on December 29, 1808, in a cabin
a few yards from Casso's tavern in Raleigh, North Carolina,
where his father, Jacob Johnson, worked as a porter until
he became the porter in a local bank. Neither Jacob nor his
wife, known as "Polly," could read or write, and she helped
her family by taking in laundry. Andrew's father was
drowned in an effort to save the life of a man who couldn't
swim and left his widow, their first son, Bill, nearly nine,
and Andrew, barely three. "Aunt Polly," as she was called
in Raleigh, could not support herself and her two boys, and
in 1814 she married Turner Doughtry, a "poor white," who
proved to be a worthless husband. "Polly" and her second
husband bound the two boys to a local tailor, James J. Sel-
by, where Andrew showed his mettle by wanting to learn to
read. Somehow, without a teacher, the youth of fourteen
or fifteen learned the meanings of simple words without regard to their spelling or use in sentences.

Bill and Andrew Johnson were threatened with prose-
cution for their part in a boyish prank, and the pair fled
from their employer in Raleigh and kept moving until they
found better opportunities in Tennessee. Andrew was succeeding in a modest way in Columbia when he learned that
his mother and stepfather were failing completely in Raleigh;
he returned at once and helped his parents transport their
few possessions in a two-wheeled cart to the region in Tennessee where brother Bill was said to be living. Their journey ended in Greenville where Andrew opened a tailor shop
in March 1827. Two months later, at the age of eighteen,
Andrew Johnson married Eliza McArdle, a girl of seventeen,
whose father, a shoemaker, had died, and whose mother
eked out a living making quilts and coarse sandals.

According to Robert Steele, Andrew Johnson's latest
biographer (1968), "Eliza was an attractive girl, well formed
and graceful. Her features expressed her character, a combination of strength, tact, gentleness and patience." In
temperament she and her husband complemented each other:

she was "patient, gentle, forbearing"; he was "passionate, ambitious, and belligerent." Photographs of Eliza Johnson taken in the 1840s when her husband first went to Congress and in the late 1860s when he was the president show a strong face with large eyes, a square jaw, and a broad brow.

Although, at the time of her marriage, Eliza McArdle had no family connections or financial resources of consequence, she did have an elementary education sufficient for her to teach her young husband to write and to do simple arithmetic. Johnson was the only president "who never attended school a day in his life." We would like to know about how the industrious tailor's wife taught him the rudiments of the education which she had acquired, but details are lacking. She had very little to share, but she gave what she had. Johnson "was never able to supply the lack of a good elementary education. His pen was not his friend; his spelling and grammar were always faulty."

With the limited instruction received from his young wife and her continued encouragement, Andrew Johnson undertook a lifelong program of self-improvement. The hours many men spend in social gatherings, hunting, and fishing Johnson devoted to studying or to useful conversations with close associates. While a member of Congress Johnson borrowed books on many subjects from the Library of Congress, and, as president, he was "an omnivorous reader." Johnson had never seen a play when he became president; he had once enjoyed a circus and a minstrel show but he preferred reading and study to such pleasant diversions. Johnson's concentration on solitary pursuits left him with very few friends; today he would undoubtedly be known as "a loner."

As a married couple, Eliza and Andrew Johnson prospered. She bore him five children, and she managed the family's business affairs while he was away. About five years after their marriage, Johnson moved his wife and their two young children into a small brick house for which he had paid a little less than a thousand dollars. Johnson thereupon purchased a whitewashed clapboard building, containing a single room, which he moved to his own lot and used as a shop. Over the entrance he hung a simple sign, "A. Johnson, Tailor," which stayed there as long as he lived. While

Johnson was in Congress, he bought another brick house
in a better part of town which was to be his family's permanent dwelling. While governor, Johnson purchased other
real property in and around Greenville including a farm on
which he established his mother and his stepfather. His
tailoring business prospered, and he and his wife worked
and saved. At the time Johnson became governor of Tennessee, he was worth about fifty thousand dollars; thrift
and prudence in investments increased this amount threefold
by the time he left the White House. After her husband became prominent nationally, Eliza would explain that she had
"remained at home, caring for the children and practicing
the economy."

    After the birth of their fifth child, Andrew, Jr.,
Eliza Johnson became a semi-invalid. She suffered from
phthisis ("slow consumption") for which her physician pre-
scribed rest and freedom from strain. Nevertheless, when
her husband's need was great, she managed to be at his
side. In December of 1860 Johnson made a great speech in
the Senate in which he declared that regardless of the
course other Southerners might take, he would stand by the
Constitution. His wife knew the criticism that her husband
would receive from Southern legislators, and she made the
trip to Washington in spite of severe weather and her weakened condition. In April of 1862, General E. Kirby Smith,
the commanding Confederate general in East Tennessee, ordered the families of Union leaders to leave; but Eliza, who
was too ill to travel, responded that she could not comply
with the general's order. When she did leave, she went
with her eight-year-old son to Nashville where she joined
her husband who had labored heroically to save the belea-
guered city. Her arrival seems to have induced her husband to follow a restrained policy in dealing with Southern
women.

    President Johnson moved into the White House on May
23, directly after Mrs. Lincoln left. The mansion was in
wretched condition; for weeks the doors had been unguarded
and strangers had carried away pictures and silver, even
pieces of furniture. The disorder was overpowering, and
Andrew Johnson called on his family for help. His resourceful daughter, Martha, and her children arrived on June 19,
and on August 6 two carriages "drove up to the White House
door and disgorged the whole Johnson family." After a

joyful reunion, Eliza and the other newcomers went upstairs
to select rooms. Eliza made the first choice, one of the
smallest in the northwest corner of the house, and here she
remained. Only twice in the next four years did she appear
downstairs for a public event, once at a reception in honor
of the buxom Queen Emma of the Sandwich Islands, and
again at the first ball for children held in the White House.

Each morning President Johnson paid a regular call on
his wife, and discussed with her prospects for the day. She
became his most trusted counselor and in his quarrel with
the Radicals in Congress, Eliza encouraged her husband to
follow the dictates of his conscience regardless of the outcome. When the president's bodyguard ran from the Capitol
to the White House with the news that Johnson had been acquitted, he dashed into her room with the cry, "He's acquitted. The President is acquitted!" She responded without hesitation, "I knew he would be acquitted; I knew it.
Thank you for coming to tell me."

Eliza's inability to function as hostess of the White
House was relieved in part by his two married daughters,
Martha Patterson and Mary Stover, especially the former
"whose dark gravity reflected that of her father." Martha
Johnson had studied for three terms in a school conducted
by Catholic nuns in Georgetown, and while a student there
she was a frequent guest in the White House of the wife
of President Polk who was a spotless housekeeper. So
Martha did not undertake her large responsibilities wholly
without preparation. She handled her mother's sizeable
mail, listened to complaints, and attended to every detail
involved in state banquets. Martha and her sister stood at
their father's right in a very large reception held in the
Blue Room on New Year's Day, 1866, and his daughters accompanied President Johnson to a reception at the home of
Chief Justice Chase during the height of a quarrel between
Congressional leaders and the Chief Executive. The other
guests were startled when the president and his daughters
were announced, but the unflappable trio "circulated among
the guests, at ease and smiling."

The three sons of the Johnsons brought many trials
for their parents. Charles, the eldest and his mother's
favorite, frequently drank to excess and was killed in a fall
from an unmanageable horse. Robert, as a boy, had bleeding

from his lungs which alarmed his parents. He, too, became
addicted to alcohol, and, like Charles, joined the resistance
movement in Tennessee. Robert studied law, won a seat in
the Tennessee Assembly, and became an officer in the Union
Army. He resigned his commission, continued his heavy
drinking, and died suddenly at age thirty-three. Andrew,
Jr., the pet of the family because he was about twenty
years younger than his brothers and sisters, developed
tuberculosis in the early 1860s and suffered severe attacks
until his death in 1879 at the age of twenty-seven.

        Andrew Johnson was a remarkably successful politician
in Tennessee. Although detested by members of the Whig
aristocracy, Johnson, as a Jeffersonian and Jackson Democrat, won almost every office within the state. He was a
hard campaigner and triumphed over opponents because he
won the votes of the working class. Frontier politics in
Tennessee in the 1830s and 1840s required physical endurance and courage to face an angry crowd, and Johnson
possessed both in generous measure. His crude speech did
not repel his listeners; instead, they responded with enthusiasm to his evangelical and rhetorical appeals. Johnson's
repeated victories at the polls bolstered his self-confidence,
because he knew that the people supported him and Johnson
believed that governments should do the bidding of working
people.

        Other than his successful sponsorship of the Home-
stead Bill, Johnson is not identified with any major legislation. He was a states' rights Democrat who decided that he
and other working people should support the Constitution
and the Union. To be sure, he was an exceptional war governor of Tennessee, but he succeeded in this role because
he was resourceful and indefatigable in encounters which
would have frightened a timorous man. And Johnson was
never timorous. Recent historians criticize Johnson's Reconstruction policies because he did not win the support of
Congressional leaders who favored their own plan, but Johnson simply tried to do his duty as he saw it. His blunders
on the day of his inauguration as vice-president and in his
attempt to rally the country behind him as he had repeatedly
done in Tennessee weakened his case but not his resolution.

        The animosity Johnson engendered was returned ten-
fold. When Congress finally voted an appropriation of

$35,000 to complete repairs and refurnish the White House, the legislation stipulated that expenditures for the purpose should be submitted to a congressional committee for approval. The weary and embittered President confided to an aide:

> I have had a son killed, a son-in-law die during the last battle at Nashville, another son has thrown himself away, another son-in-law is in no better condition, and I think I have had sorrow enough without having my bank account examined by a committee of Congress.

Johnson and his loyal friends were vindicated on January 26, 1875, when he was elected again to serve in the United States Senate. He attended a special session where he graciously greeted old friends and opponents, including thirteen of the thirty-five who had found him guilty of "high crimes and misdemeanors." After the brief session, Johnson returned to Greenville and went from there to the Stover farm in Carter County to escape from the heat. Eliza was with him when he died on July 31, 1875; she survived her husband for less than six months.

PRINCIPAL SOURCES

Eric L. McKitrick, editor. Andrew Johnson, a Profile. New York: Hill and Wang, [1969]. 224 p.

Robert V. P. Steele. The First President Johnson. The Three Lives of the Seventeenth President of the United States of America. New York: William Morrow, 1968. 676 p. ["By Lately Thomas," a pseudonym.]

SCHUYLER COLFAX, 1869-1873

Schuyler Colfax (1823-1885) was born in New York and, as a boy, moved with his family to New Carlisle, Indiana. When his father was elected county auditor the family relocated in nearby South Bend where Schuyler, at age eighteen, became his father's deputy. Colfax wrote at age sixteen for local papers, and at nineteen was a reporter for a newspaper in Indianapolis. On his return to South Bend, Schuyler became editor of the Whig Free Press which he owned in part for two decades and renamed the St. Joseph Valley Register.

After taking an active part in organizing the Republican party in Indiana, Colfax was elected to the United States House of Representatives from 1855 until 1869, and was its speaker from 1863-1869. As a congressman Colfax advocated improvements in postal service and the construction of a transcontinental railroad. His travels in the West made him widely known, and "Smiler" never lost a friend nor made an enemy. In the middle of President Grant's first term, Vice-President Colfax announced that he would not stand for reelection and thereby lost his subsequent bid for renomination in 1872.

Colfax, his second wife, and their son settled into a large, comfortable house in South Bend. The former vice-president's name was linked to the Crédit Mobilier scandal, but he publicly denied his involvement. In his later years Colfax delivered at least a thousand popular speeches on lecture circuits which brought him a larger income than he had

received previously. Colfax died in January of
1885 in Mankato, Minnesota on his way to a speaking engagement in Iowa.

*   *   *

In December of 1863 when Schuyler Colfax was first elected
speaker of the House of Representatives, President Lincoln
was said "to want confidence in Colfax whom he considered
a little intriguer--plausible, aspiring beyond his capacity
and not trustworthy." Five years later, when Colfax ran
with Grant on the Republican ticket for vice-president and
president, respectively, a Democratic paper in Cincinnati
observed: "he [Colfax] has done a larger amount of political business, on a small capital, than any person in the
country.... He was gotten up on the smallest scale, and
yet he has been fourteen years in Congress, is now Speaker
of the House, and candidate for Vice President of the United
States."

A few days after Colfax's nomination, Carl Schurz, a
leading Republican of the era, wrote to his wife, "Colfax is
a very popular man and on that account a strong candidate."
Colfax was reputed to have never lost a friend nor made an
enemy, and he deserved his nickname, "Smiler." His formal
schooling ended at age ten, and he spent his early teens
clerking in his stepfather's store in New Carlisle, Indiana,
and in working on farms in the vicinity. His family moved
in 1841 to South Bend where his father, who had been elected
auditor on the Whig ticket, appointed his eighteen year old
son to be his deputy. Schuyler's parents wanted him to
study law, which he did without serious application because
he was more interested in politics which he debated with
friends and read about in newspapers. At age sixteen
Colfax was writing for local papers, and at eighteen he arranged with Horace Greeley to prepare sketches on the Indiana scene for the New York Tribune. At age nineteen
Colfax became a Senate reporter for a newspaper in Indianapolis, and on his return to South Bend he became principal
editor of a Whig paper, the Free Press. At age twenty-two
he was a journalist with four years' experience and part
owner of the Free Press which he renamed the St. Joseph
Valley Register, the paper with which he was to be associated until more than two decades later, when he no longer
was able to give sufficient time to it.

Throughout his life in South Bend and in Washington,
Colfax was closely linked to his family, and into this group
the young man, then age twenty-one, brought his bride,
Ellen Clark of Argyle, New York. The young couple began
their married life in a house that Colfax and his father
owned jointly and moved later into a house that Colfax had
built. Mrs. Colfax found excitement in meeting Senator
Douglas and his wife at a large party in Washington, but
she distrusted the "Little Giant's" publicized opposition to
President Buchanan's acceptance of a pro-slavery plank in
the proposed Kansas Constitution. In a letter to a friend,
Ellen Colfax characterized Washington as a "wicked city,"
and she haughtily disapproved of the appearance, at the
home of the Casses, of a lady "nearly 70, with her gray hair
curled, low necked dress & short sleeves.... I was disgusted with her & most of the ladies." One activity that
Ellen probably found congenial and for which she was prepared by her background was her attendance at prayer
meetings. Many were held, but members of Congress had
no time to attend; consequently, she complained, "Their
wives have to do it all."

Ellen Colfax was an invalid during most of her years
in Washington, and in the summer of 1863 she was too ill to
return to South Bend. Colfax went with her to Newport,
but a month's stay brought no improvement and she died
there on July 10. Loss of his wife created a gap in Colfax's
life which was partly filled by several members of his family
who moved to Washington to live with him. His mother
served as hostess at receptions given by the speaker, and
in this she found enjoyment and a measure of success. As
she wrote to a friend, "Mrs. Lincoln says she is jealous of
them, for they rival hers." Refreshments consisted of coffee, cake, and ice cream but "not a drop of wine or liquor."
In 1842 Colfax had taken the pledge of a teetotaler, and his
resolve kept him from serving alcoholic beverages to guests.
Even, as one story goes, to two of his dinner guests who
found an excuse to go to Senator Morgan's home nearby
where they quickly quenched their compelling thirsts.

During his five years of widowhood, Colfax's name was
often linked to eligible women by Washington gossips, but
speculation ended when he became engaged to Nellie Wade,
niece of a senator from Ohio, who, like Colfax, was prominent among the Radical Republicans who sought to control

Southern reconstruction. The couple were married at the
residence of the bride's mother in Andover, Ohio, in November, 1868, the month Colfax became vice-president-elect,
and he could write, "Two elections in one month ought to
make a man happy and does...." At the time of his second
marriage, Colfax was forty-five and his wife was fifteen
years younger. She was "of medium size, good figure,
dark hair, brown eyes ... [and] a pleasing face, indicating
goodness and intelligence." Those who knew her considered
Nellie Colfax to be admirably qualified to serve as hostess
in the home of the vice-president, and her personality made
her a favorite at social events in Washington.

Colfax, as a member of Congress active in the improvement of postal service and in the construction of a
transcontinental railroad, made several trips to the Far West,
one in 1865 by stagecoach to the Pacific Coast and a second
in 1868 by rail to Wyoming and by stagecoach to Denver.
It was on the latter trip that Colfax became engaged to Nellie Wade. As a married couple the Colfaxes made a trip with
a few relatives and friends on the nearly completed Union
Pacific Railroad to the West Coast, and in 1883 Colfax and
his second wife traveled again to the Pacific, this time as
guests of the Northern Pacific Railroad. Colfax had been
entertained royally on all of his Western trips, but the last
was "the grandest and most delightful of my life, and the
hospitality princely."

Several times in his career as a congressman Colfax
said that he would not stand for reelection, but he repeatedly changed his mind and ran anyway. However, midway in
his term as vice-president (1870), Colfax, in a published
formal letter, announced that in 1872 he would "close my
public life absolutely." Although Colfax may have regretted
his decision, the public announcement opened the door to
other willing Republicans, and his place on the 1872 ticket
was filled by Henry Wilson of Massachusetts.

The reasons for Colfax's decision to leave public life
at age fifty are open to speculation. He may have wanted
to be out from under President Grant and available to replace
him as the head of the Republican ticket in 1872, or he may
have felt the need to spend more time with his family, which
was increased in April, 1870 by the birth of a son, Schuyler
Colfax, III. Colfax's biographer William H. Smith concluded

(1952) that the vice-president wanted to make more money; his salary simply wasn't adequate to meet his expenses. In 1871 Jay Cooke offered the vice-president $25,000 a year to represent the Northern Pacific Railroad in Washington, but the work would have obliged Colfax to resign from his office and this step he was unwilling to take. The death of Horace Greeley, friend of Colfax and long-time editor of the New York Tribune, caused a vacancy which the vice-president was invited to fill, but at the very time he was in New York to discuss details of the offer, he received word from his wife expressing her hope that he would not accept the position. His friends in South Bend did not want the Colfaxes to move to New York, and his wife understandably preferred to remain where they owned a comfortable home and would have as neighbors friendly Hoosiers who had known her husband since his family had moved there three decades earlier.

Colfax's extended family lived in a large two-story frame house in South Bend which was comfortably furnished and stocked with a private library of 1,600 volumes. Colfax's mother died of cancer in August of 1872, and his stepfather died less than two years afterwards. After the death of Colfax's parents, Schuyler Colfax, III, became the center of the diminished family circle.

In September of 1872 the Crédit Mobilier scandal broke in the New York Sun. According to the newspaper story, Vice-President Colfax and a number of other prominent officials had accepted gifts of stock from the company which had undertaken to build the Union Pacific railroad. In a speech in South Bend at the end of September, Colfax denied any involvement in the affair, but testimony delivered at the Congressional hearings on the Crédit Mobilier scandal made plain that Colfax had not told the whole truth in his earlier public statement. The amounts of money that Colfax may have received as "dividends" were not large, but Colfax's explanation about the source of $1,200 alleged to have been paid him by Oakes Ames on behalf of the Crédit Mobilier strained credulity and the vice-president's part in the affair was never clarified. The damage done to his reputation disturbed Colfax, and he tried to put himself into a better light in conversations and in correspondence. While in Boston on December 5, 1875, Colfax wrote a long letter about his involvement with the Crédit Mobilier in which he aimed to present in definitive form the facts for his family,

especially for his young son. Although this letter was addressed to his wife, Colfax did not send it but carried the
document in a pocket until his death a decade later.

Colfax's last years were spent on the lecture circuit
where he made more money than he ever had in Washington.
He traveled widely and delivered lectures on "Abraham Lincoln," "Across the Continent," based on his travels in the
West, and "Landmarks of Life," a discourse on character
and the importance of a cheerful disposition. He probably
delivered at least a thousand lectures for each of which he
was paid at least seventy-five dollars "and entertainment."
His wife wondered when Colfax would decide to remain at
home, but he continued to receive invitations to lecture and
he continued to accept them. He met his death on January
13, 1885, in Mankato, Minnesota, on his way to fill a lecture
engagement in northwestern Iowa. Colfax suffered a heart
attack as he carried his suitcase three quarters of a mile
between stations in Mankato with the temperature at 30°
below zero.

PRINCIPAL SOURCE

William H. Smith, <u>Schuyler Colfax, the Changing Fortunes
of a Political Idol</u>. Indianapolis: Indiana Historical Bureau, 1952. 475 p. (Indiana Historical Collections, Vol.
XXXIII)

Henry Wilson (1812-1875) was the name legally adopted by Jeremiah Jones Colbaith when he came of age. His poverty-stricken parents in Farmington, New Hampshire, had indentured Jeremiah as a boy to a local farmer; and when he turned twenty-one he changed his name and walked to Natick, Massachusetts, to learn the trade of shoemaking. He founded a small factory that made coarse shoes for working men and the income earned thereby enabled Wilson to pursue his true vocation, politics. He served as a Whig in the Massachusetts legislature during the next ten years (1841-1852). Wilson left the Whigs because they did not support the Wilmot Proviso in their 1848 Convention and helped to launch the Free Soil Party. A consistent opponent of slavery, Wilson later joined the American and Republican parties yet managed to hold his supporters in Massachusetts.

Wilson was elected in 1855 to the United States Senate where he continued to serve until 1873. At the outbreak of the Civil War, Wilson was chairman of the Senate Military Affairs Committee and contributed mightily to the war effort through framing and explaining legislation needed for forming and provisioning a large army. He repeatedly urged President Lincoln to proclaim emancipation as a war measure, and he drafted bills which brought early freedom to slaves in the border states. During Reconstruction Wilson favored legislation which would improve education and economic conditions in the impoverished South. After 1870 Senator Wilson's influence waned, but his name on the Republican ticket helped President Grant win reelection in 1872. Vice-President Wilson failed to complete his lengthy History of the Rise and Fall of the Slave Power in America before his death on November 22, 1875.

*   *   *

Harriet Malvina Howe of Natick, Massachusetts, a town of a
thousand people seventeen miles southeast of Boston, was
but sixteen when she married Henry Wilson on October 28,
1840. Her family could offer Wilson "nothing in the way of
social prestige, influence, or wealth." Within two years the
couple occupied a new home on Central Street, and four
years later their first and only child, a boy named Henry
Hamilton, was born. Harriet had been very ill during her
pregnancy, but her health improved several weeks after the
birth of her son. Although in poor health at the outbreak
of the Civil War, Harriet chose to remain in Washington amid
rumors of invasion and insurrection, because she believed
that she would be happier with her husband than she would
be at home in Natick without him.

The couple had planned to travel to Europe in the
summer of 1867, but Harriet became too sick to make the
trip. In 1868 her health improved, and in December she
accompanied Henry to Washington. When her husband, then
chairman of the important Senate Committee on Military Affairs, was under consideration in early 1869 for the post of
secretary of war in Grant's new Cabinet, Harriet asked him
to withdraw his name because her health had worsened. In
May of 1870 she was forced to return home, and on the 12th
of the month Henry Wilson took leave from the Senate and
followed her. Harriet died of cancer on May 28, at age
forty-six, after thirty years of marriage. Friends who expressed sympathy to her husband emphasized Harriet's "patience, humility, tenderness, delicacy, gentleness, and gen-
erosity."

The wife of Henry Wilson needed a full measure of
patience, for her husband was a self-made man who found
his vocation in politics. He was born on February 16, 1812,
the first son of Winthrop and Abigail Colbath, in a cottage
in southern New Hampshire. His parents were so poor that
the boy, christened Jeremiah Jones, was bound out at age
ten to a local farmer to work and to learn to farm until he
came of age. When he reached the age of twenty-one
Jeremiah Colbath took a new name, Henry Wilson, and
walked from Farmington, New Hampshire, to Natick, Massachusetts, to learn the trade of shoemaking. Through heroic
efforts his business of shoemaking prospered; he strove to

overcome his limited schooling through reading, discussion, and debating; and he determined to achieve recognition through a career in politics. Politics became a consuming occupation for Henry Wilson: he was prevented by inclement weather from giving a speech in Gloucester on his wedding night, and Senator Wilson had to interrupt a campaign tour to be with his wife for the celebration of their twenty-fifth wedding anniversary.

Wilson pursued his political career under the aegis of several parties--Whig, free Soil, Know-Nothing, and Republican, but throughout his political maneuverings and manipulations he was constant in his opposition to slavery, especially to the "Slave Power" of the South, and in his support of various reform movements. Wilson was not an abolitionist or a doctrinaire reformer; instead he was a realistic politician with a sixth sense of what the people of Massachusetts would support. His service in the United States Senate began in 1855 and continued until he became vice-president in 1873. As a senator Wilson chaired the Military Affairs Committee which produced important legislation during the Civil War, and he joined with the Radical Republicans during the early years of Reconstruction. For years he was a close associate of Massachusett's senior senator, Charles Sumner. Indeed, after the infamous caning of Senator Sumner by Congressman Peter Brooks of South Carolina, Wilson declined a challenge from Brooks to a duel and then wired his wife: "Have declined to fight a duel, shall do my duty and leave the result with God. If assailed, shall defend my life, if possible at any cost." The admonition at the end, "Be calm," must have been difficult for Harriet to follow in view of the message in Henry's telegram.

After 1870 Wilson's influence in the Republican party waned, and his election in 1872 to the vice-presidency was in gratitude for service given rather than in expectation of new contributions. As his political role dwindled, he found himself without a family for emotional support. His father and mother died in 1859 and 1866, respectively, and his only son, whose career as an army officer was without distinction, died suddenly at the end of 1867 while stationed at Austin, Texas.

For years Henry Wilson was away from home week after week, and his wife and son had to manage without him.

While Harriet and Henry were in Washington, the boy was sent to a boarding school; when Harriet returned home at the end of a session of Congress her husband frequently went campaigning. After the death of their son, the Senator began to spend more time at home between sessions of Congress. His nomination to the vice-presidency on the Republican ticket marked the high point of his career, but he reached it alone. Although elated with the tribute from his party and his subsequent election, he sorely missed his lost wife and son. Wilson's restless ambition caused him, in his new role, to aspire to the presidency and to work to complete his History of the Rise and Fall of the Slave Power in America in three volumes, but paralytic attacks cut him down and the eighteenth vice-president, once a cobbler, died on November 22, 1875.

PRINCIPAL SOURCES

Richard H. Abbott, Cobbler in Congress. The Life of Henry Wilson, 1812-1875. [Lexington]: Univ. Press of Kentucky, [1972]. 289 p.

Ernest McKay, Henry Wilson: Practical Radical. A Portrait of a Politician. Port Washington, N.Y.: Kennikat Press, [1971]. 262 p.

WILLIAM A. WHEELER, 1877-1881

William Almon Wheeler (1819-1887) was born
near the Canadian border in Malone, New York,
where his father died in 1827 leaving little for
the support of his family. The boy did odd
jobs to help his mother and sisters, and he
managed to work his way through the local
Franklin Academy. At age nineteen Wheeler
enrolled in the University of Vermont where
he had barely enough to eat and experienced
a severe eye problem. Two years later Wheeler
returned to Malone where he began the study
of law under Colonel Asa Hascall, who had
combined law and politics in his career. In
1855 Wheeler was admitted to the bar, and in
1847 he was elected district attorney. Thereupon he set out to strengthen the Whigs in
Franklin county, and he formed an organization which in 1849 brought his election to
the New York Assembly. In this and in the
offices he held subsequently, Wheeler mastered
the rules and procedures of the body and won
wide recognition as an able parliamentarian.
Wheeler led his county organization in 1855
into the New York Republican party, and he
was elected in 1858 to the New York Senate.
In 1860 he was elected to the United States
House of Representatives, but he did not stand
for reelection. In 1867 Wheeler served as presiding officer of the New York State Constitutional Convention, and he returned in 1868 to
Congress where he remained until he became
vice-president under President Rutherford B.
Hayes. After Wheeler returned to Malone he
found that his old political organization had a

new leader, and the former vice-president
dropped from view. Wheeler was never robust,
and he suffered a series of strokes which
brought his death at age sixty-eight.

                    *   *   *

Toward the end of President Grant's second term there was
considerable speculation among Republicans about who should
be the party's candidate in 1876. There was some sentiment
in favor of a third term for the incumbent, and there was
limited support for party leaders such as James G. Blaine
of Maine, Benjamin Bristow of Kentucky, and Roscoe Conkling of New York. The record of Benjamin B. Hayes, then
governor of Ohio, and his stand as a liberal Republican attracted attention among political commentators, and the
Hayes name was linked often with that of William A. Wheeler
to make an attractive and winning ticket in November of
1876.

    In January of that election year Governor Hayes re-
ceived a letter from a friend, General Philip Sheridan, in
which the writer said that his ticket was Hayes and Wheeler.
When Hayes wrote his wife about Sheridan's provocative
comment, he continued, "I am ashamed to say, Who is
Wheeler?" After the Hayes-Wheeler ticket received the nomination of the Republican convention held in June, 1876, in
Cincinnati, the Nation commented in an editorial that Wheeler
had gained his place "partly because he came from New York,
partly because no one knew anything against him, and partly
by pure accident." Yet Wheeler's friend, Senator George
Frisbie Hoar, wrote in his Autobiography of Seventy Years
(1904): "He [Wheeler] was a very serious, simple-hearted
and wise man. There was no man in his time who had more
influence in the House [of Representatives]."

    William Almon Wheeler was born on June 30, 1819, in
Malone, New York, about ten miles from the Canadian border.
His father, a promising lawyer and local postmaster, died in
1827 leaving little for the support of his wife and children.
His widow took in boarders from the nearby Franklin academy, and William, who was but eight when his father died,
chopped wood, hauled water, and did other odd jobs to help
his family. Throughout his life he kept his attachment to
his mother and sisters, and he suffered illnesses and physical

weakness which may have resulted from excessive work as
a youngster.

William was ambitious as well as industrious. He
worked his way through the local Franklin academy, and by
the age of nineteen he had saved enough to permit him to
enter the University of Vermont at Burlington. After two
years at the institution, during which young Wheeler lived
for six weeks on bread and water, he left because his funds
were exhausted and an eye problem kept him from studying
at night.

After Wheeler had returned from Burlington to Malone,
he began the study of law under Colonel Asa Hascall, a
leading North Country lawyer and an active Whig politician.
Following the example of his mentor, who combined law and
politics in a career, William became town clerk in 1841, and
after two years in the office he became a school commissioner.
In order to meet his expenses, the prospective lawyer taught
school from time to time; and a young woman in one of his
classes, Mary King, became his wife on September 17, 1845.
In the same year Wheeler was admitted to the bar, and he
was soon reputed to be one of the "safest and soundest"
lawyers in northern New York.

In the month after his marriage, Wheeler was appointed
district attorney to replace Asa Hascall who had become seriously ill, and in 1847 Wheeler was elected to the post on a
fusion ticket. Thereupon Wheeler set about to strengthen
the Whigs in Franklin county, and he ran the organization
with an iron hand. Wheeler's success as a political leader
in his county and his popularity among the voters led in
1849 to his election to the New York Assembly.

In his first term in the legislature Wheeler mastered
the procedures of the Assembly, and in his second he was
appointed Whig floor leader and chairman of the powerful
Ways and Means Committee. Wheeler favored legislative approval for the construction of a railroad bridge across Lake
Champlain which would permit the Northern New York railroad to connect with the Vermont Central. The proposal for
the bridge was not popular throughout New York, but Wheeler announced that the Ways and Means Committee would not
conduct any other important legislation until the bridge had
been approved. As a result of his action, the Senate passed

the bill on April 4, 1851, and the assembly followed suit on
June 30. Wheeler's success would have insured his relection, but he preferred to pursue business interests in banking and in railroads.

Although out of the legislature, Wheeler followed closely the fusion of the Whig and Republican parties in New
York, which was accomplished on September 26, 1855, at
Syracuse. After Whig leaders Seward, Fish, and Morgan
became Republicans, Wheeler led his county organization into
the new party. Wheeler was elected to the New York Senate
for the session that began on January 5, 1858, and he received the honor of being elected President Pro Tempore of
the Senate although he was a newcomer in that body. His
knowledge of parliamentary law and his tact and diplomacy
made him a strong candidate for election to Congress, and
Wheeler won the seat for his district in November of 1860.

During his first term in Congress, Wheeler concentrated on learning the rules and procedures followed in the
House of Representatives, but he did not stand for reelection
since an agreement at the time he ran provided for rotating
the office among the several counties in the Seventeenth
Congressional District. State reapportionment changed the
boundaries of his district and Wheeler could have run for
reelection without violating the outmoded agreement, but it
was not his nature to be aggressive in situations which could
be avoided.

Wheeler's career is replete with instances in which he
resigned from a place or declined an opportunity which he
should have accepted. Because of poor health, he retired
in 1863 from the bank he had helped to found and he once
declined an invitation from President Hayes to attend a public function because of the "death" of a nonexistent brother-
in-law! Wheeler's poor eyesight, one of his reasons for
leaving the University of Vermont, obliged him to give up
his law practice, and he retired from business in 1865 because of overwork. Wheeler's life was plagued with insomnia,
and he became a hopeless hypochondriac. During his last
twenty years of life, he believed that he could die at any
time. According to a close friend, Wheeler believed that
"his health was precarious and would break utterly if he
were to engage strenuously in any undertaking."

Why would anyone so lacking in physical vitality continue in a pursuit as full of stress as politics? According to James T. Otten, who wrote a Ph.D. dissertation on Wheeler and the Republican party which was accepted in 1976 at the University of South Carolina, his wife motivated him to attain high political office. She "perceived that if engrossed in politics" which were not overly strenuous, "her husband forgot his physical maladies." She encouraged her husband to seek one office after another, and she was able to dispel some of the despondency which persistently afflicted him.

In 1867 Wheeler received another accolade which recognized his skill and detachment as a presiding officer; he was named president of the New York State Constitutional Convention. In 1868 he was returned to Congress and there he remained until he became vice-president. The New York Times placed him at the head of parliamentarians in this country, and he kept clear of the scandals which flourished during President Grant's two administrations. Wheeler is often mentioned today, if mentioned at all, for his role in effecting the "Wheeler Adjustment" or "Wheeler Compromise" in 1875 in Louisiana. Different factions and contested elections had wrecked reconstruction in the state, and Wheeler was able to devise a temporary solution which brought him prestige and publicity shortly before the Republican National Convention in 1876.

James A. Garfield was a leading member of the House of Representatives early in March of 1876 when he boarded a morning train bound for New York. Garfield's entry for March 3, 1876, in his diary contains the time of his departure and this sad note: "Poor Wheeler was on board with the dead body of his wife." Mary King Wheeler had caught a cold and had died on March 3; her husband was taking her body for burial to Malone where they had been married more than thirty years before.

Friends in Washington had observed the strong bond of affection between William and Mary Wheeler. George Frisbie Hoar recalled:

> Their long living together had brought about a curious resemblance. She looked like him, talked like him, thought like him, and if she had been dressed in his clothes, or he had been in hers, either might have passed for the other.

The sudden death of Wheeler's wife was followed by a prolonged period of mourning which caused him to withdraw
completely from social life in Washington. As a lonely
widower, Wheeler had no one to encourage him in his political activities.

     The president-elect and the vice-president-elect met
for the first time when Wheeler traveled from Malone, New
York, to Fremont, Ohio, in January of 1877. The two successful candidates discussed possible Cabinet appointments,
and Hayes encouraged Wheeler to learn what he could about
Senator Conkling's role in the upcoming congressional review
of the returns in the disputed election of 1876. Wheeler
counseled his chief that Cabinet heads should be outstanding "in the matters of personal character, recognized capacity and experience," and he recommended a few individuals
for Hayes' consideration. The new president invited Vice-
President Wheeler to attend meetings of his Cabinet; the
vice-president attended one such meeting and then decided
that he was not wanted there.

     Wheeler did not support President Hayes in his pro-
posals for civil service reform and political reconstruction in
the South, and in his deferential manner he walked away
from the administration. He ceased to attend public functions with the president; Wheeler declined even an invitation
to visit Hayes in Ohio. When the mid-year elections repudiated Hayes' Southern policy, the president shifted his
ground; thereupon, Vice-President Wheeler began to take
an active part in the national administration.

     Although the president and vice-president did not
agree on every political point, the two had cordial personal
relations. Hayes appreciated Wheeler's sterling qualities,
and Wheeler reciprocated with sincere friendliness. Wheeler
liked the moral tone of the small groups that met in the
White House, and he delighted in the singing of hymns
which could be heard there on Sunday evenings. Wheeler
became especially fond of the president's wife who reminded
the vice-president of his own late wife. Wheeler abstained
from hard liquor, and his religious principles fit nicely into
those of "Lemonade Lucy" and her husband, the president.
Wheeler succeeded in inducing Lucy Hayes, accompanied by
daughter Fanny, to spend a month on a fishing trip with
him in the Adirondacks. Wheeler showed a great fondness

for another member of the Hayes family, the president's
niece Emily Platt, but their warm relationship ended when
the young woman married General Russell Hastings and the
couple moved to Bermuda.

The Hayes administration won few admirers, and the
Republican National Convention that met in June of 1880
chose a new team, James A. Garfield and Chester A. Arthur.
In late 1880 Wheeler was urged by friends to run for the
United States Senate seat of Francis Kernan, and his half-
hearted bid met with defeat. When he returned to Malone
he found that the county party that he had organized had
been taken over by another political leader. Wheeler then
dropped from public view and remained quietly at home except for a trip in the fall of 1881 to Fremont, Ohio, to visit
the Hayes family. The former president noted in his diary
for October 27, "Mr. Wheeler is in fair health. A noble,
honest, patriotic man."

Wheeler's sister, Sarah Fidelia Wheeler, had been an
invalid for twenty-five years, and William was absent from
Congress for two months in 1878 while he cared for his sister. Sarah was Wheeler's last surviving relative, and after
her death on May 28, 1879, William wrote to Lucy Hayes,
"I am all alone now, and patiently await the summons which
shall complete my family circle above." After his vice-
presidential term, Wheeler was often bedridden, and he
suffered a series of strokes. The strokes affected his
physical condition and mental capacities, and he experienced
a chill on March 3, 1887, from which he did not recover.
William Almon Wheeler died at his home in Malone on June 4,
1887, at the age of sixty-eight.

Former President Hayes traveled from Ohio to northern
New York to attend the funeral of his one-time running mate,
but President Cleveland, who was on a fishing vacation at
nearby Saranec Lake, declined his invitation to be present
for the services. Wheeler's body did not lie in state in Albany or in Washington, and no flags were lowered to half
mast to mark his passing. In his obituary in the New York
Times, the writer observed: "There is not an important
career in recent history about which the public has known
so little as Mr. Wheeler's."

Almost a century after his death, the ninteenth

vice-president of the United States lies buried in oblivion. There is no statue of its leading citizen in the town of Malone, New York, and no bronze tablets record his activities in Albany or in Washington. Wheeler's name is not associated with any major legislation, and he never wrote a book. Unfortunately, he and his wife of thirty years were childless, and no member of his family survived who might want to keep alive the memory of his impressive career.

Late in life, William Wheeler realized that he had missed several important opportunities because he had avoided strenuous conflicts, and he subsequently declared that if he had his life to live over it would be done with more aggressiveness. But it is hard to picture William Wheeler striving to vanquish an opponent, regardless of his number of chances.

PRINCIPAL SOURCES

Rutherford B. Hayes. Diary and Letters. Edited by Charles Richard Williams. Columbus: Ohio State Archaeological and Historical Society, 1922-1926. 5 volumes.

James T. Otten. Grand Old Partyman, William A. Wheeler and the Republican Party, 1850-1880. Ph.D. dissertation accepted at the University of South Carolina, 1976. 328 l.

CHESTER A. ARTHUR, 1881

Chester Alan Arthur (1830-1886) was born in Fairfield, Vermont, where his father was the pastor of a Baptist church. As his father moved from one small church to another, Arthur attended public schools in different towns; and, while the father occupied a pulpit in Schenectady, New York, the son attended Union College from which he was graduated in 1848. During the next five years Chester taught school and studied law until he was admitted to the bar in 1854 and began legal practice in New York. His law practice flourished, and his good looks and convivial personality opened doors in Republican party circles in New York. Governor Edwin D. Morgan appointed Arthur to his staff as engineer-in-chief with rank of brigadier general, an office Arthur filled with distinction until he was removed when a Democrat became governor on January 1, 1863.

Arthur's law practice declined in the late 1860s, and he turned to machine politics for an income that would enable him to continue his expensive lifestyle. With the support of Boss Roscoe Conkling, Arthur was named in 1881 by President Grant to head the New York Customhouse, a lucrative position. After the inauguration of President Hayes, Arthur's management of the Customhouse was investigated, and he was removed.

Arthur went with the New York delegation to the Republican National Convention in Chicago which selected James Garfield of Ohio to run for the presidency in 1880. Garfield's managers realized the desirability of having a New Yorker on the ticket; and when Arthur learned of the

opportunity, he seized it. As a result, Arthur
became vice-president; and six months later,
after the assassination of Garfield, Arthur became president. The new president's record
did not appear to qualify him for large responsibilities, yet Arthur's performance in the
White House surpassed public expectations.
Before the end of his term, Arthur was strick-
en with Bright's disease, but he refused to
let the ailment curtail his official activities.
After the conclusion of his term as president,
Arthur returned to New York City where he
died on November 17, 1885.

*   *   *

The night Arthur returned to his home in New York City
from the convention in Chicago that had nominated him to
be Garfield's running mate, his eight-year-old daughter
asked an aunt who was staying with her how she could
congratulate her father and was told she should bring him
some flowers. When she did so, the vice-presidential
nominee called his daughter to him to kiss her, but he
broke into tears and said "there is nothing worth having
now." His wife of twenty years had died in January of
that year (1880), and there was an emotional streak in the
man that lay just below the surface of outward appearances.
In this instance, Arthur's grief may have been tinged with
remorse, because night after night he had left his wife alone
while he sat up until two or three in the morning eating,
drinking, and talking with political cronies. Although Nell
endured her neglect in silence, her husband's nightly absence must have strained their marriage; indeed, Arthur's
grandson was told years later by his father that his parents
were about to separate when her death occurred in January
of 1880 when she was but forty-two.

Chester Alan Arthur was born on October 5, 1829,
the fifth child of William and Malvina Stone Arthur. William
was an Ulsterman who had graduated from Belfast College
before he emigrated in 1818 or 1819 to Quebec in pursuit of
better opportunities in school teaching. One of his early
appointments was in Dunham, fifteen miles north of the Vermont border, where he met Malvina Stone, a Vermonter, with
whom he eloped in 1821. By 1828 the young couple had four

children and had moved four times in northern Vermont in
search of better opportunities to provide for their rapidly
growing family. While living in Waterville, William attended
a revival meeting in Burlington and was converted to the
tenets of the Free Will Baptist church. Although the
Arthurs had been Presbyterians in Ireland and William and
Malvina had been married in an Episcopal church, his religious experience in Burlington caused William to join the
Baptist clergy. He was licensed to preach in 1827 and for-
mally ordained in 1828. His first call came from Fairfield,
Vermont, a small farming community in northwest Vermont,
where their fifth child, Chester Alan, was born on October
5, 1829. William Arthur, known better as "Elder" Arthur,
served eleven parishes before his retirement in 1864.
Throughout his career as a minister, Elder Arthur was opin-
ionated and outspoken and his tendency toward combativeness
was increased by his espousal of abolitionism, not a popular
cause in the 1830s.

During the early 1840s Elder Arthur was a pastor in
churches in and near Schenectady, and in two of these communities Chester Arthur attended academies as a preparation
for collegiate studies at Union College. Arthur entered
Union College in September of 1843 as a sophomore, enrolled
in the traditional classical curriculum, and was graduated in
1848 in the top third of his class. Arthur, then eighteen,
taught school for four years in small town academies. During his free hours he studied law and he managed to earn
enough from his small salary ($35 per month) to pay for his
move to New York where he entered the law office of E. D.
Culver, a friend of the Arthur family since their residence
ten years earlier in Union Village. In May of 1854 Chester
Arthur was admitted to the bar and joined the firm of Culver,
Parker, and Arthur. As a member of this firm, the young
lawyer played a minor role in several cases dealing with the
rights of slaves brought to New York and of free Blacks,
and in 1856 Arthur, then twenty-seven, formed a law partnership with Henry D. Gardiner, his congenial roommate in
the Bancroft House.

Chester Arthur was a handsome young man, tall (six
feet two), powerfully built, with brown hair and beard, and
black eyes. Nevertheless, he had no serious involvement
with any young woman until Ellen Lewis Herndon came in
1856 with her mother to visit her cousin, Dabney Herndon,

a young medical student who also resided at the Bancroft House. Ellen ("Nell") was then a small, rather frail girl of nineteen with a warm manner and a beautiful contralto voice. Where Nell went to school is unknown, but she had acquired the essentials of a literary education and she had learned from her prominent Virginia family a great deal about gracious living. Within a year the couple had become engaged, and in 1858 Chester Arthur made a visit of two weeks to Fredericksburg to visit the Herndon and Hansbrough (her mother's maiden name) families. Although a Northerner without a distinguished background, Arthur, then aged twenty-eight, made himself attractive to Nell's slaveholder relatives and quickly won their approval. The couple were married on October 25, 1859, in the Calvary Episcopal Church in New York and soon moved into Nell's mother's home on West Twenty-first Street where they resided at the outbreak of the Civil War.

In the late 1850s Arthur became active in the new Republican party in New York, which was controlled by Thurlow Weed who maintained his power through manipulation of the spoils system. Weed rewarded Edwin D. Morgan, a wealthy New York merchant who had held several minor offices, with the Republican nomination for governor; and, after his election, Chester Arthur, who had joined the state militia, was named to the governor's general staff with the title of engineer-in-chief and the rank of brigadier general. His duties, largely ceremonial in peacetime, involved provisioning troops raised in New York City for the Union armies and housing and feeding troops from other states who stopped in New York on their way to the front. Arthur handled his large responsibilities with energy and decisiveness, and his superior performance brought promotions to inspector general and to quartermaster general.

Governor Morgan was succeeded on January 1, 1863, by a Democratic governor, and his staff, including Arthur, lost their offices. General Arthur could have enlisted in the Union Army, but he chose to wait for the reelection of the Republicans to restore his rank and responsibilities. Nell Arthur had friends and relatives in the Confederate army, and her sympathies lay with the South. She undoubtedly was pleased when her husband's military service ended on the day President Lincoln issued the Emancipation Proclamation.

During his years as a high ranking officer in the
militia, the Arthurs lived in a showy two-story family hotel
near Twenty-second and Broadway and there their first
child, a boy, was born. Nell was a gracious hostess, and
Chester indulged his fondness for good food and fine liquor.
After Arthur's salary as a general in the militia ended, he
had a real need for money to maintain his luxurious lifestyle. The firm of Arthur and Gardiner set out to make
money, and in this they were successful, for Arthur soon
purchased a fine brownstone building for his home and hired
Irish immigrants as servants. Nell was ambitious and, like
her mother, keenly aware of society and her social obligations. The Arthurs lived in extravagant fashion, they were
seen together at the opera, she sang at special charity
functions, and they entertained frequently, including recitals
in their home.

Despite the death of their firstborn at the age of two-
and-a-half, the Arthurs appear to have flourished as a family.
A second son, Chester Alan Arthur II, called simply "Alan,"
was born on July 25, 1864, and seven years later a daughter
was born and named after her mother, Ellen Herndon Arthur. In May of 1865 the Arthurs purchased a two-story
brownstone at 123 Lexington Avenue that Nell furnished with
impeccable taste. Nell's interests were mainly social and
centered in her home; she has been described as "a woman
Jane Austen would have understood." Arthur, when at
home, was a stern and kindly father, who required his son
to address him as "sir." Recognition of his social station
came through memberships in the exclusive Century Club
and in the Union League Club, but these marks of distinction and his well-ordered home life did not fill Arthur's
need for male companionship and enjoyment of the hours
after midnight.

Chester A. Arthur was a convivial man who enjoyed
"talking politics, smoking cigars, and eating and drinking
with 'the boys'" night after night until two or three in the
morning. Although he took his family on long and expensive vacations, he often went with friends on fishing trips
to Canada or along the coast of Maine. After his return
from an excursion to Canada for salmon fishing, one of the
members of the party, Roscoe Conkling, a United States
senator and a power in New York politics, wrote to Levi P.
Morton, another friend and political associate, "Every day

& everything was enjoyable. Gen'l Arthur's constant effort
was to make everybody else happy. No wonder we all like
him." Arthur's immoderate eating and drinking caused him
to gain weight, which he tried to conceal partly with the efforts of expensive tailors. One relative commented in 1871,
"He [Arthur] looks fat & hearty," and a decade later one
observer commented that Arthur had the appearance of a
"well-fed Briton."

   Arthur's law practice declined in the late 1860s, and
he looked to machine politics to provide him with the income
to support his expensive life style. In 1869 Arthur was appointed to a newly created office as counsel to the New
York City tax commission which paid him $10,000 a year.
New York City tax levies were a source of plunder to Tam-
many Hall, and Arthur resigned his post after a year of
activities still cloaked in secrecy. Arthur returned to his
law practice to await a more congenial appointment which came
late in 1871 when, with the help of Senator Conkling, he
was nominated by President Grant to become collector of the
New York Customhouse, one of the most lucrative positions
in the federal government.

   The new collector "was tactful, sophisticated, dapper,
and suave," a much abler man than most of the political ap-
pointees with whom he associated. Arthur knew the work
of his responsible office better than several of his predecessors, but he used his influence and position to find jobs for
friends and relatives and to strengthen the Republican political organization in and outside of New York. Arthur's income from the Customhouse enabled him to enjoy living in
New York City: at times there were five servants in his
home, his children were privately educated, and the collector
was able to continue his nocturnal forays and pleasures.
In order to stay up late at night, Arthur adopted the comfortable practice of arriving at his office at 1:00 p.m., three
hours after the Customhouse opened for business. His administration of the Customhouse must have been reasonably
satisfactory, because he was the first collector in a generation to serve a full term of four years. In December of
1875 President Grant nominated Arthur for another term as
the collector in the Customhouse, and his nomination was
confirmed promptly without a dissenting vote, thanks to
Senator Conkling's ability to muster votes when he wished
to do so. After the Grant administration was succeeded by

that of Rutherford B. Hayes, the management of the Customhouse was investigated by a committee headed by J. H.
Meredith, and the report of this group led to Arthur's dis-
missal by the president.

     After his suspension from his post as collector, Arthur
returned to his practice of law, and he performed enough
legal work for his many friends and acquaintances to avoid
a severe shortage of money. Moreover, his large income as
Collector had permitted him to invest in land, and the death
of Nell's mother brought her and her husband a modest inheritance. Arthur's heart was not in his legal practice but
in machine politics in which he was recognized as an expert.
Soon after New Year's Day in 1880, Arthur and two police
commissioners left for Albany to do what they could in organizing the new legislature, and it was there that Arthur
received a telegram telling of his wife's serious illness.
Arthur took the first train to New York and hurried to his
home to find his wife under the influence of morphine ad-
ministered by her physician. Nell had caught a bad cold
while waiting outside for a carriage after a concert on January 10, and her cold soon developed into pneumonia. Arthur
remained at Nell's bedside for twenty-four hours, but his
wife never regained consciousness. Her funeral was held
in the Church of the Heavenly Rest on Fifth Avenue, and
she was buried in the family plot in the Rural Cemetery at
Albany.

     When the New York delegation headed by Roscoe Conk-
ling went in May of 1880 to the Republican National Convention in Chicago, their primary goal was to win the nomination for former President Grant who had served for two
terms before he made his triumphal world tour. After the
nomination went on the thirty-sixth ballot to James Garfield
of Ohio, several of his managers recognized that their candidate for the presidency probably could not be elected
without support from New York, and they offered Conkling
the opportunity to select Garfield's running mate. Two of
Conkling's aides overheard the offer and went immediately
to Arthur with the suggestion that he make a bid for the
second place on the ticket. Arthur, who "was never known
to overlook any political position or public office within his
grasp," indicated his willingness to accept the nomination
for the vice-presidency if the selection was to be made by
the delegation from New York. Conkling was outraged by

this development, but Arthur held his ground and won the
nomination. His record as a spoilsman caused the Democrats
to sneer at the qualifications of Garfield's running mate,
but the Republicans won the contest and Garfield was
elected president and Arthur was to become vice-president
on March 4, 1881. Six months later, on September 19, Garfield died from wounds inflicted by an assassin's bullet, and
the next day Chester A. Arthur became the twenty-first
president of the United States.

Most Americans were appalled that a machine politician
with an unenviable record, who had never held an elective
office, was to serve as president for almost three years and
a half. Arthur had not sought the office of president; indeed, he did not want it, yet he possessed better qualifications for the post than most would expect of a leading
spoilsman. Arthur "was intelligent, had extensive administrative experience, and enjoyed a number of battle-worn
friends, like former Governor Morgan, who might give useful counsel." Most Americans sympathized with the plight
of the new president and were eager for his success.
Arthur's term in office saw efforts to reform the tariff, to
introduce civil service reform, and to modernize the navy,
and the president's countrymen agreed that his presidency
went far better than almost anyone had reason to expect.

On the social front Arthur succeeded splendidly. His
occupancy of the White House was delayed by the need for
renovation, but, after he moved in on December 7, 1881,
Arthur persuaded his youngest sister, Mary Arthur McElroy, the mother of four and a resident of Albany, New
York, to leave her family for four months each year to
serve as "Mistress of the White House." Mrs. McElroy
proved to be an excellent choice, and Arthur, who was a
connoisseur of good food and drink, hosted entertainments
in the White House which have rarely been equalled. Arthur
obtained his clothes from an expensive New York tailor, and
his carriage with coachmen and driver in livery became the
talk of the capital. Yet Arthur, who cut a handsome figure
in society, wisely kept his children from the public and the
press.

President Arthur did not expect to be elected in 1884
to serve a full term in the White House, because he realized
that he had become a man without a party. The faction of

the Republican party to which he once belonged, the Stal-
warts, were disappointed in him because he had not dismissed the collector in the New York Customhouse and let
them enjoy the spoils of office. The opposing faction, the
Half-Breeds, were led by James G. Blaine who had been
Secretary of State under Garfield, but resigned after Arthur
became president in order to freely criticize the new administration and to launch his candidacy for the Republican
nomination for the presidency in 1884.

Moreover, President Arthur learned in the summer of
1882 that he had been afflicted with Bright's disease, a
mysterious malady which ordinarily proves fatal to adults.
Arthur experienced some of the mental depression sympto-
matic of the disease, and in the summer of 1882 his cousin,
a physician, who stayed some months in the White House
noted in his diary, "The President sick in body and soul."
By March 1883, President Arthur's physical condition was
rapidly worsening; he began to experience frequent nausea,
and the high blood pressure associated with Bright's disease
induced a form of heart disease. The president might have
curtailed or cancelled social events in the White House, but
to do so would have been an admission that he could not
handle the duties that had come to him through Garfield's
death. Arthur struggled on with his disease and looked
forward to his retirement from public life. He returned to
his home in New York City where his health rapidly worsened. In November Arthur asked his son to bring Jimmy
Smith, an old Customhouse friend, to his home, and Arthur
requested Smith to destroy his Customhouse files. Arthur's
son watched garbage cans repeatedly filled and their contents burned.

Chester A. Arthur died on November 17, 1885, and
his death was an occasion for public mourning in Washington
and in New York. His funeral service was held on November
22 at his wife's former parish, the Church of the Heavenly
Rest, and his body was buried in the family plot at the
Rural Cemetery in Albany.

While President, Arthur donated a stained glass window in memory of his late wife to St. John's Episcopal
Church in Washington in which she had worshiped and sung
before she moved to New York to become his wife. A heroic
statue of Arthur in bronze was unveiled in 1899 in the

northeast corner of Madison Square, a few blocks from his former Lexington Avenue residence. The sculptor's fee of $25,000 was paid by friends of the deceased president, and the presentation address was delivered by Elihu Root, soon to become secretary of war under President McKinley. After reviewing the distressing circumstances that surrounded Arthur's elevation to the presidency, Root justly observed: "Good causes found in him [President Arthur] a friend and bad measures met in him an unyielding opponent." Root's comment reflects the earnestness with which President Arthur undertook his new and vast responsibilities; before he entered onto the national scene he was known among familiars in New York political circles as the "Gentleman Boss."

PRINCIPAL SOURCE

Thomas C. Reeves, <u>Gentleman Boss, the Life of Chester Alan Arthur</u>. New York: Knopf, 1975. 500 p.

THOMAS A. HENDRICKS, 1885

Thomas Andrews Hendricks (1819-1885) was born in a log cabin near Zanesville, Ohio. In 1822 his father moved his small family to a cabin in the wilderness which became the first building in Shelbyville, Indiana, where the future vice-president grew up. After completion of the limited programs in the local schools, Thomas became a member of the class of 1841 at nearby Hanover College. After graduation, Hendricks studied law, was admitted to the bar, and opened a law office in Shelbyville. At age twenty-nine he was elected to the Indiana Assembly, and he was named in 1850 to represent his county in a Constitutional Convention. His performance there led in 1855 to his election to Congress, where he showed a keen interest in the "Homestead Bill." As a consequence, President Franklin Pierce appointed Hendricks to head the General Land Office, which he did efficiently until 1859.

Hendricks moved in 1863 to Indianapolis where he was elected to the United States Senate for a six-year term. During 1873-1877 he was governor of Indiana, one of the first Democrats to head a northern state after the Civil War. In 1876 Hendricks was Governor Tilden's running mate in the disputed election won by Rutherford B. Hayes and William Wheeler, and eight years later he ran successfully on a reform ticket with Governor Grover Cleveland. Hendricks received a warm welcome in the Senate where he had served sixteen years before. Late in November 1885, despite a feeling of illness, Hendricks attended

a reception in his honor in Indianapolis, and
the very next day the vice-president died in
his sleep.

*   *   *

A lengthy review of the life of Thomas A. Hendricks, the
twenty-first vice-president of the United States, appeared
in 1886, the year after his death. The two authors of the
book, John W. Holcombe and Hubert M. Skinner, knew their
subject personally, and in their preface they acknowledge
assistance received from relatives and friends of the late
vice-president and express special appreciation to his widow.
Consequently, it is not surprising that their treatment of
Hendricks is eulogistic, but their glowing portrait of the
man seems to have been deserved. According to this "official" biography, Hendricks' combination of wise discretion,
temperate speech, and genial disposition formed "a rarely
noble nature."

Hendricks' biography was written a century ago, and
it does not draw on personal correspondence and other material which would add interest to the story of the lives of the
twenty-first vice-president and his wife, Eliza Morgan. The
book does not claim to give "the verdict of history" upon the
career of Thomas A. Hendricks, yet its careful and detailed
presentation probably has seemed sufficient to students of
Indiana history and biography who otherwise might have undertaken a critical study of his noteworthy life and achievements.

Abraham Hendricks, the grandfather of the vice-
president, was a man of ability and character who served
four successive terms in the Pennsylvania legislature in the
1790s. He and his wife, a Jamieson, had five sons, all of
whom grew to manhood in the mountains of western Pennsylvania and emigrated to Indiana. One son, William, served in
the House of Representatives for six years immediately after
Indiana became a state in 1816, and in 1823 he became Indiana's second governor. During his term in office he
signed a bill that created a county named in his honor. The
youngest of the five sons, John, was the last to leave home
but did so shortly after his marriage to Jane Thomson, whom
he met in the home of a Presbyterian minister in Pittsburgh.

John Hendricks and his bride lived first in a log cabin near Zanesville, Ohio, where two sons, Abram and Thomas Andrews, were born. The outstanding success of brother William in Indiana drew John Hendricks and his family to Madison, the congressman's home, where they remained until 1822 when they moved to a cabin in the wilderness which became the first building in the future town of Shelbyville. In addition to being the founder of a new city, John Hendricks cleared his land, helped his neighbors, helped to organize a church in which he became the leading elder, and made his home, with its books and journals, the favorite resort of ministers and judges who came to the county seat of Shelby county. Six more children were born to John Hendricks and his wife at the Shelby homestead.

The future vice-president, who had been born in Ohio on September 7, 1819, grew up in Shelbyville and began school there, first in a log cabin and then in a small brick building which also served as a residence for the teacher. Young Thomas continued his school work in the Shelby County Seminary chartered in 1831 and in a school about twelve miles away, where he completed his preliminary studies. The boy wanted to go on to college and was assisted in doing so by his father. In the fall of 1836 Thomas A. Hendricks enrolled in Hanover College about five miles west of the town of Madison and a mile from the Ohio River.

Hendricks spent his first year at Hanover in required preparatory studies and returned the following year as a member of the freshman class to graduate in 1841. The curriculum in the Presbyterian school emphasized the classics and the Bible, and the regime of the students was strict. During his undergraduate years, Hanover College was severely damaged by a tornado and the enrollment dwindled when the school's work-study program failed, but Hendricks persevered and was graduated with his class of but four members, all of whom achieved prominence in law or medicine.

After graduation Thomas A. Hendricks began the study of law under Stephen Major, an exceptionally able young attorney who had moved to Shelbyville in 1834. A year later, lawyer Major moved to Indianapolis and Hendricks, with encouragement from his mother, entered the law school conducted by her brother, Judge Alexander

Thomson, in Chambersburg, Pa. The school was located in
a building that adjoined the home of the judge, who possessed a fine law library. The law books were studied like
text books, and the students copied countless legal documents in the local recorder's office. After spending most of
1843 at the law school in Chambersburg, Hendricks went on
to Philadelphia before he returned to Shelbyville. He had
left with two hundred silver dollars in his pocket and
reached home with only one dollar and a quarter. Although
Hendricks did not arrive in time for the regular bar examination, he was tested by three circuit judges and was immediately licensed to practice. He thereupon opened his own
law office in Shelbyville.

In the same year in which Thomas Hendricks began
his law practice in Shelbyville, Eliza Morgan of North Bend,
Ohio, came to visit her sister, Mrs. Daniel West. The visitor
was in her late teens, attractive, and cultured, and she was
pursued by the young attorney. The young couple promptly
fell in love and after Eliza returned to her home, letters
went back and forth, and Thomas visited North Bend, a
town on the Ohio River about fifteen miles west of Cincinnati. Eliza's father had died, and she lived with her mother
in an impressive stone house built by her grandfather, Dr.
Stephen Wood, a friend and neighbor of General William
Henry Harrison. The young man had won the girl's heart,
but he could not then support a wife. Two years later
Thomas Hendricks' law practice permitted him to return to
North Bend and to ask his fiancé to name the date for their
wedding. Her friends gaily proposed the next day, and the
ceremony was held on September 26, 1845. Two years later
a son, Morgan, was born on January 16, 1848. The boy
died in 1851, and his bereaved parents had no more children.

At age twenty-nine Thomas A. Hendricks was elected
to the lower house of the Indiana Assembly. Hendricks had
not sought the place that came to him because of his work as
an attorney and his reputation as a speaker. Thomas represented his constituents to advantage but found the pace of
lawmaking to be slow and tedious, and he was happy to return in January of 1850 to his law practice. Hendricks believed that he was completely out of politics.

The session of the Assembly in which Hendricks had
participated passed an act that provided for a Constitutional

Convention. Each Indiana county was entitled to two members, and Hendricks, at age thirty-one, was selected along
with James Vanbenthausen, age seventy-three, to represent
Shelby county. The Convention convened on October 7,
1850, and Hendricks was named to two important committees
where his "quiet firmness and thoughtful prudence" showed
his mettle. His eloquence in the early sessions caused his
colleagues to recognize Hendricks to be a born leader. The
work of the Convention matched his talents, and Hendricks
enjoyed it. His serious work in Indianapolis was relieved by
visits from his wife who brought their boy from Shelbyville.
After Eliza and Morgan left Indianapolis, Hendricks would
repeat to his colleagues something amusing that the lad had
said.

Hendricks, with his good looks and affability, won
friends and favor in the parties occasioned by the Constitutional Convention in Indianapolis, and the death of the elderly member from Shelby county focused additional attention
on the survivor. The Convention adjourned out of respect
for the deceased, and Hendricks accompanied his body to
his home. When he returned to the Convention, Hendricks
delivered an eloquent tribute to his late colleague.

Hendricks' role in the Constitutional Convention
marked him as a man qualified to represent his district in
Congress. The Fifth Congressional District in Indiana was
a large one which included the State capital, and the post
had been filled by outstanding men. The Democrats of Shelby county enthusiastically supported their candidate, who
won the nomination on the thirty-third ballot, the only time
in his career that Hendricks was opposed by members of his
own party. The Whigs nominated Colonel James E. Rush of
Hancock county who campaigned vigorously but lost to the
popular Democrat, Thomas Hendricks.

The new congressman served in the Thirty-second
and Thirty-third Congress, 1851-1855, and he participated
freely in the debates and committees. He had a strong interest in the Homestead Bill ("I am in favor of giving lands
upon easy terms to actual settlers."), and he stood with
other Douglas Democrats in the great controversy over the
passage of the Kansas-Nebraska Bill. The breakup of the
Whig Party led to the creation of a fusion ticket in Indiana,
and the Democrat from the Fifth District lost his bid for a
third term.

Early in 1855 Thomas and Eliza Hendricks returned
to Shelbyville. He resumed his law practice, and she re-
established their home as a permanent residence. Neither
had any thought of doing anything else until the former
congressman received late in August a completed commission
appointing him to the coveted post of commissioner of the
General Land Office. The appointment had been made without advance notice by President Franklin Pierce, and the
two Hendrickses agreed that Thomas should go to Washington to learn why he had been selected before he accepted
or declined.

After Hendricks learned that he had been named to
head the Land Office solely because the president considered him to be eminently qualified, Thomas accepted the
commission, and his wife arranged affairs at home so she
could join him in Washington. Hendricks proved to be an
efficient administrator: through his efforts each clerk in
the General Land Office processed twenty-five percent more
land patents than he had done previously and the length of
time for handling an application was reduced from four years
to four months. The new commissioner organized a law
school for clerks in his department and conducted it in the
evening despite the malarial fever he suffered in Washington.
The inauguration of President Buchanan in 1857 brought a
new secretary of the Interior who wished Hendricks to continue as commissioner of the General Land Office. Hendricks
accepted reappointment, and he and his wife anticipated a
long residence in the capital. During their stay in Washington, Thomas and Eliza Hendricks occupied suites in the
better hotels, and their rooms were a popular resort for
leading members of Washington society.

As a Douglas Democrat, Hendricks did not support
Buchanan's pro-Southern policies, and he left the Land Office to resume his law practice in Shelbyville. In January
of the next year, 1860, the Democrats in Indiana named
Hendricks to be their candidate for governor. He accepted
the nomination and arranged with the Republican nominee,
Colonel Henry S. Lane, to canvass the state together.
Eliza did not travel with her husband, but she awaited the
outcome with extraordinary interest because the Hendrickses
had decided, win or lose, to leave Shelbyville. Hendricks
lost by almost 10,000 votes, and he and his wife moved to
Indianapolis, which was to be their home for twenty-five
years.

In the year following the outbreak of the Civil War, the Democrats in Indiana met on January 8 for their regular convention. Hendricks, by acclamation, was made permanent president, and he delivered an address in which he opposed emancipation of the slaves and arming Negroes. Later in 1862, the Democrats met on July 30 in a Mass Convention, and again he was made president by acclamation. On this occasion his remarks were brief and serious, and he concluded:

> We are Indianians. We are surrounded by troubles. Our society is in an excited condition; and it is the duty of every good citizen, it is the duty of every good patriot, to maintain the public peace.

The Democrats won the election in Indiana in October of 1862; and on January 14, 1863, Thomas A. Hendricks was elected to the United States Senate for a full term of six years to begin on March 4, 1863.

Hendricks' years in the Senate encompassed the last two years of the Civil War, the assassination of President Lincoln, the impeachment trial of President Johnson, and the excesses of Reconstruction in the defeated South. His name is not linked to any major legislation, because Hendricks was a member of a weak minority in Congress. Senator Hendricks was well known and popular in Washington, and even those who opposed him in politics "early learned to value his candor, fairness and honesty, and to find pleasure in his genial companionship." The Hoosier showed himself to be a statesman, and he was mentioned at the end of his term as a likely candidate for the next Democratic nomination for the presidency.

Thomas' uncle William had moved from the House of Representatives to the office of governor of Indiana, for the rank of a governor was then "deemed far higher than that of either House of Congress." This notion continued for at least half a century in Indiana, because the Democratic State Convention that met on January 8, 1868, nominated Senator Hendricks for the office of governor by acclamation. The senator made joint appearances with the incumbent governor, Conrad Baker, in Indiana's eleven congressional districts. Governor Baker won the election by less than a thousand votes, and voting irregularities occurred in many counties.

Hendricks returned to his law practice in Indianapolis and
utilized some of his time out of office to visit the Far West
and the South. He spoke to large audiences in San Francisco and in New Orleans; "His words were calm, temperate
and encouraging."

In 1872 the Democratic National Convention in Baltimore voted to support the Liberal Republican ticket of Horace Greeley and H. Gratz Brown, and the Democrats in Indiana named Hendricks as their candidate for governor.
Greeley died soon after the election, and some of his electoral votes were cast for Hendricks, who had become one of
the first Democrats to govern a Northern state after the
Civil War. During his term as governor, the General Assembly in Indiana was controlled by Republicans, but Hendricks' courtesy and tolerance enabled him to work effectively with the legislators.

During his term as governor of Indiana, Thomas and
Eliza Hendricks lived in their own house, a substantial brick
house at the corner of Tennessee and St. Clair. Here they
hosted many dinners for legislators, and they opened their
home for public receptions. Eliza had a great interest in
her husband's duties and traveled with him to visit Indiana's
penal and benevolent institutions. She must have overtaxed
herself, because in 1875 she had to have complete rest and
a change in surroundings. Consequently, she spent three
months with relatives in California, this being the longest
period she was ever separated from her husband. After
Eliza returned to Indianapolis, she and her husband gave
up their large house and moved to a hotel where they were
readily accessible and uniformly cordial to visitors.

At the Democratic National Convention held in St.
Louis in 1876, Governor Samuel J. Tilden of New York was
nominated for president on the second ballot, and Governor
Hendricks was named without opposition to be his running
mate. This was the year of the infamous disputed election
that was won by Rutherford B. Hayes and William A. Wheeler, because members of the Republican party were able to
determine the final results in certain states where the counts
and procedures had been contested. In the next year, 1877,
Hendricks spent four months in northern Europe, and on his
return he became an active member of a leading law firm in
Indianapolis. During the late 1870s and the early 1880s

Hendricks fulfilled many important speaking engagements in
the Midwest.

In 1880 the Indiana delegation to the Democratic National Convention at Cincinnati campaigned with enthusiasm
for the nomination of Thomas Hendricks for the presidency,
but General Winfield Scott Hancock was chosen on the second ballot and William H. English of Indiana became his running mate. Hendricks worked hard for his party, but the
national contest was won by General James A. Garfield and
Chester A. Arthur. Overwork was taking its toll on Hendricks, who had suffered a slight paralytic stroke in his
right arm and had a persistent foot ailment. Hendricks
needed time in which to regain his health, and he and his
wife went to Europe with two old friends for company.
They embarked in December of 1873 and returned in April
of 1874, after having toured Italy and Spain and having
revisited favorite sites in England and France.

When the Republicans met in 1884 in their national
convention, there was widespread concern over high taxes,
speculation, and a financial panic. The situation called for
reform, yet the Republicans nominated the personable James
G. Blaine, who was opposed by true reformists. The time
was ripe for the Democrats in their convention in Chicago
to adopt a platform with specific planks for civil service reform, economy in government, and a tariff for revenue alone;
and after having done so, they nominated the reform governor of New York, Grover Cleveland, to head their ticket.
Hendricks was named for the vice-presidency and received
the vote of every delegate in the convention. At the end
of the month, Thomas and Eliza Hendricks followed their
regular practice of escaping the heat of late July in Indiana
by vacationing in Saratoga, New York, where he received
official notification of his nomination by the convention.

In November, Mr. and Mrs. Hendricks stayed at the
Fifth Avenue Hotel in New York City where they greeted
many distinguished callers, and in February, Thomas met
Governor Cleveland in Albany and returned to Indiana by
way of the South. In the last week in February, the vice-
presidential nominee, his wife, and several friends left in a
private railroad car for Washington. Thomas and Eliza participated in the inaugural ceremonies and related entertainments, but he probably received the greatest enjoyment

from an informal reception in the Capitol, which he had left
sixteen years before. The lack of physical effort required
for presiding over the Senate suited the new vice-president,
who had not completely recovered from a paralytic stroke in
1880 at the Hot Springs in Arkansas.

The special session during which Hendricks presided
over the Senate lasted but a month, after which he returned
to Indianapolis to prepare a lecture he had agreed to deliver
before the law school of Yale College. While he was preparing his address, the vice-president invited John W. Holcombe
to make the trip with him, and the young man agreed to do
so if Hendricks would also visit Harvard, his biographer's
alma mater. The vice-president welcomed the opportunity
to see more of Boston and environs, and J. W. Holcombe
told President Eliot that he intended to bring Hendricks to
the Harvard Commencement after his visit to Yale. President
Eliot was pleased that the vice-president intended to visit
Cambridge and encouraged him to ride from Boston with the
governor in the annual colorful procession.

Hendricks, his wife, J. W. Holcombe, and a state official left Indianapolis about the middle of June in 1885 and
went to Atlantic City, where the party rested and Mrs.
Hendricks remained while the others went to New Haven.
Hendricks' address on the history of the Supreme Court
is a pedestrian piece, but his audience was responsive and
generous in their comments. The vice-president met a number of Connecticut's leading Democrats and enjoyed himself
immensely. The reception Hendricks received in Boston and
at Harvard was more elaborate than the arrangements in
New Haven, and he had much of interest to tell his wife
when he rejoined her in Atlantic City.

Late in November the vice-president and Mrs. Hendricks attended a large reception hosted by prominent friends
in Indianapolis. Hendricks had not felt well on the day of
the reception, but he attended anyway because he wanted to
meet with many friends in his hometown before he returned
to Washington. Some of the guests noticed that the vice-
president appeared pale and tired, but he did not admit to
any illness. After returning home Hendricks acknowledged
that he was ill and his condition worsened rapidly. The
next day, the 25th of November, the vice-president died
while asleep; his last words were those spoken to his

physician, "I am free at last." He was free of the intense
pain he had felt around his heart.

Hendricks died on a Wednesday and was buried on
the following Tuesday. The funeral arrangements in between must have exceeded any display of mourning that
had been seen in Indianapolis before or since. His body
lay in state in the Marion County Court House, was removed
to his residence, and thence to St. Paul's Cathedral. A
long, long procession then accompanied the body to the
cemetery at the top of Crown Hill, where the emotional out-
pouring came to an overdue end.

According to his two biographers, Eliza Hendricks'
interests and ambition for her husband's success paralleled
his own. She maintained a home of refinement where Thomas' friends were always welcome, and she tried to relieve
her husband of details pertaining to the management of their
investments. She did outstanding work on the Board of
Trustees for the Reformatory for Women and Girls, and after the death of her husband, she replaced him as a director
of a large mining company in which they held stock. In the
congenial vein maintained by Messrs. Holcombe and Skinner:

> Mrs. Hendricks was a proud and happy wife, and
> Mr. Hendricks was so unfashionable as to be in love
> with his wife to the end.

In her last year of life, Eliza Hendricks gave $25,000
to Hanover College for the erection of a library in memory
of her late husband. She died at the age of eighty on
November 3, 1903, at her home in Indianapolis. In a newspaper notice of her death, the vice-president's widow was
characterized as "a woman of great learning" who "always
took much interest in politics."

PRINCIPAL SOURCE

John W. Holcombe and Hubert M. Skinner. Life and Public
    Services of Thomas A. Hendricks, with Selected Speeches
    and Writings. Indianapolis: Carlon and Hollenbeck, 1886.
    637 p.

LEVI PARSONS MORTON, 1889-1893

Levi Parsons Morton (1824-1920) was born in Shoreham, Vermont, where his father was minister of the Congregational Church. Levi attended local schools in small towns in Vermont and Massachusetts, but his schooling ended at age thirteen because family finances could not provide a college education for a second son. Instead, Levi went to work as an apprentice in a general store in Enfield, New Hampshire. Through serious application and industry, he gained more responsible posts in Concord and Hanover, New Hampshire, Boston, and in 1885, New York. There Morton expanded his business interests and moved into the field of international banking.

Not until 1873 did Morton run for political office. He was elected to Congress in 1878 and again in 1880, and for four years (1881-1885) he was the United States minister to France. Morton was vice-president during Benjamin Harrison's single term as president, 1889-1893, after which he was governor of New York for two years. In both offices Morton showed an independence and firmness that caused him to be mentioned as a candidate for the Republican nomination for the presidency in 1896, which went with little opposition to William McKinley. After leaving public office, Parsons traveled to France to renew friendships made while he was minister there, and he developed a beautiful estate of 1,000 acres, Ellerslie, at Rhinecliff, New York. Morton dissolved the firm of Morton, Bliss & Company, and formed in 1899 the

145

Morton Trust Company which in ten years became
a part of J. P. Morgan's Guaranty Trust Company.
In his eighty-fifth year, Morton was elected chairman of the board of directors of the new firm.
The former vice-president died on his New York
estate on his ninety-sixth birthday, May 16,
1920.

*   *   *

During the late 1880s, between service as minister to France
and as vice-president of the United States, Levi P. Morton
was in his early sixties, and his second wife, Anna Living-
ston Street Morton, was in her early forties. The distinguished couple and their five daughters might have been
seen on any fine Sunday morning walking to Grace Church;
en route they exchanged greetings with members of other
leading families bound on similar missions. Although on
their way to an Episcopal Church, Morton was a Puritan at
heart, and he remained true to the teachings of his family
in his strict observance of the Sabbath. His wife was the
daughter of a successful attorney who practiced in Poughkeepsie, where Anna was born. After his death, mother
and daughter moved to New York, where the girl was
brought up in a society which, in retrospect, is idyllic.
Her background and gracious manner fitted her admirably
for her place as hostess in their homes in New York, Newport, Paris, and Washington. Shortly after his election,
vice-president-elect Morton bought a home on Scott Circle
in Washington, but the improvements he authorized were
not completed in time for his inauguration and the Morton
family lodged for a time in the Arlington Hotel. After they
had settled into their newly remodeled home, their residence
at H and 15 Streets became a favorite meeting place for persons prominent in Washington society.

Before his election to the vice-presidency, the Mortons
had sold their summer home at Newport and purchased Ellerslie, a beautiful estate of a thousand acres, nineteen miles
above Poughkeepsie at Rhinecliff, and here he intended to
operate a model farm and to provide an attractive meeting
place for his children and for possible grandchildren. The
former proved difficult because of a disastrous fire and the
expense of scientific agricultural practices, but Morton viewed
the situation with humor, "I serve milk alternately with champagne. One costs the same as the other."

After Morton's term as vice-president, he served for
two years as governor of New York, and his success in this
office made him a leading candidate for the Republican nomination for president in 1896, which went with little opposition to McKinley. Instead of a quiet retirement, the Mortons
made another trip to Europe to renew friendships made while
he was minister to France, 1881-1885, and on a vacation in
1893; after their return to New York, they became involved
in the implementation of the plans for a great cathedral on
Morningside Heights. The minister of Grace Church was
one of the leaders in the campaign to raise the requisite
funds, and in this effort he was able to enlist the two Mortons. Anna Morton had a special interest in the ambitious
project, and to it she gave generously of her time and her
own inheritance. Levi Morton's gifts to the Cathedral provided for construction of the choir and the altar, and he
also gave a Skinner organ in memory of his daughter, Lena,
who died in 1904. Anna Morton died at Ellerslie in 1918,
after forty-five years as the wife of Levi Parsons Morton,
who died on his ninety-sixth birthday, also at Ellerslie.

Morton's life in politics began about the time of his
second marriage in February of 1873. Before then he had
concentrated on his business affairs, in which one success
followed another. After his political career had ended, he
arranged for the dissolution of his firm of Morton, Bliss &
Co., and the formation in 1899 of the Morton Trust Company
which a decade later became a part of J. P. Morgan's Guaranty Trust Company. Morton, then in his eighty-fifth year,
was elected chairman of the new board of directors in recognition of his long and distinguished career in business and
finance.

Levi Parsons Morton, a financier who became vice-
president of the United States, was born on May 16, 1824,
in Shoreham, Vermont. His parents were descended from
early settlers in New England, and from them young Levi
learned a respect for Puritan attitudes toward the observance of the Sabbath, gambling, temperance, and idleness.
The boy's father was the minister of a Congregational Church
in Shoreham, and there was not enough money in the family
to provide their second son with a college education. Levi
attended the Shoreham Academy and the local schools in
Springfield, Vermont, and in Winchendon, Massachusetts,
after his father became a minister in these towns, but his
formal schooling ended in his thirteenth year.

Levi Morton's business career began as an apprentice in a general store in Enfield, New Hampshire, where he engaged to work for his room and board with the family of the proprietor and a salary of $50 per year. After learning as much as he could in the small country store about simple bookkeeping, profits and losses, and varied sources of supply, Levi obtained a clerkship in a larger store in Concord, New Hampshire. His employer decided to open a branch in Hanover, the home of Dartmouth College, and young Morton was appointed manager. In Hanover Levi Morton boarded in the home of Edwin Sanborn, professor of Latin, and there he met Lucy Young Kimball, who became his wife thirteen years later. The volume of business in the Hanover branch increased through Morton's efforts until it was the largest in the area.

Levi became the sole owner of the thriving business in Hanover; but, not content with this considerable success, he moved in three years to Boston to become a member of a leading shipping firm headed by James M. Beebe. Beebe established an office in New York and named Morton to be its manager, but in 1855 Morton became the head of a large wholesale dry goods firm. Here he required his employees to follow the rigorous schedule of work that he had set for himself, and soon his finances permitted him to think of marriage. He proceeded to court Lucy Kimball, whom he had known years before in Hanover, and the couple were married on October 15, 1856, in her home on Long Island.

Lucy's father was not wealthy but he held a position of considerable influence, and her mother belonged to a family that had helped to settle Connecticut and had enjoyed a high place in the society of that state and nearby Rhode Island. In addition to the social advantages Morton's wife had received at home, she had spent time abroad while an uncle was the United States Minister to Portugal. She enjoyed her brief glimpse of public life enough to hope that her husband might seek a career in politics. In jest she predicted a notable public career for him, but in the early years of his marriage, Levi Morton chose to devote his energies to extending his business into the field of international banking. By the time Levi Morton might have been ready to consider moving into politics, his first wife died on July 11, 1871. Their only child, Lucy, had died in infancy.

In less than two years, Levi Morton had married again; his second wife brought him additional wealth and prominence, and within a few years he stood for election to Congress as the representative of the Eleventh Congressional District of New York, which contained more wealth than was to be found in many of the American states. After his election to Congress in 1878 and his reelection in 1880, he proceeded to hold higher offices in the national government and in the State of New York as recounted above.

PRINCIPAL SOURCE

Robert McElroy, Levi Parsons Morton, Banker, Diplomat and Statesman. New York: Putnam's, 1930. 340 p.

ADLAI E. STEVENSON, 1893-1897

Adlai Ewing Stevenson (1835-1914) was born in Christian County, Kentucky where he worked on his family's tobacco farm and learned to read in a nearby school. After frost killed a crop, Adlai's family moved to Bloomington, Illinois, where he taught school and enrolled in a short course at Illinois Wesleyan University. Adlai attended Centre College in Kentucky, but his father's death in 1857 obliged his son to resume teaching in Illinois. He thereupon read law, and after admission to the bar at age twenty-three, he began practice in Metamora. After Adlai's marriage in 1866, he joined his cousin in law practice in Bloomington.

In 1874 Stevenson went to Congress where he became acquainted with leaders in both political parties. He was defeated for reelection in 1876 but won again in 1878 and made more friends in Washington. At the Democratic National Convention in Chicago in 1884, Stevenson met William E. Vilas who was to become postmaster general in Cleveland's Cabinet. Vilas named Adlai to be first assistant postmaster with responsibility for replacing Republican fourth class postmasters with deserving Democrats.

In 1892 Stevenson was named to the second place on the ticket headed by former President Cleveland. As vice-president, Stevenson respected the traditions of the Senate and refrained from criticizing administration policies with which he disagreed. Party leaders wanted new programs and new candidates in 1896, but in 1900 Stevenson was named to run with the

Democrats' presidential candidate, William Jennings Bryan. The Republicans won the election, and the former vice-president became an
elder statesman. In retirement he prepared
his speeches and recollections for publication
in 1909 under the title, Something of Men I
Have Known. His death in 1914 came from
heart failure after prostate surgery in a Chicago hospital.

*   *   *

About a decade after he left the vice-presidency, Adlai
Stevenson put together a volume of speeches, anecdotes,
and reminiscences entitled Something of Men I Have Known
(1909). The book is dedicated to the compiler's wife:
"Letitia Green Stevenson, The Patient Listener to These
'Twice-Told Tales.'" Stevenson had earned a reputation as
a raconteur, and most of the stories included in his compilation probably were told many times and underwent refinement in each retelling.

After he was admitted to the bar in 1858, Stevenson
began his practice in Metamora, a town about fifteen miles
north and east of Peoria, Illinois, which then was the county seat of Woodford County. In the old courthouse at Metamora, Stevenson in his boyhood had heard Lincoln at the
bar, and as an attorney he had been moved by the eloquent
orator, Robert G. Ingersoll. During his days as a bachelor
in Metamora, Stevenson lived at the "Traveller's Home," an
inn which was especially attractive to the young lawyer because of its extremely moderate charges: "two dollars and
a half per week for board and lodging, 'washing and mend-
ing' included."

Readers of American history are familiar with the practice in colonial days and in the early nineteenth century of
sharing beds in country inns with two or three other guests,
but Stevenson's recountal of his sharing a berth in a railway
car on the way to Congress strains credulity. A complete
stranger who was ill and poorly dressed boarded the train
near Cincinnati without a reservation for a berth and no
sleeping accommodation was to be had until Stevenson offered to share his. Congressman Stevenson did not know
the identity of his bedfellow in a narrow berth until the

Monday following at a roll call in the House of Representatives when the stranger, whom Stevenson had not noticed
on the floor, responded to the call for "James D. Williams
of Indiana." This was, indeed, "Blue Jeans Williams," later
governor of the Hoosier state.

Adlai Ewing Stevenson was born on October 23, 1835,
into a family of Scotch Presbyterians in Christian County in
western Kentucky. The boy was the second of seven children born to John and Eliza Stevenson who earned their
living on a tobacco farm. Adlai, who had learned to read
in a school in nearby Herndon, did not enjoy work in the
fields, and he probably wasn't sorry when a frost killed the
tobacco crop and his parents decided to relocate near Bloomington, Illinois. Adlai, then sixteen, drove one of the three
wagons that carried the Stevensons to Bloomington on July
7, 1852, after three weeks on the road.

In Bloomington young Stevenson had educational opportunities superior to those found in the back country of Kentucky. Adlai taught in a country school and enrolled in a
short course at nearby Illinois Wesleyan University. Adlai
and a cousin, James Stevenson Ewing, then went to Centre
College in Danville, Kentucky, where they pursued scientific
and classical studies. While a student at Centre College,
Adlai met his future wife, the fourteen year-old daughter
of President Lewis W. Green. The death of his father in
1857 caused Adlai to leave college and to return to school
teaching to provide support for the family. Stevenson then
began to read law under Robert E. Williams, a college graduate and classmate of James G. Blaine. After he was admitted
to the bar, Adlai, at age twenty-three, was encouraged to
begin his practice in Metamora where he lived for the next
ten years. He promptly identified himself as a Douglas
Democrat, and in 1864 he was elected state's attorney, a
post he held for four years.

Letitia Green's father died in 1863, and the girl and
her mother joined a married sister who lived in Chenoa, Illinois, about thirty-five miles east of Metamora. Letitia met
Adlai again, and he promptly fell in love with her. The
couple were married on December 20, 1866. Letitia had been
brought up in college environments in Lexington and Danville, Kentucky, and she had attended a finishing school for
girls in New York. With her background, Letitia was

undoubtedly pleased when her husband decided to join James
S. Ewing in a law partnership in Bloomington. There the
couple had their four children, three girls and a boy, and
maintained a comfortable home in a stimulating environment.

Stevenson was nominated for Congress in 1874 and
was swept into office with many other Democrats that year.
As a congressman, he favored reductions in tariffs and government expenditures, and he became well acquainted with
political leaders such as Blaine, Garfield, Cannon, and Hoar.
Stevenson was defeated for reelection in 1876, but he won
again in 1878 and made new friends in Washington. Stevenson attended the Democratic National Convention in Chicago
in 1884 which nominated Grover Cleveland for president and
Thomas A. Hendricks for vice-president. At the convention, Stevenson became friendly with William F. Vilas of Wisconsin who was to become postmaster-general in Cleveland's
Cabinet, and he in turn named Adlai for the post of first
assistant in charge of replacing Republican fourth-class postmasters with deserving Democrats. Stevenson handled the
removals with such tact that President Cleveland named him
justice of the supreme court of the District of Columbia, but
the Republicans who controlled the Senate would not approve
the appointment of the official who had replaced forty thousand Republican postmasters.

Stevenson hoped to be nominated for the vice-
presidency in 1888, but he was not chosen. However, he
learned anew the importance of combinations of friends in
political campaigns, and he went to the Democratic National
Convention in 1892 at the head of the Illinois delegation.
He then had friends in many places and was chosen for the
second place as the ticket headed by former President Grover Cleveland. Stevenson, accompanied by his wife, campaigned strenuously in the South. His wife wrote to a
friend, "If any votes were gained by Mr. Stevenson's efforts
in N.C., he shall feel more than repaid for the fatigue he
underwent."

After Stevenson was elected to the vice-presidency,
he gave attention to unfinished business in Bloomington and
began preparations for his move to Washington. In late
February of 1893 the vice-president-elect, his wife, family,
and others boarded a train in Bloomington where two thousand people had gathered to witness Stevenson's departure

for Washington. The Stevenson party arrived on February
28, and on the next day they were the guests of honor at
a large reception hosted by the outgoing vice-president,
Levi P. Morton. Adlai and his wife occupied temporary
quarters at the Ebbitt House before they moved into a large
suite in the Normandie Hotel, which was near the White
House and enjoyed a reputation for comfortable accommoda-
tions and superior service.

Stevenson respected the traditions of the Senate, and
in his four years of presiding over the deliberations of its
members he made more friends and earned the regard of all
for his "conscientious performance of public duty." The
vice-president did not agree with all of President Cleveland's
policies, but he did not embarrass the administration through
outspoken criticism. Stevenson attended the opening of the
Columbian Exposition in Chicago in 1893 with President Cleveland, for whom he had great admiration. In his Something
of Men I Have Known (1909) Stevenson wrote, "I had excellent opportunities to know Mr. Cleveland," but his appraisal
of the man suggests that he and the president were not in-
timates. Indeed, when Cleveland underwent an operation
for a cancer of the mouth, neither the Cabinet nor the vice-
president was told about the hazard which confronted the
president.

As Adlai became prominent in politics outside of Illinois, his wife, Letitia, earned a prominent place in clubs
and other women's organizations. She was a founder of the
Congress of Mothers, a predecessor of the Parent-Teacher
Association, and a member of the Colonial Dames of America
and the Women's Clubs of America. She was especially active
in the Daughters of the American Revolution, which she
hoped would help to heal the breach between the women of
the North and the South. Letitia served four times as president of the D.A.R. in the 1890s.

The 1890s were also important years for Adlai and
Letitia's children. Their son, Lewis, had charge of his
father's campaign in 1892, and he became the vice-president's
private secretary. In November of 1893 Lewis married Helen
Davis, daughter of William O. Davis, owner and publisher of
the Bloomington Daily Pantagraph, a Republican paper. Despite their political differences, William Davis and Adlai
Stevenson had been friends for years. Son Lewis and his

wife had two children, Elizabeth, born on July 16, 1897,
and Adlai E. Stevenson, II, born on February 5, 1900, who
was the nominee of his and his grandfather's party for president in 1952 and again in 1956. The Stevensons' daughter, Mary, died in 1895 while her father was the vice-
president, and daughter Letitia made an extended tour of
Europe with her parents in late 1897.

One month after McKinley became president, he appointed a committee of three to explore the prospects for an
international conference on bimetallism. The Republicans
had promised in their platform to consider bimetallism if other major powers would do so, and McKinley was carrying out
this plank when he asked the former vice-president to serve
on a committee with Charles Jackson Paine of Boston and
Senator Wolcott of California, chairman. The commissioners
arrived on May 16 in Paris where they learned that the
French government wouldn't participate in a conference on
bimetallism without tariff concessions which could not be
promised. In London the Americans learned that the British
government preferred to hold to the gold standard and suggested that India might be more interested in bimetallism.
This suggestion led nowhere, because India had adopted a
gold standard in 1893 and was not interested four years later in a review of the subject.

Stevenson had gone to Europe without his wife, but
she planned to join him later. Mrs. Stevenson and their
daughter Letitia joined Adlai in London in July and remained
with him until the work of the commissioners was concluded.
The three Stevensons traveled on the Continent from August
until December and sailed from Naples on December 3. All
three were sick on the Mediterranean, and Mrs. Stevenson
was unwell on the trip across the Atlantic. The Stevensons
then stopped in Philadelphia for medical attention for Mrs.
Stevenson and for a visit with their married daughter, Julia,
and her family.

Adlai retired from the vice-presidency at the age of
sixty to his Victorian home on Franklin Square in Bloomington where he could romp with his grandchildren and enjoy
his large library, which was especially rich in history and
Shakespeare. The former vice-president was then about six
feet tall, erect, and well proportioned. He had blue eyes
and bushy eyebrows, but was practically bald with a fringe

of white hair which once had been reddish brown. He made
a very dignified appearance in the Prince Albert coat he
always wore in public.

In 1896 the younger leaders of the Democratic party
wanted new candidates and new programs, but in 1900 a
conscious effort was made to bring back old-line Democrats
who had deserted in 1896. Stevenson, who had run as a
liberal along with conservative Grover Cleveland in 1892,
appeared on the ticket in 1900 as a conservative to run with
the radical William Jennings Bryan. Stevenson was notified
of his nomination while he was enjoying a vacation at the
summer cottage of his daughter and son-in-law, and he went
from there to Lincoln, Nebraska, to plan strategies for the
campaign with Bryan and other leading Democrats. Stevenson then resumed his vacation at Lake Minnetonka in Minnesota and did not receive formal notification of his nomination
until early August in Indianapolis.

Stevenson spent election day in 1900 in Bloomington
with his family, and the defeat of the Democratic national
ticket elevated the former vice-president who had sought a
second term in the office to the rank of an elder statesman.
This was not hard to bear because Stevenson was studious
by nature, and he had a lucrative law practice in the community where he had many friends. At the age of seventy-
three, Stevenson was induced to run for the office of governor, because he was persuaded that he was the only
Democrat in Illinois who could defeat the Republican incumbent. Although Stevenson was late in declaring his candidacy, he came within twenty-two thousand votes of winning the election.

Honors came to the elder statesman in retirement in
Bloomington. He received in 1906 the honorary degree of
Doctor of Laws from Illinois Wesleyan University, which he
had attended in 1854, and he gave one of the principal addresses at the commemorative celebration arranged by the
Abraham Lincoln Centennial Association. Stevenson also undertook the considerable yet pleasant task of assembling
texts of his speeches and recording his backward glances
for the volume, <u>Something of Men I Have Known</u>, published
in 1909.

Letitia, who had been in poor health for years, died in

Bloomington, on December 25, 1913. Stevenson never recovered from the loss of his wife and experienced great
loneliness without her and his brothers, all but one of whom
had died. Stevenson's own health deteriorated rapidly after
1912; he had prostate trouble and was unable to control his
bladder in the year before his death. In the spring of 1914
he had contracted a rare skin disease and went to the Presbyterian Hospital in Chicago where he died on June 14,
1914. Stevenson's death was caused by heart failure which
followed prostate surgery. His body lay in state in the
courthouse in Bloomington before burial in the Evergreen
Cemetery in that city.

PRINCIPAL SOURCES

Leonard C. Schlup. The Political Career of the First Adlai
    E. Stevenson. Ph.D. dissertation accepted at the Univ.
    of Illinois in Urbana, 1973. 436 l.

Adlai E. Stevenson. Something of Men I Have Known. Chi-
    cago: McClurg, 1909. 442 p.

GARRET A. HOBART, 1897-1899

After graduation from Rutgers College, Garret Augustus Hobart (1844-1899) began the study of law in Paterson, New Jersey, under Socrates Tuttle, who had served two terms in the state legislature. Garret was licensed in 1866 to practice law, and three years later he married his mentor's daughter Jennie. Hobart's rise in his profession and in the business world was rapid; he became the director of several banks and at one time was connected with sixty corporations.

In 1872 Hobart became a member of the New Jersey Assembly and, at age thirty, its speaker. In 1876 he was elected to the State Senate, was reelected in 1879, and served in 1881 and 1882 as its president. From 1876 until 1896 Hobart attended Republican National Conventions where he made many friends and admirers. Hobart's advocacy of a gold monetary standard helped to bring him a place on the ticket headed by William McKinley in 1896. The Hobarts leased a fine home on Lafayette Square near the White House, where they enjoyed entertaining and developed a close friendship with the president and his invalid wife. Garret Hobart was stricken in the summer of 1899 with a heart attack which led to his death in November of that year.

*   *   *

Jennie Tuttle Hobart's husband was inaugurated on March 4, 1897, to serve as vice-president of the United States during the first term of President William McKinley. This event,

Mrs. Hobart wrote three decades later in her delightful
Memories (1930), "established me officially as Second Lady."
Although her new status lacked any basis in law, Jennie's
social elevation as the wife of a vice-president brought excitement and additional responsibilities. "Immediately after
the inauguration," Jennie continued, "people flocked to make
calls. They came in droves! ... I often wondered why they
came."

       After her husband had become vice-president-elect,
the Hobarts "were overwhelmed with invitations and engagements," but these did not dismay Jennie who admittedly
"was socially inclined." She had enjoyed the social activities
that came with her husband's rise to political prominence for
a simple reason, "I loved both people and politics." The
long step from society in Paterson, New Jersey, to the center of the social whirl in Washington posed no problem for
the redoubtable Jennie; the move "was merely an enlargement
of the life I had always led and enjoyed."

       According to the romantically inclined Jennie Tuttle
Hobart, her father, Socrates Tuttle, and her future father-
in-law, Addison Hobart, attended the same country school in
northern New Hampshire about the year 1830.   Their friendship grew, and after Addison settled on a farm in Monmouth
county, New Jersey, Socrates soon followed. The latter became a schoolteacher and managed to save enough money to
enable him to study law. Socrates Tuttle moved to Paterson,
but he often spent his holidays with his long time friend,
his wife, and their infant son on the Hobart farm. On one
of their visits, the two men sat under an old apple tree and
discussed the future of Addison's infant son. The young
father volunteered, "I'll make you a promise, Socrates.
When my boy grows up I'll send him to Paterson to study
law with you." Almost twenty years later, Garret A. Hobart,
a recent graduate of Rutgers College, went to Paterson to
study law in Socrates Tuttle's office. "When young Hobart
appeared," Jennie Tuttle, born on April 30, 1849, "promptly
lost her heart to him" [her words]. The young couple was
married when Jennie was but twenty and her husband was
twenty-five. Twenty-seven years later, in 1897, when Garret Hobart opened the session of the United States Senate
as vice-president, he did so with a gavel made from the old
apple tree under which his father and future father-in-law
had discussed plans for the boy's pursuit of a legal career.

Additional details about the movements and occupations
of Addison Hobart and of Socrates Tuttle may be found in a
biography of Garret Augustus Hobart by David Magie, the
vice-president's pastor in Paterson. Here we learn that Addison Hobart taught school in Marlboro, in Monmouth County,
where he married Sophia Vanderveer before the two moved
to establish a school in Long Branch, New Jersey, where
their eldest son, Garret, was born on June 3, 1844. In
1852 the Hobart family returned to Marlboro where Addison
managed a store and farmed and son Garret attended elementary and preparatory schools. The young man entered Rutgers College at age sixteen and was graduated in his nineteenth year, third from the highest in his class.

Jennie's father, Socrates Tuttle, was admitted in 1848
to the bar in New Jersey, and he served two terms in the
state legislature. His protégé, Garret Hobart, who was
licensed in 1866 to practice law, became his son-in-law on
July 21, 1869, when he and Jennie were married. The couple had two children, a daughter, Fannie, who died in 1895
in Italy from malignant diphtheria while touring Europe with
her family, and a son, Garret, Junior, who married Caroline
Frye, a granddaughter of Senator William P. Frye of Maine.

The young lawyer rose rapidly in his profession and
in the business world. He became a director of several
banks, and at one time was connected with sixty corporations. Garret Hobart never appeared to be overworked,
and he had time for his neighbors in Paterson and for politics. He became a member of the New Jersey Assembly in
1872 and speaker of that body in 1874 at the age of thirty.
He was elected in 1876 to the State Senate, reelected in
1879, and in 1881 and 1882 he was its president. Although
Hobart succeeded in both business and politics, he had recognized priorities, for he once declared, "I am a business
man; I engage in politics for recreation."

Garret Hobart attended Republican National Conventions from 1876 to 1896, and at each he won friends and admirers. His forthright position in favor of a gold monetary
standard brought him to the fore in 1896 after the Democrats had endorsed bimetalism. Before his nomination Hobart
wrote from St. Louis to Jennie in Paterson about the changes
likely to occur in their daily lives:

> When I realize all that it means in work, worry,
> and loss of home and bliss, I am overcome; so over-
> come I am simply miserable.

Jennie's response was cheerful and helpful, and, according
to her pastor, she quoted the reassuring words of Ruth,
"whither thou goest, I will go."

When the news of Garret Hobart's nomination reached
Paterson in the evening of June 18, 1896, "the city became
delirious with joy." The streets beside the Hobart residence
were filled with people, and in her home Mrs. Hobart greeted
friends who came to congratulate her on the honor received
by her husband. Four days later a reception for the nominee was held in the Paterson armory; 15,000 attended and
many more were turned away. Here Hobart spoke feelingly
of his long residence in Paterson:

> Whatever character I have has been made in the
> city of Paterson, and belongs here. Whatever of
> repute I have, or whatever I shall have conferred
> upon me, is due to my association with the people
> of the city of Paterson, and to their confidence and
> esteem.

On March 2, 1897, the vice-president-elect, his family
and a few close friends went to the railroad station in Paterson, where "a great crowd" had assembled to "say good-by
and God-speed." In Washington the Hobart party was met
by members of the Reception Committee and driven to the
Arlington Hotel, the residence of two leading Republicans,
Mark Hanna and Tom Platt. Soon after Hobart had occupied
his hotel suite, he received a courtesy call from Vice-
President Adlai E. Stevenson, and this was followed by a
request from President-elect McKinley for his prospective
vice-president to call on him at the Ebbitt House.

A fine old mansion on Lafayette Square, Senator Cameron's home, known as the Cream White House, then came
on the market. When it appeared that the Cameron mansion
might be replaced by a theater, the home was offered to
the government as the official residence for the vice-
president. A bill to achieve this end passed in the Senate
but died in the House. Fortunately, Hobart was able to
lease the Cream White House which could comfortably

accommodate large parties and was located a few hundred
yards from the White House.

Jennie Hobart greatly enjoyed her role as a hostess in
Washington, which she wrote thirty years later, "was sensible in those days." Although Congress regularly convened
the first Monday in December, the official social season did
not begin until January, "for December was the Debutante's
month." Official calls were then a ritual, and cards were
left at the homes of Senators, members of the Cabinet,
Supreme Court justices, members of the diplomatic corps,
the chiefs of the Army and Navy, and members of the House
from New Jersey. In order to accomplish this task in one
season, Jennie left her home in her carriage four days a
week and made each day from fifteen to twenty calls.

The fourth day, Wednesday, was Jennie's "official afternoon" when an average of twelve hundred people, most of
them complete strangers, came to her home. The hostess
always asked six ladies of her own age to receive with her
and six "pretty young girls to mingle with the guests."
General Grant's granddaughter, the strikingly beautiful
Julia Grant, was usually present to assist at Mrs. Hobart's
weekly afternoon receptions.

When Jennie Hobart reviewed her social calendar for the
1898/99 season she found that she had attended eighty-nine
dinners, more than forty teas and countless evening receptions and musicales. Dinners were served promptly at eight,
and when the Hobarts were the guests of honor they always
went home at half past ten. When the Hobarts entertained
at dinner, they offered their guests a choice of claret or
champagne and men could have Scotch if they desired.
Jennie never offered a cigarette to a woman in her home,
nor did she "ever hear of a cocktail until the next administration."

Jennie's social life was enlivened by her warm personality and her singular sense of humor. She especially enjoyed the mornings and luncheons for two that she and Mrs.
John Hay had together in the bay window of the Hay dining
room. She usually found that she wasn't bored when her
dinner partner "was merely a Senator"; but, she added,
this was before their election by vote of the people! When
her husband was kept in Washington longer than she liked,

it was because of "that old bugbear," the tariff. Her sallies
sometimes missed their mark. When her husband was about
to be nominated for the vice-presidency, she received in
Paterson a telegram in which an English newspaperman at the
Convention requested a photograph of the prospective nominee. Jennie replied, "I'll send it with pleasure. So sorry
you didn't want mine." This understandably gave the recipient "a shock," for he was an "Englishman who could not
see through an American joke."

        Jennie Hobart showed to special advantage in her so-
cial relations with Mrs. McKinley, who had experienced mo-
mentary seizures of unconsciousness ever since the birth of
her second child. Mrs. McKinley was unable to carry the
social burdens in the White House and turned for help to
Mrs. Hobart, not because she was "Second Lady" but because she was her "good friend." Mrs. McKinley sat in her
receiving lines, and at the suggestion of Jennie Hobart,
held in her lap a bouquet which relieved her of shaking
hands with her guests. After Jennie had left Washington,
she learned in 1901 while on a vacation at Lake Mahonk in
the Catskills that President McKinley was dying from the
wound he had received from an assassin's bullet. Jennie
immediately left with her son for Buffalo and learned on the
train on the way that the president had died. When she
reached the house where the McKinleys had been staying,
Jennie feared that Mrs. McKinley would be in shock but
heard at the door, "Mrs. McKinley is waiting for you."
Jennie and her son stayed with Mrs. McKinley for several
days and then traveled with her on the special train that
bore the late president's body to the Capitol.

        Congress continued to meet in 1899 until late in the
spring when the weather became hot in Washington, and
Vice-President Hobart presided over the Senate day after
day. At the end of the long session, Hobart was exhausted
and went to the winter home of Senator Hanna in Georgia to
recuperate. His health did not improve, and the Hobarts
decided to spend a quiet summer at Normanhurst on the
New Jersey coast near Long Branch, Garret's birthplace.
Jennie knew that her husband's heart ailment was serious,
because she was furnished with medications to administer in
case of sudden seizures. Despite his condition, Hobart in-
sisted on a visit to the president at Plattsburgh, New York,
but the excitement of the trip induced fainting spells and

the vice-president returned on August 25 on a special train
to Normanhurst. On September 20, 1899, Hobart went to
Paterson where he died on November 21.

After the death of the vice-president, the attorney
general traveled to Paterson to learn Mrs. Hobart's wishes
for funeral arrangements. Thirty days of mourning were
to be observed throughout the country, and government
offices were to be closed during the funeral services to be
held in Paterson. Twelve thousand persons viewed the
body of the deceased in his home, Carroll Hall, and the
funeral service, held in the Church of the Redeemer in
Paterson, was attended by two trainloads of dignitaries from
Washington. Among the many tributes spoken at his funeral,
the fairest appraisal came from his pastor and biographer,
David Magie:

> He had gained no great victories over his coun-
> try's foes; he had done no great deeds of renown,
> but he had won the hearts of men, the truest meas-
> ure of a true man.

Paterson honored its famous citizen by erecting a
bronze statue of Hobart to stand beside that of Alexander
Hamilton in the plaza in front of the City Hall. The unveiling on June 3, 1903, was attended by ten thousand persons
who heard Senator Lodge of Massachusetts recognize the
care with which Hobart had presided over the Senate, "He
restored the Vice-Presidency to its proper position."

Jennie Hobart spent her widowhood among friends in
Paterson. Her son, Garret Jr., and his wife presented
Jennie with a grandson on August 24, 1907, whom they
dutifully named Garret, III. During World War I, Jennie
led many Patersonians in relief efforts for helpless Belgians.
A decoration for her efforts came fifteen years later, and
the actual presentation of the royal medal and citation must
have warmed Jennie's heart. At the special dinner given in
honor of Mrs. Hobart, the flags of Belgium and the United
States were carried into the banquet hall by her two grand-
daughters, and the girls were followed by more than thirty
of Jennie's dearest friends and relatives. Garret Hobart
had received a Doctor of Laws from his alma mater, Rutgers
University, and Jennie was awarded an honorary degree from
the New Jersey College for Women at commencement in 1933.

Before the honors came to Jennie from King Albert
and from the New Jersey College for Women, her son persuaded her to put into writing some of her recollections "in
order that his children may know something of the life which
their grandfather and I led in Washington." Her efforts
produced two delightful and handsomely printed publications
entitled Memories (1930) and Second Lady (1933). No other
"Second Lady" has left such charming vignettes of society
in Washington during her husband's term in office as vice-
president of the United States.

Jennie Tuttle Hobart stayed on in Carroll Hall in Paterson until ill health forced her to leave the mansion and to
join her son in nearby Haledon. She died at the age of
ninety-one in her son's home on January 8, 1941, and was
buried beside her late husband in the Hobart family vault in
Cedar Lawn cemetery at Paterson.

PRINCIPAL SOURCES

Jennie Tuttle Hobart. Memories. Paterson, N.J.: Privately
    printed, 1930. 89 p.

_____. Second Lady. New York: Privately printed,
    1933. 36 p.

David Magie. Life of Garret Augustus Hobart, Twenty-
    fourth Vice-President of the United States. New York:
    Putnam's, 1910. 300 p.

THEODORE ROOSEVELT, 1901

Theodore Roosevelt (1858-1919) was the son
of wealthy and socially prominent New Yorkers.
The boy received elementary education at home
and made with his family in 1869-1870 and
again in 1872 long trips to Europe. After
graduation with honors from Harvard in 1880,
Theodore began the study of law but did not
like it and turned to the writing of history
and to politics. His early successes in each
were the publication in 1882 of The Naval War
of 1812 and election in 1881 to the New York
State Assembly where he made his mark in
three crowded years, 1882-1884.

The deaths of his mother and of his young
wife on the same day in February of 1884
caused Roosevelt to seek relief from anguish
in hunting and ranching in South Dakota. In
addition to these new pursuits, about which
he wrote with verve, Roosevelt continued to
write books on American history and biographies. Nevertheless, he yearned for a career
in politics and government, and in 1889 Roosevelt became a member of the United States
Civil Service Commission. After a much publicized term as a police commissioner in New
York City, Roosevelt obtained an appointment
as assistant secretary of the Navy, a post in
which he moved energetically to strengthen
the fleet for the impending conflict with Spain.

The outbreak of the War gave the dynamic
Roosevelt an opportunity to serve his country
in uniform and to gain fame which helped him
to become governor of New York and vice-
president of the United States. The assassination of President McKinley placed Roosevelt

in the presidency on September 14, 1901. In
the office, Roosevelt made dramatic moves
toward reform in interstate commerce, adulter-
ation of food and drugs, and conservation of
natural resources. He selected his successor,
William Howard Taft of Ohio, and soon disagreed with his conservative policies. After
his return from fourteen months spent in
Africa and Europe, Roosevelt led a factional
struggle within the Republican party, which
resulted in the victory in 1912 of the Democratic candidate, Woodrow Wilson. During
1913 Roosevelt made an exploration of the
Brazilian jungle where he encountered a
tropical infection from which he never fully
recovered. The exhausted advocate of "the
strenuous life" died in his sleep at his home
in Oyster Bay, New York, on January 6, 1919.

*   *   *

Three weeks after Roosevelt left the presidency early in
March of 1909, he and his son Kermit waved goodbye to
Edith, his second wife, and began their year-long expedi-
tion in Africa. Edith had packed for her husband nine
spare pairs of glasses, a supply of medicine, and thirty-
seven literary classics bound in "jungle-proof" pigskin.
The titles included several of her favorites, Spenser's
Fairie Queene and Bacon's Essays, as well as his, the
Nibelungenlied, Rob Roy, and Bret Harte's Luck of Roaring
Camp. The trip had appealed to Roosevelt because it would
give his comparatively colorless successor, William Howard
Taft, a free opportunity in which to establish his own administration and would provide the former president with
superb opportunities for hunting big game and for collecting
zoological specimens (thirteen thousand!) for the Smithsonian
Institution and the American Museum of Natural History.
Also, Scribner's had agreed to pay Roosevelt handsomely
for articles written during his trip and for expanding them
into a book after his return.

Instead of returning to the United States immediately
after his African safari, Roosevelt planned to have Edith
join him, and together they would accept some of the enthusiastic invitations to visit which had come from royalty

and other admiring people in Europe. Edith and her daughter Ethel met Roosevelt and Kermit at Khartoum in the Sudan
on March 14, 1910, and the four Roosevelts began a tour of
Europe which evoked large popular demonstrations. While
they were in Sweden, the English King Edward VII died,
and Roosevelt was asked by President Taft to be his special
ambassador at the funeral to be held in St. George's Chapel
at Windsor. Regardless of the solemnity of the service and
the presence of many other dignitaries, including Kaiser
Wilhelm, the late King's nephew, Roosevelt was the center
of attention.

     In the White House President Taft pondered the rea-
sons for the demonstrations of affection and admiration shown
his predecessor:

          I don't suppose there was ever such a reception
          as that being given Theodore in Europe now. It
          does not surprise me that rulers, potentates, and
          public men should pay him honor, but what does
          surprise me is that small villages which one would
          hardly think had ever heard of the United States
          should seem to know all about the man.... It is
          the force of his personality that has passed beyond
          his own country and the capitals of the world and
          seeped into the small crevices of the universe.

     Theodore Roosevelt's personality was nurtured in a
strong home environment. His father, Theodore Senior,
was a handsome, energetic man who became wealthy through
business and real estate; and his mother, a Bulloch from
Georgia, was a beautiful woman who was fastidious about her
person and her home. The other children, Anna (called
"Bamie"), Elliott, and Corinne had ailments, as did young
Theodore; and their parents, especially their father, tried
to improve their health. He had a back bedroom next to
the nursery converted into a gymnasium, and here his sickly
children tried to strengthen their bodies.

     The family spent a year in Europe in 1869-70, and in
1872 the Roosevelts left New York "for another terrible trip"
abroad. Before going to Europe, the Roosevelt children had
received elementary instruction from their mother's sister,
Annie, and Theodore had developed his extraordinary early
interest in natural history. He pursued these interests

abroad, but was obliged on his return from his second trip
to study under an able tutor in order to qualify for admission to Harvard in 1876. Theodore worked hard for a year
and a half to become proficient in subjects that he had neglected, and he gave additional attention to building a strong
body which he believed he would need away at college.

At Harvard young Roosevelt impressed his classmates
with his proficiency in many and varied activities. As a
freshman Theodore attended classes regularly, continued his
programs of physical exercise, "hunted in the woods around
Cambridge, taught in Sunday school, stuffed and dissected
his specimens, organized a whist club, took part in poetry-
reading sessions, followed the Harvard football team to
Yale ... and, in time-honored undergraduate fashion, ca-
roused with his friends." At the same time Theodore discovered girls, and his odd appearance and mannerisms were
concealed in part by stylish clothes and social activities.
In his junior year Theodore had settled into his routine of
recitation, study, exercise, and "sprees," when he became
a member of the Porcellian club, the most prestigious on
campus. Among its members was Dick Saltonstall, who invited the new "Porc man" to the family home on Chestnut
Hill, six miles away. Close by the Saltonstall mansion was
the home of George Cabot Lee, a partner in Lee Higgin-
son & Co. in Boston. The Saltonstalls had a daughter,
Rose, and her best friend was Alice Hathaway Lee, age
seventeen, tall (five feet, seven inches) and erect, with
honey colored hair.

In their first meeting on October 18, 1878, Alice
charmed Theodore with her sweet appearance and pleasant
manners; and after a few subsequent visits, he resolved
soon after Thanksgiving that he would make her his wife.
Lovely Alice was not to be won without a campaign; and,
the following summer, Theodore trained his mount, Light-
foot, to draw a carriage. When he returned to Cambridge
for his senior year, the young man purchased the first dog-
cart seen at Harvard, and set out to win the fair maiden.
He hoped that Alice would accept his proposal before her
debut in December, but she waited until January to do so.
Their engagement was not announced immediately, but with
family approval their wedding was set for a date late in
October, 1880. By then Theodore had graduated from Harvard, magna cum laude, had begun a book on a technical

subject, The Naval War of 1812, and had made with brother
Elliott his first hunting trip in the West.

After a brief and ecstatic honeymoon at Oyster Bay
on Long Island, the newly married couple settled into their
home at 6 West Fifty-seventh Street in New York City.
Theodore enrolled in the Columbia Law School, spent many
an afternoon in the Astor Library writing his book on naval
history, and in the evenings he went often to Morton Hall,
the Republican headquarters in the Twenty-first District.
Meanwhile, Alice enjoyed the entertainment available to the
wealthy in New York, and she soon became an intimate of
Theodore's sister, Corinne. She asked Corinne why, when
everybody else was so cordial, she could not seem to get
anywhere with Edith Carow. Presumably, Alice did not know
that her husband and Edith had been sweethearts before he
left for college and that their relationship had ended abruptly after a lovers' quarrel in the summerhouse at Oyster Bay
late in August of 1878.

Theodore's visits to Morton Hall led to his nomination
on October 28, 1881, to a seat in the New York State Assembly, and he was elected to the place about two weeks
later. His career in a political office began when he arrived in Albany in the afternoon of January 2, 1882, and
he made his dramatic entrance in stylish attire that very
evening. Alice looked for rooms in Albany for her husband
and herself but concluded that she would be happier among
friends in her new home on West 45th Street in New York.
Theodore could visit her on weekends, and this he did
regularly during sessions of the Assembly. Theodore attracted attention and supporters as an Assemblyman through
his foppish clothes, his nervous and demanding calls of
"Mister-Spee-kar!" and his charges of corruption in government by "the wealthy criminal class." He served as Minority leader in the 1883 session, but he failed in 1884 in his
effort to become the speaker for the Assembly.

Alice had become pregnant in the spring of 1883, and
the event caused Roosevelt to plan a mansion with twelve
bedrooms on Oyster Bay. He purchased additional acres in
August, and in September he left for the West to hunt buffalo. While in South Dakota he did kill a splendid specimen,
and he agreed to commit a third of his inheritance from his
father of $125,000 to a risky cattle-raising venture. When

Alice reached the ninth month of her pregnancy, she was
understandably depressed with her husband's long absence
in the Dakota country; and, when he was at home, with
his preoccupation with the contest for the speakership.
Roosevelt solved the problem by moving his wife to 6 West
Fifty-seventh Street where she would have the company of
her mother-in-law, Mittie, and her husband's two sisters,
the ever faithful Bamie and Corinne, now Mrs. Robinson,
who had recently had a baby herself. The two young wom-
en planned to run a nursery for both children on the third
floor.

Theodore was in New York City in early February of
1884, but he returned to Albany on Tuesday, February 12,
to push for the passage of his reform bills. Corinne was
away and his mother was ill with what seemed to be a cold.
He knew that his wife's baby was due soon, but reliable
Bamie was in the house, Alice's parents were in a hotel in
the City, brother Elliott was but a few blocks away, and
the family doctor was within call. The baby was born during the night of the 12th, and early the next morning Theodore received congratulations from colleagues in the Assembly. The telegram with the news of the birth of his daughter stated that his wife was "only fairly well," but there
did not seem to be reason for concern. After the receipt
of a second telegram, Roosevelt's expression changed, and
he hurried to catch the next train to New York. When he
finally reached home, his wife was comatose; she was dying
of Bright's disease and could scarcely recognize her husband.
On the floor below, his mother was dying from acute typhoid
fever. The two women died within a few hours of each other
on St. Valentine's Day. Elliott told Corinne when she arrived, "There is a curse on this house." Theodore wrote
in his diary under a large cross, "The light has gone out
of my life."

Roosevelt's wife and mother died on February 14, 1884,
and a funeral for the deceased pair was held on February
16. On the day after the funeral, Roosevelt's daughter,
Alice Lee, was christened and entrusted to the care of
Bamie, then at age thirty and seemingly destined to be a
spinster. Roosevelt was in a state of shock and showed no
interest in his baby or in the condolences of friends. On
the 18th he returned to Albany to lose himself in the work
of an assemblyman who was chairman of the New York City

Investigating Committee. Through the remainder of the
legislative session in 1884, Roosevelt shuttled between Albany and New York, but his demanding schedule did not
clear his mind. He declined renomination for a fourth term
and began to long for the open skies of the Bad Lands in
South Dakota.

Roosevelt continuously advocated the "strenuous life,"
and he delighted in his days in the saddle, his dangerous
hunting exploits, and his struggle to make a profit from
cattle ranches in South Dakota. Roosevelt managed to write
a biography of Missouri Senator Thomas Hart Benton during
lulls in activity on the range, and he lived the experiences
which he recounted with relish in Hunting Trips of a Ranch-
man and Ranch Life and the Hunting Trail. Roosevelt's
biographies of Benton and Gouvernour Morris did not receive
high praise, and the author yearned "to write some book
that would really take rank as in the very first class."
This led him to undertake a major historical work in four
volumes, The Winning of the West, which occupied him, off
and on, for nine years. As governor, with a few spare
weeks in front of him, he decided to write a life of Oliver
Cromwell. Roosevelt dictated paragraphs of his Cromwell
to one stenographer while dictating gubernatorial correspondence to another. On one occasion, while dictating to two
stenographers on different subjects, Roosevelt sat for a bar-
ber who was trying to give him a shave.

Theodore returned from the Bad Lands in September
of 1885 to aid in the New York gubernatorial campaign.
When Theodore was at Bamie's home, Edith, his former
sweetheart, kept away; but through accident or contrivance
the young couple met there one day nineteen months after
the death of Alice. The pair had known each other, almost
like brother and sister, for twenty-one years, and this sudden encounter brought to the surface a great deal of long-
suppressed emotion. Soon thereafter Theodore began to
call on Edith at her home, and he was impressed with her
self-control and maturity. In November Theodore proposed
marriage to Edith who promptly accepted. Their engagement
was to be held in secret, mainly because Theodore had been
a widower for less than two years and did not ordinarily
approve of second marriages. "They argued weakness in a
man's character," wrote Theodore, whose ardor overcame his
reasoning. The wedding was to be held in London since

Edith's mother and sister had moved to Europe to save expense, and Theodore and his sister Bamie sailed on November 6 for England. On board the ship Theodore met a
British diplomat named Cecil Spring-Rice who agreed to
serve as best man. The marriage ceremony was performed
on December 2 at St. George's church in Hanover Square
where Edith identified herself in the register as a twenty-
five year-old spinster without a profession and the groom
set down that he was twenty-eight, a widower, and, by
profession, a rancher.

In the few months immediately before his wedding to
Edith, Theodore urged Bamie to continue to keep Baby Alice
after his forthcoming marriage, but in this he was over-
ruled by his second wife. When the newlyweds disembarked
in New York on March 27, 1887, they went straight to Bamie's house at 689 Madison Avenue where they lived until
May. There they met three-year-old Alice in her best dress
and sash who handed her stepmother a bunch of pink roses.
Edith settled in and became acquainted with her stepdaughter while Theodore entertained two friends from Washington
who had come to New York to welcome the two Roosevelts.
One was Cecil Spring-Rice, the best man at Theodore's wedding, and the other was Henry Cabot Lodge, congressman
from Massachusetts and Theodore's associate at the 1884
Republican Convention.

Baby Alice became the attractive and spirited "Princess Alice" while her father was the president, and she was
married in a wedding in the White House to Nicholas Longworth, congressman from Ohio. He was her senior by fifteen years, and when she became pregnant at the age of
forty-one there were rumors in Washington about the pater-
nity of her child. Nicholas Longworth became speaker of
the House about the time he became a father, and he continued to serve in Congress until his death from an attack
of pneumonia in 1931. His widow, who lived on in Washington until her death in 1980 at age ninety-six, became a
prominent hostess and a quotable commentator on political
figures and affairs.

Alice wrote in her popular Crowded Hours (1953) and
spoke freely in her conversations with Michael Teague published under the title Mrs. L. (1981) about her troubled
relationships with her father and stepmother. After the

death of his first wife, Theodore permitted himself to act as
if she had never lived, and his conduct caused bewilderment
in their child. Her name (the same as her mother's) was
seldom spoken, and Edith tried to bridge the gap by refer-
ring to her stepdaughter as "Sister" in letters to members
of her and her husband's family. Strong-willed Alice, who
had been spoiled by her maternal grandparents with whom
she spent three weeks in every spring and fall, was not
easy to bring up. In her autobiography, published while
her stepmother was still alive, Alice summarized the problem
(which should not have been a problem):

> That I was the child of another marriage was a
> simple fact and made a situation which had to be
> coped with, and Mother coped with it with a fairness
> and charm and intelligence which she has to a great-
> er degree than almost anyone else I know.

When Edith became mistress of Sagamore Hill, the
twenty-two room mansion on Oyster Bay, she wisely accepted
the heavy masculine decor but appropriated for her own use
a parlor on the first floor. Within a few months Theodore
and Edith developed a pattern of work and recreation which
persisted for years. In the mornings Edith organized her
household, sewed, and answered letters, while Theodore
spent his time writing in his study. Afternoons found them
walking in nearby woods or boating in marshy lagoons and
winding channels. "As Theodore pulled on the oars, Edith
would read aloud from Browning, Thackeray, Matthew Arnold
and other of their favorite authors. Occasionally, on calm
Sundays, they would row clear across Oyster Bay to Christ
Episcopal Church in the village." Edith found complete
satisfaction in these quiet moments with her husband, but
her energetic and loquacious spouse felt a need for additional company.

Edith became pregnant on her honeymoon, and in her
last month of pregnancy Theodore suffered a severe attack
of asthma. During his first wife's pregnancy the prospective
father experienced a return of the asthma and cholera mor-
bus of his childhood which were relieved by a hunting trip
in South Dakota. When Edith became pregnant for the second time, her husband left for another hunting trip. His
wife was understandably depressed for it seemed that "whenever she was pregnant her husband absented himself for

long periods, leaving her with the responsibility for managing his children, his household, his farm, and his finances."
Edith bore her husband five children and proved to be an
exceptional mother. When they were youngsters, ages five
to eighteen, she could write about them to Cecil Spring-Rice
with remarkable detachment:

> I want you to see the children. Alice is exceedingly pretty, and has a remarkably steady head
> though in some ways very child like. Ted is a good
> boy and stands well at school. Kermit is odd and
> independent as always, and Ethel is just a handful.
> She is a replica of Mrs. Cowles [Bamie]. Archie
> we call "the beautiful idiot" and Quentin is the
> cleverest of the six.

Edith's pleasant life as mistress of Sagamore Hill with
her husband engaged in literary work came to an end on
October 3, 1898, when a committee arrived with the official
notice of Theodore's nomination for governor of New York.
After the ceremony Edith served lunch to thirty people, an
act that launched her own public career. After her husband
won the election, she received between five and six thousand
people in the Executive Mansion, and she undertook to make
the long-neglected residence a congenial home for herself
and her family. She joined the Friday Morning Club, a
group of young women who met for companionship and to
listen to papers prepared and read on subjects of current
interest. When an Albany winter became too confining, she
would go by train to Washington for several days of conversation with old friends or to New York for a stimulating round
of musical and theatrical performances.

When Theodore was first mentioned as a possible running mate with President McKinley in his campaign for reelection, Edith opposed the possibility because she enjoyed
her life in Albany and the state office provided a higher
salary than that of the vice-president. Also, the latter had
no official residence. Nevertheless, when the hero of the
Spanish American War was nominated for the office of vice-president at the Republican Convention on June 21, 1900,
Edith, who sat in a gallery box, after "a little gasp of regret ... broke into smiles, as she ... accepted the situation
with a grace worthy of a true patriot."

In the fall of 1900 the team of McKinley and Roosevelt defeated the Democratic candidates, William Jennings Bryan and Adlai Stevenson. The following February Theodore left for an extended hunting trip in the Rockies, and Edith busied herself by writing to her husband almost daily, attending the Oyster Bay sewing guild, studying German, and enjoying opera at the Met. By way of preparation for her removal to Washington, she negotiated the rental of a house in Washington for three thousand dollars a year and engaged a private railroad car to transport the family to Washington for her husband's inauguration.

Theodore intended to use his enforced leisure as vicepresident in the study of law, but his plans changed radically after six months in office. President McKinley was assassinated, and Roosevelt became the twenty-sixth president of the United States on September 14, 1901. He was then forty-two, the youngest man to hold the office of President, Edith was but thirty-nine, and their six children ranged in ages from four (Quentin) to just under eighteen (Alice). In less than three months after moving into the White House, Edith "was clearly in full command of her official duties, at peace with herself, and, above all, having fun." She and Theodore established a daily routine which they followed during his presidential years. After breakfast with the children at eight-fifteen, Edith and her husband walked in the garden until nine. She then went through her mail, read and clipped newspapers, and discussed with the White House steward and maids the work to be done and the meals to be served. On Tuesdays, between eleven and twelve, Edith entertained the wives of Cabinet officers, and at this hour on other weekdays she had lessons in French conversation or went for a drive in her carriage. The president usually brought several guests to lunch, after which she received callers until four when she and her husband rode in Rock Creek Park or in the Virginia countryside. At the end of each afternoon Edith would spent most of an hour talking or reading to the children, and then she would say, "Theodore, it is time to dress for dinner."

The size of the Roosevelt family required extensive rearrangements in the White House, and additional space was to be gained through construction of a new West Wing of Executive offices. The Roosevelt family returned to Oyster Bay for six months during the work of renovation and expansion, and during this period Edith had an active interest in the new arrangements and furnishings. She proposed that portraits of all of the First Ladies, "including myself," be displayed in a downstairs corridor which "could then be called the picture gallery"; for, she told the chief architect, Charles Follen McKim, "you know a name goes a long way." She also hoped that the portraits would be hung on paneled walls which sometimes lend "a certain importance to a portrait."

The former president, his wife, and two of their children received a hearty welcome when their ship from Europe steamed into New York harbor on June 10, 1910. While still on board, Edith received an invitation for her and her husband to visit President and Mrs. Taft "soon after your return," but the Roosevelts declined offering the lame excuse that a former president should not go to Washington when Congress was in session. During his first few weeks at home Roosevelt met with many influential political figures, and on June 30, accompanied by then Senator Henry Cabot Lodge, he met with President Taft in his summer home at Beverly, Massachusetts. Roosevelt sought the chairmanship of the New York State Republican Convention, but, since he did not receive support from President Taft, the post went to Vice-President Sherman. The rift between the two old friends widened, and Roosevelt complained to his eldest son, "Taft is utterly helpless as a leader."

Theodore sought the Republican nomination for the presidency at the Convention held in June of 1912, but Taft won renomination and 344 of Theodore's delegates left the floor and formed a Progressive Party with Roosevelt as its leader. His action which split the Republicans ensured the election in the fall of Woodrow Wilson, the Democratic candidate. Old friends, such as Henry Cabot Lodge remained loyal to Taft, and his daughter and son-in-law wished to support both candidates. Nicholas Longworth went down in defeat along with Roosevelt. The entire year (1912) created so much tension for Edith that she stopped making daily entries in her diary, a practice begun when her husband became the vice-president.

During the years between his major political defeat and the entry of the United States into World War I, Roosevelt focused his energies on writing, an expedition into the

Brazilian wilderness (his "last chance to be a boy"), and
on preparedness for armed conflict with Germany. He had
hoped to lead a regiment of "Rough Riders" into battle in
France, but General Pershing and President Wilson concluded that his military experience was too limited and that
his health could not withstand the rigors of trench warfare.
Their two daughters had married, and their four sons joined
the armed forces. Edith quoted Edwin Arlington Robinson,
whom her husband had appointed to a sinecure, "They have
all gone away from the house on the hill," and concluded,
"it is all quite right and best."

Shortly after his sixtieth birthday, on October 27,
1918, Roosevelt suffered crippling attacks of rheumatism,
and on November 11, Armistice Day, he went to a hospital
because of inflammatory rheumatism. Edith stayed with him
and read Shakespeare at his bedside. After she had finished reading Macbeth, she wrote to son Kermit, "Every line
is familiar, and yet ever new." Roosevelt went home on
Christmas Day, 1918, but his health did not improve. He
died in his sleep two weeks later, on January 6, 1919.

Edith survived her husband by twenty-nine years.
She made a trip to Europe to see two of her sons and to
visit Quentin's grave, and then made a long stay with her
sister at her Italian villa. In order "not to think," Edith
remained in bed until noon, took afternoon walks, studied
Italian, and played rummy with Emily. In May she returned
to live at Sagamore Hill, and, on the sixty-first anniversary
of her husband's birth, Congress awarded her the franking
privilege. An annual pension of five thousand dollars came
from a fund established by Andrew Carnegie and an additional $5,000 per annum came in 1928 from Congress.

In 1927 Edith purchased an old inn, Mortlake Manor,
with Tyler family associations, in Brooklyn, Connecticut,
and she transformed the building into a pleasant retreat
from Sagamore Hill above Oyster Bay. In 1928 she visited
friends in England, and in 1930 she went to Puerto Rico
where her son Ted was the governor. In early 1932 Ted
had been appointed governor-general of the Philippines, and
Edith made the long journey to Manila where she remained
from January 2 until February 1, 1933. Two years later
she made another trip to South America, and in September
of 1935 she delivered a speech on the adoption of the
Constitution to the National Conference of Republican Women.

During the night of November 12, 1935, Edith got up to close a window, fell, and broke her hip. The bone was slow to knit, and she remained in a hospital for five months before she was able to walk a short distance with assistance from a "walker" and a nurse. Her slow recovery was aided in the winter of 1937 by a vacation in Florida where Edith walked daily along the beach and found her spirits lifted by her lovely natural surroundings, bird songs, magnolia, and sunsets over the Gulf of Mexico. She returned to New York in late April, bought a car, and in June traveled to Mortlake where she stayed until early August.

In the winter of 1938 Edith went to Madeira but returned tired, lame, and bothered by heart trouble. In the summer she moved into the new "Old Orchard House" on land adjacent to Sagamore Hill which then was occupied by her eldest son, Ted, and his wife, Eleanor. Relations with Eleanor became strained over small charges, and her son Kermit was unable to overcome his addiction to alcohol. In February of 1939 Edith enjoyed the warm sunshine, but she did not feel fully recovered until summer when she was back in her beloved Mortlake.

In 1941 Ted went to war again in his old regiment, this time as a general, and Kermit was in and out of the British army. In 1942 he was commissioned major in the American army and assigned to duty in the Aleutians where he continued on the road to self-destruction and shot himself on June 4, 1943. Edith penned his epitaph in rhyming couplets:

> Fold in thy Heart that head so bright
> Heal him with Thy most gentle light

Son Ted died in Europe on July 11, 1944, from a heart attack after winning the Congressional Medal of Honor for his heroic leadership in the invasion of Europe, and son Archie was wounded by a grenade after he won a Silver Star for gallantry in the South Pacific. In late 1945, Edith engaged a part-time secretary to help with her correspondence. When the two were walking in the garden, the younger observed, "Mrs. Roosevelt, you've had such a sad life," to which Edith responded, "I have no regrets; it's been a full one."

Toward the end of 1945 Edith made the last entry in
her diary, and in September of 1946 she made a will which
provided that most of her estate would be divided equally
among her daughter, her surviving son, and the widows of
the other two. Stepdaughter Alice had received generous
gifts from her mother's family and would receive a modest
monetary bequest and a Sargent painting of the White House.
After the signing of her will, Edith was largely bedridden,
and she left instructions for a simple funeral, "Do not take
off my wedding ring and please no embalming." Worn out
with pain from arteriosclerosis, she fell into a coma and died
in her eighty-seventh year on September 30, 1948.

Theodore Roosevelt's second wife was a gentle mother
and companion, but she contained elements of great strength.
As a youngster she was a playmate of Theodore and his
brother and sisters, sort of a poor relation, and when she
reached womanhood, Theodore chose to first marry another.
She became his second wife and evoked from him this high
praise:

> ... she has combined to a degree I have never seen
> in any other woman the power of being the best of
> wives and mothers, the wisest manager of the house-
> hold, and at the same time the ideal great lady and
> mistress of the White House.

Edith Carow Roosevelt received her formal education
at Miss Louise Comstack's school on West Fortieth Street
where she was introduced to foreign languages, the natural
sciences, and English literature. The last was a field in
which she read widely and acquired in time a familiarity with
many masterpieces, especially the plays of Shakespeare. At
a dinner party in the White House, Theodore lectured Henry
Adams, an outstanding historian and critic, "as though he
were a high-school pedagogue," but Edith, as usual, "was
very bright and gay." In the same month she wrote to
Cecil Spring-Rice, then a close friend of the Roosevelts:

> Being the centre of things is very interesting,
> yet the same proportions remain. When I read "The
> World is too much with us" ... they mean just what
> they did, so I don't believe I have been forced into
> the "first lady of the land" model of my predecessors.

Yet Edith could be hard and, at times, somewhat cruel. Even after her own financial position enabled her to help her sister, Emily, who lived in Italy for fifty of her seventy-three years, Edith kept her at a long arm's length. And after Christmas in 1913 when son Ted chose to be with business acquaintances instead of joining the family celebration at Sagamore Hill, Edith wrote to her favorite, Kermit, "If he [Ted] was content to be 'a tin pin in a pin cushion,'" she would respect his decision. She continued:

> I realize that each child must lead his or her own life after leaving home and those who don't care to be the pearl in the satin box have at least the right of choice.

On her eightieth birthday Edith was the subject of a congratulatory editorial in the New York Times. Its author noted that Edith possessed "a well-stored mind, a gracious presence and nature, kindness as well as dignity are hers." He concluded rightly, "This is a great as well as a beloved woman."

PRINCIPAL SOURCES

Alice Roosevelt Longworth. Crowded Hours. New York: Scribner's, 1933. 355 p.

_____. Mrs. L. Conversations with Alice Roosevelt Long-worth. Edited by Michael Teague. Garden City, N.Y.: Doubleday, 1981. 203 p.

Edmund Morris. The Rise of Theodore Roosevelt. New York: Coward, McCann & Geoghegan, [1979]. 886p.

Sylvia Jukes Morris. Edith Kermit Roosevelt, Portrait of a First Lady. New York: Coward, McCann & Geoghegan, [1980]. 581 p.

Henry F. Pringle. Theodore Roosevelt, a Biography. New York: Harcourt, Brace, [1931]. 627 p.

CHARLES WARREN FAIRBANKS, 1905-1909

Charles Warren Fairbanks (1852-1918) was
born on a farm in Ohio and attended Ohio Wesleyan University. After graduation in 1872
Fairbanks worked as a reporter in Pittsburgh
and Cleveland, and in the latter he studied
law and was admitted in 1874 to the Ohio bar.
An uncle, who was general manager of the
Chesapeake and Ohio Railroad system, offered
his nephew the post of solicitor for a subsidiary; the opportunity started the young attorney on his way to fame and fortune through
railroad law and investments in Ohio, Indiana,
and Illinois.

After his marriage in 1874 Fairbanks and
his bride decided to live in Indianapolis where
Charles practiced law and undertook in 1894
and again in 1898 to advance his friend Walter Q. Gresham to the presidency. After these
efforts failed, Fairbanks undertook in 1893 to
reorganize the Republican party in Indiana
and persuaded his followers to support William
McKinley in 1896. McKinley's victory led in
1897 to Fairbanks' election to the United States
Senate. Although mentioned as a possible
running mate for McKinley in 1900, the colorless Hoosier had no chance against dynamic
Theodore Roosevelt. Fairbanks was reelected
in 1902 to the Senate, and his victory in Indiana helped him to win in 1904 the second
place on the Republican ticket. Fairbanks
campaigned hard and traveled extensively and
spoke often as vice-president, but his timid
politics and conservative life style never won
the regard of the energetic Roosevelt.

In 1916 Hoosier Republicans supported Fairbanks for the presidency, but the nomination
went to Charles Evans Hughes of New York.
Fairbanks was named for the second place on
the ticket, declined the nomination, and finally
accepted because of party loyalty. Fairbanks'
own state voted Republican in 1916, but the
Democrats won the election. After the United
States entered World War I, Fairbanks made
several speeches in Liberty Loan drives, but
the efforts led to a physical breakdown from
which he did not recover. The former vice-
president died in Indianapolis on June 14,
1918.

*   *   *

Charles Warren Fairbanks and Cornelia Cole became engaged
while they were undergraduates at Ohio Wesleyan University
in Delaware, Ohio. As students in the classical course, the
young couple had ample opportunity in which to become acquainted and to fall in love, because they were co-editors
of the college paper, the Western Collegian. Charles and
Cornelia did not marry until November 4, 1874, two years
after graduation. During this period young Fairbanks
worked as a reporter in Pittsburgh and Cleveland; in the
latter he studied law for six months and was admitted in
May of 1874 to the Ohio bar. Although Cornelia's father offered to build a home for the newly married couple in Marysville, Ohio, Charles and his bride had determined to begin
their life together in Indianapolis, then "a friendly, charming town of about 55,000."

Charles Fairbanks was a descendant of Jonathan Fay-
erbancke, who settled in 1636 in Dedham, Massachusetts.
Charles' father, Loriston Monroe Fairbanks, was a native of
Vermont and worked in a woolen mill in Massachusetts before
he became a farmer in Union county, Ohio, and married
Mary Adelaide Smith of a local pioneer family. Charles was
born on the Ohio farm on May 11, 1852, and three more
children had arrived by 1860. Nevertheless, when his
father-in-law died, Loriston had his mother-in-law and her
family move into his already crowded home. Charlie's mother
was a short, stout woman who somehow managed to accomplish the endless work required to maintain a large family

on a frontier farm. However, she was concerned about the
education of her children; when Charles was but fourteen
and away from home, she wrote:

> I am so glad to hear you was progressing in
> your studies. I am so anxious that you should
> make a smart and good man I want when you are
> advanced far enough to have you go to College.

At age fifteen Charles and a boyhood chum, Ira Andrews, entered Ohio Wesleyan University where they lived
in a tiny room near the campus for which they paid a dollar
a week. Food and clean laundry came from their parents
who made the trip from Unionville Center to Delaware by
buggy each weekend. Charles enrolled in the regular academic course in which study of Latin and Greek was required. In his junior year, Charles joined Phi Gamma Delta,
a social fraternity in which he was active long after he left
school, but he was not a leader among his fellow students.
Indeed, he seems to have lacked ordinary common sense.
When he first left for college, he promised his mother not
to leave his room after dark. On one occasion he found his
oil can empty and he "had to go down to the grocery to
get some." Consequently, overly serious Charles wrote to
his mother, "Tonight I had to disobey your instruction to
stay off the streets at night."

Cornelia's father, Philander Blaksly Cole, served in
the Ohio House of Representatives from 1850 to 1853 and in
the Ohio Senate from 1866 to 1877, and was a judge in the
Court of Common Pleas in Marysville at the time of his
daughter's wedding. Cornelia's mother, the former Dolly
Barden Whitter, had four children in addition to her attractive twenty-two year old daughter who had auburn hair
and brown eyes. Before she entered Monett Hall, the wom-
en's unit at Ohio Wesleyan University, Cornelia had attended briefly the Young Ladies Seminary at Grenville,
Ohio.

An uncle for whom Charles was named, Charles Warren Smith, was general manager of the Chesapeake and Ohio
Railroad system, and he offered his nephew the position of
solicitor for the Indianapolis, Bloomington and Western Railroad. This appointment started the young attorney on his

way to fame and fortune. Fairbanks lacked brilliance in the
court room, but his work was thorough and he developed
a reputation for diligence and reliability in railroad law.
Railroad receiverships were assigned to him, and these gave
him exceptional opportunities for profitable investments.
Fairbanks purchased farms in Illinois, Indiana, and Ohio,
and businesses in Illinois and Springfield, Ohio, and he pru-
dently entrusted their management to his three brothers and
a brother-in-law. These investments in time made Charles
Warren Fairbanks a millionaire.

Although friends and business associates advised
Fairbanks to keep out of politics, he undertook in 1884 to
promote his good friend, Walter Q. Gresham, for the presidency. This came to naught, and Fairbanks laid plans for
another and stronger effort in 1888. Gresham made a poor
showing in the Republican National Convention in 1888 which
nominated Harrison; Fairbanks campaigned strenuously for
Harrison but in 1891 he met in Indianapolis with other supporters of Gresham to plan future strategy.

Fairbanks' political career covered the "Golden Age of
Indiana Politics." Between 1868 and 1916 "eleven major national tickets bore the name of a Hoosier--all vice presidential
candidates except Benjamin Harrison.... It was during this
period that Indiana won the title, 'Mother of Vice Presidents.'"
The game had a special fascination for Hoosiers. Archibald
Butts, military aide to presidents Roosevelt and Taft, knew
the Washington scene; but a visit to Indiana prompted him
to write, "One really does not know what politics is until
one gets on the inside of Indiana and sees the situation from
the center."

When Judge Gresham denounced the high tariff policy
of the Republicans, he eliminated himself from the contest
for the party's nomination in 1892. This left Fairbanks free
to support President Harrison which he did without much
enthusiasm. After the Democratic victory and Grover Cleveland's return to the White House in 1893, Fairbanks undertook to reorganize the Republican party in Indiana, and he
and other Hoosier leaders brought their followers to support
William McKinley of Ohio. In recognition of Fairbanks' help,
he was named temporary chairman of the Convention in St.
Louis which nominated McKinley for the presidency.

The Republican victory in 1896 sent McKinley to the
White House, made James A. Mount governor of Indiana, and
led in February of 1897 to Fairbanks' election to the United
States Senate. Although Fairbanks' positions on a gold
standard, high tariffs, and other Republican tenets were
well known, he as a Senator was always "cautious, reserved
and calm." Herbert J. Rissler, who wrote a dissertation on
Fairbanks which was accepted in 1961 at Indiana University
declared:

> To many observers, Fairbanks' most exasperating
> trait was his reluctance to take a stand on major
> political issues.... His political utterances were
> thus normally composed of meaningless platitudes
> which revolved about patriotism and Republicanism.

"If a hen laid a two-yolked egg, it was suggested that Fairbanks would probably ascribe it to the ascendency of the
Republican party."

Fairbanks attendance record as a senator was excellent; he was absent but three times in eight years. As a
dispenser of patronage, he was careful to reward special interest groups and those individuals who would strengthen
his party organization in Indiana. As chairman of the Immigration Committee, Fairbanks introduced several bills designed to curb immigration, but none became law. President
McKinley named Fairbanks chairman of the American delegation on the Joint-High Commission to resolve the Alaskan
boundary dispute with Canada, but in this role the Indiana
senator was too concerned about the effect any agreement
might have on his own political future. Fairbanks did travel to Alaska with his wife and son Robert, but the dispute
was not settled until 1903 after the British Chief Justice,
Lord Alverstone, supported the American position.

The death of Vice-President Garret A. Hobart in November 1899 provoked a great deal of speculation about who
might become President McKinley's running mate in 1900.
McKinley refused to name his preference, and Fairbanks was
mentioned as a strong candidate along with Secretary of the
Navy John D. Long and Secretary of the Interior Cornelius
Bliss. During the Republican National Convention in June,
1900, the Chicago Tribune extolled the social attributes of
Senator Fairbanks and his wife:

The Fairbanks are skilled entertainers, have
enough money to see them through socially, and
would fill the gap the Hobarts left behind them.
Mrs. Fairbanks, in fact, is one of the most popular
hostesses at the capital, being charming, decidedly
handsome, and has considerable tact.

Fairbanks was no match for the dynamic Theodore
Roosevelt who appeared at the Convention in a cowboy hat
and won the nomination for vice-president. The hapless
senator from Indiana, as chairman of the Resolution Committee, had to read the long platform to the delegates, and he
read it poorly. The Philadelphia Record characterized the
reaction of the delegates to Fairbanks' performance as a
"pitiable scene," and the New York Journal disparaged Fairbanks as "Colorless."

As their financial situation improved, Charles and
Cornelia Fairbanks bettered their living arrangements and
moved up on the social ladder. Their first residence in Indianapolis was a modest house on the corner of Park Avenue
and Seventh Street, and in 1881 they moved into a new
house at 1608 Park Avenue where their five children were
born. In 1904 the Fairbanks family moved again, this time
to 1522 North Meridian Street, and seven years later Fairbanks began the construction of a palatial home in Indianapolis with twenty-six rooms and a large center hall, seventy-
five feet long and twelve feet wide. While in Washington
the family lived in the Van Wycke mansion near Dupont Circle which was admirably arranged for large parties. Their
two older children attended the college of their parents,
Ohio Wesleyan University, but the three younger boys attended prestigious schools in the Ivy League.

Charles Fairbanks was tall, six feet and two or three
inches, and very slender. His face was thin and elongated,
and he had a rosy complexion which was partly concealed by
a mustache and chin whiskers. His lean and lanky appearance was accentuated by his customary black Prince Albert
coat which reached his knees and was always buttoned in
public. He normally wore a vest, gray ribbed trousers, a
black string tie, and patent leather shoes. Fairbanks wore
very little jewelry, the most prominent piece was a long,
linked gold watch chain worn about his neck. The total effect, one wag remarked, would "turn an undertaker green
with envy."

Cornelia was an "uncommonly handsome woman" who enjoyed social and club life. Her home in Indiana held in 1885 the first meeting of the Indianapolis Fortnightly Club, and she became its first president. In 1889 she became the first woman member of the Indiana State Board of Charities, a post in which she served for four years. In 1901 she became president-general of the Daughters of the American Revolution, an office which made Mrs. Fairbanks almost as well known as her husband. During her term as the head of the D.A.R., the organization's "Centennial Hall" in Philadelphia was completed, and after her death one of the D.A.R. chapters in Indianapolis was named in her honor.

President McKinley's death on September 14, 1901, "proved to be a watershed in Fairbanks' career." The accession of Theodore Roosevelt to the presidency brought a new era in which Fairbanks was out of his element. In 1902 Fairbanks campaigned vigorously for relection to his Senate seat, and the successful outcome made him a leading candidate to become President Roosevelt's running mate in 1904. Nicholas Murray Butler, president of Columbia University, queried Roosevelt about Fairbanks' suitability for the second place on the ticket, and the man in the White House responded with a question of his own, "Who in the name of heaven else is there?"

Fairbanks had made no enemies, and his party believed that his name would strengthen the ticket, especially since Indiana was thought to be a doubtful state. After Fairbanks received the nomination for vice-president he visited almost every one of the Northern states and he traveled to the Pacific coast. Fairbanks had reserved the last week of the campaign for a final effort in Indiana. The 1,500 mile tour of Indiana went according to plan except for an incident in Evansville where someone brought bottled beer aboard Fairbanks' campaign train. Fairbanks promptly and publicly denounced this single transgression. The Republican ticket of Roosevelt and Fairbanks overwhelmed the Democrats, Alton B. Parker of New York and Henry C. Davis of West Virginia, then in his eighty-second year.

As vice-president, Fairbanks traveled about 65,000 miles and delivered more than seven hundred speeches, but he never won the regard of the president. On Memorial Day in 1907 Roosevelt was in Indianapolis to speak at the unveiling of a memorial for a Spanish-American War hero, and Vice-President and Mrs. Fairbanks hosted a lawn party and luncheon for the president and forty guests. A caterer furnished the luncheon, and someone produced cocktails, at least one of which was enjoyed by the president; Fairbanks was a teetotaler, and he was active in the Methodist church which banned alcoholic beverages. Fairbanks received a reprimand from his church for serving cocktails, and Roosevelt rightly considered the incident unworthy of serious comment. Roosevelt enjoyed repeating the response of "Mr. Dooley" when told that the president was thinking of going down in a submarine, "Well you really shouldn't do it, unless you take Fairbanks with you."

In the month after he left the vice-presidency, Fairbanks, his wife Cornelia, and daughter Adelaide began a world tour. They sailed from San Francisco on a Japanese liner to Hawaii where Fairbanks addressed the territorial legislature, and then to Japan where the visitors were guests of the Emperor. The party of three then visited Korea, Manchuria, and the Philippines, and on Christmas Eve in 1909 they were in the city of Bethlehem. The Fairbanks were the guests of the Sultan of Turkey in Constantinople and of the King of Greece in Athens. The former vice-president had arranged for an audience with Pope Pius X, but the meeting was not held since Fairbanks had agreed to address a Methodist missionary group in Rome. After Rome Fairbanks met with Kaiser Wilhelm in Berlin, and then the party spent two weeks in London where they were entertained by the Prince of Wales at a luncheon. On March 12, 1910, the three Fairbankses sailed for home on the British liner Mauretania, and eleven days later they arrived in New York. They had been out of the country for eleven months.

In the month of his return to the United States, Fairbanks declined President Taft's request to represent his country at the Argentine centennial celebration in Buenos Aires, and there were rumors that he had been offered ministerial posts and that of chief delegate to the Pan American Conference. In early December the former Vice-President and Mrs. Fairbanks spent several days in the White House as guests of President and Mrs. Taft, and on July 4 of the next year President Taft celebrated the holiday with Fairbanks and his wife in Indianapolis. In December of 1912 President Taft moved to appoint his Hoosier friend Ambassador

to the Court of St. James, but the vacancy was not filled
because only two months remained of Taft's term in office.

Cornelia's health must have declined soon after she
returned from her trip around the world, because provision
was made for an elevator for her use in the mansion which
was built in 1911-13 for the former vice-president and his
wife. The house was completed in 1913 and occupied when
word went on October 23, 1913, to members of her family
that Cornelia Fairbanks was critically ill. She died of
pneumonia on the 24th, and in her obituary in the New
York Times she was identified as one of the best-known
women in the country. Her important work for the Daughters of the American Revolution received special praise.

After the death of Cornelia, Charles confronted in-
activity and boredom. He read historical works occasionally,
but he had few other diversions. Fairbanks had little interest in most outdoor sports, and his connection with
strict Methodism kept him from playing cards and enjoying
convivial company. Worst of all, the widower had very few
personal friends. Although he had spent decades in business and politics, he was not one to share confidences and
no intimate friendships developed. "He was suspicious by
nature and unwilling to unburden his soul to any one for
fear of betrayal."

Looking forward to the Republican National Convention
in 1916, leaders of the party recognized the need for winning the electoral votes of Indiana, and the best way to
achieve this end would be to have a Hoosier on the national
ticket. The Indiana delegates agreed to support Fairbanks
for the presidency, and his candidacy was supported by the
Los Angeles Times. According to this newspaper, Fairbanks "has the confidence of the business world. And what
we need in this country today is a revival of business confidence."

The enthusiasm of the Indiana delegation did not win
votes for Fairbanks, and the nomination for president went
on the third ballot to Charles Evans Hughes of New York.
Many of the delegates at the Convention thought that Fairbanks would be ideal for second place on the ticket. When
Fairbanks learned that his name might be presented to the
Convention for the vice-presidential nomination, he stated

clearly in telegrams to his manager, "My name must not be considered for Vice President and if it is presented, I wish it withdrawn." The Convention chose to disregard Fairbanks considered statement and proceeded to nominate him by a large majority on the first ballot. Fairbanks accepted the nomination in a telephone conversation, but he did so without enthusiasm. His loyalty to the Republican Party probably was the decisive factor in his decision to accept the nomination he didn't want, but he was encouraged to do so by his daughter who hoped to return to Washington. Fairbanks campaigned throughout the country and Indiana voted Republican, but the Democrats, Wilson and Marshall, won the close election.

After the United States entered World War I, Fairbanks wanted to help in the war effort. Governor James Goodrich appointed Fairbanks to the Indiana State Council of Defense in May of 1917, and in the fall Secretary of the Treasury William McAdoo induced the former vice-president to make several speeches in support of the second Liberty Loan campaign. This effort led to a physical breakdown from which Fairbanks never recovered. He traveled in the winter to visit his son in Pasadena where Fairbanks hoped to recuperate. On his return to Indianapolis, Fairbanks kept to his bed until his death three weeks later on June 14, 1918. His physician attributed his death "to an apoplectic attack" induced by his chronic nephritis.

During his last years, Fairbanks remained an enigma to persons outside of his family. To outsiders "he appeared cold, reserved, and dispassionate"; to his critics, "he continued to seem arrogant, aloof, and conniving." Former President Taft who valued Fairbanks' qualities wrote a letter of condolence to the family:

> He was said to be cold; this was most unjust. He was genial, kindly, hospitable and human.... Since Mr. Fairbanks' retirement and my own I came to know him well and to value highly his very exceptional qualities as a public-spirited citizen and as a man I greatly mourn his death.

PRINCIPAL SOURCE

Herbert J. Rissler. Charles Warren Fairbanks: Conserva-
     tive Hoosier. Ph.D. dissertation accepted by Indiana
     University, 1961. 298 l.

JAMES S. SHERMAN, 1909–1912

James Schoolcraft Sherman (1855-1912) was born in Utica, New York, and was a graduate in 1878 from Hamilton College. A year later Sherman received a law degree from Hamilton and joined his brother-in-law's firm, but his interests were in business and politics. At age twenty-nine Sherman became mayor of Utica and limited his practice to advising clients in business matters. Sherman was a member of Congress from 1887-1891 and from 1893-1909, but his name is not linked to any important legislation. Sherman made himself an expert in parliamentary procedures and proved to be an excellent presiding officer. His rulings were fair and impartial, and he was adept and courteous in personal relations.

After the Republican National Committee in 1908 had nominated William H. Taft of Ohio for the presidency, Elihu Root of New York declined the second place on the ticket. Sherman wanted the nomination and managed to obtain "Uncle Joe" Cannon to present his name to the Convention. "Sunny Jim" received the nomination, and the Republicans won in 1908. The vice-president cut a fine figure as presiding officer of the Senate, and he and his wife conducted their social obligations admirably.

Shortly after he became vice-president, Sherman learned that he was afflicted with Bright's disease, a kidney disorder which obliged him at times to leave the chair in the Senate. Nevertheless, Sherman accepted renomination to his office, and he exhausted

himself when he spoke for thirty minutes on August 31 to the Republican Convention notification
committee. The vice-president never fully recovered from the effects of this effort and died
of uremic poisoning in Utica on October 30, 1912.

*   *   *

According to Speaker Champ Clark, "Amiability was the chief
characteristic" of James Schoolcraft Sherman who served for
twenty years in the House of Representatives before he became the vice-president when Taft became president. Sherman deserved his sobriquet, "Sunny Jim," for he was "sunny in appearance, in speech, in thought, in feeling." This
vice-president, declared Senator Charles Curtis of Kansas,
had more friends throughout the United States than "any
other one living American," yet he is today a figure devoid
of a complete personality. His face is that of a banker;
the contours are rounded and the mien is genial and self-
assured.

A photograph of the vice-president's wife, Carrie Babcock Sherman, in the gown worn at the ball that followed
her husband's inauguration, reveals a regal Victorian lady.
The accompanying biographical note in the Good Housekeep-
ing magazine for March, 1910, records that Mrs. Sherman
always provided her servants with comfortable quarters.
These, including a "servant's sitting room," they enjoyed
in the Shermans' home in Utica, New York; and the vice-
president's wife would not agree to lease an imposing house
in Washington because she was not satisfied with the accom-
modations for servants. The mistress of the Sherman resi-
dences had no trouble with domestics; they left her only to
marry or to die. "Her gentle manners endear her to every
one she meets, but in her home she is beloved."

James Schoolcraft Sherman was born in Utica, New
York on October 24, 1855. His grandfather, Willett Sherman, left a small fortune which he had made as a glass manufacturer and was said to be the proud owner of forty-six
fancy waistcoats. His interest in sartorial elegance reap-
peared in the handsome attire worn by his famous grandson.
The boy's father, Richard Updike Sherman, was an editor
of newspapers in Rochester and in Utica and was an active
Democratic politician and holder of minor offices in the state

and national governments. He understandably disapproved
of his son's entry into politics as a Republican.

Son James was a graduate of Hamilton College in the
class of 1878, and a year later he received a law degree
from the same institution. After his admission to the bar,
young Sherman joined the law firm of his brother-in-law,
but his interests lay in business and in politics. He became
mayor of Utica at the age of twenty-nine, and he limited his
law practice to advising clients in business matters. In
1887, he married Carrie Babcock, a resident of Utica who
had been born in East Orange, New Jersey. She attended
school in Utica, and, according to one account, it was there
that she met her future husband. The couple were married
in 1887 and had three sons who became prominent in business
in Utica and in New York City.

Although Sherman was a Member of Congress from 1886
until 1908 except for the years 1890-1892, his name is not
linked to any major legislation. The congressman made himself an expert in parliamentary law, and he proved to be
adept as a presiding officer in the House and, as vice-
president, in the Senate. His procedural rulings were fair
and impartial, and Sherman earned the respect of his colleagues. In personal relations he was unmatched. He went
out of his way to greet new members of Congress, and he
never exhibited ill temper or rancor. In courtesy Sherman
"rivaled Lord Chesterfield," yet he was enough of a good
fellow to attend regularly poker games at the "Boar's Nest."
Participants in the sessions included "Uncle Joe" Cannon
and two other future vice-presidents, Charles Curtis of
Kansas and John Nance Garner of Texas.

After the Republican National Convention in 1908 had
nominated Roosevelt's secretary of war, William Howard Taft
of Ohio, for the presidency, his running mate had to be
chosen. Elihu Root of New York, Roosevelt's secretary of
state from 1905 until 1909, did not want to become vice-
president, but Sherman, also of New York, did and he undertook to obtain the nomination. During the convention
Sherman proposed to his close friend, Senator James E.
Watson of Indiana, that the two go to a ball game, and while
there the New York congressman told the Hoosier of his interest in the nomination for the vice-presidency and his
desire that "Uncle Joe" Cannon should present his name to

the delegates. After he had returned to his hotel, Senator
Watson called "Uncle Joe" at Danville, Illinois, and told him
of Sherman's interest in the nomination for the vice-
presidency and of his preferred strategy. Cannon came,
and, as Watson recalled in his memoirs:

> When he finished nominating Sherman, it was all
> over but the shouting, and they did shout for "Sun-
> ny Jim," who was nominated and elected, and who
> probably never had a superior in either house as a
> presiding officer.

House Speaker Champ Clark put it succinctly, "He
wanted the place, and got it." Clark continued, "I suppose
he wanted it [the Vice-Presidency] because he felt that he
was fit for it, for he was.... He was an industrious, level-
headed, capable member [of the House of Representatives],
and a capital presiding officer." In addition to his duties
in the Senate, Sherman as vice-president had social obligations in which he was assisted by his wife. Details of these
activities are scarce, but Taft's military aide, Archie Butts,
saw the vice-president, his wife, and their three sons, "all
replicas of the Vice-President," in a box at the theater.
Butts noted that Sherman was trying unsuccessfully to speak
softly and that his voice was "one of the most discordant"
he had ever heard. "Nasal and twangy" speech comes as a
surprise from a man distinguished for polite manners and for
smart attire.

Soon after Sherman became vice-president he learned
that he was afflicted with Bright's disease, an almost incur-
able kidney malady. Four years earlier Sherman had experienced a kidney disorder which he controlled by close attention to diet. While vice-president, Sherman became so ill
one day that when he asked Senator Gallinger of New Hampshire to take the chair, he added, "I am not at all sure how
long I shall be able to continue to preside over the Senate."
Nevertheless, Sherman accepted the renomination of his party
for a second term as vice-president. Before he did so,
Sherman asked his physician whether he should accept the
renomination because of health problems, but his physician
declined to give advice on such an important and uncertain
prospect.

Before the notification committee came to Utica to tell

the vice-president of his renomination by the Republican
party, his physician advised the nominee to receive the distinguished visitors indoors and to refrain from making a
speech.   When Sherman objected to this cool reception for
the committee, his physician allowed that he could meet them
out of doors but should not talk longer than five minutes.
When the members of the notification committee arrived at
Sherman's house in Utica on August 31, he ignored the advice of his physician and talked for thirty minutes.   The
effort exhausted the vice-president, and he never fully
recovered.   His death from uremic poisoning came at the end
of October.   In addition to an uremic coma caused by Bright's
disease, the vice-president's physician noted that the patient
also suffered from heart disease and arteriosclerosis.

Vice-President Sherman was Utica's best-known citizen,
and his death brought a demonstration of respect and affection from friends and neighbors.   About a thousand residents
of Utica followed the hearse which carried Sherman's body
from his home to the courthouse where large numbers of
people, as many as five thousand in a single hour, looked
on his face for the last time.   His funeral was held on November 4 in the First Presbyterian Church in Utica, and
the eulogy was delivered by the president of Hamilton College.   President Taft and many other high government officials attended the vice-president's funeral, and the Utica
Daily Press estimated that 25,000 persons filled the streets
"on this sorrowful day."

Memorial addresses delivered at a joint session of the
Senate and the House of Representatives on February 13,
1913, reveal the high regard the speakers had for the late
vice-president, and the printed volume of the proceedings
also contains excerpts from the tributes to Sherman expressed
by distinguished Americans.   Mrs. Sherman received letters
of condolence from at least three hundred dignitaries, and
the death of the twenty-seventh vice-president was noted
officially by more than forty foreign governments.

Sherman bequeathed his entire estate valued at
$400,000 to his widow, who lived on in Utica until her death
on October 5, 1931, at the age of seventy-four.   Ten years
before her death she suffered a heart attack while a guest
of Mrs. Warren G. Harding on the presidential yacht, The
Mayflower.   Mrs. Sherman did not fully recover, and she

198 Vice-Presidents and Second Ladies

suffered a stroke in the Willard Hotel in Washington about
a year before her death. A bishop of the Protestant Episcopal Church officiated at her funeral, which was held at
the Sherman residence in Utica.

PRINCIPAL SOURCES

Champ Clark. My Quarter Century of American Politics.
    New York: Harper, [1920]. 2 v.

U.S. Congress. Senate. 62nd Congress, 3rd Session.
    Document No. 1134. James Schoolcraft Sherman. Memorial
    Addresses.... Washington: Gov. Printing Office, 1913.
    136 p.

James E. Watson. As I Knew Them. Indianapolis: Bobbs-
    Merrill, [1936]. 330 p.

THOMAS R. MARSHALL, 1913-1921

Thomas Riley Marshall (1854-1925) was born
in North Manchester, Indiana, the son of a
physician who lived in several Middle Western
communities before he moved in 1874 to Columbia City, Indiana, Thomas's home until 1909.
Marshall attended Wabash College where he
pursued a traditional course of studies and
was graduated in 1873. He then studied law
in an office in Columbia City, and at age
twenty-one was admitted to the bar. Marshall's practice flourished; he and his wife, whom
he had married in 1895, enjoyed their life in
an Indiana small town.

Although seemingly without interest in a
political career, Marshall allowed friends to
launch his candidacy for the office of govern-
or. Marshall received the nomination mainly
because Thomas Taggart, the leader of the
Democratic party in Indiana, preferred him
to the other leading candidate. Marshall and
his wife campaigned hard and won the election in 1908. As governor, Marshall strove
for an efficient administration; he opposed
child labor, prohibition, women's suffrage,
and capital punishment.

Boss Taggart went in 1912 to the Democratic Convention in Baltimore determined to
secure a plum for Indiana, and he obtained
for Marshall the second place on the ticket
with Woodrow Wilson. Marshall was not
pleased with this opportunity but he accepted
it, and he and his wife enjoyed their places
in Washington society. The Hoosier proved
to be an especially congenial presiding officer

of the Senate, and is remembered today chiefly
for his quips and salty humor. After eight years
in the vice-presidency, Marshall and his wife
returned to Indianapolis. He spent the first
five months of 1925 dictating his <u>Recollections</u>
and died in June of that year.

*   *   *

"What this country needs is a really good five cent cigar."
This pithy statement is familiar to most older Americans,
but few could identify the source or describe the circumstances under which the statement was made. A student of
American history probably would attribute the irreverant
aphorism to Thomas Riley Marshall, who served for eight
years as vice-president during Woodrow Wilson's two terms
in the White House, but he might not know that Marshall
made the quip while presiding over the Senate. During a
slack period Senator Joe Bristow of Kansas was delivering
a long speech in which he enumerated the needs of the
country. After one of the senator's oratorical flights, the
vice-president leaned over and made his pronouncement in
a voice loud enough to be heard by the secretaries of the
Senate and others nearby. Marshall's pungent comment delighted his countrymen and earned him a place in the anthol-
ogy of American folk wisdom; however, he is remembered
today for little else.

Riley Marshall, the grandfather of Thomas Riley Marshall, moved in 1817 from the mountain country of Western Virginia to Indiana where he obtained land near Marion and
sired nine children. One of these became a physician, married Martha Patterson of Pennsylvania who had journeyed to
Marion to live with a sister, and began in 1848 to practice
medicine in North Manchester where their son, Thomas, was
born on March 14, 1954. Dr. Daniel Marshall moved his family to Illinois and on to Kansas and back to Missouri to find
a climate which would improve his wife's health, but in 1860
he was back in Indiana, for fourteen years in Pierceton,
and he moved again in 1874 to Columbia City, a town of
about three thousand in Northern Indiana which was to be
Thomas' home town until 1909.

After two years in the Fort Wayne High School Thomas
was prepared to enter Wabash College in Crawfordsville,

Indiana. The course of study offered to the eighty-five
male students at the Presbyterian College was old fashioned
in its emphasis on required, traditional subjects, but young
Marshall did well in his studies and developed an affection
for the small school which continued until his death. Indeed, his widow presented her late husband's library and
memorabilia to the College which features a "Marshall Room"
in the college library.

After graduation from Wabash College in 1873, Thomas
Marshall studied law in law offices in Columbia City, and at
age twenty-one he was admitted to the bar. Two years later
he joined with William F. McNagny in a partnership, and
their practice flourished. Marshall enjoyed living in a small
town in Indiana, and he was active in the local Presbyterian
Church and in the Indiana Masonic order. He was engaged
to be married to the daughter of a lawyer in Columbia City,
but the girl died and Thomas Marshall did not fall in love
again until the summer of 1895 when at age forty-one he
met Lois I. Kimsey, age twenty-three, at a lengthy trial in
Angola, in the northeastern corner of Indiana.

After their marriage on October 2, 1895, the couple
made their home in Columbia City where the bride entered
promptly into the life of the community. She joined his
church, and traveled with her husband wherever he went.
During their entire married life they were separated only
two nights; she may have gone with him early in their marriage to keep him from drinking heavily but he became a
complete abstainer in 1898 and their practice of traveling
together became a sentimental tradition. The Marshalls were
childless, but they doted on a foster child who lived with
them for several years in Washington. Couples such as the
Marshalls usually had many opportunities to adopt children
at the end of the last century; their reason for not doing
so is not mentioned in Marshall's biography or in his Recollections (1925).

Although Mrs. Marshall receives credit for encouraging
her husband to seek a career outside of Columbia City,
Thomas did not tell his wife about his willingness to let
friends launch his campaign for governor while he and his
wife were on vacation in Petoskey, Michigan. Marshall received the nomination of the Democratic Convention because
the leader of the party in Indiana, Thomas Taggart, supported

him in preference to L. Ert Slack after Samuel L. Ralston failed to gain essential support. No Democrat had been elected governor in Indiana since 1892, and Marshall and his wife waged a clean and energetic campaign. On Saturday night before the election, Thomas ended his last speech of the campaign at midnight in Fort Wayne, and then waited until four a.m. for a train to take them to Columbia City. When they reached home, they were so tired that they slept until Monday morning and did not stay up for the returns Tuesday night. At five Wednesday morning Lois Marshall called Indianapolis and learned from Taggart that her husband was to be Indiana's next governor.

As governor, Marshall sought to keep separate the executive, judicial, and legislative branches of government, and his administration of the executive branch was characterized by salty expressions of his humane approach to the problems of individuals. He reached a satisfactory working relationship with Indiana's Boss Taggart on appointments, and he required economies in governmental operations. He opposed child labor, prohibition, women's suffrage, and capital punishment, and he was liberal in his use of the pardoning power. He did not want a prisoner near death to be kept in prison nor did he want the baby of a pregnant girl to be born within the walls of a state reformatory. He had a novel approach to certain extradition cases, but in this he tempered his theories with common sense. A Kokomo woman wanted the governor to secure the return of her husband through extradition, and he replied:

> Dear Madam:
> I do not well see how the state of Indiana is responsible for your marrying a scoundrel or how if you do know where he is the state could punish him for deserting you.

While Marshall was governor of Indiana, the state did not provide an executive mansion, so he and his wife rented a modest house and lived much as they had in Columbia City. Shortly after their move to Indianapolis, the Marshalls gained a high place in local society. The Marshalls introduced popular evenings at home in which the women who came were received in the parlor by Mrs. Marshall and the men smoked a cigar with the governor in the library. This happy state of affairs could not continue indefinitely because

Indiana's Constitution did not permit a governor to succeed
himself. Because so few states had Democrats as governors,
Marshall was mentioned as a possible candidate for the
Presidency in 1912, and Boss Taggart went to the Democratic Convention in Baltimore resolved to obtain greater
recognition for Indiana and for himself. Wilson considered
Marshall to be "a small-caliber man," but Taggart won the
nomination for him. Marshall did not know that Taggart
never expected Marshall to receive the party's nomination
for the presidency, and the governor was disappointed with
the second place on the ticket and intended at first to decline the offer. The salary of the vice-president was small,
and Marshall believed he could live better on his income as
a lawyer back in Columbia City. Mrs. Marshall preferred
the prospect of living in Washington to returning to small
town life in Indiana, and Marshall agreed to become Wilson's
running mate.

Although Marshall complained about his inadequate
salary in the offices he held, he refused to accept campaign
contributions or reimbursement for related travel expenses.
Vice-President and Mrs. Marshall were unable to afford a
house in Washington and lived in a succession of hotels.
Thomas Marshall soon learned that he could supplement his
income through lectures (he even joined the Chautauqua
circuit) and authorship of magazine articles, and he and
his wife greatly enjoyed their prominent place in the social
life of Washington. The inauguration ceremonies in 1913
and again in 1917 had a distinctive Hoosier flavor because
Marshall had the Black Horse Troop of Cadets from the Culver Military School as his guard of honor. After their second appearance the cadets were given a reception by Mrs.
Marshall to which she invited several hundred girls from
Washington's official families and nearby private schools.
Mrs. Marshall organized the Ladies of the Senate Luncheon
Club and the Diet Kitchen Welfare Center, and during World
War I she sewed for the Red Cross and spoke in campaigns
urging women to economize in their homes. During President Wilson's severe illness near the end of his second term,
the Marshalls often served as the official host and hostess
for the United States government. Marshall received criticism in some quarters for not assuming more of the duties
of the president, especially after his second stroke, but the
Constitution did not then provide a way for a vice-president
to replace a disabled president.

After the Republicans won the election in 1920 Vice-
President Marshall wired his designated successor, Calvin
Coolidge, "Please accept my sincere sympathy." After the
Coolidges came to Washington, Mrs. Marshall introduced
Mrs. Coolidge to the "ceremonial rites" of the capital. Mrs.
Marshall had been there for eight years, and Grace Coolidge
believed that she could not have had a better teacher.

After the conclusion of his second term as vice-
president, the Marshalls decided to live in Indianapolis and
spend part of each year in Arizona where Mrs. Marshall's
mother had her home. Marshall, never without a cigar,
blamed his persistent cough in the winter on the coal smoke
in Indianapolis. Thomas Marshall lived but four years after
he left the vice-presidency, and during this time he held a
place on a national coal commission to which he had been
appointed by President Harding, he continued to give lectures, he and his wife made a trip to Europe which he reported in syndicated articles, and the couple renewed their
former church and social activities in Indianapolis. Marshall
spent the first five months of 1925 dictating his Recollections, without help from a diary or detailed notes, from which
he hoped to receive about ten thousand dollars. Marshall
died on the first of June of that year, and the book yielded
almost fifty thousand dollars. Mrs. Marshall was awarded in
1929 an annual pension of $3,000 by a bill signed by Presi-
dent Coolidge, and she died in Phoenix, Arizona, on January
8, 1958, from a stroke she had suffered a week before in the
hotel suite where she had lived for many years.

Thomas Marshall's Recollections consist mainly of anecdotes which amused him and brief sketches of senators whom
he had observed while presiding for eight years over the
United States Senate. In his lifetime he had a reputation as
a homespun wit and philosopher, but his sallies evoke little
laughter today. He was a small man physically who regularly wore a mustache and a hat placed at a jaunty angle. In
his Recollections he described himself as "a light hearted
man," but his humor and manner are out of fashion today.
His lack of greatness was recognized in his own time, because the New York Post editorialized on the day after his
death, "Tom Marshall had, by ever so little, outlived his
time. The country lawyer's day in politics and statecraft
is passing ... Thomas Riley Marshall belonged to the old
America."

PRINCIPAL SOURCES

Thomas R. Marshall. Recollections of Thomas R. Marshall,
   Vice-President and Hoosier Philosopher. A Hoosier Salad.
   Indianapolis: Bobbs-Merrill, [1925]. 397 p.

Charles M. Thomas. Thomas Riley Marshall, Hoosier Statesman. Oxford, Ohio: Mississippi Valley Press, 1939.
   296 p.

CALVIN COOLIDGE, 1921-1923

Calvin Coolidge (1872-1933) was born in a small town in Vermont where his father was a farmer and kept a country store. Calvin attended local schools and nearby academies in which he prepared to enter Amherst College where he pursued without distinction regular courses in liberal arts. After graduation in 1895, Coolidge studied law, was admitted to the bar in 1897, and began in 1898 to practice in Northampton, Massachusetts where he lived for thirty-five years and held local offices including that of mayor. In 1906 Coolidge was elected to the Massachusetts House of Representatives, and five years later he went to the State Senate. He spent three years in the office of lieutenant governor, and his loyalty and work for the Republican party elevated him in 1918 to the governorship. In this office Coolidge received national attention for his stand in 1919 against a strike threatened by the Boston police.

After a small group of senators had engineered the nomination of Warren G. Harding of Ohio to be the Republican candidate for president in 1920, the convention delegates in revolt named the conservative governor of Massachusetts to be his running mate. Coolidge served as vice-president until he succeeded President Harding on his death in August of 1923, Coolidge's detachment and personal integrity reassured his countrymen as the scandal of oil leases during Harding's administration became widely known, and in 1924 he was nominated on the first ballot for the office he had held for nineteenth months.

The Republicans won the election in 1924, and
the country enjoyed unparalleled prosperity
under the hands off policies of the president.
Coolidge realized that the country needed
stronger leadership to resolve domestic and
international problems, and he declined to
run for reelection in 1928. The taciturn New
Englander returned to Northampton, where
writing and business interests occupied him
until his death on January 5, 1933.

* * *

When Calvin Coolidge was nominated by the Republican National Convention to be vice-president on the 1920 ticket
with Senator Warren G. Harding of Ohio, his wife, Grace,
wondered about the social demands which might be made on
her in Washington and whether she would live there with
her husband or remain in Northampton as she had during
the months he served in Boston as a member of the Massachusetts General Court, state senator, president of the senate, lieutenant governor, and governor. For twelve years
Calvin Coolidge rode a day coach Monday mornings across
the one hundred miles between Northampton and Boston
where he stayed in a modest room in a second-rate hotel,
the Adams House. After Coolidge became governor in 1919
he kept his room at the Adams House, because Massachusetts
did not provide an "executive mansion." His wife visited
him there occasionally when she could get away from their
two boys and the Coolidge's half of a two-family house in
Northampton.

After his election Calvin Coolidge agreed to take his
family with him to Washington, but the move did not solve
the Coolidge's housing problem. The vice-president's salary
of $12,000 per year had to cover living expenses and the
cost of keeping the Coolidge boys, John and Calvin, in a
private school. When the Coolidges realized that they could
not buy a house but would have to remain in a small suite
in the New Willard hotel, Mrs. Coolidge accepted the situation, "More hotel life, I suppose," and endeavored to make
their small quarters as homelike as possible.

While the Coolidges were occupying modest quarters at

the New Willard, Mrs. John B. Henderson, widow of a Missouri Senator, offered her home to the government for an official residence for the vice-president and his successors in the office. A bill went before Congress to accept the gift and to provide for its upkeep, but the necessary legislation was defeated. While the proposal was being discussed, Dr. and Mrs. Nicholas Murray Butler, who as president of Columbia University enjoyed the use of a splendid house on Morningside Heights, were guests at the White House and expressed their hope that the bill would pass. Their comment struck a sensitive spot in their hostess, Mrs. Harding, because she almost shouted, "I am going to have the bill defeated. Do you think I am going to have those Coolidges living in a house like that? A hotel apartment is plenty good enough for them." The Coolidges remained in the hotel until they moved into the White House after the death of President Harding in the summer of 1929, but the need for an official residence for the vice-president was in his mind when he wrote his Autobiography which was published in 1929. Here the former vice-president and president argued that holders of the second office in the Government should have "a settled and permanent habitation and a place, irrespective of the financial ability of its temporary occupant.... It would be more in harmony with our theory of equality if each Vice-President held the same position in the Capital City."

Mrs. Harding's disapproval of the Coolidges may have been caused by her reaction to the unsophisticated conduct of the vice-president and jealousy of the winning ways of his wife. According to Coolidge's most careful biographer, Claude M. Fuess, "In society Coolidge was certainly an 'odd stick,' but Mrs. Coolidge was soon as much a part of it all as if she had been brought up in Boston's Junior League and Vincent Club."

Calvin Coolidge was born on Independence Day in 1872 in Plymouth, Vermont, in the midst of rustic surroundings for which he had a lifelong affection. After preparation at nearby Black River Academy, young Calvin entered Amherst College where he had difficulty making friends and pursued without distinction courses in ancient languages, mathematics, history, and philosophy (today's "liberal arts"). Among his classmates were young men marked for success, Dwight W. Morrow, Harlan Fiske Stone, and others, but young Coolidge

was not one of their group.   After college Calvin Coolidge
read law in Northampton, Massachusetts, the town of which
he was to be a citizen from 1893 until his death forty years
later.   He served for two terms as mayor of Northampton,
and his election to this office by his fellow townsmen gave
him considerable pleasure.

It was Dwight W. Morrow, fellow classman of Coolidge
at Amherst, who first called the attention of Frank W.
Stearns, prosperous Boston merchant and a graduate from
Amherst in 1876, to the promise of the legislator from Northampton.   The two met, and with Stearns' help Coolidge's
political career acquired new momentum.   After four years
of close association Stearns was convinced that Coolidge,
then governor, possessed "many of Lincoln's strongest
qualities," and by the time he reached the White House,
others embraced Coolidge as "a man of dignity and silence,
with an odd capacity to make them smile."   A few days after
Coolidge's inauguration, Stearns wrote to Morrow, "One of
his greatest assets is Mrs. Coolidge.   She will make friends
wherever she goes, and she will not meddle with his conduct of the office."

Grace Goodhue was born in Burlington, Vermont, and
had a happy childhood in the college town along the shore
of Lake Champlain.   She attended the University of Vermont
where she made many friends and was graduated in 1902.
After graduation she enrolled in the Clarke School for the
Deaf in Northampton where she met her future husband.
As her suitor recalled, "When she had been there [in the
Clarke School] a year or so I met her and often took her
to places of entertainment....   From our being together
we seemed naturally to come to care for each other.   We
became engaged in the early summer of 1905 and were married at her home in Burlington, Vermont, on October fourth
of that year."   Grace's mother did not want Calvin to become her son-in-law, but the young man did not heed her objections.   After the wedding the couple planned to spend
two weeks in Montreal, but after a week they returned to
Northampton because the groom wanted to undertake his
first political campaign.

Although Grace Goodhue undoubtedly had good reasons
for accepting Calvin Coolidge's offer of marriage, she must
have found him irritating and at times exasperating beyond

endurance. She was a healthy, sociable person who enjoyed company, music, and dancing while he often was a
dour, inconsiderate man whose normally sour disposition
was aggravated by digestive problems. Soon after the
couple returned from their honeymoon, the groom produced
a leather bag which contained fifty-two pairs of socks in
need of repair, and Grace went to work with a darning
needle although she found darning to be a boring task.
The husband wanted his wife home promptly after any entertainment, and he left for home promptly at ten in the
evening. Calvin Coolidge as president slept an average of
eleven hours a day; he went regularly to bed at ten and he
was up at six-thirty. He also took a long nap after lunch
and catnaps on a sofa in his office whenever he wished.
Although Calvin Coolidge objected to snobbishness in any
form and in public held on to his country ways, as president he liked to use the large dining room in the White
House where Grace and he and their son John were the
only persons at the long table. "They invariably dressed,
said grace, and sat looking rather lost in the expanse of
the stately room." One day John returned late in the afternoon from a dance in Annapolis, and he stopped in the
White House sitting room a few minutes before the dinner
hour. John asked his father for permission to come to the
table without changing, and was told "You will remember
that you are dining at the table of the President of the
United States and you will present yourself promptly and in
proper attire."

     Grace Coolidge tried to compensate for her husband's
disinterest in dinner guests, but she could not do anything
to improve his treatment of his wife. He seldom gave her a
present on a wedding or birthday anniversary or at Christmas, and he would not discuss with her thoughts and events
which might involve her day or future. After the Coolidges
had been in the White House for two weeks, Grace wanted to
know about his movements in advance and asked him to have
the secret service tell her about his engagements. And to
this reasonable request, she received the chilling reply,
"Grace, we don't give that out promiscuously." Coolidge's
best remembered line, "I do not choose to run in 1928" was
handed on slips of paper to members of the press in Rapid
City, South Dakota, in the morning of an August day in
1927; after lunch when the president left for his daily nap,
Senator Arthur Capper could not keep from querying the

president's wife about the momentous news. Mrs. Coolidge
could not conceal her surprise, "He never gave me the
slightest intimation of his intention. I had no idea!"

Calvin Coolidge's short, grumpy replies spawned innumerable stories, and his wife reinforced his reputation
as a New England sage by using some of the tales in her
writings. She once was asked whether all of the tales told
about Calvin Coolidge were true, and she replied, undoubtedly with a twinkle in her eye, "The best of them are." After
he left the presidency, Coolidge wrote short daily articles
for newspapers and a volume entitled Autobiography. In his
writings Coolidge often expounded the obvious, and his
platitudes brought him ridicule. However, he became
skilled in condensed expression and was able to turn a memorable phrase. One of the best of these is a noble compli-
ment to his wife, "For almost a quarter of a century she
has borne with my infirmities, and I have rejoiced in her
graces."

After their eight years in Washington the Coolidges
returned to their half of a house in Northampton, but in
order to have more privacy they bought a larger house with
eight acres of land, The Beeches. Here Coolidge lived in
comfortable retirement until his peaceful death on January
5, 1933. Grace then made a trip to Europe with an old
friend, Mrs. Florence Adams, and both returned to Northampton to live across the street from each other. Grace,
who had led a successful drive for an endowment of
$2,000,000 for the Clarke School for the Deaf while she was
still in the White House, sponsored a centennial development
drive to enlarge and enrich programs of teaching the deaf.
Grace Coolidge was active on the Northampton home front
during World War II, and in the late 1940s and early 1950s
she continued to read and to follow professional baseball
and in 1954 she added daily watching of television. Her
son, John, and his wife and their two daughters lived in
Farmington, and there were visits back and forth and many
exchanges of letters and photographs. After 1952 Grace
Coolidge was unable to keep up with her many activities and
was obliged to remain quietly at home. She was seventy-
seven when she attended the dedication of the Calvin Coolidge Memorial Room in the Forbes Library at Northampton,
and less than a year later, on July 8, 1957, she was dead.
Although she had wished to go quietly, Grace Coolidge's

death made headlines and received official recognition from
President Eisenhower.   The New York Herald Tribune commented on the personalities of the two famous Coolidges:
"But what was austere and withdrawn in Calvin Coolidge
was warm and gracious in his wife."

PRINCIPAL SOURCES

Calvin Coolidge.   The Autobiography of Calvin Coolidge.
    New York: Cosmopolitan Book Corp., 1929.   247 p.

Claude M. Fuess.   Calvin Coolidge, the Man from Vermont.
    Boston: Little, Brown, 1940.   522 p.

Ishbel Ross.   Grace Coolidge and Her Era.   New York:
    Dodd, Mead, 1962.   370 p.

CHARLES G. DAWES, 1925-1929

Charles Gates Dawes (1865-1951) was born and
brought up in Marietta, Ohio, where he attended
Marietta College. He received a second degree
from the Cincinnati Law School and began his
legal practice in Lincoln, Nebraska, where he
formed lasting friendships with William Jennings
Bryan and John J. Pershing. Dawes' law practice flourished and he pursued business interests
which enabled him in 1894 to purchase the Northwestern Gas, Light and Coke Company in Evanston, Illinois. In May of 1896 Dawes agreed to
lead William McKinley's presidential campaign in
Illinois, and was persuaded later to handle all
of the funds for the candidate's national campaign. After his election, President McKinley
appointed Dawes comptroller of the currency,
a post from which he resigned to run unsuccessfully for the United States Senate. He
then concentrated on his business interests
in Chicago.

After the entry of his country into World
War I, Dawes was selected by his old friend,
General Pershing, to head military procurement
for the American armies in Europe; his remarkably effective work was recognized by rapid
promotions from major to general. After the
War Dawes accepted for one year the post of
the first director of the budget. In 1923 he
became head of the Allied Reparations Commission, and in 1924 he was nominated to the second place on the Republican ticket with President Calvin Coolidge. Dawes and his family
enjoyed their four years in Washington, at the
end of which he was induced by incoming

213

President Hoover to serve as ambassador to Great
Britain. In February of 1932 Dawes returned to
America to become the first head of the Reconstruction Corporation, a position which he left
after four months to reorganize his own bank
in Chicago. The former vice-president died
at his home in Evanston in 1951.

*   *   *

Two weeks after he had been nominated by the Republican
national convention to be President Coolidge's running mate
in 1924, Charles G. Dawes went to Washington to discuss
campaign plans. And on August 2 President Coolidge sent
to Dawes "one of the most unusual letters ever written by
a Presidential candidate to his Vice-Presidential running
mate." Therein Coolidge gave two paragraphs of advice
which Dawes might follow in the preparation of his speech
of acceptance of the nomination, and, as an afterthought,
the President added this postscript: "P.S. Whenever you
go anywhere, take Mrs. Dawes along." Dawes did about
the only thing he could do with this extraordinary letter
from a president whose laconism is legendary: he put it
in his lock box where it remained for the rest of his life.

Charles Dawes was born on August 27, 1865, in Marietta, Ohio. His father, Rufus R. Dawes, who rose to the
rank of brevet brigadier general in the Civil War at age
twenty-six, was a direct descendant of William Dawes who
came to Massachusetts from England in 1635, and his mother,
Mary Gates, was of New England stock. Her father, Beman
Gates, had moved from Connecticut to Marietta, Ohio, where
he became an editor, railroad builder, and bank president.
It was this grandfather who persuaded young Charles Dawes
to keep a diary; by the time of his first diary entry, Dawes
was a graduate of Marietta College and had received a degree from Cincinnati Law School. In Cincinnati he met Caro
Blymer whom he married two years later. They were married for sixty-two years; his life was one of large achievements and she was "a modest, shy, and gentle person who
found herself thrown into the spotlight because of the accomplishments of her husband."

After reaching his majority, Charles G. Dawes decided
to begin the practice of law in Lincoln, Nebraska. Here he

formed lifetime friendships with William Jennings Bryan and
John J. Pershing. Eighteen months after his arrival in Lincoln, Dawes borrowed money to return to Cincinnati and
marry Caro Blymer. She was "a delicate, dark-haired girl,
with a fine oval face, dominated by her large, dark, thoughtful eyes." Her father was a manufacturer of steam engines,
ice machines, and similar equipment, and among her ancestors were notables such as Miles Standish of the Plymouth
Colony and General Israel Putnam of Revolutionary War fame.
Years later Dawes liked to tell how the wedding check of
$500 from his wife's father paid for the couples' trip to
Lincoln and settled the debt of $100 which the young man
had borrowed to finance his journey for his marriage in
Cincinnati.

The early years of their marriage were succinctly described by the husband:

> "Mrs. Dawes and I came back to Lincoln and
> started housekeeping in a little six-room cottage
> at 1400 D Street ... it was a glorious time, when
> we figured we could live on $80 per month. It took
> close to $100. Mrs. Dawes was a good manager, or
> we could not have got through on that; but I found,
> at the end of the first year, I had earned enough
> to spend $100 per month on our living, and had
> $400 left over for furniture, and then, after a time,
> came little Rufus Fearing and then little Carolyn,
> and life was wholly complete."

During their five years in Lincoln the Dawes prospered. His law practice flourished after he won national
attention in a legislative inquiry into railroad rates, and he
became a director in a local bank. His business interests
soon included real estate and gas and light companies. The
young couple became prominent in the social and cultural
life of Lincoln; "he was always taking his pretty young wife
to see people like Edwin Booth, Henry Irving, [and] Ellen
Terry." Dawes discussed with John J. Pershing his future
prospects in the army, and he argued the silver question
with Bryan and others in the Lincoln Round Table, a discussion club representative of those to be found across the
country. Dawes red widely, played the piano and flute
at social affairs, and "for recreation, he boxed, played tennis, skated, swam, danced, and even took up ... golf." In

Lincoln he also began to explore politics and world fairs, two
activities in which he later would become greatly involved.

Late in 1894 Dawes bought the Northwestern Gas, Light
and Coke Company at Evanston, Illinois, and in January of
1895 the family moved to Chicago, the city which was to be
"home" for Charles and Caro Dawes for the rest of their
long lives.

In May of 1896 Dawes agreed to lead the campaign for
McKinley in Illinois, and the success of this effort delighted
the Presidential aspirant. After McKinley won the Republican nomination, Mark Hanna induced Dawes, not yet thirty-
one, to handle all of the funds for the forthcoming campaign.
After McKinley won the election, he discussed with Dawes
possible appointment to the Cabinet, but Dawes preferred
the post of comptroller of the currency and he was nominated
to and confirmed in this office in December of 1897.

The young comptroller of the currency and his wife
purchased a house at 1337 K Street in Washington which
was within walking distance of the White House. President
McKinley preferred working in his study to attending the
theater, and Mrs. McKinley frequently went with Charles
and Caro Dawes. After the play or concert, Dawes often
would call at the White House to discuss the happenings of
the day or plans for the morrow with the President. On
January 24, 1901, the twelfth anniversary of the wedding
of Charles and Caro Dawes, the couple had lunch with
President and Mrs. McKinley and in the evening flowers
came from the White House. This happy relationship with
the McKinleys ended abruptly with the assassination of the
president; the Daweses were at the White House when the
McKinleys left for Canton, Ohio, and they were there again
when the body of the assassinated president was brought
into the East Room.

Dawes resigned from his post as comptroller of the
currency to run in 1902 in Illinois for the United States
Senate, but in this he was defeated. He then concentrated
on his banking interests, and he worked for currency reform and as a consultant to many of the leading businessmen
in Chicago. In 1909 Dawes and his wife purchased a large,
stucco-colored brick home in Evanston which was surrounded
by large oaks for shade and a beautiful lawn which extended

to the shore of Lake Michigan. Here was ample room for
their natural children and for the boy and girl they adopted.
There also was plenty of space for Charles Dawes' rapidly
growing library and for the musical entertainments which he
and his wife enjoyed.

In the sixty-two years of their married life, Charles
and Caro Dawes were seldom separated--the longest period
was that of his World War I military service. Consequently,
his truly impressive record as the head of military procurement, for which he was selected by his longtime friend,
General Pershing, and his subsequent work on the commission to dispose of surplus goods and supplies need not de-
tain us here. After declining appointment as secretary of
the treasury in the Cabinet of President Harding, Dawes
did accept for one year the post of first director of the
budget, and in this office he introduced substantial governmental economies. In 1923 Dawes was chairman of the Allied
Reparations Commission which devised the so-called "Dawes
Plan" for German reparations, and in 1924 Dawes was nominated for vice-president by the Republican National Convention.

Vice-President-Elect and Mrs. Dawes and their two
adopted children left Chicago for Washington on March 2,
1925. The new vice-president enjoyed his return to Washington because his duties were light and permitted entertaining at their home on Belmont Street. Mr. and Mrs. Dawes
invited to their home scholars, musicians, explorers, avia-
tors, financial giants, and undistinguished old friends, and
their dinners became famous for the combinations of guests
and the absence of protocol. Mrs. Dawes cut the ribbon
at the dedication of the Peace Bridge at Buffalo, and the
ceremony was followed by an address the vice-president delivered to an audience of seventy-five thousand. In his inauguration speech Vice-President Dawes spoke of the need
for a limit on filibustering in the Senate, and in his Notes
as Vice President, 1928-1929 Dawes gave many examples of
bills passed in haste at the end of a session because certain senators had talked so much on minor topics that there
was little or no time left for serious discussion of major
ones. In his valedictory, Vice-President Dawes spoke again
of the need for rules which would facilitate the business of
the Senate. He had harped on this subject, and as he left
office, he made a final thrust, "I take back nothing." On

behalf of the Senate, Senator Robinson of Arkansas, presented to Dawes a silver tray, "selected with especial
thought of Mrs. Dawes, whose charm and modesty have won
the love of every one in official life in Washington." When
the former Vice-President and Mrs. Dawes left for Chicago
by train, "the Senate staff, including the pages" were at
the railroad station to wave goodbye.

Her husband's last month as vice-president was a busy
time for Caro Dawes who managed the packing of household
goods for shipment back to Evanston and kept up with her
social obligaitons. On February 18, Caro went to the White
House to attend Mrs. Coolidge's last tea for her official family, the wife of the vice-president and the wives of Cabinet
members, and on the 26th she and her husband had lunch
with President-Elect and Mrs. Hoover but she had to leave
immediately to preside over a luncheon of senators' wives
which Mrs. Coolidge was to attend. Her husband had gone
to see Hoover about the appointment as ambassador to Great
Britain which the president-elect wanted Dawes to accept.

Although Dawes' temperament was not that of a diplomat, he was induced to accept the appointment because of
its importance as a necessary prelude to the projected Five-
Power Naval Conference to be held in London. The Ambassador and his wife undoubtedly enjoyed their assignment in
England. They were received at Windsor Castle by King
George, who, because of illness had not received a foreign
diplomat for a year, and they entertained nobility, diplomats,
and Americans--two hundred and fifty in a single month--at
the United States Embassy. Caro and her husband even
heard his musical composition, "Melody in A Minor," played
by Fritz Kreisler at a late evening party in Belgravia.

The Ambassador returned in February, 1932, for
Dawes to become first president of the Reconstruction Finance Corporation, an agency formed to make loans to banks,
railroads, and businesses with serious financial problems.
Four months later Dawes resigned to return to Chicago to
guide his own bank, known as "the Dawes Bank" through
reorganization and to enjoy at least a few years in the spacious home they had purchased in 1909. In 1942 General
Dawes gave the property and its contents, including his
diary and other papers, to Northwestern University, but he
and his wife would keep possession during their lifetimes.

Charles Dawes died in the library of his home in Evanston
on April 23, 1951, at the age of eighty-five, and his widow
stayed in their home until her death on October 3, 1957,
at age 92.   According to the New York Times, Mrs. Dawes
had become "exceptionally popular" because of the "grace
and charm" with which she fulfilled her obligations as official hostess and helpmate to an important public official.

PRINCIPAL SOURCES

Charles G. Dawes.   Notes as Vice President, 1928-1929.
   Boston: Little, Brown, 1935.   329 p.

Bascom N. Timmons.   Portrait of an American: Charles G.
   Dawes.   New York: Henry Holt, [1953].   343 p.

CHARLES CURTIS, 1929–1933

Charles Curtis (1860-1936) was born in Topeka, Kansas, the son of Oren Curtis, who seldom remained at home, and of Ellen Pappen,
who was one-quarter Kaw Indian. After the
death of his mother, Curtis lived for three
years with his paternal grandmother in Topeka
and three more with his maternal grandmother
on a Kaw reservation where he had a great
fondness for horses and dogs but little interest in schooling. At age nine Charles returned
to Topeka where he attended elementary and
high schools and helped to pay for his living
expenses by selling magazines and newspapers
and by riding as a professional jockey. During his three years in high school, Charles
drove a hack at night and met local politicians.
These associations led Curtis to study law
with a local attorney, and he was admitted to
the bar when he came of age in 1881.

In 1884 Curtis was elected Shawnee county
attorney, an office in which he fulfilled his
campaign pledge to close saloons, and the
voters reelected him to a second term. The
young attorney then aspired to a seat in the
United States House of Representatives and
proved to be an exceptionally successful campaigner. He won his first election to Congress in 1892 and served until 1907 when he
became a senator. Curtis served in the Senate from 1907 until 1929 except for an interval of two years, 1913-1915, when he lost his
seat because of the Bull Moore uprising. In
1924 Curtis was elected majority leader of the
Senate, and he was nominated in 1928 for the

second place on the Republican ticket which put
Herbert Hoover in the White House. After his
term as vice-president, Curtis remained in Washington where he practiced law until his death
in his sleep on February 8, 1936.

*   *   *

After the inaugural ceremonies at the Capitol on March 4,
1929, President and Mrs. Herbert Hoover rode to the White
House, and they were followed closely by Vice-President
Charles Curtis and his half-sister, Mrs. Dolly Gann, who
had served as her half-brother's hostess since the death of
his wife five years before. The former senator from Kansas
wanted his half-sister to continue to help with his social
responsibilities; according to Dolly, he had informed the
State Department accordingly. The intention of the new
vice-president was not to be accomplished, however, without considerable discussion and some snickering.

Dolly first realized that she would not be accepted as
the equal of a vice-president's wife when the "Ladies of the
Senate," a club of Senators' wives, named the wife of the
president pro tempore of the Senate as their president.
This slight from women who knew her must have hurt Dolly's
pride, because it is not mentioned in Dolly Gann's Book, a
gossipy volume which reflects little credit on its author.

The outgoing secretary of state had ruled for no apparent reason that Mrs. Gann should be seated at formal
dinners below the wives of ambassadors, and Vice-President
Curtis asked the new secretary, Henry L. Stimson, to re-
scind the ruling. Stimson delayed making a decision; as
long as Dolly's status was in dispute, Washington hostesses
had to avoid inviting the vice-president and members of the
diplomatic corps to the same social function. Senator Norris,
with tongue in cheek, suggested to Secretary Stimson that
if the State Department could not resolve the matter quickly
President Hoover should be asked to refer it to the World
Court. The State Department declined to rule again on social precedence, and the ambassadors in Washington met and
agreed that in the absence of official clarification Mrs. Gann
should be given the rank she earnestly desired. The crisis
was past when Dolly attended a dinner at the Chilean Embassy and was seated at a place comparable to her brother's.

Protocol is essential for the orderly conduct of social
activities in a large capital, but for Dolly form became more
important than substance. Dolly enjoyed her high place in
official society, the second highest in the land, and she saw
herself as an expert on the niceties of social life in the
capital. Our official hostess should not let "whims interfere
with her social duties," Dolly admonished; because the safest way to select guests to attend large parties is to follow
"the rules of the game." Most women heads of official families depended on a social secretary for assistance in correspondence and in entertaining, but not Mrs. Gann. Her
long residence in Washington (more than thirty years during
most of which she was her half-brother's secretary or hostess) equipped her to manage her own social calendar and to
arrange entertainments without professional help.

After the death of his wife in 1924, Senator Curtis
moved into the large home of Dolly and her husband Billy
[Edward Everett] Gann. The three enjoyed each other's
company, and the widower had during his years of national
prominence the close support of relatives who cared about
him. During Curtis' vice-presidential term the three occupied a suite of ten rooms in the fashionable Mayflower Hotel
on Connecticut Avenue; after he left office, the trio returned to the Gann residence on Macomb Street.

Dolly, with her devotion to proprieties, probably encouraged her half-brother to lend dignity to the office of
vice-president with the result that the plain man from Kansas became a pompous bore. While he was in the House
and Senate, "Charley" Curtis enjoyed an enviable reputation
as a sharp poker player and as a keen judge of race horses,
but he refused to indulge in either pastime after he became
vice-president. As a legislator, Curtis seldom participated
in a debate; after he became a member of the executive
branch, he began to make dull speeches on public occasions.
He even commanded old friends, whom he formerly greeted
with a hearty slap on the back, "Call me Mr. Vice-
President!"

Charles and Permelia ("Dolly" was her nickname) Curtis were born in or near Topeka, Kansas; his date of birth
was January 25, 1860, hers was March 24, 1865. Their paternal grandparents descended from families who reached the
colonies in the early eighteenth century. Grandfather William

Curtis (1800-1873), while still a boy, moved west from his birthplace in New York, first to Indiana, and in 1860 on to Kansas. In Indiana he married Permelia Hubbard who bore him many children and, after her husband's death, became the matriarch of the Curtis family until her own death at age ninety-three.

Son Oren, the father of Charles and Permelia Curtis, was a rover. He was born in 1829 in Indiana where he married in 1848 a "Miss Quick" who bore him two sons. This marriage ended in a divorce, and Oren moved to Platte County, Illinois, where he remained for three years before he returned to Indiana. In 1856 he was off again, this time to Kansas where he worked in Leavenworth until he was threatened with bodily harm by pro-slavery advocates. He then traveled in Missouri and Iowa where he joined an armed troop headed for Kansas. In September of 1856 Oren left the antislavery party in Topeka where he worked at a number of jobs including the operation of a ferry owned by Louis Pappan. Oren held this job again in 1856 and 1858, and in 1859 he married the ferryman's nineteen-year-old daughter, Ellen. She had two children, Charles and Elizabeth, before her early death in 1863.

The two motherless children were left with Grandmother Curtis while their father went in the fall of 1863 with the 15th Kansas Cavalry to protect the eastern borders of the state. His company saw action against Confederates under General Price in October, 1864; two months later on December 25, 1864, while on leave in Olathe, Kansas, Oren married Lou Jay. Their daughter Permelia, born March 24, 1865, was such a tiny infant that her father could cover her entire body with his broad-brimmed hat as if she were a doll; hence her nickname "Dolly."

The fireside could not hold Oren Curtis for long. At the end of 1868 he was a quartermaster sergeant with the 19th Kansas Cavalry which was assigned to fighting Indians. Oren at age fifty-three could boast that he had traveled through twenty-nine states and nine territories and had never been sick for a day in his life. He seems to have returned to Topeka, but he probably was not there in 1888, the year of his wife's death. Oren left Topeka for Newkirk, Oklahoma Territory, several years before his death on March 28, 1898. Shortly before his death this hardy rover was busy planning a wagon trip through Arkansas.

The maternal grandmother of Ellen Pappan, Charles'
mother, was the daughter of White Plume, a Kaw Indian
chief. She married a French trader named Gonville who
lived near St. Louis; their daughter, Julie (half Indian),
married Louis Pappan. Their daughter Ellen (one-quarter
Indian) married Oren Curtis and became the mother of
Charles and Elizabeth (one-eighth Indian). Charles found
it to his advantage in politics to be known as an Indian just
as he used his father's limited service in the Civil War to
win the support of members of the Grand Army of the Republic.

After the death of his mother Charles lived for three
years with his paternal grandmother, the granitic Permelia
Hubbard Curtis; then he spent three years with his maternal grandmother, Julie Gonville Pappan, on the Kaw reservation, sixty miles south of Topeka. Curtis recalled shortly
after he became vice-president, "Until I was 8 I lived there,
happy and contented, playing, riding horses and learning
very little." He attended the mission school, but he had a
greater interest in horses and dogs than in schoolwork.
"As a boy, Curtis always thought of himself as an Indian."

At age nine Charles returned to Topeka where he
lived again with Grandma Curtis and attended elementary
school until 1875. During the winter months Charles sold
fruit and newspapers on trains to help pay for his living
expenses, and during some of his summers young Curtis
was a professional jockey. As a youth Curtis was lithe and
slender, and he knew horses from his boyhood days on the
reservation. Moreover, the pay was very good; at the peak
he was under a contract which brought him $50 a month and
ten percent of his winnings.

By the time he was sixteen, Charles probably was too
heavy to continue as a jockey, and he decided to attend
high school. He graduated three years later and was named
class orator. During his three years in high school young
Curtis drove a hack and became a "leg man" for the Topeka
Times. Through his hack driving at nights he met politicians in the Kansas capital, and he decided to study law.
At age nineteen Curtis started to study law under A. H.
Case who had known Charles as a jockey and as a hack
driver. After two years, in 1881, when Curtis became of
age, he was admitted to the Kansas bar.

Three years later, on November 27, 1884, the young attorney married Anna E. Baird, whom he had met in high school. She had been born on December 24, 1860, in Altoona, Pennsylvania, and moved in 1869 to Topeka with her parents John M. and Mrs. Baird. Charles and Anna Curtis had three children, a son, Harry, and two daughters, Permelia and Leona. While the children were growing up, Anna moved them back and forth between Topeka and Washington. She and the three children made several trips to Europe without Charles, who did not believe he could spare the time. The Curtises were married almost forty years; she, unfortunately, was an invalid for at least fifteen years before her death on June 24, 1924.

In the year of his marriage Curtis was elected Shawnee county attorney. Prohibition had been adopted in Kansas, but enforcement was lax. Curtis had promised in his campaign that if elected he would prosecute the saloon keepers; once in office, he did so with vigor. In his first thirty days in office, the new county attorney closed eighty-eight saloons. His remarkable record of law enforcement brought him recognition throughout Kansas, and in 1886 the voters in Shawnee County reelected Curtis for a second term.

Dolly Curtis claimed, without corroboration, that her mother, Lou Jay, belonged to the family of John Jay, the first chief justice of the United States. Lou's father, Minor Jay, did move his family from New York to Illinois; after his death, his widow moved with her children to Kansas. Here Lou married Oren Curtis and bore him at least one child, Permelia. When Lou became ill and died in 1888, Oren was not in Topeka; Permelia, then in her early twenties, accepted a warm invitation to live with her half-brother, Charles, and his wife, Anna. Their relationship continued to be close; Dolly wrote forty-five years later:

> Charles has always been my guide and mentor, as well as a big brother. Anna, as long as she lived, was a devoted sister, and I hope I cared for her in her later days as lovingly as she nurtured me from girlhood. [Dolly was nineteen when Charles and Anna married and twenty-three when she became a member of their household.]

After the conclusion of his second term as county

attorney, Curtis returned to his law practice. As his income increased, Charles' goal became a seat in the House
of Representatives. He enjoyed mingling with people, and he
remembered their names. He became active as a speaker
throughout the Fourth Congressional District, and each fall
he appeared at local political gatherings where he would
greet many of the residents by name. William Allen White,
the future famed newspaper editor, first met Charles Curtis
in 1891 at El Dorado, thirty miles northeast of Wichita, and
fell completely under his spell. White recalled more than
fifty years later:

> He came down from Topeka to campaign the
> county, sent by the Republican state central com-
> mittee.... He had a rabble-rousing speech with a
> good deal of Civil War in it, a lot of protective
> tariff, and a very carefully poised straddle on the
> currency question.... For his politics were always
> purely personal. Issues never bothered him. He
> was a handsome fellow, five feet ten, straight as
> his Kaw Indian grandfather [great-great grandfath-
> er!] must have been, with olive skin that looked
> like old ivory, a silky, flowing, handlebar mustache,
> dark shoe-button eyes, beady, and in those days
> always gay, a mop of crow's-wing hair, a gentle in-
> gratiating voice, and what a smile!

Curtis won his election to Congress in 1892, the year
that he began to compile his careful list of voters in his
district. In 1896 White traveled with Curtis from Emporia
to nearby Plymouth, and before they arrived the congressman pulled out a little book which contained the names of
Republicans in the township. Curtis mumbled the names to
refresh his memory; White giggled until he realized that
Curtis was in earnest. Curtis had a book which contained
the Republican poll list which he carried with him whenever
he visited a county; and, as White came to realize, for good
reason:

> In that way he survived politically for forty
> years. No matter what the issue was, it did not
> concern him. He knew that if he could call a man's
> name in a crowd, shake hands with him and ask him
> about his wife and children, whose names were also
> in the little book, he had that man's vote.

When Curtis went to Washington in 1893 to take his seat in the House of Representatives, Dolly went with him. Anna and the children were not to follow for some months; school attendance may have held them in Kansas and adequate rental housing had to be found in the capital. New members of Congress wanted to rent for a few years, because the purchase of a house might be interpreted at home as overconfidence in one's ability to retain his seat. Curtis rented a number of houses in Washington, and Anna and the children stayed with Charles during the long sessions of Congress but remained in Kansas during the short ones. When the children enrolled in schools in Washington, the visits in Kansas became shorter and shorter.

During her first summer in Washington, Dolly was overcome with homesickness. She was about to ask Charles to let her return to Kansas when he asked her to be his secretary. Most of his correspondence could be handled in a room in his home, and she could work there on Curtis' "books filled with the names of Kansas voters, the citizens of every county and town." Dolly enjoyed her work so much that she decided to continue as a congressman's secretary instead of going to college.

Curtis worked long hours as a congressman, and with Dolly's loyal help, he answered letters from constituents promptly and with a personal touch. During his fourteen years in the House of Representatives, 1893-1907, Curtis made no impact on major legislation, but he enjoyed the support of the voters in his district. He greeted them with a warm handshake and an ingratiating smile, and his voice was "strong, warm, and cordial." William Allan White, a liberal Republican, wrote about the ultra-conservative Curtis, "And what a congressman he was ... he was a kind of animated figure of political seduction whom few voters could resist."

Curtis was the first native of Kansas to serve in the United States Senate, and he served continuously from January 29, 1907, until March 4, 1929, except for the two years between March 3, 1913, and March 4, 1915, when he was a casualty of the Bull Moose split in the Republican party in 1912. During his twenty years in the Senate, Curtis made few speeches, and he was an early and strong advocate of a cloture rule which would limit unrestrained debate. Yet Curtis played a role in the Senate cloakrooms, for he believed that "everything can be fixed by friendly and confidential getting together." Surprisingly, Curtis was a strong supporter of women's suffrage. Dolly noted that her brother's move from the House to the Senate changed little in the daily life of the Curtises: "Charles moved from one end of the capital [!] to the other." Anna had her "at-homes" on Thursdays, the Senate day, instead of Tuesdays. Charles' correspondence increased after he became a senator, but no problem resulted because his secretary had become "more efficient because of experience."

In her late sixties Dolly wrote about her courtship when she was in her late forties; on a trip to Kansas in 1911 she had learned from friends about Edward Everett Gann, an attorney for the Interstate Commerce Commission. After Dolly returned to Washington, her romance began:

> In due course he came to see me. I liked him. For that matter, I liked all the men, not this one particularly; he was just another nice chap among the crowd one met in Washington.

Regardless of this cool beginning, Billy continued to call, and two years later he followed Dolly to Topeka when she went home to work in the 1914 Republican campaign. On "a lovely June evening" (June 12, 1915), Dolly, at age fifty, and Billy were married in Topeka. "Eleven hundred invitations had been sent out, and most of them were accepted, much to my joy." Mrs. Gann had pleasant memories of her wedding:

> The ceremony was performed by Dean Kaye, and the Episcopal service was used. I wore a lovely white satin gown embroidered in coin silver, of East Indian workmanship.... We received many wonderful gifts, among them fifteen silver vases. The presents ranged from tables to pincushions.

After a short honeymoon in Chicago, Dolly and her new husband hurried back to Washington. "Anna's health had been failing for years," and the simplest entertainment strained her small store of energy. Dolly wanted to see her half-brother's wife, whom she called "Sister," settled

in a comfortable home; Dolly found the house on Belmont
Road where Anna lived for the rest of her life. Dolly and
Bily lived nearby on Harvard Terrace until they bought a
larger house on Macomb Street. After her marriage Dolly
did not work as a secretary for her half-brother; instead
she made almost daily calls on his ailing wife. Anna, who
had been an invalid for fifteen years, was almost helpless
during her last three. She died at age sixty-three on June
20, 1924.

Early in the month of her death, Anna Curtis spoke
from her wheelchair in her home on Belmont Road, "Dolly,
I think Charles should be President. You ought to go to
Cleveland [the site of the Republican National Convention
on June 11 and 12, 1924] and see that he is nominated."
When it was explained to Anna that Coolidge deserved the
nomination, she responded, "Well, then, Charles should be
Vice-President." Charles had been thinking along the same
line, and he needed a personal representative at the Convention. Unable to leave his sick wife, Charles turned to
Dolly, "You and Billy, go to Cleveland," he said. The
Ganns hurried to Cleveland where they worked closely with
delegates from the large grain-producing states, but the
nomination for vice-president went to General Charles G.
Dawes of Illinois.

Soon after President Coolidge won the election in 1924,
Senator Henry Cabot Lodge, majority leader of the Senate,
died, and was succeeded by Curtis who kept his chairmanship of the Rules Committee. This responsibility entitled
Senator Curtis to ride with President and Mrs. Coolidge in
the inaugural parade. During his four years as majority
leader, Curtis worked harmoniously with the economy-minded
president, and the senator from Kansas supported legislation
in favor of farmers, prohibition, and bills which would benefit Indians.

President Coolidge announced in October of 1927 that
he did not choose to run in 1928, and Curtis promptly declared that he would be a candidate for the Republican
nomination for president. He had been in the famous
"smoke-filled room" which gave the nomination in 1920 to
Senator Warren G. Harding, and he had come to know
President Coolidge quite well. Consequently, Curtis understandably considered himself to be as well qualified for the

presidency as the last two Republicans in the office, but
Curtis' aspirations seemed ridiculous to the dynamic liberal
journalist, Oswald Garrison Villard. He saw Curtis as
platitudinous and dull. Villard recognized that Curtis was
a loyal, hard-working Republican politician but believed
him to be deficient in the important qualities which the head
of a great nation should possess.

    The Curtis family went to the Republican National Con-
vention in Kansas City, Missouri, in June, 1928, with high
hopes for Charles' nomination. The senator from Kansas
was accompanied by his two married daughters, Mrs. Leona
Knight and Mrs. Permelia George, his son Henry, and the
two Ganns. Secretary of Commerce Herbert Hoover had
broad support among the delegates, and Curtis on the defensive issued a cryptic statement, "The Republican Party
cannot afford to nominate a man for whom it will forever
after have to apologize." Curtis' warning was ignored, and
Hoover was nominated on the first ballot. When approached
about becoming Hoover's running mate, Curtis at first declined, but he agreed to accept when he learned that he
would be nominated almost without opposition. The delegates wanted to reward Curtis for his thirty-four years of
loyal service in the House and Senate, and they hoped that
his selection would make the defeat of Governor Lowden
more palatable to the farm states.

    Candidate Curtis had no talent for speaking to large
audiences outside of Kansas, but he made up for this deficiency with showmanship. His remarks on the campaign
trail were dull and repetitious, but his appearances on train
platforms or in large halls were enlivened with bands, flag-
waving, and a dancing Indian princess. Curtis' performance
may not have won many votes, but he was carried into office
along with the popular Republican candidate for president.

    Dolly's introduction to social life in Washington began
early in her half-brother's career in the House of Representatives. While serving as his secretary, she regularly
received guests with Anna at her "at-homes" on Tuesdays.
The day for the "at-homes" moved to Thursday with Charles'
elevation to the Senate; and, after Anna's death in 1924,
Dolly kept open house on the "Senatorial at-home day" after
"a long interval ... when we were in mourning and did no
entertaining." Dolly became her brother's official hostess

because every high official in Washington should have one
"in order to take his proper part in the capital's life."
Dolly took her duties seriously, the routine of her household "was shattered" when a presidential car came to her
home on Macomb Street in time for the majority leader of
the Senate to join President Coolidge in the White House for
breakfast at eight.

Dolly Gann's Book contains six chapters which deal
primarily with her life as the hostess for Vice-President
Curtis. His and her schedule of engagements was so
crowded that their free hours were needed "for rest between one entertainment and the next." Dolly pursued her
social obligations wholeheartedly; the writing of her recollections was the only undertaking which "played havoc"
with her "regular activities." In her view, "The keynote
of official entertaining in Washington is the 'at-home.'"
These receptions were appropriate for the capital of a democracy, for "anybody who wants to be there is welcome."
Dolly had been involved in "at-homes" on Tuesdays and
Thursdays, the days for congressmen and senators, respectively; but "Wednesday is the at-home day for the
Vice-President, the Cabinet, and the Speaker of the House."
The vice-president's hostess never knew how many callers
to expect at her "at homes"; the average number was between four and five hundred but one Wednesday afternoon,
she had eleven hundred visitors. She served refreshments,
coffee at one end of a long table and tea at the other with
"popular edibles" in between. Dolly had the help of friends
who talked with the guests while she remained in the receiving line; she always had "an aide, a young army officer,
in full-dress uniform," who introduced the callers as they
entered the vice-president's hotel suite.

According to Time magazine, Charles Curtis was "one
of the few men who ever genuinely enjoyed being Vice President of the United States." His working clothes, observed
the New York Times "are broadcloth, starched shirt and
white tie." Dolly devoted most of a chapter to formal dinners
she and her brother gave in the Mayflower Hotel; for most
of these she names her guests and details the menu. Many
of the Curtis' official dinners were followed by a motion picture; in 1930 President and Mrs. Hoover and other guests
of the Curtises saw Will Rogers in Lightnin' and in 1932, it
was a talking picture, Zane Grey's Heritage of the Desert.

While Anna was an invalid, Charles took her "to the movies almost nightly," and he must have been very pleased when movie mogul Louis Mayer invited him and the two Gannses to visit Hollywood in its heyday. Billy Gann had recently returned from a business trip to Europe and could not be away longer from his office, but he urged Dolly to make the trip with her brother and she did. On November 10, 1931, Charles and Dolly reached Los Angeles where they stayed in the Biltmore Hotel in a suite filled with "baskets of flowers and fruits." After a reception at seven the vice-president and his hostess sat down to a dinner for fourteen hundred including movie stars such as Marie Dressler and the Barrymore brothers.

After breakfast the next morning, Armistice Day, the visitors went to a celebration in the Olympic Stadium where the vice-president made an address "which seemed to please everyone." Luncheon was served at the MGM studio where Charles and his sister watched the filming of a motion picture, Tarzan. In the evening Charles was a guest at a stag dinner, and Dolly went to dinner and a fashion show at the Fox studio. Dolly was supposed to go with her brother to the American Legion's annual ball, but she couldn't make it, and he went alone. Later that night the vice-president and Mrs. Gann, their hosts, Mr. and Mrs. Louis Mayer, and a few others went on a private train to San Louis Obispo en route to the estate of William Randolph Hearst at San Simeon.

Mr. Hearst greeted his distinguished guests on the lawn in front of his castle and proved to be a perfect host. Sixty guests were seated at dinner which was followed by a movie, Wallace Beery in Hell Divers. The movie was shown twice in Hearst's private theater, once for the guests and again for the servants. Charles and Dolly spent the night at San Simeon and returned to Los Angeles the next day by car.

In their third day in Southern California Charles and Dolly attended in the afternoon a reception given by former Kansans and went in the evening to an opening night of The Champ, with Wallace Beery and Jackie Cooper, at the celebrated Chinese Theater. The evening ended with a short visit to the Cocoanut Grove night club with an old friend. "Spotlights were turned on our party, and we were introduced to the crowd."

On their fourth and last day, Charles and Dolly had breakfast in their hotel suite, and luncheon was hosted by Admiral and Mrs. Schofield on the battleship Pennsylvania. The vice-president received a salute of nineteen guns, and later the guests examined a submarine and an aircraft carrier. In the evening the couple from Topeka, Kansas, boarded the Golden State Limited with a collection of expensive souvenirs. Charles had a beautiful watch, and Dolly's mementoes included an evening purse and perfumes. "And," she mused, "each day I ... received corsage bouquets and basketfuls of flowers."

Toward the end of his term as vice-president, Curtis considered running again for the office of senator from Kansas. However, with the approval of President Hoover, he decided to remain on the national ticket. At the Republican National Convention in Chicago in 1932, there was some opposition to Curtis because he favored prohibition, yet no other leading politician sought the vice-presidency. As a result, Curtis was renominated on the first ballot to run again on the ticket headed by President Hoover.

In his campaign for reelection, Curtis spoke mainly outside of metropolitan areas where his longstanding support of prohibition might hurt the Republican ticket. He spoke in 1932 as he had four years earlier in favor of "the Constitution, flag, law, courts, and country." The second time around, the vice-president emphasized the need for world peace, but it must be peace with honor and without entangling alliances. Curtis tried to avoid the subject of veterans' benefits, and appealed for "Americanism" which included praise for women, mothers, education and other noncontroversial topics extolled by politicians. Curtis saw a return of good times in the near future, and he predicted a Republican victory in the election in November.

The one new element in Curtis' second campaign for a national office was sister Dolly. She made her start in the fall of 1931 with a speech before the League of Republican Women in Washington, and after this came an invitation to address a similar group in Columbus, Ohio. Before long, Dolly was added to the regular speakers' lists with the men, and she enjoyed "every bit of it--that goes without saying." During 1932 Dolly made political speeches in twenty-two states, and she was exhilarated throughout by the enthusiasm

of other Republicans and the applause of friendly audiences.
The impressions Dolly gained from her appearances in front
of scores of audiences left her "totally unprepared for the
avalanche of ballots that went against us on Election Day."

When Curtis reached the end of his term as vice-
president, he received from the senators over whom he had
presided the traditional silver tray inscribed with facsimiles
of their signatures. The former vice-president changed his
residence to Washington, and he was admitted to the District
of Columbia bar. These actions puzzled the Kansans who had
elected him to represent them for more than three decades,
and the folks at home had cause for wonder when "Our
Charley" was retained as an attorney for the notorious Dr.
John R. Brinkley, the goat gland quack who ran for govern-
or of their state. Indeed, Brinkley had run for governor
of Kansas in 1932 and 1934 and siphoned off enough votes
from the Democrats to permit the election of the Republican
Alfred Landon. In August of 1935, Curtis advocated the
nomination of Landon as the Republican candidate for president.

On February 8, 1936, a maid in the home of the
Gannses found Charles Curtis in his bed dead from a heart
attack. His body was taken to Topeka for burial near the
site of his birth. The value of his estate was not disclosed,
but he bequeathed $25,000 to Dolly and the remainder was
to go to his three children. Earlier Curtis had deeded to
his son a small property in Oklahoma which he acquired
through his connection with the Kaw Indians.

Dolly Gann lived on until January 30, 1953, when she
died at age eighty-seven. As the widow of E. E. Gann,
she continued to be active in Republican and congressional
clubs until a few days before her death from influenza. An
editorial writer for the New York Times noted her passing
with a wistful, backward glance to the quiet days in Washington when some persons believed that Dolly's concern over
social precedence was a topic of importance.

PRINCIPAL SOURCES

Marvin Ewy. Charles Curtis of Kansas: Vice President of
    the United States, 1929-1933. (The Emporia State Research

Studies, vol. 10, no. 2) Emporia: Graduate Division
of the Kansas State Teachers College, 1961. 58p.

Dolly Curtis Gann. <u>Dolly Gann's Book</u>. Garden City, N.Y.:
Doubleday, 1933. 241 p.

William Allen White. <u>The Autobiography of William Allan
White</u>. New York: Macmillan, 1946. 669 p.

JOHN N. GARNER, 1933–1941

John Nance Garner (1868-1967) was born in
northeastern Texas and attended local schools
until ill health forced him to leave. A maiden
aunt supervised his education until he began the
study of law in Detroit, Texas. Garner was
admitted to the bar and practiced in nearby
Clarksville until he learned of his tendency
toward tuberculosis. The young attorney
heard of a vacancy in a law firm in Uvalde,
four hundred miles to the southwest, and he
secured the place. In Uvalde Garner's health
improved, and at age twenty-five he was appointed county judge. In 1898 Garner was
elected to the Texas legislature where he
served two terms.

As a new member of Congress in 1903,
Garner made few speeches; but, through convivial poker games, he became an intimate
of congressmen who controlled large blocs
of votes. In 1912 Garner declined the chairmanship of the Foreign Relations Committee,
because he preferred a place on the Ways
and Means Committee which dealt with tariff
rates and tax schedules. In 1929, at age
sixty-one, Garner became minority leader
of the House and two years later its speaker. The Democratic National Convention in
1932 nominated Governor Franklin Roosevelt
of New York for the presidency, and Garner
was persuaded to accept the second place
on the ticket. Garner sought in 1940 the
nomination of his party for president, but
the Convention chose President Roosevelt

236

for an unprecedented third term. After serving
in the government for thirty-eight years, Garner
returned at the end of his second term as vice-
president to Uvalde where he enjoyed his retirement. The "Judge" died of old age, three weeks
before his ninety-ninth birthday, in November
of 1967.

*   *   *

The thirty-second vice-president of the United States and
his wife were both born in log cabins in Texas. She always
called him "Mr. Garner," and he called her "Etty," which
was short for Mariette. While he was vice-president, the
Garners lived in Washington in a hotel where they went
regularly to the cafeteria for breakfast and dinner. Mrs.
Garner ordinarily skipped breakfast and prepared her
lunch of "a little soup or a can of tamales and chile con
carne" in an improvised kitchen in her husband's elegant
offices in the Senate Office Building. However, Mrs. Garner enjoyed running her own house in Uvalde, Texas, where
she fixed the stews which her husband relished. His favorite was "cowboy stew," a mixture of sweetbreads, brains,
kidneys, and marrowguts, cut into bits, with small potatoes
and onions. The blended ingredients were cooked for hours
"in a vessel with a tight lid."

John N. Garner's widowed paternal grandmother selected the site for the homestead on the prairie south of
Detroit in Red River County, in northeast Texas. She had
moved there from Tennessee with her six children when the
future vice-president's father was four or five years old.
This son, John, married the daughter of a local banker; his
wife gave birth on November 22, 1868, to the first of their
six children, John Nance, the fourth in a line to bear the
name. The boy went to a country school until poor health
forced him to leave in the fourth grade. A maiden aunt
then supervised John's education until at age eighteen he
enrolled in Vanderbilt University in Nashville, Tennessee.
Within a week young Garner realized that his preparation for
college was deficient, and he returned to his home in Texas.
There he studied law under two local attorneys and was admitted to the bar at age twenty-one. He began his practice
in Clarksville, about fifteen miles east of Detroit, where he
learned that he tended toward tuberculosis.

The young attorney learned of a vacancy in a law firm
in Uvalde, about four hundred miles southwest of Red River
County.   After Garner reached Uvalde, a town of twenty-
five hundred, he became the junior partner in the offices
of Clark, Fuller & Garner.   The junior partner rode the
extensive judicial circuit for his firm and proved so adept
at avoiding litigation and collecting fees that his partners
agreed to increase his percentage of the profits from his
original portion of one-sixth.   Garner accepted farm animals
and other chattels instead of money, and he also took as
payment for legal services the ownership of the weekly
Uvalde Leader.   The high and dry climate of West Texas
restored Garner's health, and at age twenty-five he was
appointed county judge, a post with special responsibility
for managing county funds.

Judge Garner met Mariette on a train between Sabinal,
east of Uvalde, and San Antonio.   The young woman had
been born in a log cabin on a large cattle ranch (30,000
acres) southeast of Uvalde.   When she was less than a year
old, Mariette's mother died, and she was brought up by a
"wise and sweet" stepmother who emphasized obedience and
consideration.   Her father, Peter J. Rheiner, had come from
St. Gallen in Switzerland and had reached Texas by way of
the gold rush in California and a residence in Louisiana.
After recovering from a wound received while in the Confederate army, Rheiner acquired large holdings of land in
southwest Texas, married, and built a large log cabin on
his land for his wife and children.

Shortly after Mariette had returned from a boarding
school in Columbia, Tennessee, her father died; she and
her brother lived apart from congenial company on the large
ranch.   This was, indeed, a dull life for a spirited young
woman; although her brother objected, Mariette went with a
girl friend to San Antonio to learn shorthand.   It was on
one of the trips between her home and her business school
that Mariette met her future husband.   Within four months,
on November 25, 1895, the couple were married.   Their only
child, a boy named Tully after his father's law partner,
Tully Fuller, was born on September 24, 1896.

Mrs. Garner was a strong woman who helped to make
a strong marriage.   At the beginning of her married life,
she was "an addict of pots and pans," and the two Garners

in their four-room house would review weekly their financial
accounts. Her interest in her father's estate enabled the
Garners to acquire three banks, numerous businesses, and
a goodly number of farms and ranches. In his words, "We
kept our money rolling," and in time they became million-
aires. Mariette naturally wanted to appear well dressed, yet
during John's two terms in the office of vice-president, she
spent less than one hundred dollars a year on clothes. She
would wear with pleasure an outfit she had knitted while her
husband read or listened to the radio.

During his four years as a county judge, John Garner
learned the game of politics as it was then played in Texas,
and in 1898 he was elected to the State Legislature. Garner
had his eyes on a seat in the United States House of Representatives, and he saw a way to achieve his goal. In his
second term in the legislature, Garner was chairman of the
House committee responsible for creating congressional districts for Texas authorized by the 1900 census, and he
boldly carved out a Fifteenth District which contained his
own county. He thereupon announced that he intended to
run for the office of representative for the new district, and
the stunned legislators ratified the young man's audacious
proposal. With help from wealthy Texans, Garner moved into the seat in the House of Representatives which he had
designed for himself.

Garner was his own brand of Jeffersonian Democrat.
He believed that governments should protect the lives and
property of citizens, and he devoted his efforts to issues
which would help his party win elections. During his first
two or three terms in Congress, the Texan didn't make even
one speech. "I just answered roll calls, played poker, and
got acquainted"; yet he was aiming at the speakership. The
Texan had played poker in Uvalde county and in Austin,
and he was fond of good bourbon whiskey. These characteristics helped him to become friends with powerful men
such as Joe Cannon, Champ Clark, and Oscar Underwood;
Garner learned early that success in Congress depended
not on speeches but on the work done behind closed doors
with those who could deliver the votes.

While John ran for the seat in the House of Representatives, Mariette "brushed up" on dictation; when he
took office, she became his secretary. She later said that

she began to work for the money, one hundred dollars a
month, because "we were fairly poorly then," yet she never
quit. The Garners lived in Washington first in a rooming
house, and in his third term they rented a large apartment
where the family lived until Tully finished school and returned to Texas. Mariette said defiantly, "I never neglected
my boy any more than I neglected my secretarial job." As
her husband's responsibilities increased and his correspondence multiplied, Mrs. Garner worked even harder. "We
have neither the time nor the energy for anything but work,"
she wrote. Fortunately, she always managed to find happiness in her work; she later realized, "Work has been the
joy of my life."

When the Democrats came to power in 1912, Garner
was the ranking member of his party on the prestigious
Foreign Affairs Committee, but he declined the offer of the
chairmanship. The Texan wanted "to deal with affairs affecting American people--not foreign people," and he sought
a place on the important Ways and Means Committee. His
friends secured the appointment desired by Garner, and he
mastered the intricacies of tariff rates and tax schedules.
During World War I, Garner, although not the chairman of
the Ways and Means Committee, met weekly in private with
President Wilson to discuss legislation required for financing
the war. "Garner is responsible, more than any other man,
for the principle of the graduated income tax, and the inheritance features written into the law."

The Republicans won the national election in 1920, and
in 1923 Garner became the ranking minority member of the
Ways and Means Committee. During the Coolidge years,
Garner's outlook on tax revision combined progressive principles and pragmatic politics. During debates on major tariff
legislation, Garner never sought drastic revisions but always
tried to gain some benefit for his party. When Secretary of
the Treasury Andrew Mellon wanted to reduce wartime sur-
taxes on wealthy corporations, Garner spoke for their con-
tinuation and became known as a friend of the workingman.

In 1929 Garner, at the age of sixty-one with twenty-
six years of experience in Congress, became minority leader
of the House. At the end of a work day, Garner would
meet with his principal lieutenants, Sam Rayburn and John
McCormack, and with House Speaker Nicholas Longworth to

discuss current legislation. Other congressmen would occasionally be invited to attend meetings of the self-styled "Education Board" which was followed by a drink or two of good whiskey. Although the United States had adopted prohibition, the act of imbibing hard liquor in a room in the Capitol was pleasantly referred to "as striking a blow for liberty."

In 1931 Garner attained his goal of the speakership, and he favored a sales tax and a balanced budget. As the Depression grew, his office received as many as 3,500 letters a day; Etty went to work earlier every morning so that the mail would be ready for her husband's inspection when he arrived. "Garner for President" clubs started to appear across the country, and the speaker won the endorsement of the Texas and California delegates to the Democratic National Convention. The powerful newspaper publisher, William Randolph Hearst, who favored a sales tax and opposed international ventures such as the League of Nations, gave his support to Garner and participated in the negotiation which gave the nomination for president to Franklin D. Roosevelt, governor of New York, and the nomination for vice-president to the speaker of the House. A Texas newspaper man commented, "It is a kangaroo ticket, stronger in the hind quarter than in the front."

Only one other speaker of the House, Schuyler Colfax, had become the vice-president, and Garner described his move from the first office to the second as the "worst damnfool mistake I ever made." President Roosevelt asked Garner to represent the government at the inauguration of Manuel Quezon as president of the Philippines, and the vice-president and his wife traveled to Japan on their way to Manila. Garner attended Cabinet meetings and found some interesting and others unproductive. Three universities offered him honorary degrees which he declined as ceremonial, and he refused invitations to make speeches in which he might appear to express a point of view or policy of the president.

Traditionally, the vice-president and his wife have been Washington's most popular guests at fashionable dinner parties, but the Garners refused all of the many invitations they received except the yearly one from the White House in their honor and the only dinner party they hosted was

given each year in honor of the president at their hotel.
As the Garners grew older, life became simpler each year;
they went to bed earlier in the evening and got up earlier
in the morning. Etty regularly arose at five o'clock so that
she could enjoy "a quiet hour" before she drew her husband's bath at 6:30 and squeezed a glass of grapefruit juice
for him. After the Texan became vice-president, his wife
made only one change in their "old fashioned ways"; she in-
sisted that his suits be made to order. Etty had not been
ill with the grippe since 1916; in 1935 she regularly told
her body that it could not be sick! As a girl, Mariette
had been brought up as an Episcopalian; as an adult she
stopped going to church because she had concluded, "It's
what one really does that counts."

During the first terms in their respective offices, the
president and vice-president had cordial personal relations.
They played poker together, and Roosevelt referred to
Garner as "Mr. Common Sense." The vice-president proved
useful to the administration in facilitating the passage of
legislation needed to speed recovery from the depths of the
Depression. In his second term Roosevelt proposed enlarging the Supreme Court, he tolerated sit-down strikes, and
he proposed additional pump-priming legislation. Garner
reportedly told the president:

> Down in our country, when cattle are grazing
> and taking on fat we don't bother them too much
> and we don't scare them. We ought to have as much
> consideration for human beings as we do for cattle.

About six months later, John L. Lewis, the aggressive
leader of the CIO, appeared before a House Labor Committee
which was considering amendments on the wage-hour act and
pilloried the vice-president as a "labor-baiting, poker-
playing, whiskey-drinking, evil old man." When reporters
questioned the vice-president about Lewis' attack, Garner
chuckled, but in his hotel room he told his wife:

> There has never been anything that caused me
> more happiness than Lewis' outburst. I think that
> the majority of the people will think that anyone
> Lewis can't control is all right.

The vice-president announced in December of 1939,

"I will accept the nomination for President," and he ran
strong in the polls taken in early 1940. However, after
Roosevelt received the support of delegates in key states,
the Democratic Convention which wanted to pick a winner
in the fall nominated him for an unprecedented third term.
After Roosevelt won the election in November of 1940, Garner
returned to Washington in January of 1941 to preside over
the Senate until the end of his term. The retiring vice-
president had served in the government for thirty-eight
years, and he left Washington for Uvalde. He did not return.

At age seventy-nine, the former vice-president said
in an interview while he sat on the broad porch of his home
in Uvalde:

> I have had a lot of fun since I came back here.
> I get just the exercise I want, just the reading I
> want, just the amount of work I want, just the as-
> sociation I want. But for the fact that Mrs. Garner
> has been ill much of the time, I think I could say
> that the seven years since I came back here have
> been the seven happiest of my life.

Garner's wife for more than fifty years died in her
sleep on August 17, 1948. She had been ill for six years
with Parkinson's disease, and the day before she died she
slipped into a coma from which she did not recover. Her
husband, her son, two nurses, and a maid were with the
sick woman at her end.

In retirement Garner thought about writing his memoirs or engaging someone to do it for him. He had a record
of most of his activities during a long and useful life, but
he burned his records because he didn't want to go through
the files himself. If he had talked with an archivist or a
historian about the problem, he would have learned that he
could deposit his papers in a repository such as the Library
of Congress or the University of Texas and that the considerable labor of sorting his papers would have been done for
him. The lack of extensive files of the papers of the thirty-
second vice-president will deter biographers who otherwise
would consider writing a life of this important Texan. In
place of the correspondence files which Garner destroyed, a
serious scholar could obtain much pertinent biographical

information from the files of his contemporaries preserved
in the Franklin D. Roosevelt Presidential Library and elsewhere, but most historians would prefer to mine a file which
awaits examination. As a result of the burning of his personal papers, there is no definitive biography of John Nance
Garner, and one may not be written for years, if at all.

The "Judge," as he was known to old friends in
Uvalde, lived on until three weeks short of his ninety-ninth
birthday. During his last few years he made gifts totalling
more than a million dollars to the Southwest Texas Junior
College. He wanted to improve the educational opportunities
for young people in his and the surrounding counties, and
he gave the money rapidly because he knew that he would
not have many more years to live. He died of a very ripe
old age on November 7, 1967.

His son Tully, who returned to Texas while his father
was a congressman, managed the farms and businesses of
his parents. Tully married Ann Fraser of Texas, and their
one daughter, Genevieve, was the speaker's pet. She became Mrs. John Currie and often visited her grandfather in
retirement with her two young boys, John Garner Currie
and Tully Robert Currie. Son Tully died at the age of
seventy-one on October 3, 1968, less than a year after the
death of his famous father.

PRINCIPAL SOURCES

Mariette Rheiner Garner. "The Second Lady Speaks Her
    Mind." Ladies Home Journal, 52, 7+ (August, 1935).

Bascom W. Timmons. Garner of Texas, a Personal History.
    New York: Harper, [1948]. 294 p.

Michael John Romano. The Emergence of John Nance Garner
    as a Figure in American National Politics, 1924-1941.
    Unpublished Ph.D. Dissertation Accepted at St. John's
    University, 1974. 370 l.

HENRY A. WALLACE, 1941-1945

Henry Agard Wallace (1888-1965) was the
third Henry Wallace to be identified with
Wallaces' Farmer. "Uncle Henry" established
the publication in Des Moines, Iowa; "Harry"
edited the influential farm magazine until he
became Secretary of Agriculture in President
Harding's administration; "H.A." became editor
when his father left for Washington. In addition to managing Wallaces' Farmer, "H.A."
ran a small farm near Des Moines, and he led
in the development of hybrid corn. Wallace
left the Republicans because of their high
tariffs and was called on by President-elect
Roosevelt to submit a plan for the reorganization of the Department of Agriculture.
Wallace's response led to his being offered
the post of Secretary in February of 1933.
    Although Wallace was without political ex-
perience, he moved into his new office with
missionary zeal. He traveled widely, spoke
often, and wrote numerous articles and
books. Wallace supported all of the President's proposals for economic and social reform, and he became vice-president during
Roosevelt's third term. Wallace's liberalism
displeased conservative Democrats, and
Senator Harry Truman was selected in 1944
as the running mate for Roosevelt in his
campaign for a fourth term. Wallace became
secretary of commerce before President
Roosevelt's death and continued in office
after Truman became president. The secretary favored an accommodation with the
Soviet Union and publicly disagreed with

the president's foreign policy. As a result,
Wallace was summarily fired. After he left
Washington, Wallace edited The New Republic
and renewed his work on hybridization on a
farm at South Salem, New York. Wallace believed that world peace could be achieved
through Christianity, and he agreed to lead
the Progressive Citizens of America to achieve
his goals. Repudiation at the polls in 1948
left Wallace free to concentrate on experiments
with plants and animals which he did until
"Lou Gehrig's disease" caused his death in
Danbury, Connecticut, on November 18, 1965.

                    *   *   *

During the presidential campaign of 1940 when the Democratic National Committee requested a statement from the
wife of the candidate for the vice-presidency, Mrs. Henry
A. Wallace responded with the beginning of a recipe for
apple butter: "Wash, quarter, but do not peel juicy red
apples (Wealthy [variety] preferred.)" Ilo Browne disliked
publicity and did not accompany her husband on his speech-
making tours. She was an intensely private person "whose
life seemed to be her husband and her children." After the
death of Henry Wallace his widow gave $250,000 to Iowa
State University at Ames, his alma mater and that of their
two sons, to support a Henry A. Wallace Professorship in
Agricultural History and Rural Studies and a program of
research relating to her late husband.

    Ilo Browne Wallace was born on March 10, 1888, in
Indianola, Iowa, a county seat about twenty miles south of
Des Moines. Her father, James Browne, successively a
school teacher, merchant, and dealer in Iowa land, was
born near Fort Palmer, Pennsylvania; he married Ilo's mother, Hattie Lindsay of St. Charles, Iowa in 1877. Both were
United Presbyterians; Ilo's father was an elder in his church
and Sunday school superintendent until his death in 1911
when he left a small fortune to his heirs.

    Ilo Browne attended Simpson College in Indianola,
Monmouth College in Illinois, and Drake University in Des

Moines where she studied voice. At the last she became a
close friend of a sister of Henry Wallace, then a cub reporter on his father's farm journal. After Ilo and Henry met,
their period of courtship was brief. The couple was married on May 30, 1914, in Des Moines, and began housekeep-
ing in a small house of their own. The bride was described
as "cheerful, calm, and regal"; and, according to a family
tradition, when Henry first called on Ilo he carried with him
a classic book on agriculture in China which he read to her
aloud.

Ilo's suitor was the third in three generations of Henry Wallaces in Iowa. The first, often called "Uncle Henry,"
was born on March 19, 1836, in Western Pennsylvania, and
determined in his eighteenth year to prepare for the Presbyterian ministry. After preliminary studies in Ohio, Pennsylvania, and Illinois, he was ordained in April of 1863,
and began his ministry in churches in Rock Island, Illinois,
and Davenport, Iowa, on opposite banks of the Mississippi
River. A few months later, on September 10, 1863, Henry
Wallace married Nancy Cantwell of Kenton, Ohio, and they
started life together in one room of a boarding house in
Rock Island. After a brief period of service as a chaplain
with the Union army, Henry returned to Rock Island where
he and Nancy rented a house in which their son, Henry
Cantwell Wallace, was born on May 19, 1866. In the winter
of 1870-71 the Wallaces moved to Morning Sun, a small town
south of Davenport, where Henry preached, farmed, and
struggled to regain his health.

A physician encouraged the Reverend Henry Wallace to
stay out of doors as much as possible, and at age forty-one
he moved with his wife and four children to Winterset in
southwestern Iowa. There "Uncle Henry" managed his farms
in nearby Adair county, contributed articles on agriculture
to local newspapers, and became in 1883 editor of The Iowa
Homestead. Twelve years later he became editor of Wallaces'
Farm & Dairy which became a weekly in 1896, was moved to
Des Moines, and had its name shortened to Wallaces' Farmer.
Through the columns of this paper "Uncle Henry" became a
leader in agriculture in Iowa and throughout the country.
He died in 1916.

"Uncle Henry" and influential agricultural friends had
been active in the 1870s in the improvement of Iowa

Agricultural College at Ames; and his son, Henry Cantwell
(ordinarily called Harry), had enrolled there in 1885. Harry
was bored with his academic program and in his second year
was in love with May Brodhead of Muscatine, Iowa, who knew
nothing about farming. The young couple was married on
November 24, 1887, and Harry and his bride left college to
work as tenants on his father's farm near Orient. Here in
the small tenant house, Henry Agard Wallace, was born on
October 7, 1888. Harry and May Wallace had the help of a
married couple who lived in another tenant house on the
farm, but they had little money and few recreational opportunities. The second generation of Henry Wallaces did have
more books and periodicals and a greater interest in music
than were to be found on most Iowa farms.

In 1892 Harry received an invitation from Professor
C. F. Curtiss to resume his studies and to take charge of
the dairy herds and barns at Iowa Agriculture College, and
he moved his wife and two children to a modest house at the
edge of Ames. After Harry completed his course work, he
became an assistant professor and wrote for The Farm and
Dairy, a paper he and Professor Curtiss began to publish
in 1893.

Young Henry Agard Wallace, also called "H.A." for
short, was taught to read by his mother who also shared
with him her knowledge of familiar plants. At the age of
six "H.A." came to know George Washington Carver, then
about twenty-seven years old and a student in the Iowa
Agricultural College, who was to gain renown as a botanist.
The pair walked together in the fields and woods near Ames,
and Carver aroused in the boy a desire to master the subject of plant fertilization. Thus began a friendship which
lasted as long as the great Black scientist lived.

After Wallaces' Farmer began to prosper, Harry left
his professorship to become business manager of the paper,
and brother John solicited advertising and subscriptions by
covering Iowa on a bicycle. Daniel, the youngest brother,
helped around the shop and became one of the few who
could read his father's hurried handwriting. Harry moved
his family to Des Moines, and the family finally settled into
a large house on ten acres of land where "H.A." had many
chores. "He tended garden, cared for the chickens, milked
the family cow, and fed a pen of hogs." The boy cared

little about his appearance and often went to school in smelly
work clothes.

At age sixteen Wallace planted and worked a test plot
of five acres which revealed that the appearance of ears of
corn does not determine their yield as seed. Three years
later he reviewed his findings in Wallaces' Farmer and queried,
"What looks to a hog?" Henry Agard became a freshman at
Ames in 1906 and received a bachelor of science in animal
husbandry in 1910. Instead of returning for graduate
study, "H.A." preferred to write for Wallaces' Farmer and
to conduct his own experiments in plant breeding.

After his marriage, Henry Wallace worked as an editor
and market statistician for Wallaces' Farmer, ran his own farm
of eighty-seven acres six miles out of Des Moines, and delivered dairy products to Des Moines customers on his milk
route. His wife had a touch of tuberculosis while she was
carrying her first child, Henry Browne Wallace, but she recovered rapidly in Colorado. Back in Des Moines, Ilo helped
her husband with the milking at four-thirty almost every
morning, and she drove the milk route whenever necessary.
In 1916 Henry Agard also had tuberculosis (he maintained
he had undulant fever) and had to spend four months in the
Colorado Rockies to regain his health.

Harry Wallace was a scrapper, and in Wallaces' Farmer
he encouraged farmers to band together to fight the economic
problems which beset them after the end of World War I.
While he was out of the office busy with farm organizations,
his son "H.A." undertook more of the writing and editing.
Harry worked hard for the election of Republicans Harding
and Coolidge in 1920, and he was invited to serve as secretary of agriculture in the new administration. After he decided to accept the appointment, Harry informed his readers:

> I go to Washington ... because ... President
> Harding has taken an advanced stand for a sound
> national policy as it related to agriculture....
> Therefore he has a right to the help of every one
> of us as we can help best....
> So far as the editorial conduct of the paper is
> concerned, the responsibility will rest upon my son,
> Henry A. Wallace. He has been in the editorial
> work for ten years, and ... is fully equal to this
> larger responsibility.

Henry Cantwell Wallace was an energetic and reasonably successful secretary of agriculture. The new secretary
and the president were congenial companions at the card
table and on the golf links, and it was on the latter that
Harry received Harding's approval for an agricultural conference to be held in February, 1922. Out of the conference came thirty-seven recommendations for legislation but
nothing tangible for farm relief. The secretary of the interior, Albert J. Fall, prepared for the president's signa-
ture an Executive Order which would transfer the Forest
Service from agriculture to his department, and H. C.
Wallace threatened to resign if the transfer occurred. No
action was taken by President Harding before his Western
trip during which he died on August 2, 1923.

Secretary Wallace endorsed an export corporation to
dispose of surplus agricultural products and publicly supported the first McNary-Haugen bill, but neither was favored by President Coolidge. Harry Wallace decided to write
a book which would deal with economic problems of farmers,
but before completion he experienced intense pain from his
persistent sciatica. An operation was undertaken to relieve
pain, and the removal of his appendix and gall bladder
seemed to be beneficial. However, complications occurred
within a week, and Harry's wife wired his brothers and sons
to come to Washington. He died before they arrived on October 25, 1924, at the age of fifty-eight.

Henry A. Wallace read widely, including economic
treatises of Thorstein Veblen and a book, Economic Principles of Confucius, which described a "constantly normal
granery" utilized in China two thousand years ago. As
editor of Wallaces' Farmer "H.A." was free to attack the
administration of which his father was a part, and he advocated in his columns a plan for governmental crop insurance and an ever-normal granary according to "the Joseph
plan." The young editor concluded that high tariffs hurt
farmers, and he decided to leave the Republican party
which would not seriously consider the case for lower rates.

After Franklin D. Roosevelt won the national election
in 1932, the president-elect asked Henry A. Wallace, Rex-
ford Tugwell, and Milburn Wilson to propose plans for the
reorganization of the Department of Agriculture. In February of 1933 Wallace received Roosevelt's letter asking him to

be Secretary, and the editor seized his opportunity to work "under a chief who is definitely progressive, entirely sympathetic toward agriculture, and completely determined to use every means at his command to restore farm buying power."

The new secretary of agriculture was only forty-five and had held no administrative or political position. His appearance was unimpressive, but he entered his office as a man possessed by a mission. In his first year as secretary, Wallace traveled forty thousand miles through all of the forty-eight states, made eighty-eight speeches, and wrote twenty articles for periodicals and three books. He believed President Roosevelt to be a leader beyond compare and wholeheartedly supported measures as controversial as the proposal for enlarging the Supreme Court. Although Wallace encountered difficulties--the Agricultural Adjustment Act (AAA) was declared unconstitutional on January 6, 1936,--he could see in 1937 real progress in the formulation of plans for an ever-normal granary, free school lunches, and food stamps.

Although Ilo Wallace shunned publicity, she was interviewed by a representative of the New York _Times_ early in 1938, almost five years after her husband became a member of the Cabinet. The interview took place in the Wallace's hotel suite overlooking Rock Creek Park, and the newspaper woman was greeted at the door by Mrs. Wallace since she had encouraged her maid to see the rural arts exhibit at the Department of Agriculture. Ilo Wallace had "a pretty face and shining eyes lighted by a warm smile." She wore a dress of rough crêpe and a silver chain around her neck with a pendant of jade and silver repeated in her belt buckle. According to the interviewer, Ilo Wallace's chief interest lay in creating a home in which her husband could relax. She hoped that her two sons, then enrolled in Iowa State College, would "follow in their father's footsteps" and that daughter Jean would prepare herself to earn her own living, "not that she might have to do it, but I would want her to be able to."

Henry Wallace was vice-president from 1941 until 1945, roughly the years of the Second World War. President Roosevelt appointed Wallace chairman of the Board of Economic Warfare which was responsible for shipping and procurement of strategic materials. In this role he quarreled

with Jesse Jones, secretary of commerce, and Roosevelt resolved the dispute by abolishing the BEW and assigning its
duties to a new agency. According to the Schapsmeier
brothers, thorough students of Wallace's development as a
political thinker, "H.A.'s" part in the feud with Jones probably kept him from being renominated with President Roosevelt in 1944.

Eleanor Roosevelt wrote in The New Republic for August 7, 1944, "Mr. Wallace never was a politician and is not
a very good one now, but he has long been a thinker and
writer.... You will hear people say that they are afraid of
Henry Wallace because he is a dreamer, an impractical person,
a mystic." Wallace's "philosophy" was an inconstant mixture
of economics, politics, religion, and science which led him
toward utopian goals of social justice, improved living standards for minorities, and world peace. Many of his statements
sound like maxims, yet their meaning may have eluded his
listeners. Two of Wallace's pronouncements follow: "Parties
are of value only insofar as they make it possible to put into
action certain principles of social justice," and democracy is
the "political expression of Christian thought." The latter
was voiced in 1946 by the then secretary of commerce to a
labor organization in Mexico.

As the wife of the vice-president, Ilo Wallace stood in
many reception lines and often attended functions in place
of Mrs. Roosevelt. During World War II she sponsored the
Patrick Henry, the first liberty ship, and she served as a
Red Cross worker. Summers were spent in Iowa where she
gardened, rode horses, and discussed farm topics. When
her husband, as the vice-president-elect, drove to Mexico
from Washington, Ilo went with him accompanied by but one
aide, James Le Caron, and his wife. Later, Ilo recalled,
"Life in Washington was just party after party, luncheon
after luncheon, dinner after dinner." Once she invited so
many high ranking dignitaries to a dinner that she had to
call the State Department for help with the seating arrangements.

After the Democratic National Convention in Chicago
had nominated Harry Truman to be Roosevelt's running mate
in 1944, Wallace received from the president in San Diego a
telegram congratulating him for his "magnificent fight" in the
convention. The telegram continued, "Please tell Ilo not to

make any plans for leaving Washington in January." About
six weeks after the Convention, Roosevelt told Henry Wallace
that he could have any Cabinet post except that of secretary
of state. Wallace chose the Commerce Department because he
had learned that agriculture would not receive fair economic
treatment until businessmen of the country realized the need
for justice for all segments of the population. Wallace did
not mention that his choice would displace and embitter
Secretary of Commerce Jesse Jones.

About six weeks after Wallace became secretary of commerce, Roosevelt died and Harry Truman became president.
Wallace sought to commit the new administration to measures
which would promote full employment and world peace, and
he proceeded to comment on diverse topics, domestic and
foreign, as he had under Roosevelt. Wallace's Sixty Million
Jobs, published in 1945, advocated government participation
if needed to create jobs in the postwar years, and a Full
Employment Bill was supported by President Truman. The
legislation which resulted, the Employment Act of 1946, limited federal intervention, but it did create a Council of
Economic Advisers and a Joint Committee on the Economic
Report.

Along with Secretary of War Stimson, Wallace favored
an agreement with the Soviet Union on the control of atomic
energy, and he was disappointed in the Atomic Energy Act
which forbade regular exchange of information on atomic
energy with other nations. Unwisely assuming that he represented the Roosevelt tradition in foreign affairs, Wallace
spoke out on the need for improved relations with Russia.
Unmindful of the events which Churchill had denounced in
his "Iron Curtain" speech at Westminister College in Missouri, Wallace prepared a speech to be delivered at a large
rally in Madison Square Garden. The secretary reviewed
his speech with President Truman, but in actual delivery
Wallace omitted certain sections and in those which remained
Wallace castigated continuance of British imperialism. Ad-
verse reactions to Wallace's inept speech came from many
quarters, and these were followed by leaks to the press,
charges, and countercharges. After reviewing the facts,
President Truman quelled the tempest by asking a stunned
secretary of commerce for his resignation. Thirty minutes
later came Wallace's resignation which he had typed himself:

>As you requested, here is my resignation. I
>shall continue to fight for peace. I am sure that
>you will join me in that great endeavor.

After Wallace left the Truman administration, he accepted an editorial position with The New Republic. In order to be near his office in Manhattan, Wallace purchased a
large country home surrounded by 115 acres of land at South
Salem, New York, near Ridgefield, Connecticut. He called
his new home, Farvue Farm, the name of "Uncle Henry's"
residence, and he looked forward to further experimental
work with plants. By way of preparation for planting time,
Wallace purchased a small tractor and expected to enjoy making use of it in the following summer.

Instead of confining his efforts to his farm and The
New Republic, Wallace became a leader of the liberals opposed
to President Truman's foreign policy. The Truman Doctrine,
under which the United States would help nations in their
attempts to escape domination by the Soviet Union, seemed
to Wallace to be the equivalent of declaring war on Russia.
His speeches in England and France were cheered by radicals in Europe and in the United States; after his return, he
wrote and spoke against the Marshall Plan for economic aid
to Europe. Wallace had come to believe that the new and
untried United Nations organization should be relied on for
solutions to international problems.

Late in 1947 Wallace visited the Holy Land, and the
trip convinced him that "peace and good will" would not
prevail among men until governments followed the teachings
of Christ in their dealings with each other. Wallace's com-
mitment to world peace through Christianity led him to decide on December 2, 1947, to lead a third party "for peace
and for bringing real Americanism back again to the United
States." Although Wallace had earlier advised against a
third party movement, his idealism overcame realistic and
rational judgments. The leadership of the Progressive Citizens of America was tolerant of Communists, and Wallace
accepted support from the American Communist Party. The
result at the polls in 1948 was a disaster for Wallace; "Gid-
eon's army" received only 1,157,140 votes, far below the
predicted ten percent of the electorate.

After Wallace became convinced that United Nations

sanctions against North Korea were justified on legal and
moral grounds, he left the Progressive Party in the summer
of 1950. This left Wallace free to concentrate on his first
love, experiments with plants and animals. The seed business which he had founded in 1926 had become a multimillion-
dollar business, the Pioneer Hi-Bred Corn Company. The
company did not make a profit until 1935, but thirty years
later the estate of Henry A. Wallace was valued at $840,000.

In 1964, at the age of seventy-six, Wallace climbed a
pyramid in Central America. After he came down he noted
a numbness in one leg which caused him to limp. Medical
experts could not diagnose the cause of his muscle deterior-
ation, but additional tests revealed that he suffered from
amyotrophic lateral sclerosis, "Lou Gehrig's disease." Wallace knew that there was no cure for his terminal disease,
and he permitted doctors at the National Institute of Health
to remove sections of muscle tissue for examination and
study. With the advance of the disease, Wallace went from
crutches to a wheelchair and speech became difficult. He
died on November 18, 1965, in a hospital at Danbury, Connecticut, "with his beloved wife Ilo at his bedside."

The third Henry Wallace "did not possess the gracious-
ness of his grandfather nor the gregariousness of his father." "H.A." did not smoke or drink, and he used no jokes
or small talk to enliven conversation. At age twenty-five
he was reputed to be a "miserable speaker," and he never
overcame a streak of shyness which excluded him from the
camaraderie of political leaders. Indeed, to some Wallace
appeared to be "a kind of ascetic."

Newspaper columnist Drew Pearson once told Henry
Wallace that his public relations instincts were not sound
and that he should listen more to his wife. She did not like
many of his close associates in the Progressive Party, but
she campaigned for his election in 1948 and made speeches
in his behalf. Ilo defended her husband against charges of
disloyalty to his country but conceded that he did not always make his position clear. "I don't think my husband
always helps things," she said in an interview, "He puts
his worst foot forward." This may be the reason why she
counseled against his writing his memoirs while in retirement
at Farvue Farm.

Ilo Wallace lived until February 21, 1981, a few weeks from the ninety-third anniversary of her birth on March 10, 1888, in Indianola, Iowa. Mrs. Wallace died from a stroke, and she had suffered a series of strokes before her death. Her body was brought to Des Moines for burial in Glendale Cemetery.

PRINCIPAL SOURCES

Russell Lord. The Wallaces of Iowa. Boston: Houghton Mifflin, 1947. 615p.

Edward L. and Frederick H. Schapsmeier. Henry A. Wallace of Iowa: the Agrarian Years, 1910-1940. Ames: The Iowa State University Press, [1968]. 327 p.

_____. Prophet in Politics: Henry A. Wallace and the War Years, 1940-1965. Ames: The Iowa State University Press, [1970]. 268p.

PERSONAL NOTE

I had the pleasure of being with Mrs. Wallace and her children at Farvue Farm on two days in the late 1960s. On the first I talked with the family about the removal of Henry Wallace papers to The University of Iowa Libraries (of which I was then director), and on the second visit I made a request to the family members present for a grant of money to help in microfilming the Wallace Papers in three repositories: The University of Iowa, the Library of Congress, and the Franklin D. Roosevelt Presidential Library at Hyde Park, N.Y.

On both days I had a midday meal with the family. Mrs. Wallace sat at the head of the table and was a charming hostess. After the children and grandchildren left on the first day, Mrs. Wallace showed me the gardens and hen houses and talked about her late husband's interest in producing brown eggs, not because they were more nutritious than the white, but because they fetched higher prices in New and old England. After dinner on the second day Mrs. Wallace left promptly with her daughter to keep an appointment with a physician in New York.

Mrs. Wallace's principal concern with the transfer of
the Wallace papers from Farvue Farm to Iowa City seemed
to be whether her two sons and a daughter were pleased
with the arrangements.   After Mrs. Wallace was satisfied on
this point, most of the details were handled by her second
son, Robert, of Doylestown, Pennsylvania, in letters and
telephone conversations.

In sorting and listing the papers which came to Iowa,
a member of the Library staff discovered in Wallace's handwriting in pencil a document of eight pages entitled "Miscel-
laneous Recollections of the [Roosevelt] Interment Train.
April 14-15, 1945."   I wrote to Mrs. Wallace for permission
to publish the document, which is rich in human interest,
and she responded that I could do so if I would omit the
last sheet in which Wallace characterized President Truman
as "putty."   Since the suggested omission would detract from
the usefulness of the proposed publication, I let the matter
rest until after the death of President Truman.   When I
wrote again, Mrs. Wallace gave the desired permission, and
the manuscript was published in 1974 in facsimile with notes
by the Friends of The University of Iowa Libraries.

HARRY S TRUMAN, 1945

Harry S Truman (1884-1972) was born on a farm near Lamar, Missouri, and grew up on a farm near Independence. After graduation from high school, Harry worked as a bank clerk in Kansas city, but he left to work from 1906-1917 on his father's large farm near Grandview, Mo. When Truman's National Guard unit was mobilized in 1917, he went overseas for two years and rose in rank from lieutenant to major. On his return, before he had a job, Harry married "Bess" Wallace, whom he had courted for nine years. The Trumans invested their savings in a haberdashery in downtown Kansas City which went bankrupt, and Harry became the successful candidate of the Pendergast machine for the office of county judge (commissioner). Truman failed of reelection but became presiding judge for two terms, 1927-1935. Truman's persistent efforts to build better roads and his integrity in office led to his becoming the Pendergast candidate for the United States Senate. In his first term, 1935-1941, Truman participated in hearings on civil aviation and on railroad management; in his second, 1941-1945, the senator gained national attention as chairman of a special committee to investigate defense contracts and programs.

Senator Truman was chosen in 1944 to be the running mate in President Roosevelt's campaign for a fourth term. Roosevelt died on April 12, 1945, three months after his fourth inauguration, and Truman became president while World War II was still in progress. The new president met with the leaders of the other Allies to plan

the post-war world; but, when the Soviet Union
set its own course, Truman announced a broad
program to assist nations in danger of communist
subversion. President Truman was elected in
1948 to another term, but his administration was
beset with labor troubles at home and communist
aggression in Korea. After thirty years in public office, Truman retired in 1953 to Independence where he wrote his memoirs and spent
pleasant hours in the Truman Presidential Library. The former president died in Independence on December 26, 1972.

*   *   *

Margaret Truman tells in her <u>Souvenir</u> (1956) an amusing
story in which her father, the thirty-third president of the
United States, found her mother burning letters she had
received from him while he was overseas during World War I:

> "What are you doing?" he asked.
> "I'm burning your letters to me," she replied.
> "Bess, you oughtn't do that." He was surprised
>   and hurt.
> "Why not? I've read them several times."
> "But think of history!" admonished the former
>   President.
> "I have!" responded his prudent wife.

Fortunately, for "history" very few of Harry Truman's
letters to his family were destroyed; many letters said to
have been burned were copied before destruction and caches
of additional originals have been discovered recently. The
editor of Truman's <u>Letters Home</u> (1984) believes that Harry
wrote Bess an estimated 1,500 letters of which 1,200 have
survived. Truman also wrote many letters to his daughter,
to his brother and sister and to others in his family; generous selections from these have appeared in print during
the last decade.

While there are ample materials readily available to il-
lustrate Harry Truman's close relationships with relatives,
there is a lack of published letters written by his wife.
Correspondent Truman often mentioned the pleasure he derived from reading letters from Bess and Margaret, and he

probably kept the originals. According to Monte Poen,
editor of Letters Home, "The President saved everything--
including laundry slips--for history," yet he does not give
the location of the letters Truman received which prompted
his intimate replies.

Elizabeth Wallace was the granddaughter of George
Porterfield Gates, a successful manufacturer of pastry flour,
who had built a spacious home at 219 North Delaware Street,
the most fashionable address in Independence, Missouri.
Bess's mother, Madge, had married David Willcock Wallace,
a son of a Jackson County pioneer and a county official with
a promising career. The couple, with their daughter, Bess,
and three younger brothers, lived in a large house at 608
North Delaware, where, for reasons not known today, David
Wallace killed himself. After a year in Colorado, Madge Wallace and her four children returned to Independence and
moved in with her parents at 219 North Delaware.

At the time of the family tragedy, Bess, who had been
born in 1885, was eighteen and a graduate of Independence
elementary and high schools. Bess then attended Barstow
finishing school in nearby Kansas City, but she lived at
home where she could help her mother (later called "Mother
Wallace") in the upbringing of her three brothers. As a
young woman, Bess had superb physical coordination: she
played baseball with her brothers, and she became skilled in
skating, fishing, swimming, and in the handling of horses.
She was acknowledged to be one of the best tennis players,
male or female, in Independence.

Across the street from the Wallace's, in a little house
at 216 North Delaware, lived Ella Noland, an aunt of Harry
Truman, and her two daughters, Nellie and Ethel. One day
in 1910 when Harry, who had been born on May 8, 1884,
was visiting his aunt Ella, she mentioned that she had a
cake plate of Mrs. Wallace which should be returned. According to a family tradition, Harry seized the plate and ran
with it across the street. When Bess came to the door, "the
courtship was on."

Harry Truman was born in Lamar, Missouri, a small
farming town about 120 miles south of Kansas City. His
father, John Anderson Truman, a dealer in horses and mules,
and his mother, Martha Ellen Young, were married in 1881.

His mother had attended the Baptist Female College in Lexington, Missouri; she recognized that her children, a boy,
Vivian, and a girl, Mary, in addition to Harry, would enjoy
greater educational opportunities in a settled community than
they could have on an isolated farm.

Economic difficulties caused the Truman family to move
to other rural communities in southwestern Missouri, to Independence, and to the Young family farm near Grandview.
At age six in Independence, Harry attended a Sunday
School where he first saw Bess with her lovely blue eyes
and golden curls, and she and he were classmates in the
high school at Independence, class of 1901. The Trumans
and the Wallaces represented different social levels, and
Harry was not a member of the group in which Bess moved
and flourished.

In addition to the precarious financial condition of his
family, Harry Truman had physical problems which kept him
from participating in athletics. At age six he began to wear
heavy glasses to compensate for "flat eyeballs," and at ten
he had a case of diptheria from which recovery was very
slow. Harry's glasses and diptheria, which kept him from
sports, helped him to become a great reader. The boy,
who had been taught by his mother to read before he was
five, read through the Bible several times before he was
twelve, and he reveled in the histories and biographies he
found in the local public library. The knowledge gained
thereby as a youth stayed with Truman as an adult; as a
senator he encouraged his thirteen-year old daughter to apply herself to her studies including music, French, geogra-
phy, and mathematics. Some day, her father counseled,
"you'll be very glad that you can ... talk intelligently about
Agrippa and Genghis Khan!"

After graduation from high school, Truman lived for
four years in Kansas City where he worked in several banks
and enjoyed professional musical and theatrical productions.
During this period Harry studied bookkeeping and shorthand
in a commercial school, and he took piano lessons. Also, at
the age of twenty-one, Harry Truman, along with "some of
the boys in the bank," joined a battery of light artillery in
the National Guard. He explained that he did so deliberately:

After reading all the books obtainable in the

Independence and Kansas City libraries on history
and government from Egypt to U.S.A., I came to
the conclusion that every citizen should know something about military, finance or banking, and agriculture. All my heroes or great leaders were somewhat familiar with one or the other or all three. So
I started my grass roots military education by joining a National Guard battery, June 14, 1905.

When his parents had an opportunity to move to the
Young family farm at Grandview, Harry encouraged them to
do so and agreed to quit the bank and to return with them.
As a result, Harry Truman worked on a farm from 1906 until
1917, and he enjoyed it. The Trumans rotated crops on the
farm, and they made frequent use of a manure spreader.
The young farmer learned that "Riding one of these [gang]
plows all day, day after day, gives one time to think."

In January of 1909 Harry Truman became a Mason.
"That spring and summer I spent teaching the plow horses
all the Masonic lectures." Truman became in 1910 the first
master of a new Masonic lodge in Grandview, and he rose
in the 1930s in the grand lodge of Missouri until he became
grand master in 1940. "It is a high honor and one for which
I was most grateful to my friends and brethren."

While still on the farm at Grandview, Harry started to
call on Bess on Saturdays, and the trip to Independence by
train and streetcar required more than an hour. In 1914
Harry reduced the time required to travel' back and forth
through the purchase for $600 of a 1911 Stafford automobile.
With the car Harry could expand his walks with Bess to excursions with her and with their friends.

Harry was a devoted and worshipful suitor. In June
of 1911, when he was twenty-seven, Harry asked Bess in a
letter whether she would wear his diamond ring on her left
hand and went on to belittle his financial prospects. Bess
refused him gently, and Harry became obsessed with schemes
for immediate wealth: oil wells in Oklahoma, a ranch in
South Dakota, and a "dad blasted" zinc mine. Despite despair over his "direful financial difficulties," Harry declared
in a letter written on May 27, 1917, "I'm the luckiest guy
in the world to have you to love"; for, after seven years of
unflagging courtship, Bess had finally agreed to become his
wife.

If the newly engaged couple had plans for an early
wedding, they were interrupted when Harry volunteered for
military service in World War I. As a former member of a
National Guard unit, Harry helped to enlist new recruits and
was elected by them to be a first lieutenant in Battery F of
the 129th Field Artillery. The outfit trained at Camp Doniphan at Fort Sill, Oklahoma, where Truman became disgusted
with the physical conditions and with the overbearing atti-
tude of regular army officers toward reservists. Lt. Truman wrote daily to Bess and begged her to visit him at Camp
Doniphan. She does not appear to have done so, but his
mother and sister came. His mother, then sixty-five years
old, smiled at her son all the time she was in camp but "she
cried all the way home."

Lt. Truman went in April, 1918, with nine other officers and a hundred men of the 129th Field Artillery, to
France for additional training. In July he was given command of Battery D which was composed mainly of German
and Irish Catholics from a Jesuit high school in Kansas City.
Although the wild soldiers had broken three commanders,
Captain Truman gained the respect of his men almost immediately. Truman proved to be an officer who could lead,
and his troops became devoted to him. After the war, Truman attended many of the annual reunions of his beloved
battery, and members of the unit walked beside his limousine
in the inaugural parade in 1949. In 1980 twenty-three of
the original group of 210 men were still alive, and six of the
artillerymen attended Bess's funeral in 1982--four of the six
were there in wheelchairs.

In less than two months after his discharge, on June
28, 1919, Harry and Bess, at ages thirty-five and thirty-
four, respectively, were married in the Episcopal church in
Independence. After a short honeymoon in Chicago and
Port Huron, Michigan, the newly married couple moved into
the seventeen room house at 219 North Delaware where Bess
had lived since 1904. Truman never won the approval of
his mother-in-law, and he endured her pointed comments
with exemplary restraint.

Truman had a wife but no job or profession. In the
fall of 1919 he and his former canteen sergeant, Eddie Jacobsen, opened a haberdashery across from the Muehlebach Hotel
in downtown Kansas City. Bess kept the books for the firm,

and she handled the advertising. Business at the outset
was brisk, but a recession kept customers away and left the
partners with a large inventory of expensive apparel. Truman and Jacobsen lost their initial investment of $15,000
and found themselves saddled with debts beyond their ability
to pay. When Jacobsen declared bankruptcy in 1925, Truman
assumed the entire obligation of their partnership. Harry
carried the burden of debt for another ten years.

A few days before the haberdashery closed in 1922,
Jim Pendergast, who had been a lieutenant in Truman's army
outfit, the 129th Field Artillery, came into the shop with his
father, Mike, and encouraged Harry to run for a political
office. The Pendergasts wanted a candidate for the office
of judge (commissioner) of the rural eastern district of Jackson County. The post paid $3,600 a year, and the Trumans
jumped at the chance to run for office with the support of
the Pendergast machine. Harry was an attractive candidate
for the post: he had farmed successfully in the county, he
had a fine war record, and his wife had many influential
relatives and friends. Candidate Truman failed as a platform
speaker, but his army and Masonic connections won the election for him.

During Truman's first term as a county judge, 1923-
1925, he and Bess drove over miles of wretched roads in
Jackson County, and he laid plans for their improvement
and for an investigation of conditions in the Old Folks Home.
Regardless of support from the Kansas City Star, Truman
lost the contest for reelection, and he again had to find
work for the support of his family which now included daughter Margaret, born on February 17, 1924. Harry finally
secured a job selling memberships for the Kansas City Auto-
mobile Club which paid well, but he longed to return to
politics.

Harry approached Mike Pendergast about running for
the office of county collector which paid about $25,000 a
year, but Boss Tom Pendergast thought that Truman should
try to become presiding judge (commissioner) for the county
at $6,000. Truman held the office for two four-year terms,
1927-1935, and performed effectively in it. After the Pendergast machine had disposed of the county patronage,
"Judge" Truman worked to keep graft out of construction
contracts and to build good roads across the county. His

work as a builder of roads and of a four-million-dollar courthouse was recorded in a booklet entitled Jackson County:
Results of County Planning, copies of which were sent to
each of the courthouses in Missouri's 114 counties.

In the first week of May 1934, when Truman was in
Warsaw, Missouri, he was summoned to meet with the chairman of the Democratic committee and Jim Pendergast, "my
war buddy," in nearby Sedalia.   There Judge Truman
learned that the Pendergast machine wanted him to run for
the United States Senate.   Harry at first demurred because
he did not see himself as a legislator, but he agreed to enter the contest for the nomination against two other candidates.   Truman visited seventy-five counties during the
summer, and his friendship with county judges and clerks
helped him to win both the nomination and the election.   The
prospective senator confided to his diary, "I have come to
the place where all men strive to be at my age [fifty]."

In his first term in the Senate, 1935-1941, Truman
made an enviable record.   He was assigned to the Interstate
Commerce and Appropriations committees; and, as a member
of the former, he participated in hearings on rapidly expanding civil aviation and on graft in management of railroads.
These activities caused him to have important roles in the
adoption of the Civil Aeronautics Act of 1938 and of the
Transportation Act of 1940.

The personal life of the freshman senator from Missouri
was beset with financial problems.   Although his wife drew
$4,500 a year as a member of his office staff, Truman could
not afford to maintain comfortable homes in Independence
and Washington.   As a result, the three Trumans and Mother
Wallace occupied a succession of modest two-bedroom apartments in the capital; and, when the others in his family
returned to Independence, the lonely senator would reduce
his living expenses by moving out of an apartment and into
a single room in a hotel near the Capitol.

Worst of all, Bess never learned to enjoy the life of a
politician's wife in Washington.   She mistakenly "feared, as
any Midwestern woman might, the coldness of an Eastern
city," and she was uncomfortable in the midst of the
"sophisticated backgrounds" of her husband's colleagues.
"Most had graduated from college.   They were ex-governors,

high executives--things like that." During the years her
husband was in Washington, Bess never found a laundry
which suited her and sent the family wash to a familiar firm
in Kansas City.

Instead of making arrangements for congenial living
in Washington, Bess would leave when convenient with her
mother and daughter for long stays in Independence. During the first three of Margaret's years in high school, she
spent one semester at Gunston Hall in Washington and the
other in a public high school in Independence. Her entire
fourth year was spent at Gunston Hall and Bess remained in
Washington with her, but this happened to be at the time
Harry was traveling around the country. The long ab-
sences of Bess and Margaret continued after Harry Truman
became president, and Bess even complained that he spent
too little time with her at Christmas in 1945 when he was in
Independence and ate three turkey dinners with different
branches of his family. Surely, the only good which came
from the long separations in the Truman family was his need
to write letters to Bess, "the light in every day," and to
Margie, always his "beautiful baby."

Without help from the Pendergasts, Truman won reelection to the Senate and began his second term on January
3, 1941. Within a few months Truman became chairman of a
new Special Committee to Investigate the National Defense
Program which came to be known as the "Truman Committee."
Truman's Democratic colleagues on the Committee urged him
to seek the nomination in 1944 for vice-president, but he
always refused. The man from Missouri would repeatedly
ask the senator making the proposal to name four vice-
presidents who were not alive, and not one could do it.
Moreover, Truman enjoyed being a senator and claimed that
he wanted to remain there.

The story of President Roosevelt's selection of Senator
Truman to be his running mate in 1944 has been told and
retold. The leading candidates were the incumbent, Henry
Wallace, who was not acceptable to the party bosses, James
Byrnes, head of the War Mobilization Board, who was disliked by labor leaders, and Senator Truman, who protested
that he did not want the job. Not until President Roosevelt
telephoned at almost the last moment from San Diego was the
selection settled. Truman, still reluctant to accept the

nomination, heard President Roosevelt say that unless he
accepted the Democratic party might be broken up during a
war. Truman finally told the other politicians in the room
in the Blackstone Hotel in Chicago: "Well, if that is the
situation I'll have to say yes, but why the hell didn't he
put it that way in the first place."

President Roosevelt was in poor health in the fall of
1944, and the candidate for the vice-presidency carried the
campaign for the ticket. Truman's election to the second
highest political office brought him an increase of $5,000 in
salary, but his family remained in their apartment at 4701
Connecticut Avenue. The new vice-president found that
he had more free time than he had enjoyed as a senator,
and in part of it Truman wrote a history of his life after
graduation from high school which forms the principal part
of his published Autobiography (1980).

Three months after he became vice-president, on April 12, 1945, Truman was summoned to the White House by
Steve Early, President Roosevelt's press secretary. When
he arrived, Truman learned from Mrs. Roosevelt that her
husband had died at Warm Springs, Georgia. A few minutes
after learning that he had become president, Truman called
his apartment and asked Bess and Margaret to attend the
swearing-in ceremony which was to be held in the White
House. Members of the Cabinet were present, and Secretary of Labor Frances Perkins recalled how Bess Truman
looked:

> She had been weeping, and her eyes were red
> and swollen, and it was with difficulty that she kept
> her face straight.... She's a quickly emotional per-
> son, ... but she stood there like a Trojan, just
> startled and having to bear it, that's all. Her face
> shows it. It's a very interesting portrait, on that
> account.

After the interment of the body of the late president
at Hyde Park, New York, the train which carried the official
party returned to Washington. On the way Eleanor Roosevelt
suggested to Bess Truman that she hold her first press conference within a few days and volunteered to accompany her
and to make necessary introductions. The prospect of meeting with "the girls" in a press conference distressed Bess

until Frances Perkins told the new First Lady that she did
not need to follow the example of her predecessor. Bess
was greatly relieved and soon wrote to the chairperson of
Mrs. Roosevelt's Press Conference Association, "I do not
expect to hold press conferences." When Bess reaffirmed
her position to a reporter, "But no direct interviews under
any circumstances," she was asked, "Mrs. Truman, how are
we ever going to get to know you?" Bess quickly replied,
"You don't need to know me. I'm only the President's wife
and the mother of his daughter."

Margaret had been born five years after the marriage
of her parents who were thirty-nine and forty at the time
of her birth. She was their only child and understandably
was smothered with affection, especially from her proud and
doting father. At age twelve Margie joined the choir of
the Trinity Episcopal Church in Independence; and at age
fourteen, when her father was in the Senate, she was enrolled in Gunston Hall, a small private school for girls that
followed Southern traditions. When Margaret was graduated
in 1942, her father was the commencement speaker. Margaret
won the English prize and Spanish award at Gunston Hall
that year, and the audience was delighted when the senator
said that his daughter took after her mother in those subjects.

Margaret went to college as a day student at George
Washington University where she majored in government and
history. Again, at her graduation in 1946, her father was
on the platform at her commencement, for he received one
of his twenty-two honorary degrees on the day Margaret
received her bachelor's. During the months Margaret attended classes at George Washington University, her mother
remained in Washington, and one of her parents usually
drove her to school.

After graduation from college, Margaret wanted to
study for a career in singing. Her father, who admired
Chopin and renowned pianists, had encouraged Margaret in
her study of music since she was a child, and some singers
who had heard her (Lawrence Tibbett was one) made complimentary remarks about her voice. Margaret had made
progress in singing under a teacher in Kansas City, and
her parents (her father had become president) arranged for
Margaret to study in New York under Helen Traubel, one

of the great operatic sopranos of the day.   When Helen
Traubel tried to discourage Margaret from making a singing
tour, the pupil found another teacher who encouraged her
in plans to appear before the public.

Margaret made her debut as a singer in March, 1947,
with the Detroit Symphony Orchestra.   The concert was
broadcast over a national radio network to an audience of
an estimated twenty million people including her delighted
father at the "winter White House" in Key West, Florida.
Congratulatory telegrams came in such numbers that the
president responded uncharacteristically with a short, formal
acknowledgement.   As is well known, Margaret's singing in
public did not meet the standards set by music critics, and
her concert in December 1950 in Washington, D.C. was
roundly criticized by Paul Hume, music critic of the Washington Post.   Her father vented his anger in an incredible
letter in which he called the critic a "guttersnipe" and
threatened him with blows if they should meet on the street.
When Hume made the letter public, most of the astonished
readers indulged the impulsive father who couldn't tolerate
derogatory comments about his daughter's voice.

While in Washington the First Lady followed a regular
schedule: awake at 7:15, breakfast at 8:00 with Harry and
Margaret, worked on correspondence and menus from 9:00
until 11:00, lunch with the president at one, read a mystery
at 2:00, reception at 3:00, cocktails (one strong old-
fashioned) with Harry at 6:00, dinner at 7:00, films or conversation with husband until bedtime at 11:00.   After Bess
had settled into her routine, she agreed to answer questions
submitted in writing by reporters.   The questions were in-
nocuous, and her answers were brief, almost curt.   A few
examples follow:

Q: Would she [Bess] want to be President?
A: No

Q: What is her reaction to musical criticism of
     Margaret's singing?
A: No comment.

Q: What would you like to do when your husband
     is no longer President?
A: Return to Independence, Missouri.

Less than two months after her husband became president, Bess, Margaret and Mother Wallace left on June 2,
1945. At home they received an enthusiastic welcome, and
her sister-in-law commented, "It was as if she never had
been away."

Before unpacking, Bess started phoning her
neighbors. The next day she attended a session
of the Independence bridge club and got her hair
set at the local beauty parlor that she had frequented
for years.

Not long afterward Bess entertained her bridge club
at the White House. The eleven women with whom she had
played bridge for twenty-five years in Independence spent
four days in Washington where they had dinner in the state
dining room, sat in the presidential box at Constitution Hall
for a concert, and visited the president's Oval Office, but
Harry was away. He had chosen the time of the visit of his
wife's bridge club to go to Hyde Park to dedicate President
Roosevelt's birthplace as a national shrine.

Harry's mother, Martha Ellen Truman, visited the
White House soon after he became the president. Mamma
Truman then was ninety-four, and she walked with a cane
because she had broken a hip twice. The president greeted
his mother at the door of the airplane; and, when she saw
the crowd that had gathered, she told her son that if she
had known there would be such a crowd she would have
stayed at home. The photograph of the president greeting
his mother at the top of the steps beside her airplane won
the grand prize of the 1945 competition among the White
House photographers. Harry Truman presented the award
to "a timid little boy (forty maybe)," and wrote his mother
about the event. Son Harry commented, "It is a nice picture."

During the three years and ten months of President
Roosevelt's unfinished fourth term, his successor had to deal
with large and difficult problems for which he had no pertinent background. World War II was still in progress in Europe and in the Pacific, and the new president met in July
of 1945 with Churchill and Stalin at Potsdam, near Berlin,
to discuss bringing the war to an end on both fronts and
the shape of the postwar world. President Truman made the

decision to drop atomic bombs on Japanese cities and thereby save the lives of hundreds of thousands of American
and Japanese soldiers. The unwillingness of the Soviet Union to abide by agreements with the British and Americans
led in 1947 to the promulgation of the Truman doctrine, a
broad program to assist nations in danger of communist subversion. This led quickly to the adoption of the Marshall
Plan and within a few years to the formation of NATO.

After the end of World War II, the United States became embroiled in conflicts over prices of consumer goods
and wages for workers. The president, long a friend of
labor, came to view big labor as much of a problem as big
business. Truman vetoed the Taft Hartley bill which Congress passed over his vetoe, and he directed a seizure of
steel mills which was thrown out by the courts. Harry Truman, despite his Southern background, addressed himself
to the thorny question of civil rights, not for "social equality" but for "equality of opportunity for all human beings."

The president's countrymen wondered whether a rather
obscure man from Missouri could handle such a host of complicated problems. The new president had in his makeup
two important elements, a deeply rooted sense of right and
wrong and disciplined mental habits which made him a superb
politician. Harry noted in his diary that he had acquired
"at his mother's knee" a belief "in honor, ethics, and right
living as its own reward," and he wrote to daughter Margaret
when she was thirteen:

> Politics is a great game. Your dad has been
> playing at it for some twenty-five years. It is a
> game of people and how they act under certain con-
> ditions.... You must be able to tell the facts too,
> and to believe them yourself.

In retirement, Harry Truman explained how he reached
a final decision:

> I was always thinking about what was pending
> and hoping that the final decision would be correct.
> I thought about them on my walks. I thought about
> them in the morning and the afternoon and thought
> about them after I went to bed and then did a lot
> of reading to see if I could find some background of
> history which would affect what had to be done.

Truman's third secretary of state, Dean Acheson, dis-
cerned an uncommon quality in his chief:

> I acquired the greatest respect and admiration
> for the President's capacity to understand complex
> problems and to decide. This is one of the rarest
> qualities possessed by man. Too frequently the
> mind vacillates between unpleasant choices and es-
> capes through procrastination.

The president explained in a letter to Bess why he
couldn't leave Washington with the adjournment of Congress.
He could leave and let approximately fifty bills die from a
legal "pocket veto"; but, he wrote, "I don't want to do
that ... I have faced the music, and have never failed to
take a positive stand when necessary. So I'd better stay
and finish the job."

Harry Truman's elevation to the presidency increased
the pressures on his marriage. As a senator, he had been
able to persuade Bess to be with him while the Senate was
in session, and she did her part in the required official
entertaining. The demands of social functions in the White
House did not appeal to Bess, and she would leave with her
daughter and mother for the congenial surroundings of the
family home in Independence. The president, left alone,
would have dinner alone in the "Great White Jail," the
Trumans' name for the president's official residence.

During the 1948 campaign, Truman observed, "I'd be
much better off personally if we lose ... but I fear that the
country would go to hell and I have to try to prevent that."
If the Republicans won, European recovery might end and
his programs at home would be reversed. Political forecast-
ers didn't expect Truman to win the election in 1948, but
they underestimated the seasoned campaigner from Missouri.
With his wife and daughter, aides, secret service officers,
and reporters, Truman traveled 32,000 miles by rail and
delivered from a platform at the end of the train between
300 and 350 speeches. After he had finished his informal
remarks, the president would call Bess and Margie from their
private car to greet the crowd, and the train would pull
slowly away to the tune of the "Missouri Waltz" played by
a local high school band.

President Truman's official residence from the beginning of 1949 until the spring of 1952 was the Blair-Lee
House, because the White House was near collapse and had
to be gutted and rebuilt. Bess found the Blair House to
be a more congenial residence than the White House, but
this did not help her to find any pleasure in the ceremonies
which surround a president, countless receiving lines, sal-
utes of twenty-one guns, and frequent renditions of "Hail
to the Chief." Moreover, during her husband's full term in
office, Mother Wallace died at the age of ninety; Charlie
Ross, the president's press secretary whom she and Harry
had known in high school, died suddenly; and an attempt
was made to assassinate her husband.

Truman's "Fair Deal" of twenty-four points ran
aground in the Korean War which the president termed "a
police action," despite the deaths of 33,000 Americans along
with an estimated half a million Chinese and Koreans. The
war reached a stalemate, and General MacArthur appealed
for authority to enlarge the war, "There is no substitute
for victory." Truman fired the heroic general, and many
Americans disapproved of the president's action. In Washington, Senator Joseph McCarthy of Wisconsin created a turmoil through his charges and witch hunts of Communists in
government. Bess was understandably relieved when her
husband announced on March 29, 1952, at a Jefferson-Jackson
Day dinner in Washington, "I do not feel that it is my duty
to spend another four years in the White House."

When the Trumans left Washington they were surprised
at the size of the crowd at the Union Station, and ten thousand gathered in the station at Independence and another
five thousand stood in front of their home on Delaware Street.
The former president noted in his diary, "Mrs. T. and I
were overcome. It was the payoff for thirty years of hell
and hard work."

In retirement Truman spent his mornings working on
his memoirs or in the Truman Presidential Library. In the
late afternoon Bess would prepare dinner which often contained his favorite foods: roast beef, oven-browned potatoes, green beans or spinach, and custard pie or fresh fruit
for dessert. After dinner the Trumans would read or watch
television until bedtime at nine-thirty or ten.

Margaret, at age thirty-two, married Clifton Daniel, an editor of the New York Times, in 1956, and their first child was born a year later. The boy, nicknamed "Kif," had three brothers, and the four grandsons gladdened the hearts of Harry and Bess in Independence, on trips to New York, and on vacations in Key West. In addition to fishing with his grandsons, Harry Truman took the boys on his morning walks and read to them from the works of a classical Greek historian.

After Harry Truman left the presidency, he and Bess made two trips to Europe. In 1956 they saw "the sights," were entertained by dignitaries, and Harry received an honorary degree at Oxford University. The mayor of Philadelphia, Joseph Clark, Jr., was in the audience at Oxford, and he wrote an article about the honor and affection shown to the former president. The piece was printed in a newspaper, and Mayor Clark sent a copy to Truman. Truman was touched and penned an acknowledgment which contained a bit of self-revelation:

> I opened it [the letter from Mayor Clark], read it, read the column you enclosed, and did exactly what I did at Oxford. I wiped my eyes and my glasses.
> You know, I'm a damned sentimentalist who is as contrary as hell in fundamental things, but who can be deeply touched on a personal basis.

On their second trip to Europe, the Trumans traveled with Sam and Dorothy Rosenman who made the arrangements for a less strenuous tour. Sam Rosenman was a New York lawyer who had served as President Roosevelt's principal speech writer and became Truman's personal attorney. The Rosenmans were seasoned travelers and arranged for the Trumans special excursions such as the one to Pablo Picasso's own museum near Cannes on the French Riviera. The way to the museum led through a small chapel, and as the party entered, Picasso's secretary (also his mistress) routinely crossed herself. After the Trumans returned to their car, Bess commented on the young woman's unmarried state and ingrained religious practice, "It won't help her; it won't help her a bit."

Back in Independence to stay, Bess was asked

repeatedly by reporters and curious visitors whether she
missed living in the White House. Bess chose to answer this
rather silly question in a letter which was printed in newspapers across the country. After telling the inquisitive
lady from Iowa an amusing story about how Harry managed
to avoid running a power lawn mower by doing so on a Sunday morning "with all the Methodists and Baptists going by
our house on the way to church," Bess continued tactfully
but less than truthfully:

> Here in Independence we have a large, three-
> story house and it would be extremely pleasant to
> have some of the wonderful staff we had in the
> White House to help run it. I certainly miss them....
> For the truth is, I have two loves, and I would
> be happiest if I could live half-time in Washington
> and half-time in Independence.

During their seventies the Trumans successfully resisted the infirmities of old age. Shortly after his seventieth birthday Harry's gall bladder was removed, but his recovery was rapid and complete. At age seventy-four, a
tumor was removed from Bess's left breast, and an examination brought the good news, "no malignancy."

In 1964 Truman stumbled in the upstairs bathroom in
Independence, and his head struck against the sink. His
fall was followed by an onslaught of physical failures; his
eyesight, hearing, and resilience all seemed to go at once.
He died on December 26, 1972, in his eighty-ninth year.
This uncommon common man left a legacy of anecdotes and
precepts; at the core of his example is his simple statement,
"It takes a lifetime of the hardest kind of work and study
to become a successful politician."

After the death of her husband, Bess remained in the
house on Delaware Street in Independence. Margaret asked
her mother to live with the Daniel family in New York, but
she must have known her invitation would be declined. Bess
had told a neighbor, "I was born here and hope to die
here." Her last years were free of financial problems, for
she received a pension of $20,000 per annum, and Harry's
estate amounted to $600,000, thanks mainly to the sale of
his published memoirs. Bess managed without live-in help
until her crippling arthritis caused her to move downstairs

and to have someone in attendance. Bess died at the age of ninety-seven on October 18, 1982, of congestive heart failure. She is likely to be remembered as the first First Lady who shunned "that awful public life."

PRINCIPAL SOURCES

Robert H. Ferrell. Truman, a Centenary Remembrance. [London: Thames and Hudson, Ltd., 1984]. 256 p.

Jhan Robbins. Bess & Harry, an American Love Story. New York: Putnam's, [1980]. 194 p.

Harry S Truman. The Autobiography of Harry S Truman. Edited by Robert H. Ferrell. [Boulder: Colorado Associated University Press, 1980]. 153 p.

Harry S Truman. Letters Home by Harry Truman. Edited by Monte M. Poen. New York: Putnam's, [1984]. 303 p.

ALBEN W. BARKLEY, 1949-1953

Alben William Barkley (1877-1956) was born into a family of Kentucky tobacco tenant farmers, and as a young man worked as a janitor to help pay his expenses at the now defunct Marvin College in Clinton, Kentucky. Four years after graduation in 1897, Alben was admitted to the bar and began his practice in Paducah. At age twenty-five Alben had saved $800 which enabled him to marry and to purchase a four-room house. Ten years later when Barkley first went to Washington as a member of Congress, he went alone because he did not have enough money left after campaign expenses to move his wife and children. His family joined him in 1914 in a rented apartment, and in the early 1920s Barkley purchased a three-story house on fashionable Cleveland Avenue.

Barkley's popularity in Kentucky ensured his reelection to public office: he served without interruption for fourteen years (1913-1927) in the House of Representatives and for twenty-two more (1927-1949) in the United States Senate. He was majority leader of the Senate from 1937-1947, and minority leader from 1947-1948. He served as vice-president under President Truman from 1949-1953, and again in the Senate from 1955 until his sudden death in April of 1956 in Lexington, Va.

Barkley's first wife was bedridden with a heart ailment for four years before her death in 1947, and the senator accepted speaking engagements to augment his income. Barkley proved to be a successful raconteur, and many of his stories are retold in his published

277

recollections, <u>That Reminds Me</u> (1954). One
chapter, "Cupid and I," recounts his December
and May courtship of Jane Hadley, a widow
with two teen-age daughters. Their marriage
on November 18, 1949, was the first for a
vice-president while in office.

*   *   *

The only vice-president to be married while in office was
Alben W. Barkley of Kentucky. The date of the wedding
was November 18, 1949, six days before the groom was to
become seventy-two and the bride had celebrated her thirty-
eighth birthday less than two months before. The couple
met for the first time four months earlier on July 8, 1949,
at a party given by the Clark Cliffords on board the White
House yacht, <u>Margy</u>. The guests included Secretary of
State Dean Acheson, Under Secretary of Commerce Cornelius Vanderbilt Whitney, the Belgian ambassador to the
United States, several United States senators, Arthur Krock
of the New York <u>Times</u>, Vice-President Alben Barkley and
the house guest of the Cliffords, Mrs. Carleton S. Hadley
of St. Louis. On the night of the party the vice-president
had been a widower for almost three years, and Jane Rucker
Hadley had been a widow for five years. Her late husband
had been general counsel to the Wabash Railroad, and Jane
was supporting her two teen-age daughters by working as
a secretary to her husband's successor.

The vice-president was smitten the moment he met
Jane; he held her hand too long after his introduction and
he monopolized most of the "one enchanted evening" on the
Potomac. Jane was to stay but four days in Washington,
and on each of these she was pursued by her ardent admirer. After he wanted to host a luncheon in the Senate
on the day she was slated to be back on the job in St.
Louis, Jane telephoned her employer and obtained permission to remain in Washington for two more days.

The vice-president accepted numerous speaking engagements outside of Washington, and he arranged whenever
possible to call on Jane in her hometown. Although the first
visit was not announced to the press, the St. Louis newspapers carried the headline "VEEP VISITS ST. LOUIS WIDOW"
which told the nation about the budding romance. Subsequent

visits to St. Louis and to Paducah in which others in the
two families approved of the marriage of the "Veep" and the
St. Louis widow led to an announcement of their engagement
and eighteen days later, on November 18, 1949, to their
church wedding in St. Louis.

The Cinderella-like rise of a secretary in St. Louis to
become the Second Lady in the country within four months
delighted romantic Americans, and the Barkleys soon became
the most frequently feted couple in Washington. Indeed,
during the first season for the second Mrs. Barkley in
Washington, she and the vice-president spent only six evenings at home. Details about the social events which the
Barkleys attended, and stories about their trip to Korea
and life around the Barkley dinner table are to be found in
the book entitled I Married the Veep which Jane R. Barkley
dictated to Frances Spatz Leighton. The volume contains a
few chapters on the life of the Barkleys after Alben left the
vice-presidency, and his dramatic death on the platform of
Washington and Lee University is described with emotion
including the last words of the "Veep's" speech which also
were his last in life, "I would rather be a servant in the
house of the Lord than sit in the seats of the mighty."
Nevertheless, I Married the Veep is too long for serious
reading, and its purported author reacted at times like a
schoolgirl to the attention paid her by a celebrity almost
twice her age and to the social whirl which she enjoyed as
his wife. Almost every page contains numerous statements
in quotation marks although many of the conversations occurred seven or eight years earlier, and a reader's credulity
is challenged when he reads that Barkley at age seventy-
five chose to wash dishes in cold water. The Veep, who
had been brought up in a family of Kentucky tobacco tenant
farmers and had worked as a janitor to defray part of his
expenses at Marvin College, explained, "I used cold water....
Because the water is cool, you handle the dishes more rapidly, thus more efficiently."

A streamlined version of the Veep's courtship of the
second Mrs. Barkley is to be found in a chapter entitled
"Cupid and I" in his published recollections, That Reminds
Me. In the preparation of this volume, which was published
two years before his death, Barkley had the assistance of
Sidney Shalett who arranged and checked his recollections
for accuracy. Barkley's reputation as a public speaker was

enhanced by his robust anecdotes, and page after page of
That Reminds Me is enlivened by amusing stories which must
have delighted his listeners. The book also is our best
source of information about Barkley's first wife, who was
the mother of his three children.

At the age of twenty-five Barkley had made a start
in the legal profession and had saved approximately $800;
he thereupon proposed to Dorothy Brower, "a lovely girl,
five years my junior, who had grown up in Paducah," Alben's adopted hometown. Dorothy had moved to Tiptonville,
Tennessee, where her father had purchased a hardware
store. After she left Paducah, the couple exchanged letters
frequently, and Alben visited her whenever he could. Alben's proposal of marriage was accepted, and the young
married couple moved into a modest four-room cottage, the
purchase of which consumed most of Barkley's savings.
Nevertheless, after having lived most of his twenty-five
years in rented quarters, "I took an almost fierce pride in
having made the start toward owning my own home."

Ten years later, in 1913, when Barkley went to Washington to begin his first term as a member of Congress, his
wife and children remained in Paducah, because his campaign
expenses did not leave him money enough to move his family.
The separation proved difficult for everyone concerned, and
Alben resolved that his family should be kept together after
his two-year-old daughter did not recognize her father on
his return. After Barkley had returned to Washington he
found lodging for his entire family, and the others joined
him in 1914 and for several years they lived in rented apartments. Barkley's popularity in his district made his place
in Washington appear to be permanent, and the Barkleys
purchased in the early 1920s a three-story house on Cleveland Avenue and they engaged a cook and a yard man to
help with the household chores. In 1937, the year before
Barkley became majority leader of the Senate, he and his
wife purchased "The Angles," a rambling pre-Civil War mansion in Paducah, which as a young man he had dreamed of
owning. After needed remodeling "The Angles" was furnished with antiques which the Barkleys had acquired after
they had developed an interest in collecting years before on
a trip to New Hampshire.

During her last four years Dorothy Barkley was ill

with a heart ailment that made her an invalid. A senator's salary was not sufficient to provide the nursing care she needed, and Barkley began to accept speaking engagements in all parts of the country in order to permit the special treatment his wife required. When her health necessitated constant medical and nursing care, the Barkleys sold their home on Cleveland Avenue and returned to living in an apartment as they had done thirty years before. Barkley, at the end of a day in the Capitol, often carried home with him the Senate calendar and studied it at his wife's bedside. In 1944 when President Roosevelt ignored the recommendations of his principal advisors and returned to Congress a tax bill with a veto message which gave offense to many fair minded legislators, Barkley went into his wife's room and talked with her about the response he intended to make on the floor of the Senate. Mrs. Barkley agreed that it would be unfortunate for her husband to break with the president but recognized that he should deliver a rebuttal speech and then resign as majority leader. "Go to it, Alben," his wife said, "I'm with you." Barkley's response to the veto message and his subsequent resignation as majority leader prompted another "Dear Alben" letter from the president and his immediate reelection to the office which he had resigned, yet the position he took may have caused Roosevelt to strike Barkley's name from the list of men whom he would consider as candidates for the vice-presidency on the ticket which he expected to head in 1944.

Dorothy Barkley's health became critical in October of 1946, and he cancelled campaign speeches in order to return home. Only his intimate friends knew of the heavy burden which Alben carried at home when his wife died on March 10, 1947. By then Barkley's three children had families of their own, and Alben found that his duties as majority leader filled his days. After his election to the vice-presidency, his elder daughter, Marian (Mrs. Max Truitt) became his official hostess, and he restricted his social life to official functions. His love affair and marriage with Jane Hadley caused Barkley to break out of his established routine, and together they traveled, met new people, and enjoyed the home in Paducah which he and his first wife had purchased and decorated. In his late seventies Alben Barkley could reflect, "I feel I have been doubly blessed in life, having had the good fortune of being married to two lovely and wonderful women. No man could say more."

After Barkley's death his widow left Kentucky and returned to Washington where she became appointments secretary to Thomas Henry Carroll, president of George Washington University. Jane Hadley Barkley (née Rucker in Keytesville, Maine) died in Washington on September 6, 1965, at the age of fifty-two. She was survived by her mother, a pianist with whom Jane had traveled in Europe, a brother and a sister, and two daughters by her first husband, Carleton Hadley.

PRINCIPAL SOURCES

Alben Barkley. That Reminds Me. Garden City, N.Y.: Doubleday, [1954]. 288 p.

Jane Barkley and Frances Leighton. I Married the Veep. New York: Vanguard Press, [1958]. 316 p.

RICHARD M. NIXON, 1953-1961

Richard Milhous Nixon (1913-) was born on a lemon farm in Yorba Linda, California. When the orchard business failed, Richard's father, Frank, moved his family to nearby Whittier where his wife had relatives in the Quaker community. There Frank Nixon operated a filling station and a country store in which Richard worked while he was a student in Whittier High School and Whittier College. After standing second in his college class, Richard received a full tuition scholarship in the Duke University Law School where he had to work even harder to make expenses. After graduation in 1937 and admission to the bar in California, Nixon began his practice in a prominent legal firm in Whittier. Two years after he met Patricia Ryan, a teacher in Whittier High School, the couple were married on June 21, 1940, and began married life in a modest apartment.

After the outbreak of World War II, Nixon was commissioned lieutenant in the Navy on September 2, 1942, and he spent almost four years in service in this country and in the South Pacific. Richard was encouraged to run for Congress from his district, and he defeated the popular Democrat, Jerry Voorhis. Nixon won reelection to the House in 1948, and two years later he defeated Helen Gahagan Douglas in a bitter contest for a seat in the United States Senate. Nixon's experience in both Houses and his record as a campaigner helped him to be selected as General Eisenhower's running mate in 1952. President

Eisenhower gave Vice-President Nixon many important assignments, and he and Pat traveled
to fifty-three countries during his eight years
in office. Nixon was nominated in 1960 by the
Republicans for the presidency but lost the
close election to Senator John F. Kennedy.
The Nixons returned to California where Richard practiced law and ran unsuccessfully for
the governorship. A year later the Nixons
moved to New York where he joined a leading
law firm and undertook to win in 1968 the Republican nomination for the presidency. The
team of Nixon and Agnew won the election in
1968 and was reelected in 1972. In June of
1972 the Watergate break-in occurred, and
White House efforts to conceal involvement led
to President Nixon's resignation on August 9,
1974. The former president and his wife moved
to San Clemente, California, where they lived
in virtual seclusion for five years during
which Richard experienced cardiovascular
shock after surgery for phlebitis and Pat
suffered a stroke. The Nixons moved in
1979 to New York City and two years later
to a fashionable New Jersey suburb where
they would have more room and more privacy.

*   *   *

Four years after Richard Nixon resigned on August 9, 1974,
from the office of president of the United States his lengthy
Memoirs (1,120 p.) was published. In this volume in which
Nixon drew on notes, diaries, and the famous Watergate
tapes, the author wrote in his first chapter:

> Pat's life deserves a volume of its own, and per-
> haps someday she will write the volume herself. It
> is an exceptional story, just as she is an exceptional
> woman with great independence, keen intelligence,
> and a warm sense of humor.

Nixon's tribute to his wife is deserved, but it cannot
be accepted as written. Pat Nixon suffered a stroke on
July 7, 1976, and her disability probably would keep her
from writing an autobiography. Admittedly, Nixon may have

written the chapter on his early years before his wife's stroke, yet the former President concluded his preface in March of 1978 and he or one of his corps of assistants should have revised the statement.

Moreover, in 1978, the year in which the Memoirs appeared, a biography of Mrs. Nixon was published. Its title, The Lonely Lady of San Clemente: the Story of Pat Nixon, suggests the popular nature of the book; yet its author, Lester David, obtained information from members of Mrs. Nixon's staff and from friends and associates of both Pat and Richard. The book itself came from a well-know publisher, and it is hard to believe that Nixon knew nothing about David's work in preparation when he wrote that "Pat's life deserves a volume of its own."

Together, Nixon's Memoirs and Lester David's life of Pat Nixon, present the two Nixons and their two daughters in generous detail, but each must be used with care. The problem with the first is Nixon's distorted view of himself, his political associates, and his "old opponents"; and the second cites, in quotation marks on almost every page, statements which may or may not have been voiced. Lester David attributes some of the quotations in his book to persons whom he interviewed (Clement Conger, White House curator, and Helen Smith, Mrs. Nixon's press secretary, are examples); but a verbatim conversation between a candidate for the vice-presidency and his wife on a flight between Portland, Oregon, and Los Angeles would not be out of place in a historical novel.

Pat's parents were William Ryan, born in Ridgefield, Connecticut, in 1866, and Kate Halberstadt Bender, born fourteen years later in the state of Hesse in Germany. William Ryan had but little schooling when he signed onto a whaling ship in his teens. In his twenties he worked as a surveyor in the Philippines, and in his early thirties he sought gold in the Klondike. The lure of precious metals drew William Ryan to South Dakota where at age forty-three he married Kate Bender, a widow with two children whose husband had been killed in a mine accident. The four Ryans then moved to Ely, Nevada, where they lived in a tent city until they secured better housing after William became a mining engineer. Here the Ryans had three children, William, Junior, Thomas, and Thelma Catherine, born on March

16, 1912, who was often called "Pat" by her father since
the girl had been born only hours before St. Patrick's Day.

Kate had good reason to be afraid of the dangers met
in a mine, and she encouraged her husband to find another
occupation. In response to the urgings of his wife, Ryan
moved his family to a truck farm of eleven acres in Artesia,
California, about twenty miles southeast of Los Angeles.
Although Pat's father called the tract a "ranch" and described himself as a "rancher," life for his family was hard
and primitive. Their house of five rooms lacked electricity
and indoor plumbing, and essential water for their use and
for their produce often had to be pumped by hand at night
after their neighbors had filled their tanks. Pat slept in a
curtained area in a wide hall at the rear of the house, and
she took her turn in the nocturnal pumpings and other
chores. She later recalled, "I didn't know what it was not
to work hard."

Pat attended Artesia's grade school about a mile from
her home. She enjoyed school and caught up with her two
brothers who had to leave for extended periods to work on
the farm. Pat entered Excelsior Union High School in
September of 1925, and less than a year later her mother
died of stomach cancer. Her death left Pat at age fourteen
with cleaning and washing and the preparation of meals in
addition to her school work and helping her father pack
corn, tomatoes, and melons for market. Regardless of the
many demands on her time, Pat graduated near the head of
her class, and she managed to hold class offices and to fill
leading roles in school plays.

Pat's father died of silicosis at age sixty-four, and
his daughter decided to drop the name Thelma and to use
the name he preferred. By this time Pat had obtained a job
in a bank, had enrolled in the Fullerton Junior College,
and she continued to shop and cook the meals and do the
family laundry. After her two brothers moved to Los Angeles where they could work their way through the University
of Southern California, Pat stayed on in the little house and
her brothers would return to help with the farm work. In
1931 Pat escaped from her crunching routine when she undertook to drive an elderly couple to New York City in their
old Packard. The trip led through hot deserts in Arizona
and over steep mountain roads and Pat had to change many

flat tires, but she did reach New York where she worked
for two years as a secretary in a hospital primarily for pa-
tients with tuberculosis. Although Pat had an active social
life in New York, she decided in 1933 to return to California
and to college.

Pat moved in with her brothers in a small apartment
near the campus of the University of Southern California,
and she worked more than forty hours each week in order
to pay her expenses and to attend school. She worked in a
cafeteria, in the University library, in the Bullocks-Wilshire
department store, and occasionally as an extra in Hollywood
motion pictures, but she still was able to do well with her
studies. She completed the requirements for a bachelor's
degree in merchandising and she accumulated enough credits
for certification as a teacher, and after graduation cum laude
in 1937 she was ready to work as a buyer or as a teacher.
An opening in teaching came first.

In late August of 1937 Patricia Ryan moved to Whittier,
about fifteen miles east of downtown Los Angeles, where she
had accepted an appointment as a teacher in business education. She was an immediate success in the school from which
Richard Nixon had graduated seven years before, and she
was soon to meet him when both tried out for parts in a
play, The Dark Tower, to be performed by the Whittier
Community Players. As far as Richard was concerned, the
meeting with Pat induced "a case of love at first sight."

Richard Nixon's early years were remarkably similar to
Pat's. His father, Francis Anthony, was born in 1879 on a
farm near McArthur, Ohio, and left school after the fourth
grade. He then had a succession of jobs including that of
driving a trolley car, his work when he met and married
Hannah Milhous in 1908. She had been born into a large
Quaker family in Butlerville, Indiana; and she was a young
girl when her father, an orchard grower, moved his ten
children and his nursery stock to a Quaker colony in Whittier. Frank Nixon had been brought up as a Methodist,
but he adopted his wife's Quaker faith, and their five sons,
two of whom died while young of tuberculosis, were reared
as Quakers.

When Richard was seven in 1920, his father's lemon
orchard failed, yet Frank accumulated enough money to open

a filling station in East Whittier. The station made money,
and within a few years Frank opened next door a country
store named "Nixon's Market." Richard worked long hours
pumping gas and selling groceries, yet he was able to do
outstanding work in Whittier High School and in Whittier
College. After standing second in his class at college,
Richard received a full-tuition scholarship in the Duke University Law School in Durham, North Carolina, where he
had to work even harder to make expenses and to master
the law.

      After graduation from law school at Duke and admis-
sion to the California bar, Nixon began his practice in Whittier in the legal firm of Wingert and Bewley located in the
Bank of America building. His pay at first was but fifty
dollars per month, but he showed himself to be thorough in
in the minor cases assigned to him. Before long he was
given more important cases, and at age twenty-six he was
recognized in Whittier as an exceptionally promising young
attorney.

      When Richard first saw Pat, "a beautiful and vivacious
young woman with titian hair," at the casting tryouts for
The Dark Tower, he could not take his eyes away from her.
He pursued her with zeal, and after two years of courtship,
Pat agreed to become his wife. They were married in a
Quaker ceremony performed on June 21, 1940, in the Mission Inn, then a California showplace, in nearby Riverside.
Their wedding was followed by a trip by car to Mexico for
which they had allotted two hundred dollars; when most of
the money was spent they would return to Whittier. When
they came back on July 4, only twenty-two dollars remained.

      The newly married couple then rented a three-room
apartment about two miles from his office and her school.
Their joint incomes provided about sixty-five dollars a week
which proved to be sufficient when Pat shopped, cooked,
cleaned, washed her own clothes, and pressed his. The
apartment was furnished with a mixture of secondhand
tables, chairs, and cabinets; and Pat covered tears in the
upholstered pieces with slipcovers which she made from
yards of colorful fabric. They worked hard, and they knew
other young married couples with whom they would meet for
a modest dinner at home or for an extraordinary evening of
entertainment in Los Angeles.

The daily lives of the Nixons, which were typical of other young professional couples during the Depression, were turned upside down by the Japanese attack on Pearl Harbor. Within a month Nixon obtained an appointment in the Office of Emergency Management, and his wife followed him to Washington as soon as she could resign from her job and give up their apartment. Nixon did not like his work in the Office of Price Administration and applied for a commission in the Navy despite his Quaker upbringing. On September 2, 1942, Nixon was commissioned a lieutenant, junior grade; then followed a period of sudden moves, first to Quonset, Rhode Island, for basic training; next to Ottumwa, Iowa, for duty at a partially completed air base; and finally, in May of 1943, to the South Pacific. During the fourteen months Richard was away from Pat he wrote to her every day, and, according to his Memoirs, "She has kept all those letters to this day."

After Nixon returned in July, 1944, he and Pat lived successively in Philadelphia, New York, and near Baltimore where the then lieutenant commander wrote termination contracts for the Navy and aircraft companies, and she kept their apartment in apple pie order and saved money for the birth of the child which she was carrying. Now that Pat was pregnant, she and her husband wanted to return at the earliest possible moment to California and to reestablish their home and daily lives.

At this juncture Richard received a query from an old family friend who was manager of the Bank of America branch in Whittier:

> Dear Dick:
> I am writing you this short note to ask if you would like to be a candidate for Congress on the Republican ticket in 1946.
> Jerry Voorhis expects to run--registration is about 50-50. The Republicans are gaining.
> Please airmail me your reply if you are interested.
>
> Yours very truly,
>
> H. L. Perry
>
> P.S. Are you a registered voter in California?

Nixon and his wife discussed this new possibility as

fully as possible and decided that they would be willing to commit half of their savings of ten thousand dollars for their own expenses during a long campaign. Two days later Nixon called Perry and learned that he had written on behalf of a Committee of 100 who would be glad to meet with Nixon along with the five other candidates. Nixon flew to California for the dinner of the Committee and made his brief statement while still in uniform. About a month later Nixon learned that he had been chosen to make the contest, and he undertook a crash course in politics while he impatiently awaited his discharge and return to California.

Early in January, 1946, Richard received his discharge and left for California to begin his campaign, and Pat followed after she had done the packing for their move. On February 21 she gave birth to Patricia, soon known as Tricia, and three weeks later she was helping in her husband's campaign. Richard debated with Jerry Voorhis in schools, community centers, and missions, and Pat was always in the audience with "her hands in her lap, eyes unwaveringly on her husband, her face pale, her lips pressed together, her body tense." Although Pat hated campaigning, she proved to be good at it, and she helped her husband at age thirty-three to win his seat in Congress. Richard recalled three decades later:

> But nothing could equal the excitement and jubilation of winning the first campaign. Pat and I were happier on November 6, 1946, than we were ever to be again in my political career.

The Nixons moved into a two-bedroom unfurnished apartment in Park Fairfax, Virginia. Pat cooked, cleaned, shopped, and cared for Tricia, and her daily life in a small apartment became even more hectic after the birth on July 5, 1948, of Julie. Pat worked long hours each day, yet she did attend some of the official functions open to a congressman's wife. Two years later the Nixon family purchased for $41,000 a small two-story white brick house in the northwest corner of Washington; the new house provided more space but it added yard work to Pat's household chores.

In his first term in Congress, Nixon served on the Education and Labor Committee along with another freshman representative, John Kennedy of Massachusetts; and he received two additional assignments from the Republican Speaker, John Martin. The first was a place on the controversial House Committee on Un-American Activities where Nixon won national prominence in the Alger Hiss case, and the second was his appointment to the committee headed by Congressman Christian Herter of Massachusetts to tour Europe and to prepare a report regarding the proposed Marshall plan for monetary aid to the European countries devastated by World War II.

Nixon won in 1948 reelection to the House, and two years later he decided to run for the Senate seat held by Democrat Sheridan Downey. Helen Gahagan Douglas, a musical comedy star and wife of one of Hollywood's leading men, Melvyn Douglas, also served in Congress; and, as a Democrat, she defeated Downey in the California primary. The contest between Mrs. Douglas and Richard Nixon which followed received national attention for bitter charges and countercharges and was won by Nixon by a plurality of almost 700,000 votes, the largest achieved that year by any candidate for the United States Senate.

After General Eisenhower wrested in 1952 the Republican nomination for the presidency from the able and conservative Robert A. Taft, the qualities desired in his running mate pointed to the junior senator from California. Nixon represented a populous state in the West, he had served in both Houses of Congress, he was a seasoned and successful campaigner, and his selection would please the traditionalists in the party who had backed Taft, fondly known as "Mr. Republican."

About two months after Nixon's nomination for the second place on the Republican ticket, several leading newspapers carried screaming headlines about Nixon's secret fund which enabled him to travel to California and to communicate with his constituents. The furor over the fund became so great that Nixon considered leaving the ticket, but he was told by Pat that to do so would cause Eisenhower to lose the election and would irreparably damage his own career. Nixon decided to explain the fund and its use in a televised speech which became known as the "Checkers speech." Nixon's defense was maudlin, but the popular response was overwhelmingly in his favor. Eisenhower wasn't satisfied that one speech cleared up all the questions and asked Nixon to

meet him in Wheeling, West Virginia. Counselors who knew
the general encouraged Nixon to make the trip which led to
an enthusiastic endorsement by Eisenhower, but the fund
episode left Pat with deep scars. She resented attacks on
her husband's integrity in financial matters and the taste-
less invasion of their privacy.

During Richard's eight years as vice-president, he
and Pat traveled together to fifty-three countries. Shortly
after Nixon took office, President Eisenhower asked him to
visit the Far East to improve diplomatic relations and advised, "Take Pat." This initial journey lasted ten weeks
during which the Nixons traveled more than forty-five thousand miles and visited twenty-one countries. While the
vice-president sat in meetings, his wife visited "schools,
hospitals, orphanages, clinics, museums, and marketplaces
to meet the people and to let the people meet her." In
Venezuela the Nixons' car was stoned and Pat was spat
upon, but most of her trips were immensely successful.
She received a decoration from the President of Peru for
her work in earthquake relief in that country, and she was
the first Second Lady to serve as the president's official diplomatic representative abroad. In 1972 she returned from
the inauguration of the president of Liberia and from meetings with heads of state in Ghana and the Ivory Coast "fresh
as a daisy." Pat showed love for the people of the countries she visited, and they responded with demonstrations
of affection toward her.

After Nixon was reelected to the vice-presidency, he
sold his house in Spring Valley and bought a larger one in
a secluded part of Wesley Heights. The new home had
eleven rooms which provided a bedroom for each of the girls
and for a live-in couple, Sue and James Johnson. Nevertheless, Pat continued to repair and alter Tricia's and Julie's
clothing as well as her own, and she continued to press her
husband's suits. Although in her middle forties, Pat's
energy was "awesome." She was up at six-thirty in the
morning to prepare breakfast for her family before they left
for the office and school, and she struggled to provide a
normal home environment for her two girls despite the fact
that their father's work schedule ordinarily kept him from
coming home in time for a family dinner.

On election night in 1960 the Nixon family awaited the

returns in their suite in the Ambassador Hotel in Los Angeles. The race with Kennedy was close but the final outcome
appeared likely to be in his favor, and Nixon proposed to
make a public statement in which he would acknowledge the
apparent trend in the election. Pat opposed making any
such statement and said that she would not go with him to
the ballroom where the party workers had gathered, and
Richard began to make a few notes to use in his remarks.
Within a few minutes Pat returned and said, "I think we
should go down together." Nixon observed in his <u>Memoirs</u>:

> I do not know which quality I loved more--the
> fight or the warmth. It is at such moments, when
> you see the effect it has on your family, that the
> ache of losing is the greatest.

After Nixon lost the election in 1960, he accepted an
offer from a law firm in Los Angeles, and the Nixons were
settled before the end of 1961 in a large new house with a
swimming pool. Richard had not been back in California
long when former political associates encouraged him to run
for governor; Pat was opposed but she agreed to campaign
with her husband if he decided to run against the incumbent, Pat Brown. Nixon lost, and he conceded his defeat
in a meeting with newspaper writers in which the candidate
said, "You won't have Nixon to kick around anymore because, gentlemen, this is my last press conference...."
Nixon's listeners were stunned; and, although he was to
hold many more press conferences, he wrote later that he
had never regretted his combative remarks to the men and
women of the media.

Close and influential friends of Nixon told him that he
and his family would find a more stimulating life in New
York, and Pat and the girls were willing to move. A
change in residence would keep Nixon out of politics in 1964,
and this factor appealed to Pat. The Nixons settled into a
twelve-room apartment on Fifth Avenue where Nelson A.
Rockefeller and William Randolph Hearst, Jr. were tenants.
Nixon worked downtown in a prestigious law firm which paid
him enough for membership in country clubs and for his
daughters to attend the expensive Chapin School. Just two
weeks after the Nixons had occupied their new apartment,
Pat looked across the dinner table and said to her husband,
"I hope we never move again."

Two years later, in 1965, Nixon was considering his
chances for running for the presidency in 1968, but he did
not then discuss the subject with his wife and daughters
because he knew that they would be disappointed. "But,"
wrote Nixon, "I had finally come to the conclusion that there
was no other life for me but politics and public service."
In college the Whittier football coach, Wallace "Chief" New-
man, an American Indian, instilled in his teams a highly
competitive spirit and a determination to fight again whenever you lose; and the coach's creed helped to develop
Nixon's "highly competitive instinct." Nixon's values became
those of the street fighter: He believed that John Dean
possessed "the kind of steel and really mean instinct"
needed for overdue reorganization in several large departments, and Nixon concluded in 1972 "that John Connally was
the only man in either party who clearly had the potential
to be a great President." For Connally had, according to
Nixon, the "necessary political 'fire in the belly.'"

During 1965 Nixon began to receive a large number of
political inquiries and invitations to speak, and in January
of 1966 he engaged Pat Buchanan, a young editorial writer
for the St. Louis Globe-Democrat, to help in research and
in speech writing. On Christmas Day in 1967 Richard discussed with Pat and his daughters the possibility of his
running for the presidency, and his wife responded that she
was happy with her life in New York but would help if he
decided to campaign. On December 28 Nixon left for Florida
where he would join his friend Bebe Rebozo and make up his
mind. After Nixon returned and told his family that he had
decided to run in 1968, Pat responded, "Now that the decision is made, I will go along with it."

On election night in 1968 the Nixons awaited the returns in two separate hotel suites, the candidate in one and
his family in the other. Richard thought that this arrangement would lessen the strains on all of them. After he had
won, the president-elect joined Pat who told him that the
uncertainty over the outcome in Illinois had brought on
waves of nausea. After Richard assured Pat that victory
was certain, he held her and "she burst into tears of relief
and joy."

At the end of the day of Richard's first inauguration
as the thirty-seventh president of the United States, his
family came together on the sofas in the West Hall of the

White House, and Pat volunteered, "It's good to be home." She worked with help from the White House curator and an architect on redecorating the mansion, and in five and a half years she was able to complete improvements in fourteen rooms. Pat also provided the impetus which led to flooding the building with light after dark; if the Lincoln Memorial and Washington Monument could be lit through the night, she asked, "Why not the White House?"

Pat was an active First Lady in many other respects. In her first three years in the White House she entertained more than a hundred thousand guests at dinners, receptions, luncheons, and teas, making her the busiest hostess in the history of the mansion. She traveled with her husband to China and Russia, and she worried with him over ending the war in Viet Nam. After peace finally came, the president asked Kissinger to share the news with Mrs. Nixon, and she "was enormously pleased." Pat tried to persuade her husband to appoint a woman to the Supreme Court, but none could be found who met "the strict constructionist criterion" he had established. At times Richard kept Pat in the dark about topics which involved both of them personally; for example, President Nixon talked with Jerry and Betty Ford about the congressman's selection for the office of vice-president before he shared the news with his wife. When he did so, she responded, "Good, I guessed it."

President Nixon learned first about the Watergate break-in from a short newspaper story in the Miami Herald for June 18, 1972, while he was vacationing with Bebe Rebozo at Key Biscayne. The next day Bob Haldeman, Nixon's chief of staff, told the president that the burglary of the Democratic National Committee headquarters involved someone on the payroll of the Committee to Re-elect the President directed by Attorney General John Mitchell. The president and Bob Haldeman had two conversations of approximately one hour each on June 20, mainly on the break-in; and Nixon was satisfied that no one from the White House was involved. Also on the 20th Nixon talked briefly with John Mitchell on the telephone, and the president was convinced that his attorney general had no knowledge of the episode in advance.

During the next few days Haldeman furnished his chief with additional details about the break-in and Mitchell's possible involvement, and the two agreed that an investigation of the caper by the FBI would reveal other embarrassing activities conducted by employees of the Committee to Re-elect the President. On the 23rd Haldeman and the president discussed a plan to have the CIA request the FBI to halt its investigation, and Nixon approved of the proposal which would clearly be an obstruction of justice. The tape recording of this conversation would prove two years later to be the "smoking gun" which brought down the president.

More than four years after his resignation, Nixon appeared on a popular television show in France and was flustered by a question about his having lied in the cover-up investigation. After Richard had regained his composure, he replied:

> The responsibility was mine. Mistakes were made--very grave mistakes. If one makes a mistake and does not correct it, he makes another mistake; that was my mistake in Watergate.

Nixon knew that he should begin his investigation of the Watergate break-in by interrogating the head of the Committee to Re-elect the President, but he did not do so. Ten months later Nixon overcame his "hypersensitivity" regarding Mitchell and asked Haldeman to query Mitchell about his part in the affair. Nixon did not challenge Mitchell himself, and the Attorney General responded to Haldeman with an evasive reply. But by this time, three months after Nixon's second inauguration in January of 1973, the break-in and the cover up began to unravel in the court presided over by Judge Sirica and in the hearings conducted by a special Senate committee chaired by Sam Ervin of North Carolina.

John Dean, who became White House Counsel in 1970, had a special responsibility for keeping track of developments relating to Watergate; and he told the President on March 21, 1974, about the "growing cancer" surrounding his office. When John Dean testified for five days before the Ervin Committee at the end of June the country became aware of the White House involvement in Watergate, and documentation for his account became a real possibility when Alex Butterfield told the Committee about the existence of the White House taping system. From then on the president strove to retain the tapes, and he stood almost naked when

the Supreme Court ruled on July 24 that the president could
not withhold any of the incriminating recordings.

Instead of recognizing his egregious involvement in the
Watergate cover up, President Nixon hoped at the end of
April, 1974, that the people would become impatient with the
topic. Incredible as it may seem, Nixon stated in his Memoirs that he "was good at being President, at the really important things." As his position crumbled, Nixon blamed
scapegoats instead of himself, "Rightly or wrongly, I convinced myself that I was being attacked by old opponents
for old reasons." Regardless of the serious violation of his
responsibility to execute the laws of the land, Nixon saw
himself as the victim of larger and stronger political forces.
He was proud of the support he had received from his
Cabinet and from his White House staff, but "from the beginning we had been hopelessly outmanned." Even the
House Judiciary Committee "was a stacked deck" which would
vote for impeachment of the president regardless of his guilt
or innocence because it numbered seventeen Republicans
and twenty-one Democrats, eighteen of whom "came from
the party's liberal wing or had reputations as hard-core
partisans."

After the "smoking gun" tape of June 23, 1972, was
made public, Nixon considered resigning his office as president. After he had decided to leave, he called General
Haig, his chief of staff, and Ron Ziegler to his office and
told them of his intention to leave gracefully and without
rancour. Nixon finally said to the two men with him, "Well,
I screwed it up good, real good, didn't I?" His question
did not require an answer.

After the debacle, Nixon's family closed ranks around
the president. Nixon talked the night before his resignation
with Kissinger and then walked alone to the White House
where his family had gathered in the Solarium. "Pat was,
as always, the strongest of all." Later in the evening when
Pat, Ed (Cox), and Tricia went to third floor to say good
night to Julie and David (Eisenhower), "We," wrote Tricia,
"all broke down together, and put our arms around each
other in circular, huddle-style fashion. Saying nothing."

The morning of August 9, the date of President Nixon's
resignation, Pat joined her family in the White House wearing

dark glasses to hide the signs of two sleepless nights of preparations for leaving and the tears which had come that morning. She removed her glasses for her walk to the helicopter, and the photograph taken then of Pat reveals a face grimaced with pain. On the helicopter flight to Andrews Air Force Base where they would board Air Force One for the trip to California, Pat remarked "to no one in particular, 'It's so sad. It's so sad.'"

The disgraced former president and his distraught wife went into self-imposed exile in their home, La Casa Pacifica, in San Clemente, California. Pat had collected Richard's favorite possessions from his bedroom in the White House, and soon after their arrival in California she placed them in the master bedroom in an arrangement similar to the one to which he had been accustomed as the president. Richard intended to use the free time ahead of him for reading and possibly some writing and for the healing of his emotional wounds. Pat began a garden and spent hours each day planting and cultivating flowers and vegetables.

Richard carried with him to California serious legal, monetary, and physical problems. The first, his criminal involvement in the Watergate cover-up, was relieved by President Ford's full pardon for "offenses against the United States" during Nixon's presidency, but questions about the ownership and custody of his papers would bring bills from lawyers for legal fees. Nixon saw his way partly through his entanglements when he signed a contract for the publication of his Memoirs for two-and-a-half million dollars to be paid as he progressed with the preparation of the book. His physical problem was an aggravation of the phlebitis which Nixon had experienced off and on since 1964 and had reoccurred in an acute form on a trip to the Middle East in June of 1974. After examining the swelling in Nixon's leg and considering the potential for an embolism, his physicians ordered him to go to the Long Beach Memorial Hospital for treatment. Nixon arrived on September 24, and after tests and treatment, he was released twelve days later. About two weeks later, Nixon was back in the hospital where he almost died from internal bleeding following surgery. The patient had gone into cardiovascular shock which continued for three hours; afterwards his condition was critical for several days but he recovered and was released from the

hospital on November 24. After Nixon returned to La Casa
Pacifica, Pat supervised his diet and medications, but he
was not able to read at length or to dictate his memoirs until the middle of January when he felt better, mentally as
well as physically.

The Nixons broke out of their confinement in San Clemente when they went at the end of February in 1975 to
Wallace Annenberg's estate in Palm Springs. A few old
friends had been invited to dinner in honor of Nixon who
had appointed Annenberg ambassador to the Court of St.
James. In response to a toast made by his host, Nixon
thanked Walter and Lenore Annenberg for their friendship
and commented on the beauties of their large house. He
then began to ramble about how a large house is filled with
friends "when you are on top," but afterward, "You don't
need a house so large." Nixon did not use the word "down"
but it hung in the room; he went on, "But let me assure
you--I'm not out."

Within a year Richard and Pat went to China on a
plane provided by the People's Republic. The Nixons received many courtesies similar to those they had enjoyed
when they made an official visit in 1972. Toward the end
of the tour Nixon began to tire, but his trip to China
proved to be a needed tonic. "On his return, Nixon
plunged back into his work, alert and refreshed, as if in-
jected with new life."

In the afternoon of July 7, 1976, Pat sat on the patio
of La Casa Pacifica reading Woodward's and Bernstein's The
Final Days which portrayed Nixon as emotionally unstable
and no longer intimate with his wife. Pat suddenly felt
weak and went to bed. The next morning Nixon noticed
that Pat's speech was slurred and that she was having difficulty moving her left side. Richard called his physician,
and soon Pat was taken to the Long Beach Memorial Hospital
where the diagnosis was stroke. Two weeks later when Richard wheeled his wife in a wheelchair out of the hospital, Pat
remarked to the onlookers, "I feel fine. But I'm a little
frightened about the driver." Pat then underwent months
of strenuous physical therapy, but she was cheered by the
receipt of one hundred thousand cards and letters, mostly
from schoolchildren.

Four years after his resignation Nixon began to move freely outside of California. He returned for the first time to Washington on January 13, 1978, to attend the funeral of an old friend and political rival, Hubert Humphrey. Nixon made public speeches in Hyden, Kentucky, and in Biloxi, Mississippi, where he received an ovation. After his appearance on a television show in Paris, France, Nixon went to Oxford, England, where he told eight hundred men in the Oxford Union, "I'm not just going to fade away and live the good life in San Clemente." Nixon regained social respectability when he was invited by President Carter to attend on January 29, 1979, the White House dinner in honor of Teng Hsiao-ping, a Chinese leader, whom the former president had met in China.

Nixon had never intended to remain permanently in California; he expected to move someday to "the fast track" in New York. Pat was agreeable because she was conscious of people staring when she shopped on Rodeo Drive in Beverly Hills, and the drive to and from Los Angeles was long and tiring. Moreover, by March, 1979, there were three grandchildren in the East, and residence in New York would permit frequent and long visits. Consequently, the Nixons sold their home in California and purchased a fine house on East Sixty-fifth Street in Manhattan. Now Nixon could be in his downtown office at 7:30 in the morning and return home for a nap and an afternoon of reading or visiting Tricia and her family. On weekends Richard and Pat often drove to Berwyn, Pennsylvania, to be with Julie and David Eisenhowever and their daughter, Jennie, born in August of 1978.

Although life in the fashionable East Sixties met most of Nixon's requirements, after eighteen months he was ready to move again, this time to the suburbs. The Nixons wanted to stay within commuting distance of downtown New York, but they wanted more privacy and space than they had on Sixty-fifth Street. Nixon's chief of staff, Nick Ruwe, found a home in Saddle River, New Jersey, which had fifteen rooms, a library, and a wine cellar, and was located on four-and-a-half wooded acres at the end of a cul-de-sac. The Nixons purchased the property for more than a million dollars in 1981 and had it beautifully decorated in a bright contemporary manner. The New Jersey property was offered for sale in early 1984 for $2,300,000. Pat had had a second stroke in August of 1983; and, although she suffered no paralysis or speech problems, the Nixons decided to find a smaller home.

Nixon had planned since 1971 to have a presidential library constructed to house his papers, but the foundation organized to raise the requisite funds dissolved after Watergate. In 1975 Nixon offered to donate his papers to Pat's alma mater, the University of Southern California, but nothing came of the proposal. In 1981 the president of Duke University talked with Nixon about building a library for his papers on the campus of the school where Richard had studied law, but Terry Sanford, Duke's president, found that his faculty was strongly opposed to the prospect. A third concrete proposal provides for a two-story building of almost 82,000 square feet to be constructed on thirteen acres of land six miles north of La Casa Pacifica. Plans for the structure in the Spanish colonial style have been drawn by architects from Newport Beach, and a Nixon Presidential Archives Foundation has been established to raise the twenty-five million dollars needed to build the library building.

Richard Nixon was in the headlines in November of 1985, and again he was the center of a controversy. The major league baseball team owners and the umpires union chose Nixon to arbitrate a dispute about how much umpires should be paid for the two games added to the league playoffs. The new commissioner of organized baseball didn't think a "tiny dispute" should involve a former president. "And it dredges up all the problems Richard Nixon faced." Ueberroth explained that he "didn't slam the table" when the two sides ignored his advice, but he did slam the table when the two sides said they were going to have the hearings in St. Louis on the first day of the World Series. "No," said Commissioner Ueberroth, "You go someplace and you get it done, and I don't want to hear about it again."

Arbiter Nixon ruled in favor of the umpires.

PRINCIPAL SOURCES

Robert Sam Anson. Exile; the Unquiet Oblivion of Richard M. Nixon. New York: Simon and Schuster, [1984]. 360 p.

Lester David. The Lonely Lady of San Clemente; the Story
    of Pat Nixon. New York: Crowell, [1978]. 235 p.

Richard M. Nixon. RN; the Memoirs of Richard Nixon. New
    York: Grosset & Dunlap, [1978]. 1120 p.

LYNDON B. JOHNSON, 1961-1963

Lyndon Baines Johnson (1908-1973) was born
in a farmhouse in the Texas hill country about
sixty miles west of Austin. After graduation
from the Johnson City High School at age fifteen, Lyndon worked as a laborer until 1927
when he entered Southwest Texas State Teachers College in San Marcos. Before he was
graduated in 1930, Lyndon taught school in
Cotulla, Texas, and after graduation he taught
public speaking and debate for two years in
Houston. He left the classroom to become
secretary to Representative Richard Kleberg
of Texas and soon showed in Washington his
capacity for hard work and organization.
These traits and the support of Texas congressmen helped Lyndon become at age twenty-
seven director of the National Youth Administration in Texas, a post which he held until
he ran successfully two years later for a seat
in the United States House of Representatives.
He was reelected five times and served in the
House until 1948. Although defeated in 1941
in a special election for the United States
Senate, Johnson became a senator in 1948
and was reelected in 1954. In the Senate,
as minority and majority leader, Johnson
demonstrated his exceptional ability to muster the votes necessary for the passage of
liberal legislation.

After the Democratic convention in 1960
nominated their candidate for president, Senator John F. Kennedy, he personally selected
Johnson to be his running mate because of
the Texan's strength in the South and among

minorities. President Kennedy made his vice-
president the spokesman for the administration
throughout the world and gave him many important responsibilities. After the assassination
of President Kennedy on November 22, 1963,
Johnson moved quickly to induce Congress to
adopt the liberal legislative program proposed
by the late president. Johnson was elected
president in 1964, and the program to correct
inequities among Americans was enlarged and
dramatized, but funds needed to achieve "The
Great Society" were consumed by the Vietnam
War. President Johnson lost support at home
for the costly and futile conflict in Asia; and
he announced on March 31, 1968, that he would
not accept the nomination of his party for another term. After Lyndon Johnson left office on
January 20, 1969, he returned to the LBJ
ranch in Texas where he died of a heart attack
on January 22, 1973.

*   *   *

A few days after her husband became the thirty-sixth president of the United States, Claudia Alta Johnson, usually
called Lady Bird, began to create her White House Diary
(1970). Shortly after the assassination of President Kennedy, Mrs. Johnson realized that she had an exceptional opportunity to record the momentous events which her position
enabled her to observe, and she wanted to help herself recall details and to share her experiences and reactions with
her children and grandchildren. The challenge of preparing
a daily record of activities, the "discipline" of it, had an
appeal; and Lady Bird enjoyed writing: "I like words."
As she continued with the arduous task, she felt an obligation to permit others to learn about her rich and varied life
in the White House.

    Most of Lady Bird's diary was created by her talking
into a tape recorder at the end of a workday. With a manila
envelope full of aids to memory (a list of appointments,
speech cards, guest lists, menus and entertainment programs, or travel schedules) collected by her secretary, Lady
Bird talked about her activities when she could find time to
do so, usually between seven and nine in the evening or

whenever Lyndon came home to dinner. Her diligence produced a suitcase full of tapes which when transcribed
yielded a manuscript of 1,750,000 words. From this enor-
mous record Lady Bird selected one-seventh for her published Diary, a book of eight hundred pages, and deposited
all of the tapes and the transcripts in the Lyndon Baines
Johnson Presidential Library for the use of historians.

Although the reader of her White House Diary does
not know what she chose to exclude ("Editing was not
easy"), Lady Bird's published recollections provide us with
an unparalleled record of life in the White House during the
presidential term of her husband and countless comments on
her activities or reactions thereto. Although a reader may
become tired of reading about her "big days" ("Today
[January 18, 1965] is the first of the big days!), Lady
Bird in her Diary is a sensitive and alert person who gave
her best to her many and varied activities and derived enjoyment and satisfaction from doing so.

Lady Bird enjoyed words, and she craved "the ability
to make words march and sing and cannonade and speak with
the cool voice of reason." Lady Bird had a sharp eye, and
she could describe her perceptions accurately and with feeling. Neither she nor her husband liked artist Peter Hurd's
portrait of the president; in her words, "The hands were
not Lyndon's gnarled, hardworking hands which have so
much strength and fight in them." She especially enjoyed
the beauty of nature. On a flight over Japan she "saw
one of the great sights of my whole life--Mount Fuji--rising
like a dream from a soft ocean of white clouds." Thanksgiving Day in 1969 was spent with her family and close
friends at the Ranch in Texas:

> Today was one of those glorious days when just
> to be alive is enough. There are green velvet
> patches of oats here and there, and the Spanish
> oak outside the picture window of the dining room
> is a blaze of red. On the hillsides the oaks are
> turning from red to russet--the sumac here and
> there more brilliant, but some of its leaves have
> fallen, for fall is advancing.

Claudia Alta Taylor was born on December 12, 1912,
at Karnack in East Texas. She was named after a wealthy,

unmarried uncle, Claude, but her nickname came from a
Black nursemaid who looked at the brown-eyed baby girl
and exclaimed, "Why, she's as purty as a lady bird." When
she entered a new school at age thirteen she wanted to be
called Claudia, but old friends appeared who called her
Lady Bird and the nickname prevailed.

Lady Bird's father, Thomas Jefferson Taylor, II, was
brought up in southern Alabama where he went to school
with his future wife, Minnie Lee Patillo. The Taylor family
farm did not prosper, and Tommy left to establish a general
merchandise store in Karnack, Texas, near the Louisiana
state line. His business venture proved successful, and
young Taylor expanded his activities into farming and cattle
raising. He then returned to Alabama to persuade Minnie
Patillo to become his wife, and the young couple returned
to Karnack where she tried to continue some of the cultural
interests she had enjoyed in Alabama. Two sons, Thomas
Jefferson Taylor, III, and Antonio J. Taylor, were born
before Lady Bird. Her father then owned 18,000 acres and
was considered to be wealthy, but his home lacked electricity and indoor plumbing.

Before Lady Bird was six her mother died, and the
girl went to live in Alabama with her mother's sister Effie.
Aunt Effie soon returned with her charge to Karnack and
remained to take care of her. Lady Bird began school in
a one-room schoolhouse with grades from one to seven.
When she went to high school in Jefferson, Aunt Effie went
with her, but in her junior and senior years she lived at
home and drove to and from school in Marshall, the county
seat. High school was followed by two years in the St.
Mary's Episcopal School for Girls in Dallas where she was
accompanied by faithful Aunt Effie. For her junior and
senior years Lady Bird went to the University of Texas in
Austin. Here she drove a new Buick and had a charge account at Neiman-Marcus in Dallas. She received her bachelor of arts degree in 1933, and remained in Austin for a
bachelor's degree in journalism which came in 1934.

A few weeks after graduation Lady Bird returned to
Austin where in the office of a friend from Karnack, Eu-
genia (Gene) Boehringer, she met Lyndon Johnson. Lyndon
had met Gene four years earlier in Austin, and he would
stop by her office when he was in the city doing work for

Congressman Richard Kleberg, a member of the family who
owned the famed King Ranch. Lyndon asked Gene, Lady
Bird, and another girl friend to join him for a drink after
work, and in this first date Lyndon asked Lady Bird to
join him for breakfast the next morning. That day Lyndon
discussed personal finances, talked about his goals, and
asked Lady Bird to marry him. She was uncertain whether
he was serious, but before the week was over they went
together to meet his parents, the Klebergs at the King
Ranch, and finally her father at Karnack.

Lyndon wrote or telephoned Lady Bird almost daily
after he returned to Washington, and in less than two months
when he returned to Texas he made his first stop at the
Taylor home. Lyndon renewed his proposal, but Lady Bird
could not make up her mind. Although Aunt Effie and
friends advised Lady Bird to wait at least six months before
marriage, Lyndon pressed his suit: "We either get married
now or we never will," and the young woman acquiesced,
but not without misgivings. Lyndon B. Johnson and Lady
Bird Taylor were married at the St. Mark's Episcopal Church
in San Antonio on November 17, 1934.

Lady Bird's ardent suitor was born in the Johnson
farmhouse in the Texas Hill Country about sixty miles west
of Austin on August 27, 1908. His father was Sam Ealy
Johnson, Jr., a farmer and great talker who served two
terms in the Texas state legislature; and his mother, Rebekah Baines, was a graduate of Baylor College in Waco, Texas
where her grandfather, a Baptist minister, had been president. Truth and legend in the Texas Hill Country are in-
tertwined, but it seems clear that Rebekah hoped to realize
in her son some of the distinction she had lost through mar-
rying his easygoing father. The Johnsons had four more
children, but her eldest was Rebekah's pride and joy. She
recalled that Lyndon, at age two, knew the alphabet and
juvenile poems of Tennyson and Longfellow and would run
to the country schoolhouse where he chose to follow the
teacher instead of playing with the other children.

At age fifteen Lyndon graduated from the Johnson
City High School and told his family that he was through
with going to school. He was then tall for his age, six feet
three, but there was no work to be had in the depressed
community. Lyndon thereupon joined with five or six other

young men from the Hill Country and drove to California in
a Model T Ford. After failing to find a good job in San
Bernardino, Lyndon became homesick and hitchhiked back
to Texas. After driving a gravel truck in Johnson City,
Lyndon finally listened to the urging of his parents and decided to go to Southwest Texas State Teachers College in
San Marcos, about thirty miles south of Austin.

At San Marcos Lyndon showed some of the traits which
were to become prominent. He had to work to help defray
expenses, and he sought and obtained a job in the office of
the college president. His favorite professor taught government and debate, and Lyndon excelled in both. Professor
Greene also enjoyed stories that reeked of the barnyard,
and Lyndon contributed to their exchanges of earthy, robust humor.

Lyndon left college before his senior year to teach at
the grade school level at Cotulla, a community of Mexican
Americans, halfway between San Antonio and Laredo. Many
of his pupils were hungry and disinterested in organized
activities, but Lyndon as principal organized basketball and
baseball teams. In addition he completed correspondence
courses at SWTSC from which he received his degree in
August of 1930. Lyndon next spent a most successful year
as debate coach in Sam Houston High School in Houston.
The following summer Lyndon made his first political speech
and ran part of the campaign for a candidate to the state
senate, and these activities brought him the post of private
secretary to Congressman Richard Kleberg.

Congressman Kleberg was not interested in the details
of running his office, but Lyndon was and he organized the
work and directed the staff. Here Johnson began his practice of requiring members of his staff to work long hours,
almost as long as those he set for himself. Johnson frequently represented the congressman in his district, and on
two of these trips he met and married Lady Bird. Congressman Kleberg raised Lyndon's salary, and the newlyweds
settled into a one-bedroom apartment in Washington. Lyndon ran Kleberg's successful campaign for relection, and he
attracted attention in congressional circles through his leadership of the organization of congressional secretaries called
the Little Congress. Lyndon's successes seem to have displeased the congressman's wife; in any case, he left after

three and a half years when it was time for him to engage
in other activities.

The National Youth Administration, a program designed
to help young people continue their education, was established in 1935; and Lyndon, not yet twenty-seven, wanted
to head the organization in Texas. After enlisting the assistance of Sam Rayburn and other Texans in Congress,
Lyndon received the appointment on July 26, 1935. The
Johnsons had been married less than nine months, but they
welcomed their move to Austin. Lyndon recruited several
old friends to work with him, and together they launched a
vigorous program which won the admiration of the national
administration in Washington. Aubrey Williams, head of the
N.Y.A., described Lyndon's work in such glowing terms to
Eleanor Roosevelt that she made several trips to Texas to
see the remarkable accomplishments with her own eyes.

Lyndon's service for the National Youth Administration
was short, because he decided to seek the congressional seat
vacated on February 22, 1937, by the death of Congressman
James P. Buchanan. Former state senator Alvin Wirtz told
Johnson that he would need at least ten thousand dollars for
his campaign, and Lady Bird secured the sum by calling her
father. Lyndon launched his campaign in San Marcos and
ran hard as a supporter of President Roosevelt's plan to enlarge the Supreme Court. Lyndon won the election and
went to Washington where he became a staunch New Dealer
and earned recognition from leaders in the administration
including President Roosevelt.

The twelve years Lyndon served in the House of Representatives (1937-1948) included those of World War II.
On Pearl Harbor Day, December 7, 1941, Lady Bird was in
Alabama where she had gone because of the death of Uncle
Claude who had left a sizeable estate. Before the end of
the month Lyndon was commissioned lieutenant commander
in the Naval Reserve and assigned to desk duty in San
Francisco. Lady Bird followed Lyndon to the West Coast
and tried to be his secretary, but soon returned to Washington to live in their apartment and to run his Congressional office. During May and June, 1942, Lyndon as deputy to Secretary of the Navy Forrestal made with two other
officers a trip to the South Pacific to determine whether
General Douglas MacArthur's reports on men and supplies

were reliable. On June 9 Johnson flew a dangerous combat
mission for which he was awarded a Silver Star by Mac-
Arthur. On July 1 President Roosevelt ordered all congressmen in uniform to return to their legislative duties,
and on July 16, 1942, Lyndon returned to his seat in the
House.

During the winter of 1942-1943, Lady Bird purchased
radio station KTBC in Austin for $17,500 which she had re-
ceived from an inheritance. The Johnsons were still childless, and Lady Bird sought a business opportunity in a
field, communications, in which she had related academic
preparation. Approval for the purchase came promptly from
the FCC. Station KTBC became a CBS affiliate, and Lady
Bird and Lyndon were on the road which in time brought
them considerable wealth. Management of the station was
primarily Mrs. Johnson's responsibility, but Lyndon occasionally intervened and upset staff and routines. Afterwards
Lady Bird would restore calm and essential order.

Lady Bird had three miscarriages before the birth on
March 19, 1944, of Lynda Bird, a name which combined
those of her parents. The young mother's physician suggested that she not have any more children, but in 1946
she underwent a tubular pregnancy which ended in another
miscarriage and endangered her life. Nevertheless, before
the end of the year, Lady Bird was pregnant again, and a
second daughter, Luci Baines, was born on July 2, 1947.
Lyndon had close and loving relationships with both girls,
who grew up in Washington, married, and brightened his
last years with energetic grandchildren.

Lyndon ran in 1941 for a seat in the United States
Senate and was defeated, but he ran again in 1948 and won
in a hotly contested election by such a small number of
votes that wags referred to him as "Landslide Lyndon."
This brought Lyndon into the arena where he proved to be
a master of mustering the votes necessary for the enactment
of liberal legislation. Johnson was the minority leader of
the Senate in the 83rd Congress and a remarkably successful majority leader in the 84th, 85th, and 86th Congresses.

When Senator Kennedy was nominated by his party for
president in 1960, Johnson was persuaded to accept the second place on the Democratic ticket because he could attract

votes in the South and among minorities where Kennedy
lacked support. After the Democrats won the election,
Johnson was loyal to his chief; but, like most vigorous
vice-presidents, he was restive in the office.

The new vice-president and his wife wanted a commo-
dious house but nothing available seemed to match their
needs. Impulsively, Johnson leased a suite of eight rooms
in the apartment wing of the Sheraton Park Hotel, but
Lady Bird continued to look for a spacious home. She was
delighted when she found Perle Mesta's beautiful French
chateau, "The Elms" on a hilltop in the Spring Valley section of Washington. This house had everything: parquet
floors in the library, a dining room and a drawing room
which had been shipped from France, wood panelling from
Versailles, and Waterford crystal chandeliers. Years later
Lady Bird looked back:

> When he became vice-president, I had a ball. I
> loved it. I had a great time once I was in it. We
> bought a beautiful home. We took a sizeable share
> of entertaining the visitors; we did a lot of travel-
> ing--all things I enjoy and had done very little of
> before.

Although Lyndon Johnson had substantial grounds for
personal happiness, a loving family, wealth, and national
prominence, he possessed a mean streak which he showed
to close associates, especially subordinates. His press secretary, George Reedy, described Johnson as "a miserable
person--a bully, sadist, lout, and egotist," and wrote a
book, Lyndon B. Johnson, a Memoir (1982) "to get him out
of my life at last." Jack Valenti, who responded to Johnson's dynamic personality in their first meeting in 1957 and
joined the staff of the vice-president as a close associate,
also wrote a book about the man entitled A Very Human
President (1975). Herein Valenti characterizes Johnson as
"an awesome engine of a man" and utilizes thirty adjectives,
some mutually contradictory ("patient, impatient; terrorizing,
tender; compassionate, brutal") to limn his portrait. John
B. Connally, who probably knew Johnson better than anyone else outside of his immediate family, observed, "There
is no adjective in the dictionary to describe him," but he
made an attempt ("cruel and kind, generous and greedy,
sensitive and insensitive, crafty and naive" and so on).

Connally gave up in despair: "it would take every adjective in the dictionary to describe him."

How could anyone live with such a man? According to Jack Valenti, "She [Lady Bird] ministered to him, and he needed her with a largeness that all of us close to the both of them saw and understood." When Lady Bird was making plans for the Johnson Library in Austin, she visited the Truman Library where President Truman, "cane in hand," and Mrs. Truman greeted her on the front steps. Lady Bird noted that Bess Truman's "first interest is rightly [italics added] to take care of him [President Truman]." The Johnsons were church members, but they often visited different churches. One Sunday morning when the disasters in Viet Nam were encircling the president, Lady Bird suggested that they go to a particular church where the minister is "a comfort to him." Lady Bird was cognizant of her solicitousness: "I seek out comforts for him like a mother seeking medicines for a sick child." The president's wife admired the way her husband utilized every minute to advantage, yet she never questioned the wisdom of his excessively long work days--as many as eighteen hours. On the day of Luci's church wedding, August 6, 1966, "Lynda and the bridesmaids left on time, followed by Lyndon and Luci," and the bride's mother observed: "He looked so handsome. a cutaway was meant for a tall man--a commanding man."

Occasionally Lyndon overawed his wife. Thirty-two sat down for dinner at the Texas Ranch on August 27, 1966, the president's fifty-eighth birthday. After dinner the group, which included Governor Connally and his wife, went to Lyndon's office to open his presents. Lady Bird had given her husband a seaman's chest in which a family of German immigrants had brought their possessions to this country in the 1840s, but her present "was no great hit." The petulant recipient remarked, "If I live long enough I guess Lady Bird will get enough of these chests!" Instead of indignation, Lady Bird felt chagrin:

> There must be something I could give him that
> would surprise, excite, elate him. The only thing
> I can think of is to learn how to do my hair, keep
> my lipstick perfect, and be devoid of problems.

There is no way to train for the role of the president's

wife. At the outset, Lady Bird told Nellie Connally, a close
friend, "I feel like I am suddenly on stage for a part I
never rehearsed." Lady Bird learned that she had to rapidly "shift gears, mentally, physically, and emotionally, and
go on to the next appointment." She succeeded splendidly.
Her Social Secretary, Bess Abell, recalled in an interview:

> She had this great ability to be able to compart-
> mentalize her life. We'd be working on something--
> maybe a trip, maybe a guest list, maybe a batch of
> mail--and one of the girls would come in from school,
> and she would shift gears and suddenly all of her
> attention was devoted to that child--that particular
> child, that problem, or the thing that was going to
> happen.

Official entertainments in the White House during the
Johnson administration--visits of heads of states, dinners
for members of Congress, and receptions for the Diplomatic
Corps--are recounted in detail and with relish in Lady
Bird's Diary. She ordinarily includes the names of special
guests, mentions unusual items on a menu, quotes a line or
two from remarks made by her husband, and identifies the
dress she wore for the occasions. For instance, Lady Bird
recorded that she wore her Stavropoulos dress for the state
dinner for the Shah of Iran. Lady Bird often attended
three or more social functions in a day, and she needed a
large wardrobe. This she obtained by spending a few days,
usually in February and August, in New York. Although
she enjoyed these forays, she felt at times "that it is probably not right to spend so much time and money on clothes."

Lady Bird tried hard but with little success to induce
her husband to eat dinner at a reasonable hour. One evening early in their occupancy of the White House, Lady Bird
learned that her husband would take a swim and then join
her for dinner, probably about eight. Then she heard that
he had gone from the swimming pool to the Cabinet room for
a meeting of fourteen people, and she anticipated the outcome. At 9:30 she dismissed most of the kitchen help, at
10:30 she ate her supper from a tray, and at 12:30 she went
to bed. Lyndon did not eat until two in the morning. Lady
Bird was concerned about her husband's health, and she
watched his weight. When he reached 226 pounds, he began
to diet but not for long. "His undoing is those 10 and 11

o'clock dinners, before which he has had little lunch or no
lunch, and tea and melon for breakfast. And so he's raven-
ous and eats hugely, especially desserts."

Lady Bird was careful with her own health. New
Year's Day in 1965 began with black coffee and orange juice,
because she had gained five pounds. Late in the same
year she was so pleased with her weight, 115¼ pounds, that
she had nothing but black coffee for breakfast. Lady Bird
recognized her need to exercise at least three times a week,
and she went frequently to the pool where she would swim
twenty or thirty laps or to the bowling alleys. She was
pleased and excited when her score for a game was 188,
"the best score I've ever made."

The Johnson daughters, Lynda and Luci, were in their
late teens and early twenties when they lived in the White
House. Lady Bird realized that the girls deserved attention, and she would invite them to her room for conversation. The younger, Luci, was a "self-starter" and decided
on her own to join the Catholic Church. After receiving the
necessary instruction, Luci was baptized in St. Matthew's
church in the presence of her family and sponsors. Lady
Bird viewed Luci's act as a separation but admitted the girl
had never been happier. Both girls were married and had
babies while their father was still the president. Their
mother was pleased to see that the girls had become com-
panionable and were enjoying each other's company. "It
has not always been so, as every parent knows."

Although Lady Bird had a busy schedule with official
entertaining, ministering to her husband, and devoting time
to her two daughters, she undertook and advanced several
activities of considerable importance. The one for which she
is best known, beautification, was her favorite. Her efforts
to clean up and to plant vacant corners and the land beside
highways led to the planting of thousands of bulbs and
trees in and around Washington, and this example was followed in cities and beside highways across the country.
Her leadership in the work of creating an attractive environment was recognized by changing the name of Columbia
Island in the Potomac River, in which many daffodils had
been planted, to "Lady Bird Johnson Park."

Lady Bird continued Mrs. Kennedy's work directed

toward improving the furnishings and decoration in the
White House, and in doing so she gave special attention to
works of art which could be displayed there. She hoped
to replace the posthumous portraits of John Adams and
James Madison and wanted at least one work of each important American artist to hang in the mansion. On a singular
day when her schedule was relatively free (March 11, 1966),
she went to the National Gallery of Art where she proved
adept at identifying the artist behind each work in an ex-
hibition of French Impressionists.

After President Johnson decided that he would like to
have his papers housed in his own presidential library, he
turned the project over to Lady Bird. She visited the established presidential libraries in West Branch, Iowa (Hoover), Hyde Park, N.Y. (Roosevelt), Independence, Mo. (Truman) and Abilene, Kansas (Eisenhower), and contributed to
the planning of the building after the site was selected.
The University of Texas wanted the Johnson Library to be
on the campus in Austin and offered to establish there a
Lyndon Baines Johnson School of Public Affairs. The latter
prospect pleased Lyndon because he wanted leaders in government to come from universities away from the Atlantic
coast and California. He never overcame his hatred for the
Eastern Establishment! Selection of the Austin campus site
must have pleased Lady Bird because she loved the city and
had determined that a presidential library should be located
"where the scholars are, where students come on a university campus."

Early in 1965 Lady Bird hosted a tea and cocktail party for members of the Advisory Council of the War on Poverty and for concerned Cabinet members, about thirty-five
in all. Lady Bird participated in a serious discussion of
how best to salvage people, and she was invited by the
chairman of the council to accept an honorary chairmanship
of the Head Start program. She accepted although she
didn't like being just "honorary." "If I take it on, I want
to work at it," she said; and "work at it" she did. Six
months later she went to New Jersey to see two quite different Head Start projects, one in urban Newark and the
second in depressed Lambertville. She saw youngsters from
homes where ordinary words are seldom spoken learning the
names of things commonly found in a kitchen. Almost two
years later she visited the Mathis family with their seven

children in a two-room shack in the mountains of western
North Carolina and rode with the Mathises in a school bus
to the consolidated school where the children sang and
danced and Lady Bird made a little speech to the Head
Start students.

In her five years in the White House Lady Bird made
forty-seven trips and logged over 200,000 miles. Her travels took her to every corner of the continental United States,
to Korea, the South Pacific, and to Israel. When she was
well into her fourth year Lady Bird met privately with her
husband's physician, Dr. Willis Hurst, who was concerned
about symptoms of serious fatigue shown by the president.
Lady Bird asked how she could help, and Dr. Hurst replied, "I think you ought not to travel so much. I think
it matters to him for you to be with him. Stay home."
Lady Bird responded that she intended to do so after she
had completed trips scheduled for the following week, but
three months later she spent a morning with her principal
assistants going over innumerable invitations and a proposal
about "the best trips to take." In her last year in the
White House Lady Bird went without her husband on official
visits to Padre Island, Texas; Tarryton, New York; Timber-
line Lodge on the slope of Mount Hood in Oregon; and to
Louisville, Kentucky. With him she made half a dozen trips
to the Ranch in Texas, and in November of 1968 they went
together to Cape Kennedy in Florida to view the elaborate
preparations made for the first landing on the moon.

Six months after he became the president, Lyndon
talked with Lady Bird about how he could gracefully leave
the office. She sympathized with his desire to leave the
problems in Washington and retire to the Ranch in Texas,
but she could think of no one capable of succeeding him.
In a curious exchange on August 25, 1964, the day after
the Democratic Convention had opened, Lyndon showed
Lady Bird the draft of a statement in which he would tell
the convention that he did not wish to be nominated because
of felt inadequacies, and she responded in an affectionate
letter that it would be wrong to step out now. He, of
course, accepted the nomination, won the election, and
within a year Lyndon's plans for the Great Society bogged
down in Viet Nam. Lyndon and Lady Bird then agreed that
he would not seek reelection in 1968; the only question to
be decided was when should he make the announcement.

Lady Bird never criticized her husband in her <u>Diary</u>
except to note in passing that his remarks were too long
or lacking in humor. Since a President has no close advisors other than those he has appointed, Lady Bird should
have questioned the wisdom of her husband's policy in
Viet Nam. Criticism of this sort probably is too much to
expect, yet Lady Bird did learn that a competent successor
to Secretary of Labor Arthur Goldberg could be found.
She thought at first that any successor would be inferior,
but she learned, "I was wrong. Many different men can fit
into the work of this country."

Immediately after leaving the White House, the Johnsons retired to the LBJ Ranch where Lyndon busied himself with details of ranch management and with efforts to
launch symposia at the Lyndon Johnson Institute of Public
Affairs. His weak heart did not improve, and he died alone
of a heart attack on January 22, 1973.

Lady Bird spent the first year or two of retirement
on the publication of her <u>Diary</u>, and on her seventieth birthday, December 12, 1982, she helped to dedicate the National
Wildflower Research Center, ten miles east of Austin, for
which she had provided a gift of $125,000 and sixty acres
of prime land along the Texas Colorado River. The Center
has one hundred species of wildflowers under cultivation
and serves as an information center for wildflowers grown
in and outside of Texas. At the dedication of the Center
Lady Bird remarked, "You might say I'm sort of paying the
rent for space I've taken up in this highly interesting
world."

Lady Bird saw herself as a "controlled person" who
needed "a little aloneness" in her life. Her daughter,
Lynda, identified a key element in Lady Bird's character
when she said that her mother was like a character in Vol-
taire's <u>Candide</u>--whatever is going on it's "the best of all
possible worlds." The problem of fairly representing Lady
Bird Johnson was confronted by Jack Valenti, one of the
president's assistants:

> There is the temptation to go overboard in heap-
> ing laurels on her. Yet the record is plain and
> untarnished. How she managed to combine several
> lives, wife, mother, adviser, activist, ceremonial

White House partner, and retain her composure and
her good humor is still not clear to me. She always
did her job, uncomplainingly.

PRINCIPAL SOURCES

Lady Bird Johnson. A White House Diary. New York:
    Holt, Rinehart and Winston, [1970]. 806 p.

Doris Kearns. Lyndon Johnson and the American Dream.
    New York: Harper & Row, [1976]. 432p.

Merle Miller. Lyndon, an Oral Biography. New York:
    Putnam's, [1980]. 645 p.

George Reedy. Lyndon B. Johnson, a Memoir. New York:
    Andrews and McMeel, [1982]. 159 p.

Marie Smith. The President's Lady. An Intimate Biography
    of Mrs. Lyndon B. Johnson. New York: Random House,
    [1964]. 243 p.

Jack Valenti. A Very Human President. New York: W. W.
    Norton, [1975]. 402 p.

HUBERT H. HUMPHREY, 1965-1969

Hubert Horatio Humphrey (1911-1978) was born in a room above the family drug store in Wallace, South Dakota, and attended elementary and high schools in Doland. Hubert attended the University of Minnesota in 1929-1930 but left to work in his father's drug store which was moved in 1931 from Doland to Huron, South Dakota. In 1932-1933 Hubert qualified for a degree from a college of pharmacy in Denver, Colorado, and he worked until 1937 as a pharmacist. In 1936 Hubert married Muriel Buck of Huron, and with her modest savings the couple moved to Minneapolis. Within two years Hubert completed three years of academic work in the University of Minnesota and was graduated in 1939 with honors in political science. The Humphreys spent 1939-1940 at Louisiana State University where Hubert obtained a master's degree. He returned in 1940 to the University of Minnesota to work for a doctor's degree in political science, but his persistent need for money caused Humphrey to accept a full time position with the Works Progress Administration. Labor union friends induced Humphrey at age thirty-two to run for mayor of Minneapolis. He lost but realized that he needed broader support to win, and he led a movement to join the Democrat and Farmer Labor parties. The new organization (DFL) made Humphrey mayor of Minneapolis from 1945-1949 and United States senator from 1948-1964. In the Senate as majority whip Humphrey skillfully managed the adoption in 1964 of controversial civil rights legislation.

Humphrey repeatedly sought a place on a Democratic national ticket but did not succeed until President Johnson chose the Minnesota senator to be his running mate in 1964. Humphrey disagreed early with the president's intention to escalate the war in Viet Nam; but, after a brief visit to the country, he reversed his stand. After President Johnson decided not to run in 1968, Humphrey became his party's candidate for president; but his unwillingness to repudiate the administration's policy in southeast Asia cost him the support of liberals and possibly the election. The former vice-president taught at the University of Minnesota and Macalester College before he returned in 1970 to the Senate. The senator learned in 1973 of the cancer which was to waste his body and to cause his death on January 13, 1978, at his home in Minnesota.

*   *   *

At the age of twenty-four Hubert Horatio Humphrey went to Washington, D.C. to attend his sister Frances' graduation from George Washington University. During her years in college Frances had lived with Uncle Harry, senior plant pathologist in the Department of Agriculture. Hubert stayed during his visit to the city with Uncle Harry who showed him the outstanding tourist attractions, including the Jefferson Memorial and the Capitol where the young man sat in the Senate gallery and saw Huey Long make a dramatic entrance in his flashy attire, a suit the color of cream, white shoes, and orange tie. Washington thrilled Hubert to his "very finger tips," and he shared his excitement in a letter to his sweetheart in Huron, South Dakota:

This trip has impressed one thing on my mind, Muriel. That impression is the need of an education, an alert mind, clean living, and a bit of culture.... I don't necessarily mean more college is necessary, but I need to do more reading, more writing, more thinking, if I ever want to fulfill my dream of being someone in this world.... I can see how someday, if you and I just apply ourselves and and make up our minds to work for bigger things,

how we can someday live here in Washington and
probably be in government politics or service. I
intend to set my aim at Congress.

In his autobiography, The Education of a Public Man.
My Life and Politics (1976), the former vice-president wrote,
"I have been overwhelmingly shaped by two influences: the
land of South Dakota and an extraordinary relationship with
an extraordinary man, my father." He should have added
two more, his thirst for education and a restless ambition,
because these enabled him to escape from the gloom of
South Dakota in the Depression and from the dominion of his
father who needed his son's help in his drug store yet paid
him no salary.

Hubert was born in a room over the family drug store
in Wallace, South Dakota, in 1911, and four years later the
Humphreys moved to Doland, about fifty miles to the south
and west. Here young Humphrey went to elementary and
high schools, and here he began at age ten to work behind
the lunch counter. The store opened at seven in the morning and did not close until late at night. Hubert's father,
a free thinker in politics and religion, discussed many subjects with friends who came to the store, and young Hubert
listened intently. Although customers often paid for their
drugs with farm produce, if they could pay at all, Hubert
never doubted that he would go to college. In the spring
of 1929 his family discussed whether the boy should go on
to school in Mitchell, South Dakota, or at nearby Brook-
ings, but his father wanted Hubert to attend the Unviersity
of Minnesota where two of his brothers had studied and his
preference prevailed.

Hubert did part time work to pay his expenses at the
University, but at the end of his first year he left to permit
his brother, Ralph, to return to college. One of the two had
to remain at home to help in the drug store which failed to
make a profit. At Christmas Hubert received a gift of fifty
dollars from Uncle Harry in Washington "to start you back to
school," and his father agreed that Hubert should go since
the future in Doland was so bleak. After Hubert returned
to the University and to his former rooming house and lunch
counter, his father came one day and told his sons that he
would relocate in Huron, South Dakota, if the Minneapolis
Drug Company would extend the necessary credit. The move

to Huron was made in the spring of 1931, and the two
brothers left the University at the end of the term in order
to help their father. In the following year Hubert expected
to continue indefinitely in the drug store, so he went to
Denver to study at the Capitol College of Pharmacy.
Through intense application Hubert completed the course in
six months and then was able to qualify as a pharmacist.

Hubert's life on a treadmill became brighter after he
met Muriel Buck, a student at Huron College. She was "a
shapely, attractive girl, shyly charming and independent."
Muriel and her girl friend would drop into the drug store
for a soft drink, and Hubert shortly asked her for a date.
Hubert had learned to dance at the University, and the
couple would go whenever possible to a public dance hall
about a mile outside of Huron. During intermission they
would sit in the car, drink orange pop, and talk.

Muriel's family, in the produce business, felt the financial pinch, and the young woman left college and went
to work in the local power company. When her father sold
his interest in the produce business, he opened a fishing
resort at Big Stone Lake on the Minnesota-South Dakota
border. During the summers Muriel would take leave from
her regular job to help her father, and Hubert would try
to join them one hundred and forty miles away on Saturday
nights. The young couple would swim and fish in the summer and hunt for ducks and pheasants in the fall. Muriel
and Hubert became engaged in December, 1935, and the
couple were married on September 6, 1936. Hubert neglected to obtain a marriage license until after the court
house had closed, but the wedding was held as scheduled
and the honeymooners had but five free days, most of them
spent on the North Shore of Lake Superior.

Dust storms followed by grasshoppers convinced Hubert and Muriel that they should leave South Dakota. They
dreamed about the joys of a cruise in the Mediterranean,
but Muriel decided they should go to the University of
Minnesota which Hubert had praised enthusiastically. Although Hubert's father had counted on his son's help, he
agreed that Hubert should make a change if he was unhappy, and the young couple left for Minneapolis in September,
1937.

Although Hubert had been away from the University
for six years, he undertook a heavy load of courses, and
he and Muriel both worked since the money she had saved
($675) would not carry them through his projected academic
program. Within two years Humphrey had completed three
years of academic work and was graduated magna cum laude
after election to Phi Beta Kappa. During these busy two
years, the Humphreys became good friends of Evron Kirk-
patrick, a young and stimulating professor, and of Orville
Freeman, later governor of Minnesota and secretary of agriculture. Their first child, Nancy, was born on February
27, 1939, two months before Muriel's father suffered a heart
attack. The Humphreys borrowed a car and drove 175
miles to Millbank, South Dakota, so that Muriel could care
for her father; Hubert returned at once to Minneapolis in
order not to miss school and work.

With his bachelor's degree in political science, Hubert,
with Muriel's encouragement, decided to pursue graduate
work towards a doctor's degree and a teaching career.
Hubert went alone to Louisiana State University, where he
had an assistantship, and Muriel and Nancy came after he
had secured an apartment. Hubert's annual stipend was
small, $450, and Muriel worked as a typist in the Department
of Government. She also made sandwiches each morning
which her husband sold to fellow students for a dime. Before the year was half over, Muriel went home to help her
father, and Hubert worked to complete the requirements for
a master's degree. His thesis on the Political Philosophy
of the New Deal was published forty years later (1970) by
the Louisiana State University Press.

In June of 1940 the Humphreys returned to Minnesota
where Hubert expected to continue graduate work. The
chairman of the Political Science Department helped Hubert
to obtain a temporary post in Duluth which paid $200 a
month, and Muriel returned with Nancy to South Dakota to
save money. In the fall Hubert and his family were settled
into rooms near the University of Minnesota, and Hubert
was given a teaching assistantship which paid $600 a year.
Humphrey knew that he would need more money and arranged with the department head to teach more hours and
to receive eleven hundred dollars. At this time Humphrey
was offered a post with the local WPA which paid $150 per
month and required close work with trade unions. Tired

of trying to make ends meet for his family, Humphrey accepted the directorship of the Workers Education Program
and left unfinished his Ph.D. program at the University.
However, he continued to live near the University and saw
frequently friends in the Political Science Department.

When Hubert decided to run for mayor of Minneapolis
he "was thirty-two years old, married, a father, on a new
job, with an unfinished doctoral degree hanging in abey-
ance, and broke." Several of his labor union friends were
trying to find a candidate for the office of mayor, and
asked Humphrey if he would be interested. After consulta-
tion with friends at the University, Hubert decided to enter
the race. He campaigned hard for nineteen days, received
enough votes in the primary to qualify for the general election, but lost there in a close contest to the Republican
candidate.

Hubert recognized that his base of support, labor,
university people, and minorities, would have to be broad-
ened, and he made an appeal to business leaders. He also
led a movement for the fusion of the Democratic and Farmer
Labor parties which was needed to defeat Republican candidates. With his added support, Humphrey won election
to mayor in 1945, and then wrested the leadership of the
combined DFL party from its Communist leaders. The new,
cleansed party named Humphrey to be its candidate for the
United States Senate in 1948.

While Hubert was engaged in ridding the DFL party
in Minnesota of Communist leaders, he played an active part
in the formation of the Americans for Democratic Action, a
group of liberals who feared that the nation might slide into
blind reaction in the aftermath of World War II. Among the
leaders of the ADA were well known New Dealers such as
Eleanor Roosevelt, Leon Henderson, Walter Reuther, and
Reinhold Niebuhr. This organization furnished the spring-
board which lifted Humphrey into national prominence. At
the Democratic National Convention held in 1948 in Philadelphia, Humphrey behind closed doors led the fight in the
platform committee for a strong plank in favor of civil rights
legislation but lost by a vote of about seventy to thirty.
Humphrey had reserved the right to speak for the minority
on the floor of the convention; and leaders of the ADA, unwilling to accept defeat, arranged with Sam Rayburn, convention chairman, for the necessary time.

Before delivering his argument, Hubert talked with
his father, a delegate to the convention from South Dakota,
who encouraged Hubert to follow the dictate of his conscience
and with Muriel. Although his political future might be damaged beyond repair through leading a divisive fight on the
floor of the convention, Muriel told him he must stay the
course. Humphrey's speech thrilled the convention and led
to the adoption of a liberal civil rights plank which may have
helped Truman gain the minority votes needed for victory.
One line near the end of his speech probably is Humphrey's
best known: "The time has come for the Democratic party
to get out of the shadow of states rights and walk forth-
rightly into the bright sunshine of human rights." Hubert's
conviction and eloquence brought him national prominence
and enmity among intransigent leaders of the South.

Humphrey expected less than cordial treatment from
certain Southern senators after he took his seat in the Senate in January, 1949, but he was hurt deeply by a remark
made for his benefit by Senator Richard Russell of Georgia,
"Can you imagine the people of Minnesota sending that damn
fool down here to represent them?" The new senator added
to his troubles when he questioned the value of a particular
committee under the wing of Senator Harry Byrd of Virginia.
Any merit in Humphrey's case was lost in his challenging
Senator Byrd when he was not on the floor, a violation of
an honored tradition of the Senate. On the very next day
about twenty-five senators spoke in defense of Byrd's committee and humiliated the junior senator from Minnesota.
Humphrey did not want to discuss his damaged feelings with
friends or members of his staff, but Muriel gave him the
support he needed. Without it, as he recalled in his autobiography, "I might have given up."

The move to Washington in the years shortly after
World War II was hard for Humphrey's family. With a loan
from a Minneapolis friend, Humphrey bought a new house
in a raw development, and he went ahead to arrange for the
unloading of furniture. Muriel and the children, Nancy,
age nine, Skip (Hubert, III) at six, Bob, four, and Doug,
ten months, came by train and moved into a house full of
unpacked boxes and misplaced furniture. Muriel made
draperies for the windows, seeded the lawn, and drove the
children to school, music lessons, and, as required, to a
doctor or a hospital. At the end of six months, Muriel felt

so exhausted that she entered a hospital in Baltimore for
tests which revealed nothing organically wrong. As soon
as school was out she drove the four children to a lake in
Minnesota, and Hubert joined them for a few days when he
could manage to be away from Washington. This was the
pattern for vacations the Humphrey family followed for years.

In Humphrey's campaign for reelection to the Senate
in 1954 his whole family went with him to county fairs, and
Muriel worked closely with the Minnesota Women for Humphrey. Although a shy person when young and not comfortable on a podium, she developed into a valued campaigner.
"Her speeches were short, thoughtful, and filled with good
common sense and humility." As she became more experienced, she acquired confidence in herself in public, and,
as she grew older, she became more photogenic. In Hubert's words, "Her warmth and her decency, her compas-
sion and her sincerity came through."

Hubert Humphrey was elected four times to serve in the
United States Senate by the people in Minnesota, but he did
not fare as well in his repeated attempts to win higher national office. Even before his first election to the Senate,
Hubert hoped that he might become President Truman's running mate in 1948, but the nomination went to Alben Barkley. Humphrey had reason to believe in 1956 that he would
be named as Stevenson's running mate, but the choice was
left to the Democratic convention and Estes Kefauver was
selected.

In 1960 Humphrey sought the Democratic nomination
for the presidency, and made his first bid in the Wisconsin
primary. Humphrey's wife could not match the glamour of
the women John Kennedy brought to Wisconsin, but she won
admirers for what she was, "a warm and loving woman, sensitive and concerned." Humphrey lost badly in Wisconsin,
but he decided to try again in West Virginia. Here, Muriel
surpassed her performance in Wisconsin. She would load
the Humphrey station wagon with campaign literature and a
five-gallon coffee urn so that she could greet prospective
voters at plant gates. In spite of their heroic efforts
Humphrey was crushed by the Kennedy steamroller. After
the returns were in, Robert Kennedy telephoned from his
brother's headquarters and asked if he could call on the two
Humphreys. Hubert encouraged Bobby Kennedy to do so,

and after he came in he gave Muriel a friendly kiss on the
cheek. Muriel rarely became angry in a political contest,
but on this occasion she "stiffened, stared, and turned in
silent hostility."

Shortly after the election of President Kennedy,
Humphrey had lunch with Adlai Stevenson in Senator William
Benton's apartment in the Waldorf Astoria Hotel in New York.
Stevenson had hoped to be named secretary of state in the
new Cabinet, but Kennedy had offered him the ambassador-
ship to the United Nations. Stevenson was inclined to re-
ject the offer, Benton encouraged him to hold out for the
post he wanted, but Humphrey tried to persuade him to accept. At this moment, Humphrey received a call from the
new vice-president, Lyndon Johnson, from which he learned
that he was the favored candidate for majority whip of the
Senate. Stevenson did not believe Humphrey should forfeit
his independence as a legislator, but Humphrey accepted the
post in which he helped his party in Congress to adopt important liberal legislation.

A few days after the assassination of President Kennedy, Humphrey met in his office with four trusted political
advisers, and he opened the discussion by telling them, "I
want to become president, and the only way I can is to become vice president." All four of the men opposed Humphrey's wish, because they feared that he would be emascu-
lated by President Johnson. Humphrey persisted, "Look,
I'm a poor man.... I just can't do it on my own. The
only way I can become president is first to become vice
president, and I want you to help me." His friends acquiesced, and they began to hold weekly strategy sessions.

Although Humphrey was the outstanding contender for
the Democratic nomination, President Johnson talked about
other possibilities, Secretary of Defense Robert McNamara,
New York Mayor Robert Wagner, Governor Edmund Brown
of California, and Minnesota's other senator, Eugene Mc-
Carthy. When Humphrey despaired of receiving the nod,
James Rowe came from the White House to discuss the kind
of working relationship the president wanted with a vice-
president. Thereupon in a telephone conversation with
Johnson, Humphrey pledged complete loyalty, but the president left him on tenterhooks.

After the opening of the Democratic Convention in Atlantic City, word came from the White House that Humphrey
was to receive the nomination, but the president's assistant,
Jim Rowe, told Humphrey, "You can't even tell Muriel."
Humphrey protested, "This is ridiculous; a man can't even
tell his own wife." Rowe then allowed Humphrey to share
his momentous news, but the offer did not become definite
until Humphrey flew to Washington and renewed his fealty
pledge. The President then telephoned Muriel and told her
in folksy Texas speech, "We're going to nominate your boy."

Immediately after the convention at which Humphrey
was nominated for vice-president, Johnson ordered Hubert
and Muriel to fly with him to his ranch. The reason given
for the trip was the need to plan the campaign, but Johnson
did not treat his running mate with consideration and respect. The president produced a cowboy's outfit several
sizes too large for Hubert and ordered him to put it on and
to mount a spirited horse. Humphrey was not a horseman,
and his embarrassment furnished the president with a good
laugh and the photographers present with an opportunity for
taking an amusing but not newsworthy picture.

Hubert found it difficult to accommodate his bouncy
personality to the wishes of a domineering man, but "Muriel
and I talked it out ... and made up our minds we would be
loyal and helpful to the President." When the President
was at his Texas ranch recuperating from a heart attack,
Humphrey groveled:

> I'm learning a great deal from you. You're the
> one teacher who makes a fellow like what he's being
> taught. Hurry up and get back to Washington.
> I'm lonesome.

Later, when Johnson went to the Bethesda Naval Hospital for a gall bladder operation, Muriel promptly sent a
pair of blue pajamas to the hospital room, which the president wore when Hubert came to visit. In return, when
Johnson was pleased, he showed it. Muriel and Hubert went
to the White House several times in May of 1966 for dinner
and movies, and on the vice-president's birthday, May 27,
Johnson called in the press and photographers and showered
him with gifts: a watch, an electric razor, and "three pictures of the two of us together."

In less than a month after his inauguration, Vice-President Humphrey sent the president a carefully reasoned memorandum in which he advised restraint in escalating the war in Viet Nam. The president was furious, and Humphrey was excluded from top level discussion of the War. After a year of cool relations between the two, the president asked Humphrey to visit Viet Nam and several other countries in Asia. In but two days in Viet Nam, Humphrey found the tide of battle had turned in our favor, and, in but eight days in Asia, the vice-president perceived "the big picture," China's role in support of Viet Nam, which "Mansfield, Fulbright, Morse all missed." Humphrey's fifty-page report was "revised" by the White House and the State Department to seven pages, yet Humphrey became the principal spokesman in favor of the disastrous War. As he wrote later, "I came to feel, strongly and not indifferently, that what we were doing had to be done."

The war wore on until loud protests against the bloody violence caused President Johnson to seek peace. In the morning of March 31, 1968, when Muriel and Hubert were packing for an official trip to Mexico City, President Johnson, his daughter Luci and her husband, called on their way home from church. Johnson told Humphrey about the speech he would give that evening including two alternate endings, in one of which was the announcement of his withdrawal from the 1968 election. As the Johnsons left, the president hugged and kissed Muriel who sensed something amiss, but Hubert made light of the surprising visit. That evening before a formal dinner for the president of Mexico Muriel and Hubert sat in the library of the Ambassador's residence, heard Johnson's speech and his final line, "Accordingly, I shall not seek, nor will I accept the nomination of any party for the Presidency of the United States." The two Humphreys looked at each other; Muriel demanded, "Why didn't you tell me?" and hurried from the room to conceal her tears. "Part of the reason for Muriel's tears was concern for me, for us. Part was the resentment that there had been no warning for us that permitted rational planning."

The year 1968 was a troubled one for the United States and a disaster for Lyndon Johnson. Martin Luther King, Jr. and Robert Kennedy were assassinated, and Humphrey won the Democratic nomination for president under

circumstances that almost precluded victory in November.
President Johnson did not attend the convention in Chicago
but controlled many of the proceedings from his ranch in
Texas. Most importantly, the president would not tolerate
a plank on Viet Nam which repudiated his policy, and
Humphrey was unwilling to oppose him. Good friends who
recognized Hubert's predicament thought that he should
resign as vice-president and announce that he had done so
in the speech to the convention in which he accepted the
Democratic nomination for president. Humphrey refused,
"it would look like a gimmick.... And it will enrage the
President."

A year later in his favorite vacation spot in the Virgin
Islands, the defeated candidate reflected:

> It would have been better that I stood my ground
> and remembered that I was fighting for the highest
> office in the land.
> I ought not to have let a man who was going to
> be a former President dictate my future.

In retirement Humphrey had teaching positions at Macalester College and the University of Minnesota, and, through
his friend William Benton, he obtained a highly paid con-
sultantship with the Encyclopaedia Britannica. These activities did not provide the excitement of politics, and Hubert
hastened to run for the Senate seat which Eugene McCarthy
had decided to leave. He won the place in the Senate but
found the work dull in comparison with the yeasty days when
he was a junior senator. Humphrey thought that he might
gain the nomination for president again in 1972, but this
time he was defeated by a protege, George McGovern, who
won enough primaries to ensure his nomination.

Late in 1973 Hubert Humphrey learned that he probably had cancer; and when he told Muriel, she replied,
"Well, Daddy, that's all I need to know. We'll work together." X-ray treatments induced anemia, and chemother-
apy caused Humphrey to lose his hair. One operation left
him without a bladder, and a second resulted in a colostomy.
Humphrey's body was wasting away, yet he tried to continue
to work. In a contest for Majority Leader, Humphrey lost
to Senator Robert Byrd; but his friends in the Senate created for him a new post, deputy president pro tem, which

brought with it a higher salary, a chauffered limousine, and a Capitol office.

Humphrey died at home in Minnesota on January 13, 1978, and his body was flown to Washington to lie in state in the Rotunda. His most fitting tribute came from another protege, Walter Mondale, who then was the vice-president:

> He taught us how to hope and how to love, how to win and how to lose. He taught us how to live, and, finally, he taught us how to die.

Two weeks after the death of her husband, Muriel Humphrey was appointed to his seat in the Senate by Governor Rudy Perpich of Minnesota. She was to serve until the November election with the option of running for the remaining four years of Hubert's term, but she announced on April 8 at the first annual Hubert H. Humphrey dinner in St. Paul that she would not continue. Although she wanted to further her late husband's legislative program and to encourage other women to aspire to a seat in the Senate, she decided to leave because of poor health. She had high blood pressure and had been hospitalized briefly for exhaustion during Hubert's last few months of life. Moreover, she told a writer for a popular women's magazine, "My children say those ten grandchildren of mine need me at home."

The number of Muriel's grandchildren jumped to fifteen on February 8, 1981, when she married Max Brown, founder of a radio station in Lexington, Nebraska, whom she had known in high school in Huron, South Dakota. Muriel had attended in Huron the dedication of an airport named after her late husband where she learned from Max Brown's sister that his wife had died. Muriel wrote a letter of condolence, Max answered, and a correspondence ensued. After they met they must have found interests in common besides Huron and the high school they had attended more than fifty years before, because Muriel announced toward the end of January in 1981 that she would marry Max Brown and their wedding was held early in the very next month.

PRINCIPAL SOURCES

Edgar Berman. Hubert. The Triumph and Tragedy of the
    Humphrey I Knew. New York: Putnam's, [1979].
    300 p.

Hubert H. Humphrey. The Education of a Public Man. My
    Life and Politics. Garden City, N.Y.: Doubleday, 1976.
    513 p.

Carl Solberg. Hubert Humphrey, a Biography. New York:
    Norton [1984]. 572 p.

SPIRO T. AGNEW, 1969-1973

Spiro Theodore Agnew (1918-   ) was born in
Baltimore, Maryland, where his father, an immigrant from Greece, ran a restaurant. After
graduation from high school, Spiro (nicknamed
"Ted") enrolled as a chemistry major in Johns
Hopkins University but withdrew after two years
because he had tired of extended laboratory
work. Ted then worked as a clerk in the Maryland Casualty Company and studied law in the
evenings at the Baltimore Law School. Agnew
was drafted into the army in September, 1941,
and received a commission on May 24, 1942.
In March, 1944, Agnew went overseas where
he spent twenty months with the Tenth Armored
Division.

On his return Agnew concentrated on legal
studies in the University of Baltimore from
which he received a degree in 1947. After admission to the bar, Agnew found it difficult to
make a living from legal practice, and he held
various jobs in which his knowledge of law proved
useful. After Agnew moved his family to Towson,
the seat of Baltimore county, he obtained his first
political office. In 1962 Agnew was elected Baltimore county executive, an office in which he resisted demands for open housing. In 1966 he
was elected governor of Maryland, and he followed a hard line in dealing with student pro-
testers and with rioters.

While governor, Agnew met Richard M. Nixon,
and the two found that they had much in common. Agnew was candidate Nixon's choice for
his running mate, and the Republican Convention in 1968 approved of the selection. In the

campaign Agnew made blunders which Nixon took
in stride, and the Republicans won the election.
Vice-President Agnew visited many countries for
the president, and he became popular with audiences for his rhetorical attacks on important
groups such as the media. Agnew was reelected
in 1972; but, before the end of 1973, he resigned
from office because of charges against him for
kickbacks received while governor of Maryland.
Agnew was disbarred and turned for income to
writing a novel and to serving as a consultant
to leading figures in government and business
in the Orient and the Middle East. The former
vice-president's autobiography, Go Quietly ...
or Else, appeared in 1980.

*   *   *

In the evening of September 13, 1973, when Spiro T. Agnew
first told his wife that he had decided to consider resigning
the office of vice-president of the United States, Judy
swooned. In her husband's words:

> My wife had been suffering from the strain of
> the long struggle even more than I. She was stand-
> ing by the foot of the bed. Suddenly, her knees
> buckled, her eyes turned up, and she slumped to
> the floor. I rushed to her and lifted her to the
> bed. Her skin was waxen, clammy. Fear gripped
> me.
> But before I could move, she came around. Then
> came the tears. I tried to comfort her, but I didn't
> trust myself to talk. It was all I could do to keep
> myself under control. Finally, she forced a smile.
> "It's such a shock," she said in a small voice,
> "but it's not the end of the world. You still have
> us, and we believe in you."

Spiro Agnew's account of the emotional scene with his
wife in their bedroom was published seven years after his
resignation in disgrace and four years after the appearance
of his novel which brought the author ridicule from critics
and not less than half-a-million dollars in advances and
royalties. This approximates the amount which the former
vice-president paid to cover damages, taxes, and legal fees

related to the $147,500 in kickbacks which he had received during his two years as governor of Maryland.

Students who want to learn about the lives of the thirty-ninth vice-president and his wife, Judy, encounter two difficult problems. The first is the superabundance of detailed information about him and the shortage of facts about her, and the second is a need to determine what to believe. A solid book on the rise of Spiro Agnew entitled White Knight (1972) carries the story through his first term as vice-president without any suggestion of kickbacks and bribery in his political offices, and the same author (Jules Witcover) collaborated two years later with a Washington Post reporter (Richard Cohen) in a volume which gives a blow-by-blow account of Agnew's illegal financial gains which led to his resignation on October 10, 1973, less than nine months after the beginning of his second term in the second highest political office in the land. Six years later came Agnew's self-serving apologia, Go Quietly ... or Else (1980) in which he declared in his very first sentence:

> I am writing this book because I am innocent of the allegations against me which compelled me to resign from the vice-presidency of the United States in 1973.

Agnew's wife, Judy, appears briefly in books about her husband and is featured in several articles written for popular magazines, but few facts are presented. She was brought up in Baltimore in a lower middle-class environment similar to her husband's, yet the date of her birth has gone unnoticed. Judy did not attend college; for, as she told an interviewer while her husband was vice-president, "I majored in marriage." She and her husband had four children before he was able to support a family. His need for money was real; after he entered politics in 1958, he had opportunities to supplement the modest salaries received from the offices he held. How much Judy knew of the illegal payments her husband received is unknown, yet she must have realized that her family was able to live better in the 1960s than his regular income would permit. The former vice-president wrote in Go Quietly ... or Else that he and Judy entertained Allan Green and his wife at dinners in the Sheraton Park Hotel when the Baltimore County engineer came once a year to "present a small holiday remembrance." Agnew continued,

"The gifts were expensive.... They usually gave us watches or pieces of jewelry," and added in extenuation, "I doubt that the Agnews were the only recipients of gifts from Green."

Undoubtedly, it would be a waste of time to try to respond to Agnew's denial of the charges with which he was presented; the sensible thing to do here is to tell the story of the two Agnews in a straightforward manner and to leave to researchers the explication of Agnew's illegal operations and the extent of Judy's knowledge thereof. Shortly after his resignation, Agnew, with help from his librarian and volunteers, undertook to sort, arrange, and pack the papers for his vice-presidential years for transfer to the University of Maryland. After recording this important donation of his files, Agnew wrote, "No tax deduction was taken for the gift," without noting that none was then permitted under Federal law.

Spiro Theodore ("Ted") Agnew was born in Baltimore on November 8, 1918. His given names followed the Greek custom of reversing those of his father, Theodore Spiro Anagnostopoulos, a strong, hard-working immigrant who ran a restaurant near his family's small apartment. His mother, born Margaret Akers in Bristol, Virginia, had a son, Roy, by her previous marriage to Dr. William Pollard, a veterinarian. The Pollards ate frequently in the Agnew restaurant; and after the death of Dr. Pollard, his widow and the restaurant owner started going together. They married, and their son, Spiro Theodore, was born about a year later.

When his small restaurant prospered, Spiro's father opened a restaurant in downtown Baltimore, and he moved his family to a neighborhood of upper-middle-class homes. Residence in the Forest Park section permitted Ted Agnew to attend successively P.S. 69, Garrison Junior High School, and Forest Park High School. Spiro was not outstanding in anything in high school, but his grades were good enough for him to be accepted at Johns Hopkins University. He entered in 1937 as a chemistry major and withdrew two years later after he had become tired of prolonged work in laboratories.

Ted then attended Baltimore Law School in the evenings while he worked full time as a clerk at the Maryland Casualty

Company. A fellow worker in the insurance firm recalled
that young Agnew was "friendly and cordial, with a dry
sense of humor, and 'immaculate' in his dress." Back files
at Maryland Casualty were kept downstairs and could be
obtained from a clerk, Elinor Isabel Judefind ("Judy") who
worked behind a counter. Ted went with increasing fre-
quency to the records counter, and observant fellow employees thought that he and Judy would make a fine couple.

Ted Agnew was drafted into the army in September of
1941; and, after basic training at Camp Croft in South Carolina, he was assigned to officer candidate school at Fort
Knox, Kentucky. He was commissioned on May 24, 1972,
and three days later the junior officer and Judy were married. They lived in apartments close to Fort Knox and Fort
Campbell, Kentucky, until Lt. Agnew was sent in March,
1944, to Europe to join the 10th Armored Division. Their
first child, Pamela, had been born before her father left the
United States.

After twenty months spent overseas, several in combat
in Germany, Agnew rejoined his family in Baltimore. He
could have returned to his old job at the Maryland Casualty
Company, but he preferred to complete his legal studies at
the University of Baltimore law school under the GI Bill of
Rights. Ted worked as a law clerk-trainee in the firm of
Smith and Barrett and succeeded in being admitted to the
bar six months before graduation from law school. The
fledgling attorney then asked for an increase in his modest
salary but was refused, because the firm, which had an office in Towson, the seat of Baltimore County, planned to
close the Baltimore branch. Agnew then opened his own office but did not meet with success.

With help from a friend at Maryland Casualty Company
and law school, Agnew in late 1948 joined Lumberman's Mutual
Casualty Company as an investigator and claims adjuster.
Legal training enabled Agnew to carry a minor case to a
conclusion, but his salary was only $3,600 per annum. A
year later Ted tried again to establish a private law practice,
but he failed a second time. Thereupon he became an assistant personnel manager in a supermarket chain run by four
Schreiber brothers.

Agnew's work for the supermarkets which specialized in

the sale of meats to blacks in Baltimore was interrupted by
a call from the Army to serve in the Korean War. By this
time the Agnews had three children, yet the Reserve Army
officer was sent to Fort Meade and to Fort Benning, Georgia,
preparatory to being sent overseas. Before he left, however, the Army realized that a man with three children was
not required to serve abroad and he was released. Agnew
went back to Schreibers' where he became "a kind of glori-
fied store detective-judge" to whom suspected shoplifters
were brought for restitution of stolen goods and stern warn-
ings.

Agnew made a third attempt to have his own law practice in Baltimore, and this time he was moderately successful.
Butchers at Schreibers' belonged to a strong union which
engaged Agnew to represent it in negotiations with other
Baltimore area stores; and he helped black fishermen in Kil-
marnock, Virginia, who fish in the Atlantic for menhaden,
to obtain better returns for their catches. In order to supplement his fees, Ted worked on a county committee studying
a charter form of government. When his former mentor,
Lester Barrett, was appointed a judge in Towson, Agnew
and two associates opened a law office across the street from
the Baltimore County courthouse.

Ted and Judy then moved with their children to a row-
house in a Towson subdivision, Loch Raven Village. The
neighborhood suited the Agnews, and Ted became president
in the P.T.A. at the nearby junior high school. The Agnews
also joined a group of husbands and wives who met on Saturday night each month for drinks, dinner, singing, and dancing. Ted could play popular tunes on the piano, and he
usually spent some time in the evening responding to re-
quests. The group continued to meet regularly after Agnew
became vice-president, and the couple would go to the hotel
in Washington when it was the Agnewses' turn to be the
hosts.

As Ted became better known in Towson through his
participation in P.T.A. and Kiwanis, his law practice improved, and he decided to engage in local political activities.
Lester Barrett had told Agnew, raised as a Democrat, that
he would be able to rise more rapidly in Maryland in the
smaller Republican party; and Ted volunteered to work for
the election of Brigadier General Devereux, Republican

candidate for Congress. The General won the office, and
Agnew turned to work for county charter reform. The proposed charter was adopted in 1956, and Agnew sought unsuccessfully a seat on the new council. The councilmen
named Agnew to his first political office, a place on the zoning appeals board for one year at an annual salary of $3,600.
Zoning was an important matter in the rapidly developing
county surrounding the city of Baltimore, and Agnew took
the work seriously with the result that he was reappointed
in 1958 to a full three-year term on the board.

Although there was no vacancy on the bench of the
Baltimore County circuit court, Agnew announced in March,
1960, that he would run against one of the sitting judges
who ordinarily were relected as long as they performed sat-
isfactorily. Ted was advised against entering such an un-
equal contest, but he did regardless and finished behind
the three sitting judges who won reelection in November.
Ted's campaign made him so well known in the county that
the seven Democratic members on the council chose to replace him on the zoning board. Ted wanted to keep his post
and fought for it but went down to defeat. Agnew claimed
that he had been a victim of the Democratic machine and
wished to run for Congress. An older Republican was favored for the seat in Congress, but the county party leaders
recognized Agnew's hard work on the appeals board plus
his popularity and agreed to support him for the office of
county executive, a post similar ·to that of the mayor in a
large city.

The Democrats had an overwhelming majority in Baltimore County, but there was a deep division between the
former county executive, Michael Birmingham, and the incumbent, Christian Kahl. Birmingham tried to give Kahl
orders which he resisted, and Agnew became the candidate
who would free the voters in the county from the Birming-
ham-Kahl machine. Ted's friends in P.T.A., Kiwanis, and
county Republican clubs rallied to his standard, and he won
the election from the divided Democrats. Moreover, since
the other Republicans running for important posts in the
county lost their contests, Agnew found himself at the head
of his party in the State.

When Agnew became Baltimore County executive in
December, 1962, he was confronted by activists pressing for

civil rights for blacks. One group wanted the new executive to create a county human relations commission and submitted a list of topics which deserved attention. Agnew
cautioned the leaders of the black community about "intemperate haste," but a large demonstration at an amusement
park which banned Blacks caused the county executive to
urge the county council to create the human relations commission. Agnew thereupon named the eleven members of the
new commission but only one person was selected from the
list of twenty-one prepared by leaders of the activists.
Agnew named among others one of his own law partners and
an enthusiastic and energetic young man, Michael G. Holofcener. Holofcener's direct approach to the problems before
the commission won the approval of his fellow members, and
he was elected chairman. The young chairman led his group
to advocate desegregated private swimming pools and open
housing. The latter, according to Agnew, conflicted with
property rights, and he fought for his belief. A conservative county councilman observed, "If he [Agnew] sticks to
this, he can be elected governor."

    Near the end of his four year term as county execu-
tive, Agnew realized that he probably could not be reelected,
so he decided to run for governor. For, as he told the
leader of the Republican party in the county, "If I'm going
to be defeated, I'd rather be defeated for governor than for
county executive." When Agnew began his campaign, Maryland had had fifty-four governors, only four of whom were
Republicans, so he met no real opposition in securing the
endorsement of his party. His speeches reached few voters,
so Agnew engaged Bob Goodman's advertising firm to enliven his campaign. Goodman changed the words of Frank
Sinatra's hit song, "My Kind of Town, Chicago Is" to "My
Kind of Man, Ted Agnew Is," and kept the catchy tune.
Under Goodman's direction, Agnew was presented as a sincere, hard working public servant, and his name became
well known among the voters in Maryland even before the
Democrats had settled on their candidate for governor.

    The unpredictable fortunes of politics which helped
Agnew to win the office of county executive in 1962 permitted him to become governor of Maryland in 1966. Two
strong, liberal candidates sought the Democratic nomination,
but the pair split the vote of the majority of the party, and
the primary was won by an ultra-conservative, George P.

Mahoney, who had lost seven statewide races. Mahoney's
tenets and remarks made Agnew, basically a conservative,
sound like a liberal, and he was elected governor of Maryland by a plurality of more than 80,000 votes.

The forty-eight-year-old governor earned high marks
for his first year in office, and early in his second he introduced a fifteen-point legislative program including pure
water and initiatives for improvements in mental health,
housing, and highways. He promised to accomplish these
goals without an increase in taxes, and he did sponsor the
passage of an open-housing law which would apply only to
new apartment buildings with twelve or more units and to
homes in new subdivisions. The law would not operate in
established neighborhoods where property values might be
affected by sales to unwanted individuals. The new open-
housing law in Maryland had very limited application; nevertheless, it was the first open-housing bill passed south of
the Mason-Dixon line.

In the spring of 1968 the governor was confronted by
several serious disruptions in which he showed himself willing to deal with moderate leaders such as Roy Wilkins and
Whitney Young but not with militants who advocated riots
and destruction. Students at Bowie State College, a school
attended largely by Blacks, disrupted classes to call attention to the wretched condition of many buildings on campus.
Agnew believed that "students always have objections to the
way colleges are run," and he emphasized that he would not
deal with students at Bowie State while they occupied buildings at the College.

Two nights after the assassination of Martin Luther
King, Baltimore was in flames. Rioters and looters ran wild
in the streets, and responsible Blacks who tried to control
the lawlessness were ignored. The situation outgrew the
capabilities of the city and state police, and the governor
issued a call for the National Guard. He also asked the attorney general to send in federal troops, and they helped
to stop the damage and destruction. The human toll was
awesome: six dead, seven hundred injured, and five thousand arrested.

Governor Agnew invited about a hundred moderate
Black leaders to meet with him two days after Dr. King's

funeral. After the group had assembled in the legislative
council room of the tightly secured State Office Building,
Agnew berated the Black leaders for letting the lawless run
wild in their city. In his view, civil rights leaders pressed
continuously for change and improvements but did nothing
to check the extremists who marched under their banner.
Agnew's stern remarks did not please his stunned listeners,
many of whom had tried to quell the rioters, but they made
sweet music to many in the white community who longed for
a restoration of law and order. Indeed, within a very few
months, Agnew, without conscious intent, had become prominent nationally as a "hardline law-and-order" man.

Agnew had met Nelson Rockefeller at governors' conferences and was so impressed with his manner and capabilities that the Marylander endorsed the New Yorker for the
Republican nomination for president. The New York governor hadn't declared himself to be a candidate, yet he authorized the opening of an office in Annapolis into which
grass-roots support for Rockefeller could be funneled. Agnew was pleased to have near his office the initial spearhead
of Rockefeller's campaign, and he assumed with good reason
that he was privy to the New Yorker's intentions. When
Rockefeller announced that he would give his decision on
national television on March 21, 1968, Agnew assembled reporters in his office to hear the New York governor declare
that he would be a candidate in 1968. Agnew had gone out
on a limb, and he looked foolish when Rockefeller reiterated
"unequivocally" that he was not a candidate for the presidency. Moreover, Agnew was deeply hurt, because a courteous telephone call from Rockefeller or one of his aides
would have saved the Marylander needless embarrassment.

Only a few weeks before Rockefeller took himself out
of the 1968 race, Agnew and Nixon met for the first time at
a reception for Republican women in New York. The two
men found that they had much in common, and Agnew told
the press, "I like Nixon ... if Rockefeller can't be brought
in, he may well be my choice." After Rockefeller announced
that he would not be a candidate, Nixon's close advisers
moved quickly to arrange a second meeting between Agnew
and Nixon on March 29. This time the two men talked for
more than two hours, and they found themselves to be in
agreement on politics and issues. About a week after the
assassination of Robert Kennedy, Agnew went to Nixon's

apartment on Fifth Avenue where the pair discussed civil
disorders and demonstrations, and in late July, Nixon was
Agnew's guest for dinner at the governor's mansion in Annapolis. Before leaving Nixon quipped to the other guests,
"If I'm elected, I assure you there will be two piano players
in the White House."

Former President Nixon wrote in his Memoirs that he
and his campaign manager, John Mitchell, tentatively agreed
two weeks before the Miami Beach convention that Agnew
should be his running mate. "Here was a good, strong,
tough guy that maybe nobody had thought of." Moreover,
Agnew lived in a Border state, and he could be counted on
to draw votes away from George Wallace, a declared third-
party candidate. After Nixon received the nomination of the
1968 convention on the first ballot, he held meetings with
three groups of prominent Republicans to discuss the final
selection of the nominee for vice-president. Candidate Nixon
managed to keep Agnew's name at the head of the list of
persons qualified for the second place on the ticket; and,
after the conclusion of the "consultations," Nixon turned to
Roger Morton, one of six insiders invited to a final unan-
nounced meeting, and said, "Call Agnew." After Ted came
on the line, Nixon invited him to be his running mate, and
Agnew accepted at once. Thereupon he turned to Judy and
said simply, "I'm it."

On the campaign trail "Spiro Who?" made himself known
through a series of egregious misstatements. He said that
Hubert Humphrey was "squishy" soft on Communism, which
he wasn't, and he referred to a Polish American as "a Polock."
In Chicago he called on his audience in "Illi-noise" to help
win the election, and his error in pronunciation evoked deri-
sion. After Agnew had condemned civil disobedience on a
television panel, he was asked whether Jesus, Gandhi, Thor-
eau, and Dr. King had not practiced it, and he blundered,
"The people you have mentioned did not operate in a free
society." Candidate Nixon took Agnew's missteps in stride
and assigned to him a seasoned speech writer. Agnew referred to a reporter, Gene Oishi, as "a fat Jap," and the
incident was featured in Honolulu papers when Agnew's
plane reached Hawaii. The hapless candidate had his finest
hour when he spoke feelingly on Maui:

If I have inadvertently offended anyone I am truly

sorry. To those of you who have misread my words,
I only say you've misread my heart.

Right after the election President-elect Nixon invited
Ted and Judy to Key Biscayne for discussions of the role of
the vice-president in the new administration. Agnew was
given an office near the president's in the White House, but
the vice-president preferred the suite once occupied by Lyndon Johnson in the Executive Office Building. For a few
months Agnew presided regularly over the Senate, but other
responsibilities intervened. The president sent Ted and
Judy on a twenty-three day tour of eleven nations in Asia,
but Agnew made his mark as a speaker before large audiences of enthusiastic Republicans.

Agnew's oratorical style captured middle-class America,
"the silent majority." He was careful in his dress and personal appearance, and he stood on a platform with serene
self-confidence. His words, usually supplied by a professional speech writer, were delivered calmly and without bom-
bast, regardless of their inflammatory message. Words held
a fascination for Agnew, and he delighted in extravagant
alliteration. The speech writer who coined two of Agnew's
most quoted phrases, "nattering nabobs of negativism" and
"hopeless hysterical hypochondriacs of history," asked the
vice-president which one he wanted to use in a speech.
Agnew's fondness for uncommon words triumphed over taste
and discretion. "Oh, hell," said the vice-president, "let's
use 'em both."

Agnew fired his salvos of reckless rhetoric at targets
across the country. At a fund raising dinner in New Orleans, the vice-president characterized the leaders of the
Vietnam Moratorium as an "effete corps of impudent snobs";
and the next night in Jackson, Mississippi, Agnew castigated
verbally the critics who contended that the Nixon administration should move faster on integration. In Des Moines
Agnew tore into the news commentators based in Washington
and New York who wield great power over the opinions of
millions of Americans, and in South Carolina the vice-
president claimed that the Nixon administration was the first
"to welcome the South back into the Union." When the Nixon
administration extended the war in Viet Nam to Cambodia,
violent eruptions followed on college campuses, tragically at
Kent State Unviersity in Ohio. Agnew dismissed the incident

at Kent State as "a tragedy that was predictable" and proceeded to attack "a general malaise that argues for confrontation instead of debate."

Many leading Republicans objected to Agnew's incendi-
ary speeches, but Nixon didn't and the "silent majority"
wanted more. Invitations for Agnew to speak at fund raisers poured in, as many as fifty a day, and the donations
followed. In the congressional elections in 1970 Agnew tried
to purge the "Radiclibs" in the Senate, not very successfully, and then he was given the congenial job of promoting
revenue-sharing among the governors whom he knew. In
his fourth year as vice-president, Ted Agnew had "the satisfaction of having been the office's busiest and most talked-
about occupant." Some of Nixon's advisers hoped he would
replace Agnew when he ran again in 1972, but Agnew had
strong support among his large constituency, "the silent
majority," and he was kept on the Republican ticket.

Judy Agnew was not a "political wife." She never
made a speech, and she enjoyed a quiet evening with her
husband and others in her family. When the four Agnew
children were growing up, their mother tried to control their
dating by means of flexible curfews, and she provided a
family room for their games and encyclopedias for their
study at home. Judy occasionally played golf with her husband, and she often served his favorite meals, seafood or
spaghetti. Although Ted was an Episcopalian and his two
daughters received instruction in that denomination, Judy
held to the faith of her father, a Methodist. She told one
interviewer, "My husband and I respect each other as well
as love each other, and this is the core of our philosophy
of marriage." In the words of one well-known Washington
journalist, the wife of the vice-president was not a liberated
woman but "a devoted hausfrau."

The remarkable rise of Spiro Agnew from a minor governmental post in Baltimore County to vice-president of the
United States within eleven years came to a disastrous end
in less than a year after his reelection in 1972. George Beall,
the U.S. attorney for Maryland, was investigating kickbacks in Baltimore County, and one of the engineers sub-
poenaed told his lawyer that he had been "paying off the
Vice President." As Beall and his three energetic assistants
probed deeper, they found other records of illegal payments

to Agnew. The Baltimore investigative team presented their
information to the attorney general, Elliot Richardson, who
had to plan the next move. After the president was told of
the payments which Agnew had received, he agreed that
Agnew should resign in order to save the country a long
trial or impeachment proceedings in the House of Representatives.

The vice-president repeatedly denied the accusations
made by the Department of Justice, but he came to realize
that he had lost the support of the White House. After the
president's assistants, General Alexander Haig and Bryce
Harlow, told Agnew that his resignation was desired, Agnew
met with Nixon but "felt there was no need for me to bring
up the subject!" After seven months in a "pressure cook-
er," Agnew, with concern for his wife and family, asked his
attorneys to explore the best deal he could obtain. After
learning that he would not be sent to jail, Agnew agreed to
resign and plead nolo contendere (no contest) to one incident
involving tax evasion. He also admitted in court that he
knew the contents of a forty-page document which detailed
other charges against him.

After Agnew paid the fine of $10,000 imposed by the
federal court in Baltimore, the Internal Revenue Service demanded that he pay $150,000 in back taxes, interest, and
penalties. Agnew was without funds, and he borrowed
$200,000 from his loyal friend, Frank Sinatra. Early in 1974
Agnew was disbarred from the practice of law and found himself "without any visible means of income." Surprisingly,
he decided to write a novel, because "doing something crea-
tive" would restore his lost confidence. After he had told
his wife, his daughter Susan, and his secretary about his
plan, he worked for three hours a day writing the story in
longhand. He found it easier to dictate the dialogue. The
book entitled The Canfield Decision dealt with an imaginary
vice-president who became the dupe of militant Iranians who
wanted to provoke a serious confrontation between the United
States and the Soviet Union.

While vice-president, Agnew had traveled to the Middle
East and the Orient where he became well acquainted with
leading figures in government and business. Many of these
individuals admired Agnew and were pleased to have him furnish goods and services from the United States, and Americans

who wished to make foreign investments were willing to pay
Agnew for assistance in locating profitable opportunities.
Agnew organized a firm, Pathlite, Inc., to handle his lucra-
tive business, and he opened an office in Crofton, near
Annapolis, Maryland. His payments on his home in Bethes-
da, Maryland, which cost $190,000 loomed large, and Agnew
sold the property and relocated to a modest house in Arnold,
Maryland, close to his Crofton office.

In May of 1974 Ted Agnew was in the Middle East when
he learned by telephone that Judy had been taken to a hospital for blood clots which developed after an operation performed three weeks earlier. The former vice-president flew
home on the first available plane, and he was with his wife
until she was permitted to recover at home. Agnew's business expanded to Europe and South America, and Judy went
with him on trips where conditions did not oblige him to travel alone.

With encouragement from Frank Sinatra, Agnew sold his
house in Arnold, Maryland, and bought a beautiful home in
Rancho Mirage near Palm Springs, California. Here he could
play golf and tennis with cronies and swim during the winter
in warm sunshine. Ted and Judy have their favorite rest-
aurants in the desert playground, but the Agnews avoid
public functions except for events such as the fundraiser
for the Desert Hospital hosted by Frank Sinatra. Judy does
some volunteer work at the Eisenhower Medical Center where
daughter Susan is a nurse. During the summer months when
heat is excessive in the desert, the Agnews go to their
beachfront condominium in Ocean City, Maryland, where they
enjoy meeting with friends and relatives.

In the "Epilogue" to Go Quietly ... or Else (1980),
Agnew mentioned a lawsuit against him in a Maryland circuit
court. The former lawyer observed, "It continues to be a
source of irritation, but I intend to fight it through to the
bitter end." The end of the suit came early in January of
1983 when the Maryland court required Agnew to pay
$268,462 to compensate the state for bribes and kickbacks
received during his two years as governor. Students in a
course in legal activisim at George Washington University,
with financial assistance form Stewart H. Mott, a liberal
philanthropist, argued successfully that the taxpayers had
to make up the sums that went into Agnew's pocket. In

April 1981 a county circuit judge ruled that Spiro Agnew
"had breached the public trust," a ruling which was upheld
in June, 1982, by an appeals court. The state's highest
court refused to review this decision.

In the summer of 1985 the wire services carried a
photograph of Ted and Judy Agnew enjoying a stroll beside
the surf at Ocean City, Md. The former vice-president wore
no shirt, and he appeared to be trim and tanned. Judy wore
a robe to protect her from the sun, but her uncovered head
revealed that her hair is completely white. According to the
description printed beside the picture, the Agnews "often
walk along the beach without attracting too much attention."

PRINCIPAL SOURCES

Elinor Isabel Agnew. "Don't Be Ashamed to Call Yourself
    'Housewife'!" Today's Health, Vol. 49, 21-23, 68-70
    (July, 1971).

Spiro T. Agnew. Go Quietly ... or Else. New York: Mor-
    row, 1980. 288p.

Richard M. Cohen and Jules Witcover. A Heartbeat Away.
    The Investigation and Resignation of Vice President
    Spiro T. Agnew. New York: Viking, [1974]. 373 p.

Robert Pack and Peter S. Greenberg. "In Search of Spiro
    Agnew." The Washingtonian, Vol. 18, 147-153 (April,
    1983).

Nick Thimmesch. "Private Anguish of Judy Agnew." Mc-
    Call's, Vol. CI, 44-46, 125 (January, 1974).

Jules Witcover. White Knight, the Rise of Spiro Agnew.
    New York: Random House, [1972]. 465 p.

GERALD R. FORD, 1973-1974

Gerald Rudolph Ford (1913-   ) was born in Omaha, Nebraska, and moved with his adoptive parents to Grand Rapids, Michigan, where he finished high school in 1931. Jerry Ford was an outstanding football player in high school and at the University of Michigan from which he was graduated in 1935. He received a law degree from Yale University and was admitted to the bar in Michigan in 1941, and he served from 1942-1946 in the Naval Reserve. After the completion of his tour of duty, Lt. Commander Ford returned to Grand Rapids to practice law. He was elected in 1948 to the United States House of Representatives where he continued without interruption from January 3, 1949 until December 6, 1973. Ford became minority leader of the House in 1965 and held the office until he became the vice-president.

After the resignation of Vice-President Spiro Agnew on October 10, 1973, his successor was chosen by President Nixon as provided by the Twenty-fifth Amendment to the Constitution. The president's nominee was confirmed by large majorities in both Houses of Congress, and Gerald Ford was sworn into the office of vice-president on December 6, 1973. On the day of President Nixon's resignation, August 9, 1974, Vice-President Ford became the thirty-eighth president; and within a brief period he pardoned his predecessor for any crimes committed against the government. President Ford's reasons for issuing the pardon were not appreciated at the time by his countrymen and may have contributed

to his defeat at the polls in 1976 by a former
governor of Georgia, Jimmy Carter. After he
left the White House, President Ford moved his
family to Palm Springs, California.

*   *   *

The day after President Nixon announced on national TV
that he had selected Gerald R. Ford to succeed Spiro Agnew
as vice-president of the United States, the minority leader
of the House, and his wife, Betty, flew to Cedar Springs,
Michigan, to march for the twenty-fifth time in the annual
Red Flannel Day parade. But this time, on October 13,
1973, the Fords flew in a plane provided by the president.

When the Fords returned to their comfortable home on
Crown View Drive in Alexandria, Virginia, the street was
crowded with reporters and with members of the Secret
Service. The latter wouldn't permit the news people on the
property of the Fords, and a hospitable neighbor permitted
the reporters to use her garage and other essential facili-
ties, and the Secret Service converted the Ford garage into
a command post. The driveway had to be rebuilt to bear
the weight of the armored limousine assigned to the vice-
president, and bulletproof glass was installed in the windows
of the house which had been their home since 1955. After
the Secret Service had made changes for improved security
such as new wiring and the installation of smoke detectors,
the Fords had to pay $4,800 to make their home as livable
as it had been before.

The vice-president-designate and his wife and their
four children then came under the protection of the Secret
Service, and photographers and reporters pursued all members of the family. Betty's new role as president of the
Red Cross Senate Wives obliged her to obtain the appropriate Red Cross uniform with signs bearing her name and state
to be attached to a necklace. The selection of the prospective vice-president by the president as authorized by the
Twenty-fifth Amendment to the Constitution had to be approved by both houses of Congress after almost four hundred agents of the Federal Bureau of Investigation had in-
terrogated more than 1,000 witnesses and compiled 1,700
pages of reports. Confirmation of Jerry Ford's nomination
finally came from the Senate on November 27 and from the

House on December 7. and the fortieth vice-president took
the oath of office in the evening of that day. However, as
Betty Ford wrote, "Jerry's Vice Presidency must have been
one of the shortest on record--from December to August--
but those eight months were incredibly busy for both of us."

As minority leader of the House, Jerry Ford and his
wife received each week invitations to between forty and fifty
social events, and the number increased almost ten fold after
he became vice-president. Betty had planned to work three
days a week in a hospital, but her husband's new duties and
her new role left her no time for volunteer work. Congress
had designated the Admiralty House at 35th and Massachusetts Avenue, N.W., as the official residence of the vice-
president, and had provided some money for the transfer
from the Navy of the Victorian residence of the Chief of Naval Operations on the grounds of the Naval Observatory.
Betty Ford selected the silver and the china with cobalt blue
and gold trim and the vice-presidential seal on the borders,
and she scheduled a trip to New York on August 8 to look
at suitable pieces of furniture for their new home. Plans
for this trip were cancelled on August 5, and on August 9
Betty Ford became First Lady when she and her husband
moved into the White House after the resignation of President
Nixon.

Certain events in Betty Ford's life during her husband's
two and a half years in the presidency and in retirement in
Palm Springs, California, are familiar to Americans because
she has been open about newsworthy psychological and physical problems and these are discussed with candor in her autobiography, The Times of My Life (1978). Her life before
she became a celebrity is sketched in this volume, and additional details can be found in her husband's autobiography,
A Time to Heal (1979), which presents many personal activities but gives more attention to political events during his
term as president.

Betty (née Bloomer) was born in 1918 in Chicago, but
her family moved to Grand Rapids when she was but two
years old. Her life as a youngster and teenager in Grand
Rapids was a happy one, and she did well in school and in
her dance classes which ranged from tap to ballet. She
spent two summers at the Bennington School of Dance where
she studied under Martha Graham, and she enrolled in

Martha Graham's studio in New York. Her mother induced
Betty to return for six months to Grand Rapids, and she
went to work again for a department store as a fashion coordinator. At age twenty-four she married Bill Warren, who
had serious health and personal problems, and five years
later their marriage ended with a divorce.

In the fall of 1947, Betty Warren had her first date
with Jerry Ford, football hero in high school and in college,
who had returned to live in Grand Rapids after completion
of law studies at Yale and service as an officer in the Navy.
The couple found that they had many things in common and
missed each other intensely when they were apart. Betty
and Jerry were married in the Grace Episcopal Church in
Grand Rapids on October 15, 1948, a little more than two
weeks before his first election to Congress as the representative of Michigan's Fifth District.

Betty and Jerry Ford began their life in Washington
in an apartment on Q Street, N.W. Their first child, Mike,
was born on March 14, 1950, while the Fords still lived at
2,500 Q Street. A second son, Jack, was born a year later, and Betty then "started militating for a house." Three
years later they occupied a house which they had built in
a new residential development in Alexandria, Virginia. A
third son, Steve, was born on May 19, 1956, and a daughter, Susan, was born on July 6, 1957. The children grew
up in a congenial and stimulating environment in Alexandria
and enjoyed vacations in Vail, Colorado, and elsewhere, but
their father who became minority leader in 1965 was obliged
to be away on numerous demanding political assignments.
Betty suffered a great deal of pain from a pinched nerve and
arthritis, and Jerry realized in 1972 that his goal of becoming Speaker of the House probably was unattainable because
his party had gained so few seats in the House of Representatives. Jerry Ford and his wife discussed their future
and concluded that he would run one more time and in early
1975 he would announce his retirement. The Fords considered Florida as a place to live during their projected retirement, but Betty was confident that "no matter where we retired to, we'd keep our house in Alexandria."

Before President Nixon announced his selection of
Jerry Ford to succeed Spiro Agnew as vice-president, he
asked the congressman from Michigan about his political

aspirations. Jerry Ford told the president of his promise
to Betty to leave public office after January of 1977, and
the president expressed pleasure over the intention of the
Fords, because, said Nixon, "John Connally is my choice
for 1976." That evening at seven President Nixon called
the Fords and told the two of them that he would nominate
Gerald Ford to become vice-president. The Fords had to
change and then hurry to the White House to participate in
the announcement ceremony to take place on TV at nine.

After President Nixon's resignation, the Fords forgot
about their plan to retire. In Betty's words, "Jerry had
to become President. He was Vice President. He had no
choice."

PRINCIPAL SOURCES

Betty Ford and Chris Chase. The Times of My Life. [New
    York]: Harper & Row, [1978]. 305 p.

Gerald R. Ford. A Time to Heal, the Autobiography of
    Gerald R. Ford. [New York]: Harper & Row, [1979].
    454 p.

NELSON A. ROCKEFELLER, 1974-1977

Nelson Aldrich Rockefeller (1908-1979) was born at Bar Harbor, Maine, where his parents, John D. Rockefeller, Jr. and Abby Aldrich Rockefeller, had an estate. Nelson had dyslexia which made spelling and reading difficult, but he did well enough in the Lincoln School at Teachers College in New York City to gain admission to Dartmouth College. After graduation with a Phi Beta Kappa key in 1930, Nelson worked as a rental agent for the Rockefeller Center, then under construction, and he held several positions in banks with ties to his family. Nelson's desire for a career with a challenge led him to Standard Oil Company oil fields in Venezuela where he became interested in the health and economic conditions of workers in the area. Rockefeller's concern for the people of Latin America led him to propose to President Roosevelt a program for economic aid, and the president appointed him to head a new agency, the Coordinator of Inter-American Affairs. Rockefeller's concern for the improvement of conditions in Latin America brought him a responsible post in President Truman's "Point Four" program, and President Eisenhower named Rockefeller to head a Committee on Government Organization which recommended the creation of a new department of Health, Education, and Welfare (HEW).

Rockefeller's friends induced him to run as a Republican against the Democratic governor of New York, and Nelson was elected by a wide margin and he was twice reelected. Governor Rockefeller's widely publicized achievements

made him a leading candidate for the Republican
nomination for president in 1964 and 1968, but
the prize escaped him. After Gerald Ford became president, he had to select a vice-president;
and he chose Nelson Rockefeller mainly because
of his responsible experience in government.
After the conclusion of his term as vice-president,
Rockefeller returned to New York City where he
died on January 26, 1979.

*   *   *

Nelson Aldrich Rockefeller was born on July 8, 1908, with a
gold spoon in his mouth, and he died on January 26, 1979,
in his town house at 13 West 54th Street in New York, in
the company of Megan Marshack, an exuberant young woman
in her middle twenties who had worked closely with the vice-
president during his last year in office. At the end of his
term, Rockefeller sold his Foxhall Road estate in Washington
and returned to New York where he devoted part of his restless energies to the publication of books and reproductions
based on his personal art collection. Megan, who then
worked as Rockefeller's principal assistant on the art project, lived at 25 West 54th Street in an apartment which she
had bought with the help of a loan-gift from her wealthy
employer.

     The Rockefeller children, Nelson, his sister Abby, and
four brothers were given a strong sense of responsibility by
their wealthy parents, John D. Rockefeller, Jr. and his
mother Abby, daughter of a Rhode Island farm boy who rose
to become a political leader in the Republican party and a
United States senator. The family began each day with
prayers, a custom which was followed in Nelson's own home.
The children had modest allowances and grew up surrounded
by the advantages, tennis courts, and swimming pools to be
expected of a family with fine homes in midtown Manhattan,
Pocantico Hills, an estate of four thousand acres near Tarry-
town, thirty miles north of New York City, and a summer
retreat with a fine harbor and miles of roads in the woods
at Seal Harbor on Mount Desert Island in Maine. The boy
enjoyed his active life with his family and had no extraordinary characteristics except his left-handedness and a tendency to transpose figures and letters, a condition now
identified as dyslexia, which made spelling and reading difficult throughout his life.

Nelson's mother retained the letters written to her by
her children when they were separated from her, and most
of those written by the boy of thirteen or fourteen reveal
his intense enjoyment of the many activities in which he participated: firing a cannon at summer camp, dancing lessons,
and even the opera.   Almost everything for young Nelson
was "great" or "peachy," and in some of the letters which
he wrote about events and sentiments he must have pleased
his parents.   At age seventeen he wrote about his school
work ("four and five hours of home work every night") and
concluded, "I am just beginning to realize what wonderful
parents I have."

Young Nelson's application to studies came too late for
him to make the marks required for admission to Princeton
where his older brother, John, was enrolled.   Instead, the
second son of the only son of the first John D. Rockefeller
went to Dartmouth where he roomed with a boy from a family
known to his mother and where he began his career as an
undergraduate by calling on Dr. Ernest Hopkins, president
of the college and a respected friend of Nelson's father.
The example of Nelson's roommate, who was elected to membership in Phi Beta Kappa in his junior year, caused young
Rockefeller to study diligently, and his grades brought him
a Phi Beta Kappa key.   Nelson's major field was economics,
and his honors thesis dealt with the Standard Oil Company.
Nelson's father arranged for his son to draw on a biography
of John D. Rockefeller, Sr. in manuscript, and the reading
of this work induced ecstasy in the grandson, "I realized
the significance of his life and its influence for good on this
earth and I was just left speechless."

During Nelson's years at Dartmouth he had dates with
many young women, but his interest in Mary Todhunter Clark
of Philadelphia, whose family usually spent their summers on
Mount Desert Island, never flagged.   In the winter of 1929
Nelson's parents and his brother, David, made a trip to
Egypt, and Mary Clark went as their guest.   "Mary has been
a great success," wrote Nelson's mother, and the young man's
ardor glowed, "She is the only girl that I know who measures
up anywhere nearly to the standards set by you, Mum."
Nelson and Tod became engaged early in his last year of college, and the young couple were married immediately after
Nelson's graduation from Dartmouth.   The wedding was held
at Bala-Cynwyd, a fashionable suburb of Philadelphia, and

was attended by fifteen hundred invited guests. The young
couple began their honeymoon at Seal Harbor, where they
could be alone "except for twenty-four servants and a housekeeper," and continued it for almost a year on a trip around
the world, a wedding trip provided by the groom's father.
This was no ordinary trip for a young married couple; instead they were "often shepherded around by representatives
of the oil company [Standard, of course], the American Express, the Pennsylvania Railroad [Tod's grandfather was
president], the Matson steamship line and others at almost
every stop."

        Mary ("Tod") Rockefeller came from a family which
held a high place on Philadelphia's Main Line. She was tall,
five feet and ten-and-a-half inches, and skilled in riding,
tennis, and golf. She had been educated at the Foxcroft
School in Virginia and spent a year in Paris living with a
family and studying French literature. She possessed an
orderly mind and a sharp wit, and her accustomed restraint
provided a useful foil for her young husband's many enthusiasms. He was a year her junior and a half-inch shorter
than his wife; indeed, she wore felt slippers under her wedding gown to lessen the apparent difference in their heights.

        After the young couple returned to their workaday
world of an apartment on Fifth Avenue and a cottage at
Pocantico Hills, Nelson sought a career with a challenge.
He dabbled in real estate, especially leases for Rockefeller
Center then under construction; and he held several offices
in the Chase National Bank, headed by his uncle Winthrop
Aldrich. Nelson's quest for work he wanted to do led him
up the Orinoco River in eastern Venezuela to visit company
oil fields, and there he found a new vocation, to induce
companies interested in exploiting the resources of Central
and South America to improve the health and economic conditions of workers in the area. Rockefeller's concern for
the people of Latin America led him to propose to President
Roosevelt that the United States strive to win the people of
the Green Continent away from the influence of Nazi and
Communist propaganda through economic aid; and at age
thirty-two Nelson Rockefeller was named to head a new
agency, the Office for Coordination of Commercial and Cultural Relations between the American Republics, later the
Coordinator of Inter-American Affairs, or CIAA. In this
new, wartime office, Rockefeller "was far more a creature of

lunging enthusiasms than cool celebration." The young director led his staff at an exhausting pace; some of the projects initiated by his agency succeeded but others failed
miserably. Rockefeller seemed oblivious of the intrusion of
his agency on the established territory of the State Department, and he found himself in a pointless dispute with Under
Secretary Sumner Welles which was resolved by a polite
reprimand from the president.

Meanwhile, Rockefeller purchased an estate of twenty-
seven acres on Foxhall Road in Washington and into his
Colonial mansion he moved Tod and their five children, the
eldest, Rodman, was then nine, and the twins, Michael and
Mary, were but three. As in his own boyhood, Nelson's
children received modest allowances, from a quarter to a
dollar a week, and their days began with family prayers or
with their father reading from the Bible. Their summers
were spent with their mother at Seal Harbor in Maine where
they were joined for weekends by Nelson who commuted whenever possible by plane.

According to Rockefeller's most perceptive biographer,
Joseph Persico, his speech writer for eleven years (1982),
"The marriage of Nelson and Tod underwent a deep if common enough metamorphosis during the war." By the time
the Rockefellers moved to Washington, they had a large,
young family and Tod's role as a mother was established; but
his work left him little time for the traditional roles of husband and father. "He began to display that paradox of a
certain breed of man, a fanatical obsession with work that
seemed only to generate excess energy to be exhausted elsewhere." Nelson Rockefeller had many relationships with capable young women that seemingly ended without animosity on
either side; the damage done thereby to his own marriage
"was not immediately fatal" but the beginning of its "pro-
tracted death."

At the end of 1944 President Roosevelt appointed
Rockefeller to serve as assistant secretary of state in charge
of Latin American affairs under the new secretary, Edward
R. Stettinius, Jr. Rockefeller won few friends in the Department, and he offended some of his colleagues at the
preparatory conference for the United Nations in San Francisco in May and June of 1945. By the time Rockefeller returned to Washington, the new secretary, James F. Byrnes,

had made changes in the Department of State, and the controversial Assistant Secretary was forced to resign.

Rockefeller did not turn his back on Latin America;
instead he persuaded his brothers to establish in July of
1946, the American International Association for Economic
and Social Development (called the AIA) to promote improved
social programs in underdeveloped areas. The mixed results
of AIA programs led to the creation of the International Basic
Economy Corporation, or IBEC, a commercial enterprise into
which the Rockefeller family invested $16,000,000. IBEC
formed a subsidiary known as the Venezuelan Basic Economy
Corporation (VBEC) which received Rockefeller's personal
attention but yielded little financial return.

Rockefeller's work in Latin America fitted him to participate in President Truman's "Point Four" program of technical assistance to underdeveloped countries, and in November
of 1950 Rockefeller was named chairman of an International
Development Advisory Board to recommend policies to be followed in the new activity. The report of the Board covered
more than the Truman administration was willing to undertake
at the time, and Rockefeller resigned for, as he saw it, his
usefulness had ended.

After the election of President Eisenhower, Rockefeller
returned to Washington to head the President's Advisory
Committee on Government Organization. He undertook this
task with his characteristic vigor and recommended the creation of a new department of Health, Education, and Welfare
(HEW) and a reorganization of the armed forces. After the
Health, Education, and Welfare Department was created in
April, 1953, by Congress and Mrs. Oveta Culp Hobby was
nominated by the President to be the first head, Rockefeller
was appointed under secretary and became "general manager"
of the large department. Within a year and a half, Rockefeller believed that the organizational work was done, and in
December of 1954, he was appointed special assistant to the
president for foreign affairs. This was another office in
which he had conflicts with the Department of State, now
headed by John Foster Dulles; and, with a sense of futility,
he resigned in December, 1955.

After Rockefeller returned to private life he persuaded
the Rockefeller Brothers Fund to support a Special Studies

Project under the title of <u>America at Mid-Century</u>. Rockefeller engaged a panel of notable experts such as Henry
Kissinger, Henry Luce, Edward Teller, and Chester Bowles,
and he served as chairman and had a hand in the preparation of the final reports. These received national attention
in newspapers, and he was named by Governor Harriman to
head a Temporary State Commission on the Constitutional
Convention. Meanwhile, leaders of the Republican party in
New York concluded that Rockefeller was the man best able
to defeat Governor Harriman in his contest for reelection,
and they prevailed on Rockefeller to try for the nomination.

According to an adulatory biography of Rockefeller by
Joe Morris published in 1960, the first consideration for the
not reluctant candidate was the effect that politics might
have on his immediate family. Tod knew of her husband's
aspirations and interposed no objection, and his children
welcomed the prospect. His wife and their five children,
plus a daughter-in-law, were in the limelight when ten thousand spectators cheered the nomination of Rockefeller in the
great hall of the Rochester War Memorial on August 25, 1958.
Rockefeller's family proved to be good campaigners, and his
wife worked with her husband from dawn to dark because he
aspired to a political career.

On election night Rockefeller struggled through a roaring crowd in the ballroom of the Roosevelt Hotel followed by
Tod and the children who could reach the platform only by
pulling each other along in single file. Rockefeller's wife
added a distinctive touch to life in the governor's mansion
in Albany. She presided effectively over official functions,
and at an office party she demonstrated how the Charleston
was danced in the 1920s. She even kicked off her shoes
with high heels which would cause her to tower above a
group of women reporters in a group picture.

During his first term as governor, Tod and her husband had ceased to live as husband and wife. Even before
the 1958 campaign he had fallen in love with Margaretta
"Happy" Murphy, a married woman eighteen years his junior
with young children. Happy was the wife of Dr. James
Murphy, a microbiologist at the Rockefeller Institute for
Medical Research. The Rockefellers and the Murphys had
been friends, and Happy had worked in his first gubernatorial campaign. Tod and Happy had similar backgrounds;

both came from distinguished Philadelphia families and had
attended fashionable finishing schools. In temperament and
appearance, the two women were poles apart; Happy was "a
man's woman, radiating an elemental warmth and unaffected
physicality." She considered President Johnson to be "a
magnificent animal" and added, "I guess it takes one to know
one." One apologist for the governor's conduct observed,
"'Tod' was simply not a political wife" although she had
earned commendation for her performance as the successful
candidate's wife.

Although the public seemed to accept the estrangement
between the governor and his wife of thirty-one years, his
marriage to Happy in May of 1963 had many repercussions.
Certain members of his family disapproved, and the public
saw Happy as an adventuress who was willing to break up
two homes to satisfy her desires. After their marriage the
couple went to the governor's ranch in Venezuela, and pictures of the newlyweds in jeans and sport shirts were not
admired by Americans who saw them in newspapers published
across the country. Happy felt the sting of public disapproval, but her husband "forged ahead in simultaneous pursuit of his personal and political happiness.... He believed
he could have it all. He always had."

Nelson Rockefeller served for fifteen years as governor
of New York, and his record of state expenditures and control of subordinates is chronicled in detail in books such as
I Never Wanted to Be Vice-President of Anything! by Michael
Kramer and Sam Roberts (1976) and need not be recounted
here. Happy had her say on political issues "involving
the poor, minorities, and women." She strongly supported
her husband's stand in favor of legalized abortions, and she
was instrumental in having the Rockefeller name added to
that for the Empire State Plaza, the extravagant center for
state government in Albany built during his years in office.
She even suggested drugging the food of the inmates as a
possible solution to the disturbance which became a tragedy
at Attica prison!

Tod Rockefeller lived at the opposite side of Westchester County while Nelson and Happy made a home for themselves at Pocantico Hills. The couple lived in Kykuit House,
the principal residence on the estate, but Rockefeller in the
early 1970s had a Japanese house built for Happy at a cost

of $650,000. While they lived at Pocantico, Nelson employed
no valet and Happy did not have a personal maid. For
her forty-first birthday party, Nelson engaged the director
of stage operations at Radio City Music Hall to decorate and
light their Westchester home. The couple had two sons,
Nelson, Jr., and Mark, before Happy learned of her need
for breast surgery. She was then forty-eight and physically
active, and she described herself as a person "who loved
being in touch with nature." Her surgery and his confirmation hearings before congressional committees came at about
the same time, and each provided emotional support for the
other. However, married life with Nelson Rockefeller was
not always easy; he decided on the menu and selected the
wine and china when they entertained and he continued to
enjoy intimate relations with other women.

In his autobiography, A Time to Heal (1979), President
Ford gives his reasons (largely responsible experience in
government) for offering the post of vice-president to Nelson
A. Rockefeller, and his confirmation hearings extended over
four months. Here were made public Rockefeller's practice
of making generous gifts to subordinates, somewhat in the
manner of a feudal lord, and of his family's financing the
publication of a derogatory biography of Arthur Goldberg,
Nelson's opponent for governor of New York in 1970. When
Rockefeller did take office he expected to have the principal
responsibility for recommending initiatives on the domestic
front, but his elaborate proposals for social and energy developments did not win the support of Donald Rumsfeld, the
White House chief of staff, or of others in key positions in
the Ford administration. Two years later President Ford
asked Rockefeller to withdraw from the 1976 ticket, and the
vice-president gracefully withdrew and showed his loyalty
to the president and the party by nominating his replace-
ment, Senator Robert Dole of Kansas.

Nelson and Happy had been married almost twelve
years when he received at Seal Harbor a telephone call from
President Ford in which he learned of his opportunity to be
appointed vice-president. The two Rockefellers went for a
long walk in the woods during which it was agreed that he
would accept the place but that she would not move to
Washington. She did not wish to disturb the school arrangements for their two sons, and she preferred living in
New York. Their principal home would continue to be

Pocantico Hills, and her husband, the vice-president of the United States, would travel to and fro each weekend.

When Nelson Rockefeller had a conversation with President Ford in the Oval Office, he learned that he would "have to live" in the home which Congress had finally provided for the vice-president. According to President Ford, Rockefeller assented, yet Nelson and his wife spent but one night in this comfortable, somewhat old-fashioned mansion. The new vice-president and his wife gave nine separate housewarming parties for three thousand guests. The visitors were wined and dined under a large green-and-white striped tent on the grounds around the Victorian mansion, and they toured the inside which was decorated with art objects from the vice-president's personal collection and a celebrated bed adorned with mink and mirrors for which the creator received $35,000.

During the four weeks devoted to unveiling the new home for a vice-president, the Rockefellers lived at their estate on Foxhall Road, and here Rockefeller remained and entertained during the weekdays--and nights--when he was in Washington. Hugh Morrow, Rockefeller's longtime press secretary, lived there in a guest room, and was present one evening for dinner with the vice-president and Megan Marshak. Afterwards Hugh Morrow went to bed, but several hours later he was awakened by Nelson who said, "I guess your friend wants to go home now." According to his son, Lance Morrow, in The Chief (1984), "So my father got dressed and drove Megan Marshak home."

In the evening of January 26, 1979, this same Hugh Morrow, confidant and employee of Nelson Rockefeller for nearly two decades, told reporters that the former vice-president had died at his desk on the fifty-sixth floor of 30 Rockefeller Plaza. Although he had escorted Megan Marshack out of the hospital emergency room where Happy, brother Laurence, and others in his family had gathered, Morrow made his announcement "solely ... to protect the widow and her children." In spite of his gallant effort, the details of Nelson's whereabouts during his last hours were ferreted out by newspapers and shared with a wide public.

Nelson Rockefeller's funeral was held in Riverside Church built in the 1920s with money from his father and was

attended by both President Ford and President Jimmy Carter.
The Reverend Martin Luther King, Sr. offered a prayer,
Roberta Peters of the Metropolitan Opera sang a hymn, and
his son, Rodman, and his brother David read eulogies. At
the end of the ceremonies, Nelson's family led the way out.
Happy Rockefeller bore "an expression of absolute resignation," and Tod, the first Mrs. Nelson A. Rockefeller, looked
like "a composed, distant relative."

PRINCIPAL SOURCES

Michael Kramer and Sama Roberts. "I Never Wanted To Be
    Vice-President of Anything!" An Investigative Biography
    of Nelson Rockefeller. New York: Basic Books, [1976].
    420 p.

Joe Alex Morris. Nelson Rockefeller, a Biography. New
    York: Harper & Brothers, [1960]. 369 p.

Joseph Persico. The Imperial Rockefeller, a Biography.
    New York: Simon and Schuster, [1982]. 314 p.

Michael Turner. The Vice President as Policy Maker:
    Rockefeller in the Ford White House. Westport, Conn.:
    Greenwood Press, [1982]. 252 p. (Contributions in
    Political Science, No. 78).

WALTER F. MONDALE, 1977-1981

Walter Frederick Mondale (1928-   ) was born
in a small town in southern Minnesota; his father
was a Methodist minister and his mother led the
church choir.   The family moved in 1937 to Elmore, near the Iowa border, where Walter (ordinarily called Fritz) grew up.   Fritz worked
after school and in summers to help his family,
yet he saved enough to enroll in 1946 at Macalester College in St. Paul.   There young Mondale met Hubert Humphrey, mayor of Minneapolis,
who introduced Fritz to his campaign manager,
Orville Freeman.   The three became fast friends
and zealous coworkers for the Democrat-Farmer
Labor party (DFL).
   Fritz's father died in December of 1948, and
his widow and their three sons had to make new
plans.   Fritz spent a year (1948-1949) in Washington as executive secretary for the Students
for Democratic Action.   The work convinced him
that he needed more education, and Mondale enrolled in 1950 in the University of Minnesota
from which he was graduated with honors in
1951.   After graduation Fritz spent two years
(1951-1953) in the Army, and then entered the
University of Minnesota law school where he
ranked near the top of his class.   Fritz was
admitted in 1956 to the Minnesota bar and practiced law from 1956-1960.   While in law school
and during his busy practice, Mondale worked
for the DFL party, including managing Governor
Freeman's successful campaign for reelection
in 1958.   Two years later the governor appointed Mondale to be attorney general, a
post to which he was elected in 1960.   Mondale

held the office until Governor Karl Rolvaag ap-
pointed him in 1964 to fill the seat in the United
States Senate vacated by Vice-President-elect
Humphrey.

In the early 1970s Senator Mondale was mentioned often as a likely candidate for the presidency in 1976, but late in 1974 he announced
that he would not run the race. Twenty months
later Mondale agreed to run with Jimmy Carter,
the Democratic candidate for president, and the
team won the election. President Carter and
Vice-President Mondale were defeated for reelection in 1980, and Fritz set out to win the Democratic nomination for president in 1984. Mondale
won the nomination and selected a New York
congresswoman, Geraldine Ferraro, to be his
running mate. They lost to the Republican in-
cumbents, Ronald Reagan and George Bush.

*   *   *

He was the son of a Methodist minister, Theodore Mondale,
who was fated to serve poor congregations in small towns in
southern Minnesota; she was the daughter of a Presbyterian
minister, John Maxwell Adams, who became in 1947 chaplain
of Macalester College. The young couple from somewhat similar yet greatly dissimilar backgrounds met in the summer of
1955 on a blind date and became engaged fifty-three days
later. They were married before the end of the year, on
December 27, 1955, by her father in a candlelight service
in the Macalester Chapel; among the wedding guests, mostly
upper-class, conservative Republicans, were the two stal-
warts of Minnesota's Democratic Farmer-Labor (DFL) party,
Senator Hubert Humphrey and Governor Orville Freeman.

Theodore Mondale was the grandson of an immigrant
from Norway, who, like the other members of his family,
was a member of the doctrinnaire Norwegian Lutheran church.
At the time of his marriage, Theodore joined the Methodist
church, and a few years later he had a religious experience
which qualified him at age thirty-five for the ministry. He
proved to be a patient and tolerant pastor who was not disturbed when his eldest son, Lester, became a Unitarian minister, because he recognized that there may be more than
one way to achieve salvation.

The Reverend Theodore Mondale surmounted a number
of serious misfortunes, the worst of which was the slow
death of his wife from encephalitis. During her long illness,
Jessie wondered who would help her husband to bring up
their three sons, and she suggested that after her death he
should try to persuade Claribel Cowan to become his second
wife. Theodore dutifully began to correspond with Claribel,
and this led to their marriage on June 29, 1925. Claribel
Mondale was a remarkable woman; she had a college degree
in music and she added instruction in playing the piano and
direction of the church choir to her household duties.

The second Mrs. Mondale bore her husband three
more sons, the second of whom, Walter Frederick Mondale,
was born on January 5, 1928, in the tiny town of Ceylon,
near the southern border of Minnesota. In 1937, when the
Reverend Mondale was sixty-one, he moved his family to
Elmore, a town of less than a thousand people near the Iowa
border. The family remained for nine years in Elmore where
the boys, Pete (for Clarence), Fritz (for Walter), and Mort,
were brought up. Their lives in a white frame house on a
large lot combined the hard work and pranks characteristic
of energetic youths in small, rural, Midwestern communities.

While in Elmore Walter held various jobs after school
and in summers to help his financially pressed family, but he
did manage to enroll in 1946 as a freshman at Macalester College in St. Paul. There young Mondale met Hubert Humphrey, the dynamic thirty-five-year-old mayor of Minneapolis
who became Mondale's lifelong friend and political mentor.
Mayor Humphrey introduced his collegiate admirer to his
campaign manager, Orville Freeman, who gave Fritz Mondale
the routine tasks of distributing campaign literature and ring-
ing doorbells in the Mayor's campaign for reelection. When
the national office of the Americans for Democratic Action
sent organizers to Minnesota to assist Humphrey in his effort
to rid the DFL of Communist sympathizers, Fritz Mondale
formed a chapter of the Students for Democratic Action on
the Macalester campus. When Humphrey ran in 1948 for the
United States Senate, Mondale left Macalester to win votes in
the normally Republican Second Congressional District (which
contained Elmore) for his hero who won in the District and
throughout the State.

The death of Theodore Mondale in December of 1948

obliged his capable widow, Claribel, and their three sons
to make new plans, but Fritz was out of money. Consequently, when Mondale was offered the post of executive
secretary of the SDA in Washington with a monthly salary
of $250, he seized the opportunity. In his year as an execu-
tive secretary, Mondale led a fight for civil rights in a meeting of young Democrats in Chattanooga, and he headed a
tour of England sponsored by the SDA. The year was especially important for Mondale, because through it he came to
realize that if he aspired to become a politician he needed
more education.

In the winter of 1950 Fritz Mondale enrolled in the
University of Minnesota from which he was graduated with
honors in 1951. Although he studied harder in his last two
years of college, Mondale agreed to manage Freeman's campaign for the office of attorney general. Freeman did not
expect to win, and he didn't; but the campaign made the
candidate better known and linked Mondale with a rising
political star.

Almost immediately after graduation, Mondale went into
the Army where he spent two undistinguished years. He
was discharged in 1953 and promptly entered the law school
of the University of Minnesota. While in law school Fritz
lived with his widowed mother who at age sixty-one had become an expert in religious education. Fritz showed to advantage in courses relating to political issues, and he did
well enough in the others to place him near the top if his
class which brought in his senior year a clerkship with a
highly regarded justice of the state supreme court. However,
he did find time in 1954 to have a small part in Freeman's
successful campaign for the office of governor.

On June 21 of the very next year, 1955, Fritz Mondale
met Joan Adams at a dinner in the small apartment of her
sister, Jane, who was the wife of another law student, Bill
Canby. Joan had lived in St. Paul since 1947, and she was
a graduate of Macalester College, but her background was
decidedly different from Fritz's. Joan had been born in
1930 in Eugene, Oregon, where her father was the Presbyterian chaplain on the University of Oregon campus. When
she was six her father accepted a position with the Church's
Board of Christian Education in Philadelphia which required
him to travel a great deal. While Reverend Adams was away,

the family pursued regular activities in Wallingford, about
fifteen miles southeast of Philadelphia. Joan later remarked
that the way her mother handled the household chores while
her father was away for months at a time was an excellent
example for the future wife of a politician.

When the Adams family moved in 1947 to St. Paul they
purchased an old farmhouse in Highland Park, a rural neighborhood which in time became fashionable. Joan and her
two sisters attended the Summit School, where girls from
fine families prepared for admission to Eastern colleges, and
they dated boys from the comparable St. Paul's Academy.
Instead of going east to college with her schoolmates, Joan
chose to attend Macalester where her father was chaplain.
There she majored in history with minors in art and in
French, but art became her principal interest after Joan
spent a brief vacation with her uncle, Philip Adams, then
director of the Cincinnati Art Museum. After her return to
Macalester, Joan became a volunteer at the Minneapolis Institute of Art. After graduation from Macalester, Joan
worked for a year in the slide library of the Boston Museum
of Fine Arts which she left when the Minneapolis Institute
offered her a salaried position in its education office.

During the summer of their courtship, Fritz traveled
up and down Minnesota for the DFL, and he was on the road
every weekday night. His old car made the hour of his arrival on Saturdays uncertain, but Fritz's schedule and lifestyle were for Joan a welcome change from her bland friends
in the SPA-Summit crowd. He was committed to liberal
causes and she was devoted to art; the meeting of the two
on eight weekends brought their engagement during Fritz's
final year of law school. Joan was then twenty-four, and
Fritz was two years older.

Within a few years of their marriage at the end of
1955, Joan had had her first child, a boy born in 1958 and
named Theodore; and Fritz had established a busy law practice and had managed Governor Freeman's successful 1958
campaign for reelection.

Now thirty, Mondale had proven himself a master
at helping someone else get elected.... Missing
from Walter Mondale's life was the challenge of put-
ting himself on the line, of running for office in

his own right and letting the voters judge his worth
as a person, as a politician, as an embodiment of a
set of principles.

Late in 1959 the Mondales moved from St. Paul to a
middle-class neighborhood in south Minneapolis where he
could run in 1962 for one of the three seats in the legislature created as part of a reapportionment plan. However,
in the very next year, 1960, the state's attorney general
quit in a huff, and Mondale was appointed to fill the responsible post by his friend and political associate, Governor
Freeman.

The day the governor announced Fritz's appointment
was a memorable one in the Mondale household. Joan recalled:

> Eleanor was a baby. She was four months old
> and I was changing her in the bassinet and the
> phone rang, rang, rang, and she rolled off and
> fractured her skull on the bathroom floor ... a
> hairline fracture.
>   I also got a call from the bank and I was over-
> drawn forty dollars, which knocked me out. It had
> never happened before. It was just insane.

Fritz's term in his important office was to expire in
six months, and he and his wife spared no effort to win the
upcoming election. Attorney General Mondale made long
trips throughout the state, and his wife worked in the DFL
headquarters and went on campaign tours with the wives of
other candidates in her and her husband's party. Fortunately for their careers, the attorney general found in his
office the file of an investigation into possible fraud in the
Sister Elizabeth Kenny Foundation for the treatment of polio,
and the release of the facts pertaining to the scandal brought
Mondale favorable publicity and helped to win the election in
the fall of 1960.

Mondale's extraordinary good fortune in politics continued. He chose not to run against Karl Rolvaag, the DFL's
choice for governor in 1962, and thereby made himself available for an appointment in 1964 to the U.S. Senate. At the
Democratic National Convention in Atlantic City in 1964,
Mondale devised a compromise plan for seating rival black

and white delegations from Mississippi; and Senator Humphrey was chosen by President Johnson to be his running
mate. A few days after the election, on November 17, 1964,
Governor Rolvaag announced that he had decided to appoint
Walter Mondale to the seat in the United States Senate to be
vacated by the elevation of Vice-President-elect Hubert
Humphrey.

On his thirty-seventh birthday, January 5, 1965,
Walter Mondale took his seat in the United States Senate,
and his mother observed the proceedings from the gallery.
The newly-appointed senator's committee assignments were
less than exciting, and he would have to run for election
in 1966. Meanwhile, Joan was trying to settle the family
into an unpleasant rented house in Chevy Chase, and she
missed the involvement in art and politics which she had
greatly enjoyed in Minneapolis. The pressures on the junior
senator from Minnesota were intense, but he kept his ears
attuned to the needs of his constituents and they voted for
him in 1966. He was elected on his own to the United States
Senate, and he had six more years in which to serve and to
improve on his initial performance.

The next year, 1967, was a memorable one for the
Mondales. Fritz accepted the challenge to lead the fight in
the Senate for open-housing legislation, and the family moved
into an older and larger house in the Cleveland Park district
which had some of the characteristics of the home they had
enjoyed in Minneapolis. Joan undertook to make a book out
of talks on art she had delivered to women working for the
DFL in Minnesota. The slight volume of seventy-one pages
with its ambitious title, Politics in Art, was printed in 1972
in Minneapolis. Included in the book are reproductions of
a small number of paintings with the compiler's comments on
their political relevance.

Mondale's leadership of the open-housing provision in
the civil rights bill which passed the Senate and the House
of Representatives in the spring of 1968 along with his work
to resolve the credentials controversy at the 1964 Convention brought him recognition as a politician who could handle
knotty problems with skill and restraint. The senator
showed to a disadvantage, however, in his willingness to
rationalize the war in Viet Nam. His perception of wrongdo-
ing was clouded by his loyalty to Vice-President Humphrey

who was President Johnson's man, and he even let an assistant secretary of state talk him out of making a break with the administration on a course which had great moral implications. Mondale later regretted his indecision, and called on September 17 for a halt in the bombing over North Viet Nam. Candidate Humphrey, still trying to ride two horses, commented, "Mondale is a good friend ... and I welcome his view."

After the inauguration of Richard Nixon as president in 1969, Mondale was free of the restraints which resulted from his loyalty to former Vice-President Humphrey, and he undertook to champion solutions to neglected problems such as the health of migratory workers and the need for day-care centers for children of working mothers. Mondale's Subcommittee on Children and Youth produced the Comprehensive Child Development Act of 1971 which was vetoed by the president. The senator also became chairman of the Select Committee on Equal Educational Opportunity and argued for forced busing until he came to realize that it was but one of many ways to equalize educational opportunities. Mondale's liberal concerns won wide support because they were related to desirable social issues, but he came in time to realize that not every family problem can be cured by legislation.

Mondale's activities as a senator in the early 1970s caused him to be talked about as a likely Democratic candidate for the presidency in 1976, and he made publicly remarks which fanned the speculation over whether he would or would not make the race. Mondale called a press conference on November 21, 1974, to announce his decision and he surprised his audience when he said that he would not seek the nomination in 1976. Even Joan seems to have been surprised:

> Suddenly, I remember sitting there in my red president suit, saying to myself, "I am unemployed." And I was indeed, because I had cleared my life to go campaigning with him.

Mondale explained at his press conference that he lacked the "overwhelming desire to be president which is essential for the kind of campaign that is required," and he added, "I don't think anyone should be president who is not

willing to go through fire." Mondale had observed the price
paid by Humphrey for seeking the presidency, and he decided not to follow his friend's example.

Mondale's decision not to run in 1976 for the presidency was firm, but his announcement in late 1974 was not his
last word on the subject. His decision, Mondale wrote in
1975, "was a fairly simple personal one because it reflected
my own priorities." This somewhat enigmatic statement appeared in a curious book, The Accountability of Power, which
Mondale wrote in 1975 with a great deal of help from his
legislative assistant, Roger Colloff. Although the book began as a joint effort to expand a speech Mondale gave in the
Senate, the final product is a blend of some of his attitudes
as a freshman senator and considerable sophomoric theorizing
about how to correct abuses of power exercised by "imperial"
presidents. Ten years earlier, when Mondale entered the
Senate, he viewed the president as a likely moral leader of
the country, but he became disillusioned by the ruthlessness
of presidents Johnson and Nixon, especially the latter. The
seasoned senator made a number of concrete proposals for
reform including the repeal of the Twenty -fifth Amendment
to the Constitution which provides for the selection of a
vice-president when the office has been vacated, because
this procedure bypasses campaigns and elections, truly a
surprising comment from a politician who had been appointed
to two important offices by two different governors of Minnesota.

Twenty months after Mondale took himself out of the
1976 contest for the Democratic nomination for the presidency,
he sought and obtained the honor of becoming Jimmy Carter's
running mate. Although his campaign as a member of the national ticket would make great demands on Fritz and his wife,
the candidate, as his biographer observed, would be risking
nothing:

> Victory could move him, relatively effortlessly,
> across the threshold of national power. Defeat
> would send him back to the Senate, where it would
> be easy to accept the outcome gracefully, especially
> if he had acquitted himself honorably in the party's
> service.

When Jimmy Carter, the prospective nominee of his

party in 1976 for president, asked Walter Mondale, about
the kind of a role he wanted to play if he became the vice-
president, the senator from Minnesota responded that he
would want to be active in the Georgian's administration.
After the Democrats won the election, Mondale submitted to
the president-elect a number of proposals which he hoped
would be adopted; President-elect Carter was receptive but
very few of Mondale's recommendations became priorities in
the new administration. Three days after he became the
vice-president, Mondale made a trip of almost 25,000 miles
to greet the NATO allies and to Japan; the trip was followed
by others including one to the Middle East and another to
China.

Walter Mondale's family was the first to live in the
residence for vice-presidents finally provided by Congress.
This meant that the Mondale home in Cleveland Park could
be leased, and Joan undertook to wash windows and to paint
rooms for her new tenants. She was spared the work of a
final housecleaning when friendly neighbors did the job in
her absence. On Inauguration Day Joan and her family
moved into the large, Victorian white house on a hill near
35th and Massachusetts Avenue which is surrounded by
twelve acres of land carefully maintained by naval personnel.

Joan's move into her new home made her a Washington
celebrity, and she took the change in stride with more attention to clothes and personal appearance. Her new role
and residence gave her an opportunity to feature artistic
work which she loved, and she decorated the vice-president's
house with contemporary American paintings and with pottery
she had made in a class under the tutelage of a recognized
master. "Joan of Art" also persuaded the National Park
Service to offer for sale in souvenir shops examples of crafts
produced in a locality. And before long, Joan induced the
administrator of the General Services Administration to increase the percentage of total construction costs allocated to
art in new or renovated federal buildings.

Joan Mondale told a newspaper man in 1984 that she
and Fritz recognized in August of 1979 that the team of
Carter and Mondale would be defeated for reelection in 1980.
After the victory of the Republican national ticket, the Mondales returned to their home in Cleveland Park. Their three
children, two boys and a girl, had attended public elementary

schools in the District of Columbia but went on to private
secondary schools. Within a few years, the boys, Theodore
and William, were undergraduates at the University of Minnesota and Brown University, respectively, and their sister,
Eleanor, aspired to a career as an actress in New York or
in Hollywood.

When her husband won the hardfought Democratic
nomination for President in 1984, Joan was asked about the
role she would play if her husband won the election, and
she had resolved to promote the arts and to strengthen the
American family. Joan favored the adoption of the Equal
Rights Amendment and programs for "flex time" and day
care centers which would help young women to work and to
have a family.

After Mondale had defeated the other candidates, mostly senators, for the Democratic nomination for president, he
selected a woman, Geraldine Ferraro, a congresswoman from
New York, to be his running mate. In doing so, according
to Ferraro, My Story, Mondale was "urged on by his wife
Joan," but he did not make the selection until after he had
interviewed other candidates including two women besides
Ferraro, two black mayors of large cities, one Hispanic
mayor, and two white males. According to Ferraro, the list
of persons interviewed by Mondale "sounded like a lineup
for Noah's Ark." This process which got Mondale into a
"bind" was followed only because the candidate from Minnesota was "trying to emulate Carter's vice-president selection
process." Jimmy Carter's example is a lame excuse for Mondale's doing anything which would seem ludicrous to any of
the candidates, especially to the one selected.

After Mondale's selection of Ferraro was ratified by
the delegates to the 1984 Democratic National Convention in
San Francisco, no cloud was to be seen on the horizon as
Ferraro and her husband shared a bottle of champagne with
Fritz and Joan Mondale. Fritz's campaign, according to
Ferraro, made a poor start because the Democratic candidate
predicted a necessary increase in taxes. Moreover, again
according to Ferraro, Fritz was perceived as dull by television audiences while "I, on the other hand, was being seen
as feisty and irreverent." Despite the embarrassment caused
by an examination of Ferraro's and her husband's financial
dealings and the resounding defeat of the Democratic national

ticket, Geraldine considered her candidacy for the office of
vice-president to be "a bond between women all over America."

     Ferraro recognized that if she had not been on the
ticket with Fritz, Joan "would have been the focus of attention." Ferraro continued, "Never once, however, did she
display anything but the warmest feelings toward me."

     Joan Mondale's reaction to Geraldine Ferraro is not
apparent, but she did comment directly on her husband in
several newspaper interviews. In one she said that the key
to Fritz is "Norwegian charisma," whatever that may be; and
in another she said that her husband "never shows emotion.
He handles it." Mondale's political record is impressive,
and his hobbies, fishing and the reading of history, appeal
strongly to Americans. Yet, despite his obvious virtues,
Mondale excites few voters outside of his home state; for,
as one Texan voiced his lack of enthusiasm for the Democratic candidate for president in 1984, "He's too pale for
me."

PRINCIPAL SOURCES

Geraldine A. Ferraro and Linda Bird Francke. Ferraro, My
   Story. New York: Bantam Books, [1985]. 340 p.

Finlay Lewis. Mondale, Portrait of an American Politician.
   New York: Harper, [1980]. 287 p.

Joan Adams Mondale. Politics in Art. Minneapolis: Lerner
   Publications, [1972]. 71 p.

Walter F. Mondale. The Accountability of Power; Toward a
   Responsible Presidency. New York: McKay, [1975].
   284 p.

PERSONAL NOTE

     I had the pleasure of meeting Mrs. Mondale on three
separate occasions while her husband was the vice-president.
All three pertained to the formation of a small collection of
books pertaining to the vice-presidency and to the individual

vice-presidents which occupy shelves in the vice-president's house in Washington. Mrs. Mondale is a slender, gracious person with a warm, sincere smile. When the book collection was opened, the vice-president was in Yugoslavia to attend the funeral of Tito. Mrs. Mondale greeted the guests, mainly authors of the books on the shelves and descendants of former vice-presidents who lived in Washington, and she delivered an amusing and appropriate speech. At the end of the evening when I expressed my thanks to Mrs. Mondale for her interest in forming the collection of books on the vice-presidents and for the pleasure my wife and I had had in attending the party, I added that I was pleased she hadn't been called that evening to the White House for the installation of Senator Muskie as the new secretary of state. Mrs. Mondale's quick rejoinder was that she would not consider leaving her guests, and I sensed that she meant it.

GEORGE BUSH, 1981–1989 (?)

George Herbert Walker Bush (1924–   ) was
born in Milton, Massachusetts; his father was a
successful businessman who moved to Connecticut where he became a United States senator
and his mother was the daughter of George
Herbert Walker of Walker Cup fame.   George
attended Greenwich Country Day School and
Phillips Academy in Andover, Massachusetts,
where he was a standout in academic subjects,
student government, and sports.   On his
eighteenth birthday George enlisted in the
Navy's pre-flight training program and became in 1943 the youngest pilot in the United
States Navy.   During a combat mission in the
Pacific theater, George's plane was shot down,
and the twenty-year-old pilot escaped with
his life after dropping heavy bombs on enemy
installations.   After discharge from the Navy,
Bush entered Yale University where he played
on the college baseball team and received in
1948 an honors degree in economics.

Instead of moving to Wall Street, George
Bush located in Texas where he bought and
sold oil properties and headed an offshore
drilling company.   After selling his firm,
Zapata Petroleum, for a substantial sum, Bush
was elected to Congress from his district,
which included Houston, and was reelected
in 1968.   In 1970 Bush ran unsuccessfully for a
seat in the United States Senate and was named
by the White House to head the United States
mission to the United Nations.   Two years later
Ambassador Bush resigned to become chairman of
the Republican National Committee, an office which

he held during the Watergate crisis. After
the resignation of President Nixon, Bush was
named by President Ford to head the American
Liaison Office in China. Before he left China
in late 1975, Bush had agreed to head the Central Intelligence Agency where he earned high
marks for his leadership which ended when
President Ford left office in January of 1977.
Bush returned to Texas, and a year later he
began to campaign for the Republican nomination for president in 1980. During 1979 Bush
won several primaries but not enough to win
the nomination which went in 1980 to Ronald
Reagan. Bush promptly accepted Ronald
Reagan's invitation to be his running mate,
and the Republican team won the election.
President Reagan and Vice-President Bush
were reelected in 1984.

*   *   *

After more than a year of very active duty aboard the light
aircraft carrier USS San Jacinto, Lt. George Bush's squadron was replaced and dispatched to San Diego where their
ship arrived on December 23, 1944. George reached home
in Greenwich, Connecticut, in time for a joyous Christmas
celebration, and he promptly called on Barbara Pierce, the
girl to whom he had been secretly engaged while he was in
the South Pacific. Within two weeks, on January 6, 1945,
the couple were married in a large family wedding in the
bride's hometown, Rye, New York. Barbara, then nineteen,
in her second year at Smith, left college to begin her married life as the wife of a naval training officer stationed at
Norfolk, Virginia.

Barbara was the daughter of Marvin Pierce, publisher
of the Redbook and McCall's which then embraced a magazine
and a pattern company. Barbara recalled that her father
often brought home pattern catalogs which she and her
friends cut into paper dolls. This marked the beginning of
Barbara's interest in sewing and needlecraft which she has
carried into the Tuesday meetings of senators' wives on
Capitol Hill.

When she was but sixteen Barbara met George Bush
at a dance in Rye. On their "first real date," George made

sure that his car radio was in working order because he
was afraid the pair might not have anything to talk about.
However, according to Barbara, George "shouldn't have
worried. We started talking that night and we haven't
stopped for [more than forty] years." Her admirer, a
super-achiever at Phillips Academy at Andover, Massachusetts, was the "nicest, handsomest, funniest man," Barbara
recalled; and she added, "He still is."

     George Bush is a descendant of two outstanding fam-
ilies. His father, Prescott, was a graduate of Phillips Academy and Yale College who served as an officer in World War
I before he entered a business firm which caused him to
move to Milton, Massachusetts, where George, his second
son, was born on June 12, 1924. Another move brought
Prescott to Wall Street and his family to a large house in
Greenwich, Connecticut. During the 1930s and 1940s, Prescott Bush was active in Connecticut Republican politics, and
this led to his appointment to a seat in the United States
Senate. After the 1956 election made Prescott a senator by
vote of the people, he served for six years and retired in
1962 to his comfortable home in Greenwich where he died ten
years later.

     George's mother, Dorothy, was the daughter of George
Herbert Walker, who gave his name to a trophy, the Walker
Cup, for world golf competition. He established an investment firm in New York which enabled him to build a summer
home at Kennebunkport, Maine, where George, his three
brothers, and a sister spent delightful summers replete with
sailing, picnics, golf, and tennis. At Christmas the Bushes
would travel to South Carolina to spend the holidays on
Grandfather Walker's plantation. There members of the
family and guests enjoyed riding, hunting, and feasting on
the superb food prepared by a cadre of capable servants.

     At home in Greenwich the Bushes escaped the harsh
blows of the Depression, and George entered along with his
older brother, Prescott, Jr., the nearby Greenwich Country
Day School. After his completion of the elementary program,
George followed his brother to Phillips Academy in Andover,
twenty miles north of Boston. Here George was a standout
student in his class of over two hundred; the activities
listed in the yearbook for his class at the time of graduation, 1942, show him to have been a leader in student

government and the captain of baseball and soccer teams.
According to his biographer, the handsome George Bush at
age eighteen was a "big man" on the Andover campus.

The Bushes and the Walkers were Yale men, and
George intended to go to New Haven after graduation from
Andover.   Although he had been admitted at Yale, George
chose instead to enlist on his eighteenth birthday in the
navy's flight-training program.   George lacked the two years
of college preparation ordinarily required of candidates for
commissioners, but he did qualify in the fall of 1943 as the
youngest pilot in the entire United States Navy.   The new
ensign's lack of college experience surprised his squadron's
executive officer, but the youthful pilot soon proved his
mettle.

George Bush had been assigned to the San Jack (short
for San Jacinto) which was commissioned in December, 1943,
and headed west across the Pacific after shakedown cruises
in the Caribbean.   Bush was a member of a torpedo bomber
squadron which saw action first in support of the landings
on Saipan in the Marianas.   Bush's ship and squadron participated in operations in the Marshall Islands and in the
Palau campaign; it was the latter in which on September 2,
1944, George's plane was hit by Japanese antiaircraft shells.
One of Bush's two crewmen was killed, but the twenty-year-
old lieutenant (j.g.) dropped several large bombs on enemy
installations before he bailed out of his damaged plane.
Bush paddled hard in his life raft to elude the Japanese and
was rescued by an American submarine in which he spent a
month before he went to Hawaii for rest and recreation, after which he returned to the San Jacinto for action in the
Philippines.   The young pilot's exploits brought him three
Air medals and the Distinguished Flying Cross.   His actions
on the day his plane was shot down were remarkable for
"heroism and extraordinary achievement" in the face of enemy
fire.

After the decorated pilot, not yet twenty-one, returned home and married Barbara, the newly married couple
shared a house with three other couples at Virginia Beach.
In 1945 the war in Europe and in the Pacific ended, and
Lieutenant Bush was discharged from the Navy in September,
1945.   Two months later George was enrolled in Yale as a
member of the largest freshman class in the history of the

institution, and he and his wife moved into an apartment
near the campus where their first child, George Walker
Bush, was born in 1947.

George Bush's brief career as an undergraduate at
Yale was another success story. He earned an honors degree in economics, played first base on the Yale baseball
team for three years, and was active in a Greek social fraternity and in the senior society known as Skull and Bones.
At age twenty-four Bush was ready to move into a prestigious firm in New York's financial district; but, partly out
of a desire to move out from under the shadow of influential
relatives, he and Barbara decided to locate in Texas.

Although young George Bush knew nothing about
drilling for oil, he proceeded to make a fortune in petroleum
enterprises in west Texas. He and Barbara, with son
George, moved into a house in Odessa, Texas, where they
shared a bathroom with occupants of nearby trailers. George
began at the bottom of the oil business; he swept warehouses
and painted drilling machinery for $375 a month. Hard work
and long hours brought a better job as a salesman of drilling
bits in Bakersfield, California, but George soon decided to
make a fresh start in Midland, Texas, where he had a part
in organizing and operating the Bush-Overby Development
Company which bought and sold oil properties. Three years
later Bush and the two Liedtke brothers put their resources
and energies into the Zapata Petroleum Corporation (named
after the motion picture Viva Zapata!) which developed a rig
for offshore drilling. The venture prospered, but George
began to think of moving to Houston and a career in public
service. The death of daughter Robin from leukemia in 1953
may have caused her parents to review their goals.

In 1958 Bush moved the headquarters of Zapata Petroleum to Houston, and the Zapata Offshore drilling company
prospered in the early 1960s. The offshore drilling business
had been Bush's signal success, but he realized the pre-
cariousness of the operation. A large drilling rig was lost
without a trace during Hurricane Betsy which swept the
Gulf Coast in September of 1965. Bush took leave of his
company in 1964 to run unsuccessfully for the seat in the
United States Senate held by Ralph Yarborough who had the
support of another Texas Democrat, President Lyndon Johnson. Candidate Bush tried to link his campaign to that of

Barry Goldwater, the Republican presidential nominee in
1964, but this did him little good for Bush outran the national candidate by 200,000 votes in Texas.

Bush sold his interest in Zapata petroleum in 1966,
for by then he had made his first million dollars. He then
won election to Congress from the Seventh Congressional
District, which included Houston, and he was reelected to
the House of Representatives in 1968. The Bushes bought
a three-story brick home near the National Cathedral in
Washington. Their daughter, Dorothy, attended the Cathedral School, and their two younger boys went to St. Al-
ban's. Their two older boys were then away at college.

As a Republican congressman from Texas, Bush was
the first freshman in sixty years to be appointed to the
important Ways and Means Committee. Congressman Bush
showed himself to be a congenial colleague, and he supported
the Civil Rights Act of 1968 with its controversial provision
on open housing for minorities. His vote on the legislation
was not well received by constituents in Houston, but Bush
never regretted following his conscience when the bill came
up for a vote in the House.

Bush voted also to abolish the draft and to expand
birth control programs. He was among the first in Congress
to employ women in key staff positions, and he made friends
everywhere. His correspondence from his district was heavy,
and he wrote personal notes to constituents and appeared
often on Saturdays at his office to help his staff clear his
desk of correspondence.

Instead of running for a third term in the House of
Representatives, Bush tried again in 1970 for a seat in the
United States Senate and lost. Instead of abandoning politics, Bush asked the White House for an appointment and
was named Permanent United States Representative to the
United Nations. Although young and without diplomatic experience, Bush became head of the United States Mission to
the U.N. on February, 1971. Despite his government's unsuccessful effort to block the admission into the United Nations of the People's Republic of China, Ambassador Bush
won the admiration of the diplomatic community and the
press. The Nation described Bush as a "mixture of Gary
Cooper and John Lindsay--with money."

During the two years Bush was ambassador to the
United Nations his residence provided by the U.S. government was an apartment in the Waldorf Towers, high above
Park Avenue, with a splendid view of New York City.
Barbara decorated the apartment with paintings borrowed
from the Metropolitan Museum of Art, which lends pictures
from its storerooms to American embassies around the world.
Barbara selected mainly paintings in black-and-white done
early in this century, but she displayed in the entrance hall
of the apartment a portrait of an early Secretary of the
Treasury, Albert Gallatin, done by a master, Gilbert Stuart.

The Bushes probably enjoyed their life in New York
while George was in charge of the Mission at the United Nations, but he resigned in less than two years.   President
Nixon wanted Bush to replace Senator Bob Dole as chairman
of the Republican National Committee (RNC), and George
could not refuse.   His explanation for accepting the party
post was a simple one, "When the president wants you to do
something, in my kind of civics you ought to do it."

The new chairman headed the party committee for
eighteen months which included the Watergate revelations
and the resignation of President Nixon.   The president and
George Bush admired each other, and the RNC chairman believed at the outset that his chief was telling the truth.   In
April, 1974, Bush confided to a national committee meeting
that he had become "plagued with doubts" about the president's involvement in the scandal, and Bush may have privately urged Nixon to resign.   But he never criticized Nixon
publicly.   Instead, he struggled manfully to keep the party
strong while Nixon's administration crumbled.   Most Republicans respect Bush for his posture during his chairmanship
of his party's national organization, but he has been criticized for his "imitation of the last defenders at the Alamo."

In recognition of his loyal performance as captain of
the party's ship, President Ford named Bush to head the
American Liaison Office in Peking.   As the second envoy of
the United States to China, Bush headed a mission of 226
Americans, and he and his wife lived in a compound surrounded by a wall which enclosed their residence and the
mission's offices.   The Bushes studied the Chinese language,
rode bikes all over the city, and visited the principal sights
in the land of mystery.   Surprisingly, Bush's official duties

left him time for recreational reading. In an interview four
years later, Bush talked about his hobbies:

> Some reading at times, especially when I was in
> China. I read all the time over there, something I
> haven't done a lot of in my life, not light reading,
> fiction and things like that....
> What I like to read, I suppose is just about any-
> thing. In China, for instance, everything from
> Teddy White's stuff to novels to foreign policy
> treatises.

Before he left China in December of 1975, Bush had
agreed to become director of the Central Intelligence Agency
which had been involved in assassination plots and in spying
on antiwar groups in this country. These and other extra-
legal activities led to an investigation of the agency which
caused it to be demoralized before Bush became its head.
Bush's new job was a hard one; he spent hours in being
briefed on the myriad activities of the CIA, and he would
meet weekly with the president to report on important developments. Because the nature of the work was secret,
Bush "elected on this job to keep all the information to myself. It didn't make it any easier for Barbara." Bush as
director of CIA provided the leadership needed by the agency, and he won praise from the chairman of the Senate's
Select Committee on Intelligence who had earlier voted
against his confirmation. When President Ford left office
on January 20, 1977, Bush left the CIA, but not until he
had received the Intelligence Medal of Merit, one of the
agency's highest awards.

In 1977, after ten years in five different key posts in
the United States government, Bush returned to Houston to
the chairmanship of the First International Bank and to positions on several other corporate boards. However, in late
1977 and in 1978 Bush explored his chances for the presidency by campaigning for Republican candidates in forty-
two states. His travel expenses were paid by an organization he had established, the Fund for Limited Government
headed by an old friend, millionaire Texas lawyer James A.
Baker III. By the end of 1978, Bush had decided to mount
an energetic campaign for the Republican nomination in 1980,
and the "George Bush for President Committee" was formed
on January 5, 1979, with James Baker as chairman.

George's mother, then in her late seventies, did not want her son to seek the presidency because of the intense pressures which had aged holders of the office, but the rest of his family did not object. Barbara was willing to forego her own interests to stand beside her husband on political platforms; moreover, she once calculated that she and her husband had lived in twenty-eight houses in seventeen cities during their thirty-four years of married life. When George Bush officially launched his campaign on May 1, 1979, at the National Press Club in Washington, Barbara was there with the rest of the family.

During 1979 candidate Bush spent 328 days on the road and logged 246,000 miles. He won the first big test, the Iowa caucuses on January 21, 1980, and was criticized by the press for trying to limit the debate in New Hampshire to Reagan and himself. Reagan won overwhelmingly in Florida, but Bush recovered in Pennsylvania and Michigan. By Memorial Day, Bush's campaign was in serious trouble; funds were low and it was clear that he would not go to the Republican National Convention in Detroit as the choice of the voters in the primaries.

As George Bush's chances for obtaining the Republican nomination in 1980 for president disappeared, he must have considered the possibility of becoming Ronald Reagan's running mate. Bush knew that he has been passed over for the post on three occasions, and he stressed during the campaign that he was not a candidate for the second place on the ticket. Nevertheless, when Reagan at the Convention invited Bush to accept his party's nomination for vice-president, he accepted at once. As the principal runner-up in the primaries, Bush's selection was received with enthusiasm by delegates at the Detroit Convention. Bush strengthened the Republican ticket among the Eastern Establishment; for, in the opinion of the New York Times, Bush was "a serious, able and likeable man."

After the Republicans won the 1980 national elections, the support teams organized independently by candidates Reagan and Bush were merged. The most visible appointment of a member of one team to the other was the naming of James Baker, Bush's campaign manager, to become President Reagan's chief of the White House staff. The new president followed the example of President Carter in giving

the vice-president important assignments, and George Bush,
"the handyman of American politics," made himself useful in
the new administration. Vice-President Bush observed a
simple rule, "To get along, go along."

The Bushes redecorated the Vice-President's House.
The abstract modern paintings favored by Joan Mondale were
replaced by works of American impressionists borrowed from
museums. Almost $200,000 donated by friends of the vice-
president were expended on rugs, draperies, and furniture
for the first floor; the new sofas were covered with Chinese
chintz and fabrics in green and salmon were selected for the
upholstered chairs. The vice-president's study was installed
on the second floor, and a treadmill for Barbara was put in
place on the third.

As the wife of the vice-president, Mrs. Bush continued
to enjoy sewing and needlework, and she has learned that
handbags are "small enough to take with me to work on when
I travel." She spent eight years on a room-size rug, fourteen feet in length, which she began in China. Stitched into
the rug are Barbara's name in Chinese characters, the in-
itials of her children and grandchildren, and the outline of
a flower native in her home state, Texas.

Barbara Bush has focused attention on the decline in
literacy in this country. She purported that while ninety-
nine percent of Americans could read in the 1950s, the figure
declined in 1982 to seventy-seven percent. Mrs. Bush observed in 1984, "About one in every five [Americans] can't
read or write well enough to cope with everyday life."

In order to do something of consequence about illiter-
acy in this country, Barbara Bush has talked to national library associations and she has contributed money to two
organizations concerned about literacy which are based in
Syracuse, New York. At the suggestion of Nelson Doubleday, a publisher friend of the Bushes, Barbara undertook
to compile a book about her family as seen through the eyes
of their cocker spaniel, C. Fred. The book, which contains
sixty-two photographs of the dog, netted $65,000 which
Barbara gave to help increase literacy. Mrs. Bush's work
for illiterates brought her in 1983 special recognition at the
sixth annual dinner of the Joint Center for Political Studies,
a nonpartisan research organization which focuses on topics
of importance to Black Americans.

During her husband's first term as vice-president,
Barbara traveled with him to fifty-five countries and served
as hostess for six hundred events in his official residence.
The Second Lady also attended, during three-and-a-half
years, 287 Republican party events and 231 fund raisers
for literacy.

In the heat of the 1984 campaign for George's reelection, Barbara told reporters that the Bushes were worth
about $2,100,000 and remarked that the sum was about half
of the wealth possessed by the Democratic candidate for the
vice-presidency. Barbara did not name Ferraro but referred
to her as a person often designated by a term which rhymes
with "rich." Before the end of the day Barbara called
Geraldine at her Sheraton Centre headquarters in New York
to apologize for her unguarded remark, and Ferraro graciously accepted Mrs. Bush's explanation. Barbara, relieved,
exclaimed, "Oh, you're such a lady," and the telephone
conversation ended. In her Ferraro, My Story, Geraldine
attributed her restraint in the exchange to the training she
had received as a youngster in a convent school.

The two Bushes form a team. She works as hard as
he does in a campaign, and she tries to keep pace with him
in his varied activities. He is tall, six feet and two inches,
and slender; and Barbara has a quick, athletic stride and a
crown of prematurely white hair which distinguishes her in
a crowd. The Bush image is one of success:

> The lip and leg service paid to education, intel-
> ligence, the sure knowledge of human relations, even
> playing tennis well and being in respectable physical
> condition, testifies to the desirability of the Bush
> model or method.

Indeed, the accomplishments of the Bushes and their
many gifts "sometimes seem too easily come by, too good to
be true."

PRINCIPAL SOURCES

Nicholas King. George Bush, a Biography. New York:
    Dodd, Mead, [1980]. 146 p.

Arthur E. Wiese. <u>George Bush, Interview on the Issues</u>.
   Washington: Political Profiles, Inc. 1979. 30 p.

INDEX